THE NEW JEWISH CANON

Emunot: Jewish Philosophy and Kabbalah

Series Editor: Dov Schwartz (Bar-Ilan University, Ramat Gan)

ACADEMIC
STUDIES
PRESS

THE NEW JEWISH CANON

IDEAS & DEBATES 1980-2015

Edited by **Yehuda Kurtzer** and
Claire E. Sufrin

Boston
2020

Library of Congress Cataloging-in-Publication Data

Names: Kurtzer, Yehuda, editor. | Sufrin, Claire E., editor.
Title: The New Jewish canon / edited by Yehuda Kurtzer and Claire E. Sufrin.
Description: Boston: Academic Studies Press, 2020. | Series: Emunot: Jewish
  Philosophy and Kabbalah
Identifiers: LCCN 2020009720 (print) | LCCN 2020009721 (ebook) | ISBN
  9781644693605 (hardback) | ISBN 9781644693612 (hardback) | ISBN
  9781644693629 (adobe pdf)
Subjects: LCSH: Jews--Intellectual life. | Judaism--20th century. | Judaism--
  21st century. | Jewish philosophy--20th century. | Jewish philosophy--21st
  century. | Jews--History--1945-
Classification: LCC DS113 .N39 2020 (print) | LCC DS113 (ebook) | DDC
  305.892/4--dc23
LC record available at https://lccn.loc.gov/2020009720
LC ebook record available at https://lccn.loc.gov/2020009721

ISBN 978-1-64469-360-5 (hardback); ISBN 978-1-64469-361-2 (paperback)
ISBN 978-1-64469-362-9 (electronic, Adobe PDF);
ISBN 978-1-64469-470-1 (ePUB)

Cover design by Dov Abramson
Book design by PHi Business Solutions

Published by Academic Studies Press.
1577 Beacon Street
Brookline, MA 02446, USA
press@academicstudiespress.com
www.academicstudiespress.com

To our teachers, who taught us the canons that we have inherited; and to our students, who will surely compile and write the ones that will emerge.

Contents

Acknowledgments

A great many people were involved with contributing to, aiding, stewarding, and supporting this massive project with its so many discrete components.

Multiple research assistants moved this project along from inception to completion by gathering and typing excerpts, tracking down citations, coordinating with authors, acquiring permissions, organizing the manuscript, and scheduling countless video conferences between editors working in two different time zones. Daniel Atwood and Talia Harcsztark helped get the project off the ground. Josh Flink collected the bulk of the excerpts and was a valuable thought-partner in helping to define this body of primary sources. Hannah Kober and Sam Hainbach stewarded the project towards completion. We are grateful to all of these emerging scholars for their support, their hard work, and for the various marks their own learning has left on the final product. Our gratitude as well to Naomi Adland, Tova Serkin, and Rob France for their leadership of the iEngage summer internship program at the Shalom Hartman Institute, which brought several of these folks into our orbit.

This book has also benefited from the help and support of many individuals at the Shalom Hartman Institute, including Daniel Price, the librarian of the Institute in Jerusalem, who aided in tracking down many references and citations; Miri Miller and Becca Linden, who have supported the production of this book as a project of the Institute; and the program and marketing team at SHI for integrating the book into programming at the Shalom Hartman Institute of North America. The Shalom Hartman Institute also supported the project financially, especially by providing funding towards permissions, subvention, and publicity; and we are grateful to the staff and board of the Institute and especially the leadership of Donniel Hartman who supported and encouraged this project throughout.

We also thank Claire's colleagues at the Crown Family Center for Jewish and Israel Studies at Northwestern University for their encouragement and support of this project. The collections of the Northwestern University Libraries came through in many a bibliographic pinch. Special thanks to Alissa Schapiro and Arielle Tonkin for their help generating ideas for cover art and to Barry Sufrin for his good counsel.

Erica Brown, Ariel Picard, Sonja Pilz, and Shlomo Zuckier submitted essays that for various reasons could not be included in the final manuscript, and we appreciate both their time and their flexibility. We thank the authors and publishers of the material reprinted in this book for granting us permission to do so.

The dozens of scholars who submitted essays have endured a long and winding timeline as this book has grown and evolved, and we thank them for their patience in the process!

Dov Schwartz welcomed *The New Jewish Canon* into Emunot: Jewish Philosophy and Kabbalah, the series he edits for Academic Studies Press. ASP has been a wonderful partner in producing the book; we thank Kate Yanduganova and Kira Nemirovsky especially, as well as the many editors and others who shepherded our manuscript through the stages of its production. Finally, we thank Dov Abramson and his studio for their thought partnership in designing a cover that communicates the purpose and pathos of the volume.

As we have envisioned *The New Jewish Canon* as a teaching tool, the book has benefited from a variety of contexts in which its ideas and choices have been explored together with students and colleagues. This includes a convening at SHI NA on post-Holocaust Jewish thought in 2014, organized by Yehuda and Rabbi Dr. Joshua Feigelson, where we first began exploring the idea of a "canon" of contemporary Jewish thought; a study group in New York taught by Yehuda and organized by Abigail Pogrebin; a reading group at SHI NA for David Hartman Center Fellows, organized by Rabbi Sarah Mulhern; and countless of our own classes where we have read and taught contemporary sources. We thank our students for helping us refine the parameters of this project, and helping us understand—and now make possible for others to understand—the significance of living through a period of an expanding canon.

Some of the very best Jewish learning does not happen in seminar rooms, synagogues, or online but at home around the kitchen table or sitting on the couch. We thank our most important learning-partners and supporters: Stephanie Ives and Noah, Jesse, and Sally Ives-Kurtzer; and Michael Simon and Jacob and Ethan Simon.

Finally, we want to thank you, our reader, for picking up this very large book; for reading it in whatever way you choose, whether cover to cover, or by following the thread of a particular interest, or by opening it at random and reading whatever you find on the page. We beg your forgiveness in advance for quibbles you may have about what we chose to include and what we excluded; we know the book is imperfect. It is intended to start, not close, the conversation.

Introduction

The State of Jewish Ideas:
Towards a New Jewish Canon

If periods in Jewish history can be described in reference to major themes, then contemporary Judaism deserves its own place in the timeline, and we are bidden to characterize and understand its defining ideas. Contemporary Judaism constitutes something of a paradox. On the one hand, the late twentieth and early twenty-first centuries witness a great Jewish "settling down" after the ruptures, revolutions, disruptions, and dislocations of the mid-twentieth century. The majority of Jews in the world are found now split between Israel and North America and experiencing a new Jewish economic and political stability based in remarkable social, economic, and political conditions. Patterns of migration over the last three centuries, the destruction of Eastern European Jewry in the Holocaust, and the mass exodus of Middle Eastern Jewry to Israel since its founding, have resulted in the overwhelming majority of world Jewry now living between these twin poles. One dominant story of contemporary Jewishness is thus a story of at-home-ness both in Israel and America. On the other hand, this very stability—in demographics, geography, and relative security—has enabled the flourishing of new diversities in ideological and political foments *within* these two primary sites of Jewish community. Stability generates entropy. And as a result, Jewish life in North America and Israel is witnessing large-scale and fast-moving change in the realms of identity (who is a Jew?), ideology (what is Jewishness?), and infrastructure (what are the institutions of Jewish life in and through which Judaism is lived, studied, and practiced?).

In short: we are living in a period of the mass production and proliferation of Jewish ideas. Even while Jewish life is incredibly diverse, it is also increasingly unstable. While it can be frightening for some, mass instability in the structures of Jewish community and identity enables and exhibits new forms of Jewish expression: some that are entirely new, and many that constitute the remaking of the textual and ideological traditions inherited from the past. In this process, the nature of Jewish authority is being transformed, both within the formal power structures of established institutions as well as in less formally structured communities that can also produce (and control) what constitutes authoritative Jewish knowledge.

Meantime, the modes and means of the production of ideas are changing dramatically as well. The digital revolution has created new and cluttered public squares: American, Israeli, and Jewish. The mass culture of blogging has a democratizing quality to it, as it shortens the distance between writer and reader and the time between the inception or incubation of an idea and its publication. The same culture also risks diminishing the quality and meaning of the written word, and certainly eliminates the implication that publication necessarily grants or recognizes authority. And the possibility for misrepresentation and falsehood—either deliberate or accidental—has dramatically increased. This means that the structures of authority and authenticity are teetering at the same time as there are many new claimants to authority and authenticity, and this contributes to both the calcification and reification of structures of authority in some parts of the Jewish world, and the total collapse of authority structures in others.

The New Jewish Canon is an effort both to acknowledge the revolutionary times in which we are living and to offer a conceptual roadmap to make sense of all these changes. It combines some of the best writing from the late twentieth and early twenty-first centuries with perspectives drawn from some of the best scholars of Jewish thought today. Together, these writings continue an ages-old conversation on what it might mean to be Jewish, to live a Jewish life, to be part of a Jewish community, or to identify with the Jewish people.

In studying the Jewish past, we often seek to identify the tension between continuity, on the one hand, and change, on the other. The discipline of studying Jewish ideological and behavioral trends is also pulled in two directions, between what "Judaism" is said to be and what Jewish people actually do. But the central story of contemporary Jewish life appears to be one of fast moving change, which departs from the past both in its relationship to time and the pace of change, and in challenging our attempts to understand Jewish life holistically. This contrast between the past and the present helps shape some of what we see as dominant contemporary ideas, as Jews struggle with how the pace of change is influencing the production of ideas and the evolution of communities; and as we witness implicit contests between the sociologists, the historians, and the philosophers on the authority and capacity to best describe and understand the present moment.

From the standpoint of Jewish intellectual history, it is also hard to classify and understand the most recent period. Are we still in the period known as modernity? Have we entered postmodernity? Or perhaps we are further still, in a post-postmodernity? Do any of these terms help us to make sense of what we see before us? Older anthologies of modern Jewish thought—whether focused on post-Holocaust Jewish thought, the Jewish political tradition, the history of Halakhah, or other themes—often end in the 1970s. They tend to focus on the immediate aftermath of the Holocaust and the birth of the State of Israel, and in so doing they confine the story of Jewish thought to the mid-twentieth century and its particular challenges. The ideas of the late twentieth and early twenty-first century still entail a rethinking of Judaism prompted by these twin massive historical events, to be sure, and they thus represent a form of continuity with the thematic centerpieces of the recent past; but they also demonstrate a shift to wider theaters of politics, law, theology, and religious practice that imply some rupture and some opening of new conceptual possibilities for Israel and the Jewish people. The canon of Jewish ideas continues to develop and grow relative to new challenges faced by the Jewish people. Enough time has elapsed—enough new ideas have been articulated—that it is time to expand the canon more formally with a volume like this.

A canon project represents a kind of search for order in chaos. Like all other forms of boundary-drawing, it bears witness to an underlying culture of complexity and anxiety. It is hegemonic, to be sure, but maybe—if conducted with transparency—it can still be useful. Forming and naming a canon is also an act of authority, imposing a false superstructure atop a set of disparate ideas and disconnected written pieces, and of course also drawing exclusionary lines that separate— whether intentionally or more arbitrarily—between what counts as "in" and what counts as "out." The process of canon formation combines the descriptive and the prescriptive: some pieces find themselves in the canon because they are already known to be "canonical," having acquired value from their widespread familiarity or because they are considered foundational to the emergence of later ideas and/or to shaping the discourse. Other texts find their way into the canon because the canon-formers, whether consciously or not, are making explicit decisions to elevate their status, to hold them alongside those texts that are more universally acknowledged as canonical, and in doing so to change the arc of an intellectual history. The postmodern canon-former differs from the canon-formers of the past only in the self-awareness and transparency through which this unscientific exercise is undertaken. And as with any such exercise, we completely anticipate the most obvious criticism of this project: why this and not that?

In the interest of transparency, a few words on the process that led to this particular take on the new Jewish canon. This anthology focuses on non-fiction prose, in part on the theory that the inclusion of fiction, culture, and art would render the project unwieldy, and in part because the core definitional question that vexes such efforts—what makes a piece of work Jewish?—is far more complicated in the realm of fiction and art than it is in politics, law, and theology. In this volume, many if not most of the authors would self-consciously acknowledge that they are working in the realm of the "Jewish," which is more than can be said about many Jewish fiction authors who are vexed by an ethnic or religious classification of what they see as a work of art. While a focus on non-fiction prose simplifies some matters, it also effectively excises much of the lived experience and social history of contemporary Jews in their economic lives, foodways, travel, and cultural creativity.

Canons are also textbooks, which is a goal for this book as well. Beyond making a cultural argument about the ongoing production of Jewish ideas, the complicated state of Jewish political and social diversity, and the still unfolding central categories of Jewish history and identity, *The New Jewish Canon* invites debate both about why these documents and ideas help us understand the present moment, as well as whether they should—and what is left behind of contemporary Judaism as a result.

Canon formation has been a surprisingly common activity in recent Jewish publishing. There are many such books that reflect efforts to make sense of how "contemporary" Judaism had come to manifest its complexity and diversity through a study of the modern Jewish experience up to the recent past. In fact, one could even construct a canon of late twentieth-century canons, each with its own ideological underpinnings and implied boundaries within the larger body of Jewish literature from which they are making their selections. These include Jehuda Reinharz and Paul Mendes-Flohr's magisterial *The Jew in the Modern World,* a chronologically and thematically-organized survey of major texts of Jewish modernity (with an emphasis on the religious and the political); the mulit-volume *Jewish Political Tradition* collection, which uses categories from political theory and thought to organize ancient, classical, premodern, and modern Jewish writings, together with analytical essays by contemporary philosophers and legal theorists, into an effort towards a comprehensive thematic survey; Arthur Hertzberg's *The Zionist Idea* and now Gil Troy's revamping of Hertzberg into *The Zionist Ideas*; David Roskies's *The Literature of Destruction*; and Ruth Wisse's *The Modern Jewish Canon,* with its emphasis on twentieth-century literature. There are also countless collections of major papers and academic essays in all fields of Jewish Studies, as well as meta-analyses of trends in Jewish Studies that help us understand trends in the field of how scholars in the present understand the Jewish people's history and its present realities.

As noted above, we seek to go beyond these existing acts of canonization by focusing on a later period that carries us into the present, to bear witness to the contemporary canon—from 1980 to 2015. Despite this different focus, we were determined to use what we saw as the "best practices" of the best of these anthologies. Thus, this book is composed of excerpts of primary sources written during the period in question alongside essays from scholars written specifically for this volume. The excerpts from the primary texts were chosen with the intention of capturing something representative of the larger work, whether in an essential theme, a characteristic of style, or a particularly memorable section of prose. In some cases, the primary texts may not reflect the most famous contribution of the writer, but will be more useful as a vehicle to engage with the writer's ideas and their enduring legacy. The accompanying essays are intended to provide historical context for the primary sources and also to indicate why the ideas expressed in these sources were significant when they appeared and how they have continued to evolve. The essays, in turn, constitute a canon in their own right; essayists received broad guidelines and followed a broad stylesheet, but the diversity of their responses help us understand the complexity of "reception history" of contemporary Jewish ideas as much as the primary text selections. In some cases, one of us wrote the essay. The book in its total package also strives for and struggles with all forms of diversity—in the background and identities of the authors of primary texts, in the background and identities of essayists, in the chosen and rejected parameters of the criteria for inclusion of topics and genres—which, in itself, constitutes a text of sorts for the present moment.

Though the term "canonization" has religious connotations, our choice to include the work of any particular scholar or writer in the selection of primary texts is not an endorsement, morally or otherwise, of them, their ideas, or their actions. Our goal in this book is to capture the dominant ideas and debates of the period 1980–2015. At times this has meant including the work of individuals who are known to have committed bad acts in their personal and/or professional lives or whose ideas we personally find offensive or even dangerous. In some cases, these opinions or actions are plainly essential to why the ideas were important enough to merit inclusion, as with authors who promoted violence or advanced radical or polarizing ideas that had major ramifications for Jewish and/or Israeli society. In other instances, it is more challenging to draw a direct line between the bad acts of individuals and the substance of their ideas or their popularity as authors with lay and scholarly audiences. With both cases, we struggled with the impossibility of separating the artist from the work. This "tarnished legacy" problem is not unique to us but beguiles the history of literature, art, philosophy, and more. For our book, the stakes of this debate are intensified by the fact that we are working with living subjects, whose legacies are not fully established.

We struggled most in debating whether to include the work of several authors accused of abusive behavior toward women. More specifically, between 2016 and 2018 and in the context of the #metoo movement, Steven M. Cohen, Ari Shavit, and Leon Wieseltier were each accused of patterns of sexual impropriety, and each acknowledged his bad behavior. An important scholarly and public debate has emerged in the wake of this movement as to whether we should understand their patterns of abusive behavior toward women as correlating to their work in some way, even though none of that work directly addresses sexual ethics. Whether or not there is such a correlation between the behavior of these scholars and their ideas, we recognize that the power and charisma that allowed them to succeed professionally and to promote their ideas is the very same power and charisma that they are accused of abusing in their predatory actions. We recognize and regret that the continued publication of the works of these individuals risks rehabilitating their reputations and also risks re-traumatizing the victims of their bad behaviors.

We recognize the courage of the women who bore witness to the pain and humiliation they suffered. We identify with the cause of the #metoo movement in which they stepped forward, and each of us has participated in and led actions to call out abusive behavior in our Jewish community. We will continue to do so.

Despite our concerns, we decided to move forward with publishing the works of these men and other individuals who are known privately or publicly for problematic personal or political views or behavior. This is because we believe that the ideas they express and the pieces included here were central to the Jewish communal conversation in the years 1980–2015, particularly among American Jews, and that we cannot understand the period without reckoning with this material.

We hope that the coming phase of Jewish history is characterized by greater integrity, moral and intellectual, than the period we are chronicling: to get there, we believe, requires an intimate understanding of the recent past, in all its complexity.

We also want to acknowledge that some of the scholars we invited to comment were resistant to the very notion of creating and publishing a canon of recent Jewish ideas. They asked whether this project might risk damaging the very diversity it means to chronicle. This criticism hinges on an understanding of the wild contemporary Jewish ecosystem as "postcanonical," or at least on the belief that that ecosystem needs more time to flourish before we can meaningfully differentiate between the ideas that will or should endure and those that will or should become quickly dated. But this choice *not* to engage in canon formation is its own political choice, and it also risks abdicating the process of curating ideas either to canon-formers with more tendentious political ideologies or to processes of chance. To stand outside the canon process and to resist it in defense of diversity creates an even greater risk that the ideas not preserved now will be lost to a history we cannot fully control. We choose instead to advocate for a more diverse canon.

To take a previous moment in Jewish history as a point of comparison: the creation of the biblical canon by the early Rabbis, and then the rabbinic canon by later Rabbis, constituted careful sets of choices from within a vast sea of biblical forebears, Second Temple literature, and the literary output of these Rabbis themselves. The Rabbis were making choices, sometimes self-evidently and with unapologetic self-awareness (as in Mishnah Yadayim 3:5). We can speculate as to the political circumstances or ideological dispositions animating certain choices made by the Rabbis about what belonged in *the* Bible or in *the* Talmud, though we are not fully privy to the larger cultural context in which they worked and how it might have circumscribed the range of their own canonizing power. At the same time, as several historians have demonstrated, rabbinic power was not entirely the product of their own making, but emerged as a result of their positioning within their particular societies, which was enabled by imperial structures. That is, the Rabbis were also aided in the forming of their canons by history and political circumstances beyond their own control. Canon formation is always an interplay of hegemonic decisions made by the canonizers with purpose and intent, and forces beyond the canonizers that they themselves might not even be able to see. To think that we can escape such forces in our own time would be an act of foolish hubris. But to refuse to canonize would be to submit entirely to these forces. And so we proceeded in our task with both humility and confidence. We are humble because we anticipate that readers of later generations will see things in our choices that we cannot ourselves see; we are confident because we believe our work will be meaningful even to its very first readers. While there is only one Bible and only two Talmuds, perhaps this book might in some small way shape the Jewish identities and ideologies of Jews who will follow us. Time will tell.

* * *

The material gathered in *the New Jewish Canon* is organized chronologically within a few major themes that characterize the zeitgeist: Jewish Politics and the Public Square; History, Memory, and Narrative; Religion and Religiosity; and Identities and Communities. By organizing Jewish thought into these categories, we seek to enable the reader to trace the conceptual evolution of specific issues that continue to matter in our own time.

The central theme in **Jewish Politics and the Public Square** is the shift, as has become clear in the past decade, of the State of Israel functioning as an organizing force in American Jewish life toward it becoming the most powerful disorganizing force, as demonstrated today in both the widespread narrative of the "distancing" of American Jews from Israel, as well as in the ways that Israel serves as the site for intracommunal conflict in the American Jewish community. At the same time, politics have long served as the dominant discourse of the Israeli public square, with prevailing questions about the character of its democracy, the fight for religious pluralism, and the ongoing conflict with the Palestinians. The new rise of nationalism, especially as it is mapped onto religion, is an essential theme of the contemporary State of Israel for both its ideological adherents and its critics. Violence and the threat of violence—both corollaries of power—course throughout this section, whether in the costs of occupation, in the acts and ideologies of internecine zealotry, or even in the emergence of a drumbeat hostility that now characterizes public discourse on Israel. And Israeli law also emerges as a critical instrument to understand contemporary debates about the nature of Israeli democracy and its applicability to questions of enabling or choosing between different visions of Jewishness in the Israeli public square, and the applicability of Israeli and international law as part of Israel's ongoing occupation of the West Bank. Our volume includes several examples and critical analysis of the enormous legacy of Chief Justice Aharon Barak of Israel's Supreme Court, a tenure which raised significant enduring controversy in Israeli society around the question of judicial activism.

The Jewish conversation about **History, Memory, and Narrative** has been heavily informed by Yosef Yerushalmi's articulation of a distinction between the first two terms in his book *Zakhor* and has played out in the unfolding interpretation of the meaning of recent history for contemporary Jews. Here we find major developments in the culture of preservation of the legacy of the Holocaust. This includes analysis of the principal architects and exhibits of this culture as well as their discontents, and the emerging awareness of all the ways that contemporary Judaism shatters the legacy of the inherited and mimetic past even as it desperately tries to preserve it. Here too we encounter the twin legacies of the emergence of the American and Israeli experiences from the precariousness of the previous century, and the efforts—some still nascent—to try to define some coherent narratives and leitmotifs that tell its story most effectively.

In the section on **Religion and Religiosity**, using Martin Buber's terms differentiating between the lived experience of the holy (religiosity) and the instantiation of the holy in fixed forms (religion), we witness the end of the great first phase of postwar theology and its attempts to grasp with a rapidly unfolding pace of change, and the emergence of new forms of theology, prayer, and ritual that situate themselves squarely in the late modern and postmodern turn. It can be argued that both Israeli and American Jewish societies are in the midst of a religious revival, as American Jews shift away from the "peoplehood" identification that dominated Jewish life in the twentieth century and seek new forms of identifications and affiliations that privilege sincerity and experience, and as Israeli Jews wrestle with the politics of *hadatah*—a phenomenon that often appears in the news to describe charged efforts to lead towards a religious awakening in Israeli society. Throughout the global Jewish world, the rise of ultra-Orthodoxy also bears witness to a reclassification of the place of religion and its dominant expressions within the broader sector of Jewish identity.

The **Identities and Communities** section bears witness most explicitly to the entropic shifts in Jewish identity in both North America and Israel, and in particular the aftereffects of the widespread embrace of intermarriage between Jews and non-Jews, the intermixing (especially in Israel) of Jewish ethnicities, the demise of the idea of a single shared Jewish language and culture, the influence of major shifts in the understanding of gender and sexuality, and the emergence of a desperate search by American Jews for content and frameworks through which to understand and transmit Jewishness to its next generation, often perceived as being increasingly disinterested. Coursing through these two sections is also a reckoning with the continued force that Halakhah, Jewish law, continues to have for a growing percentage of the Jewish public, even as its defining questions exhibit a distinctly contemporary set of interests, and even as the nature of Jewish legal authority in the modern world is contested and affirmed differently in different communities.

Each section is organized chronologically based on the publication date of the primary texts. This allows for fluid understanding of the evolution of certain ideas, but also can be a bit confusing as there are multiple overlapping intellectual histories between the different sections. In some cases, we have also grouped together several independent primary texts if they reflect similar themes, so that they might be analyzed together. This emphasis on chronology also helps us understand the influence of the new forms of media and publication vehicles on the proliferation of ideas, as in some cases the internet-based publications near the end of the chapters will make implicit and explicit use of the earlier material. The internet often stretches the applicability and visibility of earlier ideas to radically new audiences. The transformation in how ideas are disseminated is one of the major new ideas itself in the history of Jewish knowledge that is being written about the present moment, and this collection captures merely the earliest phase of this ideological revolution.

As in any act of canonization, there is a lot left out. This collection privileges the American Jewish and Israeli experiences, and the reality of contemporary Jewish life as defined primarily by these two poles, as its own idea, and as a departure from the previous history of more diverse diasporas. If these contemporary conditions were once merely the product of population migrations in the twentieth century, they are now a defining characteristic of contemporary Jewry. We have thus focused on Israeli and American ideas, and we have privileged the relationship between these two poles, in our volume. The collection leaves out "culture," broadly construed, and also remains intentionally lean on academic Jewish scholarship, including a few such books and essays but leaving out even those works of scholarship in Jewish Studies that have represented paradigm shifts in their subfields. The works in this collection largely present a direct line between their ideas and their impact on the Jewish general public; and while new research in rabbinics, for instance, may travel through rabbinical school education and inform thousands of Jews who encounter Talmud through their rabbis, with only few exceptions do such works of scholarship travel directly to end users or course quickly into Jewish sensibilities. The book also includes excerpts from works that are already broadly understood to be canonical and ones whose canonical status is yet to be tested by the arc of history. The book almost certainly makes mistakes. There are items that should be included and are not, or are included but should not be, and the disproportionate perpetuation of certain ideologies and identities, or at least an interest in them, that are the product of the editors' own proclivities and blind spots. Some if not all readers will, no doubt, find something that disappoints them about our choices. But the overall success of the book will be measured, we hope, on its ability to catalyze conversation on its principal themes and the effectiveness of how they are represented.

More than anything else, *The New Jewish Canon* invites debate. The ideas that it preserves of contemporary Judaism, and the pedagogy of seeking to understand how ideas can be influential, seeks to launch a provocative new conversation in the Jewish community and beyond about our most important ideas and trends, about the way in which new ideas are produced, and about the central concerns facing Jewish life today in religion, history, identity, community, and politics. If the conditions of contemporary Judaism are ripe for a democratization of Jewish power structures, and if we are witnessing entropy in questions of authority and continuity, then this is as good a moment as any to remember that the citizen is sovereign in the writing of the next phase of Jewish history and tradition. We invite you into conversation.

The Editors

I

Jewish Politics and the Public Square

1. Michael Walzer, *Exodus and Revolution*

Michael Walzer, *Exodus and Revolution*, New York: Basic Books, 1985

Dr. Michael Walzer (1935–) is Professor Emeritus at the Institute for Advanced Study in Princeton, New Jersey and Co-Editor Emeritus of *Dissent*.

Since late medieval or early modern times, there has existed in the West a characteristic way of thinking about political change, a pattern that we commonly impose upon events, a story that we repeat to one another. The story has roughly this form: oppression, liberation, social contract, political struggle, new society (danger of restoration). We call the whole process **revolutionary**, though the events don't make a circle unless oppression is brought back at the end; intentionally, at least, they have a strong forward movement. This isn't a story told everywhere; it isn't a universal pattern; it belongs to the West, more particularly to Jews and Christians in the West, and its source, its original version, is the Exodus of Israel from Egypt. My purpose in this book has been to retell the story in its original version, to give a reading of the Exodus that captures its political meaning—and then to reflect upon the general character and internal tensions of Exodus politics. This is not, of course, the only way of reading the biblical account. It is an interpretation, and like all interpretations, it highlights some features of the account and neglects or suppresses others. But I am not reading Exodus in an idiosyncratic way. I am following a well-marked trail, moving backward from citation and commentary to primary text, from enactments to acts or, at least, to stories of acts. The Exodus may or may not be what many of its commentators thought it to be, the first revolution. But the Book of Exodus (together with the Book of Numbers) is certainly the first description of revolutionary politics.

The Exodus, or the later reading of the Exodus, fixes the pattern. And because of the centrality of the Bible in Western thought and the endless repetition of the story, the pattern has been etched deeply into our political culture. It isn't only the case that events fall, almost naturally, into an Exodus shape; we work actively to give them that shape. We complain about oppression; we hope (against all the odds of human history) for deliverance; we join in covenants and constitutions; we aim at a new and better social order. Though in attenuated form, Exodus thinking seems to have survived the secularization of political theory. Thus, when utopian socialists, most of them resolutely hostile to religion, argued about the problems of the "transitional period," they still cast their arguments in familiar terms: the forty years in the wilderness, write the Manuels in their chapter on Robert Owen, were "a deep ... cultured memory and the death of the old generation [was] an archetypal solution." (It was even a solution for "scientific" socialists like Marx or, in this century, Lincoln Steffens.) This sort of thing is never merely a matter of rhetorical convenience. Cultural patterns shape perception and analysis too. They would not endure for long, of course, if they did not accommodate a range of perceptions and analyses, if it were not possible to carry on arguments inside the structures they provide. I don't mean to defend an essentialist view of revolution or of radical politics generally. Within the frame of the Exodus story one can plausibly emphasize the mighty arm of God or the slow march of the people, the land of milk and honey or the holy nation, the purging of counterrevolutionaries or the schooling of the new generation. One can describe Egyptian bondage in terms of corruption or tyranny or exploitation. One can defend the authority of the Levites or of the tribal elders or of the rulers of tens and fifties. I would only suggest that these alternatives are themselves paradigmatic; they are *our* alternatives. In other cultures, men and women read other books, tell different stories, confront different choices.

But we in the West also have a second way of talking about political change, a second pattern, the intellectual offspring, as it were, of the Exodus, though unlike it in crucial respects. The second pattern is, in Jacob Talmon's phrase, "political messianism." Messianism is the great temptation of Western politics. Its source and spur is the apparent endlessness of the Exodus march. The long drawn-out tale of human progress is shadowed by error and catastrophe wrote the young Ramsay MacDonald in a book called *The Socialist Movement*, "by wearisome journeys in the wilderness, by Canaans which, when yet lands beyond the Jordan, were overflowing with milk and honey, but which, when conquered, were almost barren. ..." MacDonald professed himself bound to continue the march, but one might well decide to give it up (as he eventually did)—or, alternatively, to opt for a far more radical hope. Why be content with the difficult and perhaps interminable struggle for holiness and justice when there is another promised land where liberation is final, fulfillment complete? History itself is a burden from which we long to escape, and messianism guarantees that escape: a deliverance not only from Egypt but from Sinai and Canaan, too. It may seem odd to expect such a deliverance from politics—even from revolutionary politics and apocalyptic wars. Theological or philosophical arguments in defense of that expectation are always complex, invoking divine purpose or history's providential course along with this or that political program, just as the Book of Exodus does. What is important here, however, is that the messianic program is very different from the one adopted by Moses in the wilderness and at Sinai. (12–13)

COMMENTARY BY WILLIAM GALSTON

No American scholar has done more than Michael Walzer to bring the classic texts of Judaism into the mainstream of contemporary thought. Walzer first signaled the importance that Jewish political thought would attain in his career with his book *Exodus and Revolution*, which explores the impact of the Exodus story on liberation movements throughout Western history. This story and its later reading, he argues, "fixes the pattern" for subsequent accounts of revolutionary events. Because of the centrality of the Bible for the Western tradition, this pattern "has been deeply etched into our political culture" (134), and it remains operative today, as its centrality to the narrative of the US civil rights movement attests.

For this reason, *Exodus and Revolution* moves back and forth between the biblical text and its appropriation by centuries of revolutionary leaders, each illuminating the other. Walzer is alert to the risks of "presentism" this strategy presents, but he believes—plausibly—that the historical resonance it generates more than compensates for any lack of interpretive fidelity.

The template of the Exodus story, Walzer contends, comprises four themes, arrayed sequentially: the experience of oppression; liberation, understood as both breaking the bonds of oppression and the difficulties that attend this first encounter with negative freedom; covenant or, more generally, the constitution of authority and mutual responsibility that transforms a mass of individuals into a people; and finally, the hope for a better life, the Promised Land or utopian vision that gives direction to the people's movement through time.

Walzer links his reading of the biblical text to contemporary themes. For example, he interprets the Israelites' incessant grumbling and episodic rebellions against Moses's leadership as evidence of the ambiguous effects of oppression on the character of the oppressed. Yes, the experience of coerced subordination can purify the soul and make us more sensitive to the sufferings of others. But it can also induce a slavish preference for security over liberty. As Walzer observes, the tribal leaders Dathan and Abiram accuse Moses of leading the Israelites away from, not toward, a land flowing with milk and honey

(Num. 16:13). We may not have been free, they imply, but at least we were not enduring the world's most boring diet and experiencing the constant threat of dying in the wilderness. This retreat from novelty and risk, which the poet John Milton called "backsliding," is a perennial challenge to all movements seeking to upend an unjust status quo.

In another striking move, Walzer connects the Sinai covenant to the psychology of freedom. Liberation produces what philosophers term negative freedom—the absence of impediments to the exercise of will and choice. When negative freedom is attained by throwing off oppressive bonds, it creates a sense of exhilaration. But this intense sentiment cannot last because, Walzer asserts, the condition of negative liberty is in practice "unendurable" (75). (Here he echoes the postwar theme of the "escape from freedom" through which many intellectuals sought to comprehend Europe's embrace of totalitarianism.) Individuals—and even more, peoples—cannot live with endless possibility and pure fluidity. They need solidity and form. The only question is whether a people's form comes from outside through coercion or whether from within through consent. The Hebrew Bible, says Walzer, offers a hitherto unknown pathway to forming a people: "Covenant is the political invention of the Book of Exodus" (74).

Walzer anticipated that his foray into Biblical interpretation would raise some scholarly hackles. He described his new book as a movement back and forth between the Torah and the literature of radical politics—between a field where he was an "amateur" and his home base of professional experience, between the enthusiasm of the novice and the caution of the experts. And he acknowledged that if he had erred, it was in the direction of enthusiasm (ix).

If this cheerful admission was designed to ward off criticism from the field into which he had trespassed, it did not work. Zeev Falk's review in the *Journal of Religion* was tersely dismissive. Jacob Neusner's review in the *Journal of the American Academy of Religion* was more expansive but no less critical. We must begin by understanding classic stories in their original context, he insisted, which permits us to understand "their points of stress, nuances, generative tensions." When we read them out of context, which Neusner taxed Walzer with doing, we hear "only those messages that we did not need the story to convey to us—only what we knew before." Reviews by sociologists, political theorists, and law professors were less critical but far from thoroughly positive.

In contrast to these scholarly critiques, *New York Times* reviewers raved, and *Exodus and Revolution* was selected as one of the "Books of the *Times*," where it was characterized as a "rewarding" book—"elegantly written, subtly argued, full of stimulating suggestions." In *Sunday Book Review*, Robert McAfee Brown, a professor of Christian theology, praised the book as a "brilliant tapestry" that wove together strands of the biblical story, commentaries, and accounts of revolutionary activists who drew on this tradition.

These assessments gave *Exodus and Revolution* currency within a wide community of lay readers. They also set the stage for a passionate public debate between Walzer and Edward Said, the noted literary theorist and Palestinian activist. In the course of a "Canaanite Reading" of the book, Said accuses Walzer of minimizing key aspects of the narrative—in particular, the injunction to extirpate the previous inhabitants of the Promised Land. Said links these omissions to the obvious parallels in contemporary politics, and he claims that Walzer's refusal to distance himself from the consequences of Israel's military victories suffuses his work with an "unattractive moral triumphalism." It is Walzer's unswerving loyalty to his people, the foundation of the "connected criticism" he so often praises, that leads, Said says, to a tragic impasse: "you cannot both 'belong' *and* concern yourself with the Canaanites who do not belong." The exchange Said's critique triggered made *Exodus and Revolution* a *cause celebre*.

This controversy only elevated Walzer's stature within the American Jewish community, most of which identified with his brand of liberal, social democratic Zionism. Bernard Avishai's shrewd review took this link a step farther. Scholars such as Walzer, he argued, could help solve the identity crisis of American Jews who do not identify with either Orthodoxy or the secular world of Jewish immigrants, by making Judaism's classic literature part of these Jews' ethical imagination.

To be sure, Avishai continues, there are difficulties with Walzer's this-worldly interpretation of Exodus. He asks whether it is possible to understand how the story unfolds without seeing the "longing for God" as its driving force. This question leads to another: when the Jewish community is commanded to be holy, is this merely a matter of justice and solidarity among human beings? Doesn't holiness require purity as well as righteousness? If so, is holiness fully compatible with the "secular social contract" that provides the fulcrum for Walzer's account? If not—if revolutions made in the image of Exodus have an ecstatic as well as rational dimension, is there not reason to worry about the charismatic leaders who so often lead these revolutions?

Avishai's review highlighted the contestable secular thrust of Walzer's analysis. This did nothing to weaken its appeal to the majority of American Jews, who were encouraged to learn that their leanings were compatible with a respected scholar's reading of the tradition. And—to state the obvious—it did not hurt that Walzer took as his text the Jewish story that Jews not raised in the tradition know if they know anything at all. Most of the Jews who reject ritual and the calendar of Jewish holidays somehow find themselves at a Seder every year. In this context, *Exodus and Revolution* has taken its place as an accessible reworking of this most familiar of stories for two generations of American Jews.

Throughout his career, Walzer has been a man of the left—specifically, the social democratic left. The tension between democratic and non-democratic radicalism is the most explicitly contemporary issue he brings to (and finds in) the Exodus story. Following Maimonides, he insists that human beings change only gradually and that efforts to accelerate this process lead inevitably to coercion or worse. As Maimonides explains in the *Guide for the Perplexed*, "It is not in the nature of man that having been brought up in slavish service, ... he should all of a sudden wash off from his hands the dirt [of slavery]." This is why God caused the Jewish people to wander in the desert for so long—to allow them to become more courageous and to buy time until a new generation arose that was not accustomed to the humiliation of servitude. And it is why Moses patiently tries to shape an often ungrateful and rebellious Jewish people through rhetoric, persuasion, and law.

Acknowledging "shameless anachronism," Walzer describes this as the "social democratic version" of the Exodus narrative (54). But as he admits, the story has its "Leninist" moments as well (65). Moses's brutal response to the sin of the Golden Calf mobilizes the Levites as the revolution's "vanguard" and generates the first documented "purge" in the history of revolutionary movements (59). For Machiavelli, Walzer observes, this was a pivotally instructive moment.

Unlike some squeamish interpreters, Walzer does not shy away from this episode. Nor does he surrender to it. "Was it the purging or the teaching," he asks, "that made the decisive difference?" Although, as he says, the text can be read either way, he insists on what he regards as its plain meaning: the people's resistance to God's law cannot be defeated by force alone:

> God and the Levites could easily kill all the people who yearn for the flesh-pots (or idols) of Egypt. But then the Levites would arrive in the promised land virtually alone, and that would not be a fulfillment of the promise. The promise is for the people, and the people can only move in gradual stages from bondage to freedom. (69)

In rare circumstances, brutality may be an unavoidable necessity, but it cannot be the principal strategy of a successful revolutionary movement. The Cultural

Revolution did not "reeducate" China's intellectuals; the Khmer Rouge's killing fields did not "purify" the Cambodian people; and the waves of purges Lenin's heir launched did not create the New Soviet Man. In the end, there is no substitute for the slow processes of education and persuasion rooted in the experience of the people themselves.

When Walzer moves from means to ends, the same distinction is in play. On the one side we find what he calls "Exodus politics"—the movement not from our fallen state to the kingdom of God on earth, but rather from slavery and oppression to a real-world politics where human beings can live with a measure of security, liberty, and above all dignity. Exodus politics rejects the idea of a final solution of anything. Politics is always in need of radical reform; the work of reform is endless.

Walzer grounds Exodus politics, so understood, in classic texts of the tradition, such as Maimonides's depiction of the messianic age in the "Laws of Kings." Human nature is not transformed, and neither is the nature of politics. As Walzer summarizes Maimonides, "The messiah ... will be a human and historical figure, exactly as Moses and David were, and the world into which he comes will 'continue in its accustomed course.'" The lion and the lamb will not lie down together; at best, Israel will dwell securely among the nations (123).

By contrast, utopian messianism—which Walzer dubs "the great temptation of Western politics"—yearns for total transformation of human nature and political relations, typically through an apocalyptic event that sweeps away our corrupt and compromised world and ushers in a world of justice without conflict.

As an interpreter, Walzer frankly acknowledges that Exodus can be read as the source of messianic politics as well as the alternative to it. As a social critic, he makes his preference clear: the best reading of Exodus focuses on its "tough realism" (121), and Exodus politics is best understood as "cautious and moderate." In this world, anyway, the most we can hope for is dignity, not redemption (149). And however much we may be tempted to see God's presence in current events, we must resist this impulse, because it makes the everyday politics of compromise and gradual change impossible to sustain. If we are too quick to identify God's will with our own, we end up with the politics of Pinchas.

2. George Steiner, "Our Homeland, the Text"

Judith Butler, "Remarks to Brooklyn College on BDS"

George Steiner, "Our Homeland, the Text," *Salmagundi* 66 (1985)

Dr. George Steiner (1929–2020) taught English and Comparative Literature at the University of Geneva, the University of Oxford, and Harvard University. He was an Extraordinary Fellow at Churchill College at the University of Cambridge and the author of countless essays and reviews published in the *New Yorker* and elsewhere.

The notion that the appalling road of Jewish life and the ever renewed miracle of survival should have as their end, as their justification, the setting up of a small nation-state in the Middle East, crushed by military burdens, petty and even corrupt in its politics, shrill in its parochialism, is implausible. ...

The State of Israel is an endeavor—wholly understandable, in many aspects admirable, perhaps historically inescapable—to normalize the condition, the meaning of Judaism. It would make the Jew level with the common denominator of modern "belonging." It is, at the same time, an attempt to eradicate the deeper truth of unhousedness, of an at-homeness in the world, which are the legacy of the prophets and of the keepers of the text. ...

Locked materially in a material homeland, the text may, in fact, lose its life-force, and its truth-values may be betrayed. But when the text is the homeland, even when it is rooted only in the exact remembrance and seeking of a handful of wanderers, nomads of the word, it cannot be extinguished. Time is truth's passport, and its native ground. What better lodging for the Jew? (24–25)

Judith Butler, "Remarks to Brooklyn College on BDS," *The Nation*, February 7, 2013

Dr. Judith Butler (1956–) is Maxine Elliot Professor in the Departments of Rhetoric and Comparative Literature at the University of California, Berkeley.

Only if we accept the proposition that the state of Israel is the exclusive and legitimate representative of the Jewish people would a movement calling for divestment, sanctions and boycott against that state be understood as directed against the Jewish people as a whole. Israel would then be understood as co-extensive with the Jewish people. There are two major problems with this view. First, the state of Israel does not represent all Jews, and not all Jews understand themselves as represented by the state of Israel. Secondly, the state of Israel should be representing *all* of its population equally, regardless of whether or not they are Jewish, regardless of race, religion or ethnicity. ...

The second point, to repeat, is that the Jewish people extend beyond the state of Israel and the ideology of political Zionism. The two cannot be equated. Honestly, what can really be said about "the Jewish people" as a whole? Is it not a lamentable [stereotype] to make large generalizations about all Jews, and to presume they all share the same political commitments? They—or, rather, we—occupy a vast spectrum of political views, some of which are unconditionally supportive of the state of Israel, some of which are conditionally supportive, some are skeptical, some are exceedingly critical, and an increasing number, if we are to believe the polls in this country, are indifferent. In my view, we have to remain critical of anyone who posits a single norm that decides rights of entry into the social or cultural category determining as well who will be excluded. Most categories of identity are fraught with conflicts and ambiguities; the effort to suppress the complexity of the category of "Jewish" is thus a political move that seeks to yoke a cultural identity to a specific Zionist position. If the Jew who struggles for justice for Palestine is considered to be anti-Semitic, if any number of internationals who have joined [this] struggle from various parts of the world are also considered anti-Semitic and if Palestinians seeking rights of political self-determination are so accused as well, then it would appear that no oppositional move ... can take place without risking the accusation of anti-Semitism. That accusation becomes a way of discrediting a bid for self-determination, at which point we have to ask what political purpose the radical mis-use of that accusation has assumed in the stifling of a movement for political self-determination.

When Zionism becomes co-extensive with Jewishness, Jewishness is pitted against the diversity that defines democracy, and if I may say so, betrays one of the most important ethical dimensions of the diasporic Jewish tradition, namely, the obligation of co-habitation with those different from ourselves. Indeed, such a conflation denies the Jewish role in broad alliances in the historical struggle for social and political justice in unions, political demands for free speech, in socialist communities, in the resistance movement in World War II, in peace activism, the Civil Rights movement and the struggle against apartheid in South Africa. It also demeans the important struggles in which Jews and Palestinians work together to stop the wall, to rebuild homes, to document indefinite detention, to oppose military harassment at the borders and to oppose the occupation and to imagine the plausible scenarios for the Palestinian right to return.

COMMENTARY BY JULIE E. COOPER

In "The Jewish State and the Jewish Problem" (1897), Ahad Ha'am objects that, in their preoccupation with the establishment of a Jewish state, Zionists have ignored the spiritual predicaments of Eastern European Jews. For assimilated Western Jews, Ahad Ha'am concedes, the establishment of a Jewish state could remedy the crisis precipitated by the failure of Emancipation. Yet, in Ahad Ha'am's diagnosis,

> The eastern form of the spiritual problem is absolutely different from the western. In the West it is the problem of the Jews; in the East, the *problem of Judaism*. The first weighs on the individual; the second, on the nation. The one is felt by Jews who have a European education; the other, by Jews whose education has been Jewish. The one is a product of anti-Semitism, and is dependent on anti-Semitism for its existence; the other is a natural product of a real link with a millennial culture.[1]

Among Eastern European Jews, the most pressing spiritual concerns surround the fate of Jewish culture in modernity. In diaspora, Ahad Ha'am warns, Judaism's national character is at risk—"in danger of losing its essential being"

---

1   Arthur Hertzberg, *The Zionist Idea* (Philadelphia: Jewish Publication Society, 1997), 266.

through foreign influence and "in danger of being split up into as many kinds of Judaism, each with a different character and life, as there are countries of the dispersion."[2] As Ahad Ha'am defines it, the "problem of Judaism" involves the preconditions both material and spiritual for preserving national unity and reinvigorating national culture.

Ahad Ha'am's distinction between "the problem of the Jews" and "the problem of Judaism" provides a helpful rubric for understanding what is distinctive about the form that debates surrounding Israel and Zionism have taken in recent years. Although these controversies are noteworthy for their volume and vehemence, I want to highlight a different facet of these contentious debates. In academic contexts, the debate surrounding Israel largely turns on the "problem of Judaism," rather than the "problem of the Jews," which is thought to have been resolved for the vast majority of the world's Jews, who reside in Israel and North America. Writing from Britain and the United States, Steiner and Butler warn that the State of Israel poses a grave threat to *Judaism*: to ethical traditions, developed in diaspora, of co-existence. Yet, from Ahad Ha'am's time to our own, the nature of this "problem" has changed markedly. For Ahad Ha'am, the "problem of Judaism" was a *collective* predicament arising from exposure to modern culture, which threatened to fragment the nation. For Steiner and Butler, by contrast, the "problem of Judaism" surrounds the moral integrity of Jewish *individuals*—the predicament of those who refuse to be conscripted for national projects. Steiner and Butler worry that, with the establishment of the State of Israel, Judaism no longer produces—or, perhaps, is no longer hospitable to—independent thinkers who protest injustice and deceit.

Writing after the First Lebanon War, Steiner mobilizes an evocative—albeit highly romanticized—vision of diasporic Judaism to counter what he considers the "collective mendacities" of nationalism (21). In lieu of a physical homeland, Steiner argues, diasporic Jews sought shelter in the text, and, within this mobile dwelling, cultivated a fanatical devotion to the truth. I will not enumerate Steiner's oversights and omissions—for example, his utter neglect of communal institutions such as the *kahal*—required to arrive at this idyllic portrait of diasporic moral genius. After all, Steiner aims less for historical veracity than for ethical resonance. Rather, I want to highlight the extreme individualism of Steiner's moral vision. Although Steiner locates "our" homeland in the text, he devotes scant attention to the role that textuality played in sustaining a collective identity among a dispersed people. Instead, he valorizes the ethical

---

2   Ibid., 267.

code that textuality ostensibly produces: a clerical code dedicated to "*a politics of truth*" (18). The partisans of the text are few—"a handful of wanderers, nomads of the word"—and the political virtues associated with textuality are those of the gadfly (Socrates), the heretic (Spinoza), and the "conscientious objector" (24, 21). In other words, Steiner celebrates diasporic culture for its ability to produce exceptional individuals. Uncompromising in their pursuit of truth, Steiner's exemplary clerics resist "the conventions of expediency, of moral approximation and irresolution" that are part and parcel of mundane politics (18). "A true thinker, a truth-thinker, a scholar, must know that no nation, no body politic, no creed, no moral ideal and necessity, be it that of human survival, is worth a falsehood, a willed self-deception or the manipulation of a text. This knowledge and observance *are* his homeland" (20). Steiner's essay reads as an elegy for a "Judaic sensibility" exhibiting "unique strengths and purities of disinterested purpose"—a sensibility that produced exceptional intellects and, by extension, moral exemplars (17).

Although Steiner warns that with the establishment of the State of Israel, "the text may, in fact, lose its life-force, and its truth values may be betrayed," he has not forgotten the "problem of the Jews" that the state promises to remedy (24). Indeed, Steiner acknowledges the perceived elitism of his lament for a Judaism that encouraged heroic gestures of individual refusal. What consolation does a politics of truth provide to the survivors (and other beleaguered Jews) who "hunger, desperately, for the common condition of man upon men" (23)? In other words, the "problem of the Jews" remains present to Steiner as a live question, and he allows that the establishment of the State of Israel may constitute a necessary solution to these material predicaments. Steiner remains torn between two imperatives: the need to establish a "refuge," a "place of physical gathering in which a Jewish parent could give to his child some hope of a future," and the fear that these children will forsake the legacy of principled dissent (22).

At first glance, "the problem of Judaism" seems remote from Butler's concerns: she defends the principles of academic freedom, rather than a specific Jewish inheritance. On closer inspection, however, Butler displays marked affinities with Steiner. For both thinkers, Israel's establishment poses an acute challenge to Jewish *individuals*, who are forced to accept or resist the state's claims upon their allegiance. In Butler's 2013 lecture, individual ethical dilemmas overshadow collective Jewish projects. We can see as much if we look at the role that self-determination plays in Butler's appeal. Butler defines the BDS movement as a movement "organized and led by Palestinians seeking rights of political self-determination." Butler never mentions Jewish self-determination, presumably because, unlike Palestinians, Israeli Jews enjoy rights of self-governance. Yet Butler also neglects to indicate whether self-determination remains a positive value or aspiration for Jews. Would a just resolution to the Israeli-Palestinian conflict include institutions that facilitate Jewish self-determination? Butler does not address this question, nor does she articulate a collective Jewish vision.

Rather, in this lecture, the challenge for Jews (and others) is to exercise autonomous judgment. Butler assumes that, their diverse ideological commitments notwithstanding, her listeners have "come here to exercise critical judgment." By attending Butler's talk, audience members confirm their "right to form and communicate an autonomous judgment, to demonstrate why you think something is true or not, and you should be free to do this without judgment and fear." The principles of academic freedom that Butler invokes are a precondition for exercising this important right. In the immediate context of the controversy surrounding Brooklyn College's decision to host the event, the judgment surrounds the BDS movement. Yet, as Butler proceeds to rebut the arguments of those who deny the movement's legitimacy, she also invites individuals to exercise critical judgment with respect to hegemonic identity claims. Against those who "suppress the complexity of the category of 'Jewish'" in an attempt "to yoke a cultural identity to a specific Zionist position," Butler reminds her listeners that "most categories of identity are fraught with conflicts and ambiguities." Thus, individuals must exercise autonomous judgment when confronted with claims about what Judaism means or requires. "In my view, we have to remain critical of anyone who posits a single norm that decides rights of entry into the social or cultural category determining as well who will be excluded." Moreover, Butler links this kind of criticism, animated by appreciation for diversity, to a diasporic Jewish ethos. "When Zionism becomes co-extensive with Jewishness, Jewishness is pitted against the diversity that defines democracy, and if I may say so, betrays one of the most important ethical dimensions of the diasporic Jewish tradition, namely, the obligation of co-habitation with those different from ourselves." Here, Butler implies that diasporic traditions cultivate the political values—openness to diversity, critical judgment, suspicion of reigning norms—that individuals are called to exercise. It is incumbent upon each of us to decide whether to accept dominant definitions of Jewishness, whether to "be complicit with the occupation," and whether to join a political movement to protest injustice. Like Steiner, Butler invokes diasporic traditions to encourage modes of individual judgment ostensibly threatened by Zionism's ascendance.

I have showcased Steiner's and Butler's concern for the moral integrity of Jewish individuals to get at what I consider a limitation of the discourses that remain popular on the academic Jewish left. Clearly, we must encourage and valorize individual acts of dissent, and we must support movements dedicated to truth and frank speech. Yet a culture of refusal and dissent does not provide a sufficiently powerful counterweight to the non-egalitarian Zionism that rules in Israel and continues to shape diasporic Jewish politics. To mount a credible challenge to in-egalitarian, state-centered Zionisms, Jewish leftists must articulate an alternative, positive vision, a vision that addresses both the "problem of the Jews" and the "problem of Judaism" (recognizing the collective dimensions of the latter predicament).

3. Jonathan Woocher, *Sacred Survival*

Jonathan Woocher, *Sacred Survival: The Civil Religion of American Jews*, Bloomington: Indiana University Press, 1986

Dr. Jonathan Woocher (1946–2017) was Professor of Jewish Communal Studies at Brandeis University, Founding President of the Lippman Kanfer Foundation for Living Torah, and both President and Chief Ideas Officer of the Jewish Education Service of North America.

The American Jewish civil religion which Robin's words invoke is, as detailed in the previous chapter, the product of an evolutionary process which has woven together strands from American Jewish folk religion and from the elite ideologies affirmed by important segments of American Jewry's institutional leadership. Its tenets reflect this process and the successful synthesis of diverse sentiments into an encompassing worldview and ethos. The social values of this civil Judaism bespeak its origins in the philanthropic ethos of the communal establishment. Its grounding in a firm sense of Jewish peoplehood reflects the intensity of ethnic sentiment among the masses of Eastern European Jews who migrated to America during the last century. The civil religion's commitment to Jewish continuity constitutes a clear response to the threats to Jewish survival which have become manifest in recent decades. And its affirmation of America as a setting for Jewish success and achievement expresses a nearly universal American Jewish conviction that here they are no longer in exile, but part of a pluralistic society which offers unprecedented opportunities for both integration and Jewish self-expression.

These themes were firmly established as part of the civil religion by the middle of the 1960s. It was during the years following Israel's Six Day War in 1967, however, that civil Judaism truly came of age as a force in the American Jewish religious consciousness. The late 1960s and the decades which have followed have been a period of Jewish renewal in North America. Despite frequently cited manifestations of assimilation on the part of some Jews (e.g., rising rates of intermarriage), the American Jewish community experienced as well as new wave of energy. Across a broad variety of fronts—in the development of new religious institutions, in the burgeoning of Jewish Studies in American universities, in growing political activism—Jews became more self-confident in their Jewishness and more creative in its expression.

Nineteen sixty-seven will surely be remembered as a watershed year in Jewish history. The impact of the events of that year on the State of Israel has obviously been enormous. Its impact on American Jewish life was only slightly less monumental. The traumatic days of May and June 1967, when Israel first seemed threatened by a new Holocaust, only to win a magnificent, almost miraculous victory culminating in the reunification of Jerusalem, galvanized American Jewry and launched a chain of response which eventually acquired momentum independent of its original impetus. The Six Day War was not alone responsible for the intensification of Jewish activity in America which followed. The seeds had begun to be planted even before the war. Indigenous factors—the general mood of social activism, the reawakened ethnic consciousness of many groups, the discomfort of some Jews with the direction of the civil rights movements, and later a broadly renewed interest in religion and spirituality—all played a role in sustaining the resurgence. But 1967 marked a clear turning point, and especially so for the federation-framed polity and its civil religion.

The most dramatic manifestation of the growing centrality of the polity in American Jewish life in the period following the Six Day War is the tremendous increase in the funds raised by federations and the UJA. In 1967 and again in the wake of the Yom Kippur War of 1973, American Jews gave unprecedently, both in numbers and in amount. Moreover, the primacy of the federation/UJA campaign was accepted by virtually every institution on the American Jewish scene. Though giving fell back when the immediate crises had waned, new plateaus were established, and from the post-1973 plateau annual contributions have risen again to surpass $600,000,000.

Even more important, however, is the extent to which the UJA/federation movement and its leadership have emerged clearly as a preeminent force in Jewish communal life in the post-1967 period. It is perhaps the link to Israel through fundraising which made this rise to preeminence possible. But Israel has hardly been the entire focus of the polity's efforts or the sole source of its expanded influence. The impact of polity institutions has come to be felt in every sphere of Jewish activity. The federations and UJA have become a focal point for Jewish identification, and a rallying point for those seeking to strengthen Jewish life in all its dimensions. The Jewish polity has ridden the broad wave of intensifying Jewishness in North America; it has also helped to feed and to steer its currents.

The "Judaization" of the federation/UJA structure which has given it credibility as a "central address" for American Jewry came as a result of both pressure from without and a process of self-discovery from within. The self-discovery had been taking place for several decades as the polity moved ever more firmly toward a survivalist agenda. Its climax was the 1967 war, during which thousands of American Jews, including many of those who had been active leaders in the community, discovered a depth of Jewish concern and commitment in themselves they had not previously recognized was there. The push to translate that heightened Jewish consciousness into an intensified programmatic thrust came often from activist Jewish youth. They turned to the federations and demanded that verbal professions of concern for Jewish survival be matched by a greatly augmented financial and programmatic commitment to Jewish education as the best guarantor of Jewish continuity. (65–66)

COMMENTARY BY SYLVIA BARACK FISHMAN

How did American Jews in the second half of the twentieth century define their Jewishness? That question animated the research agendas of several major scholars of American Jewry from the 1960s through the 1980s, when identification with Jewishness and affiliation with the Jewish polity had effectively become voluntary—rather than an ethno-religious identity ascribed at birth—for American Jews. Social scientists Marshall Sklare, Charles Liebman, Jonathan Woocher, Calvin Goldscheider, Steven M. Cohen, Herbert Gans, and others analyzed the parameters of this American Jewishness-by-choice, creating the vocabularies and sketching out the conceptual frameworks utilized by many subsequent sociologists and policy makers.

The postwar era opened new opportunities for Jews educationally, professionally, and economically. Sklare examined the Jewish identity, experiences and attitudes of Jews migrating from urban Jewish neighborhoods to previously gentile suburbs, in his landmark study with Joseph Greenblum.[1] Two decades later, by the time Woocher published *Sacred Survival: The Civil Religion of American Jews,* Jewish geographic migration—and an equally significant upward socioeconomic mobility—had transformed American Jewish life. But while Sklare's *Jewish Identity on the Suburban Frontier* discussed primarily

---

1 Marshall Sklare and Joseph Greenblum, *Jewish Identity on the Suburban Frontier: A Study of Group Survival in the Open Society* (Chicago: University of Chicago Press, 1967).

Jewishly ambivalent trailblazers relocating far from organized Jewish life, at least temporarily, Woocher spotlighted American Jewish organizational leadership, a group deeply devoted to secular Jewish institutions like local and national Jewish federations. The two studies, in other words, examined disparate Jewish populations. Nevertheless, their questions were startlingly similar. How were American Jews distinctively American? How were they also distinctively Jewish, simultaneously rooted in "Jewish unity and distinctiveness on one hand" and "in American society on the other" (131)?

Even secular American Jews with little interest in Judaism often experienced a heightened sense of their own and Jewish communal vulnerability before and after World War II, which galvanized a self-conscious—and frequently defensive—awareness of Jewish peoplehood. Woocher posited that American Jews were obsessed with "Jewish survival in a threatening world." The organizational leaders he studied displayed little concern about the continuity of the sacred, spiritual, or cultural Jewishness, about Jewish education, or the preservation, revitalization, or transmission of Jewish culture; "Survival" meant "first and foremost the physical survival of Jews and the Jewish people," whether in the United States, other Diaspora communities, or in the Jewish State of Israel. This focus on physical survival was precipitated by the lessons of Jewish history: "Since the Holocaust, no leader of the Jewish polity is prepared to take even this level of continuity for granted" (72–73).

In framing the beliefs and values of American Jewish leadership as a "civil religion," Woocher adapted iconic concepts of Robert N. Bellah, who himself traced the concept of civil religion back to Rousseau's *The Social Contract*.[2] Bellah saw American civil ideals as a "religion" rendered sacred by "a genuine apprehension of universal and transcendent religious reality … as revealed through the experience of the American people" (9). In similar fashion, Woocher insisted, the Jews he studied subscribed to a "civil religion" incorporating a sweeping, universalistic goal: "American Jewish civil religion is an activist religion emphasizing the pursuit of Jewish survival and social justice" (131). With its two-pronged dedication to tribal wellbeing and universalistic ideals, Jewish civil religion was based on three central animating myths (132): first, a narrative of 'Holocaust to rebirth"—which spotlighted not only the Holocaust as "awful proof" of historical Jewish vulnerability, but also the critical importance of Israel as "preeminent symbol of that new condition, that new power, or a new era in

---

2   Robert Bellah, "Civil Religion in America," *Daedalus: Journal of the American Academy of Arts and Sciences* 96, no. 1 (Winter 1967): 1–21.

Jewish history" (134–135); second, an insistence that "America—and American Jews—are different"; and third, a renewed embrace of the ancient concept that Jews are "a chosen people, a people with a special destiny," as understood by the "folk"—"bearing witness against injustice, laboring for brotherhood" (142).

Sacred Survival's conceptualization of American Jewishness was critiqued by Jonathan Sarna in his aptly entitled *Commentary* magazine review, "Federation Judaism."[3] Woocher's observations accurately described organizational leadership, but not ordinary Jews, Sarna charged. Moreover, Woocher "abandons the role of the religious sociologist and casts himself as the prophet of a new Jewish religious movement." Espousing "a form of civil Judaism" which, in Woocher's own words, "places at the center of its world not Torah, but the Jewish people, and makes the maintenance and expression of Jewish peoplehood its primary religious obligation," Jewish civil religion ignores the traditional religious content of home, school, or synagogue. Performed "in the public square," Sarna wrote, "communal and political work" become the Jewish leader's "sacred calling."

Nevertheless, Woocher's "civil religion" gained impressive traction in Jewish policy conversation, bolstered by another innovative positive understanding of the secularization and Protestantization of American Jewishness, "transformationalism," as proposed by Calvin Goldscheider and Steven M. Cohen, and popularized by Charles E. Silberman.[4] "Transformationalism" hypothesized that Jewish communal life remains vibrant as long as Jews comprise a cohesive group, even if the specifics of that cohesiveness are transformed. Goldscheider argued that immigrant American Jews had been stratified by poverty and outsider status, but in the 1980s Jews were a cohesive group stratified by high levels of education, high social status occupations, and liberal political attitudes; this cohesiveness is cemented by mostly Jewish friendship circles and mostly endogamous marriages. Goldscheider, Cohen, and especially Silberman created a triumphant picture of the broad center of American Jewry enjoying ever-increasing opportunities, yet simultaneously remaining distinctive and retaining pride in their Jewish heritage. Like Woocher, Goldscheider, Cohen, and Silberman suggested this survival was successful regardless of the *cultural content* of the Jewish societies that survived.

---

3   Jonathan D. Sarna, "Federation Judaism," *Commentary* (December 1987).

4   Calvin Goldscheider, *Jewish Continuity and Change: Emerging Patterns in America* (Bloomington: Indiana University Press, 1986); Steven M. Cohen, *American Assimilation or Jewish Revival* (Bloomington: Indiana University Press, 1988); Charles Silberman, *A Certain People: American Jews and their Lives Today* (New York: Summit Books, 1985).

In striking contrast, Sklare, Liebman, and Gans may be termed "content survivalists." That is, these three expressed profound concern not only about survival but even more so about the *cultural content* of surviving Jewish societies. Liebman saw liberal values as a dangerous diluter of Jewish distinctiveness for "the ambivalent American Jew";[5] he suggested that Jewish distinctiveness required "deviations from contemporary standards of behavior," and that, significantly, "Jewish commitment of all kinds is associated with religious performance."[6] Gans's much quoted *cri de coeur* exposed what he called, "symbolic ethnicity." Gans belittled in pointed detail the then growing popularity of "ethnic symbols ... individual cultural practices which are taken from the older ethnic culture" but are "pulled out of its original moorings."[7] Unlike ethnic practices that bind individuals to the ethnic group, individualized symbolic ethnicity is inauthentic, in Gans's estimation, because it "does not require functioning groups or networks," and thus is no guarantee of "the persistence of ethnic groups or cultures."

A comparison of interpretive frameworks reveals the differences between Woocher the survivalist and Sklare the content survivalist. Woocher's *Sacred Survival* includes a section examining American Jewish "norms for 'good Jewishness'" (123–128), a conceptual framework that usefully reprises Sklare's famous attitudinal and behavioral tables in his "The Image of the Good Jew in Lakeville" chapter (Sklare, 321–332).

His respondents' Jewish "personal belief systems may be inconsequential," Woocher writes approvingly; they worry about Jewish physical survival: "All of the items rated very serious by a majority of the respondents can be seen as immediate threats to the physical continuity and communal integrity of the Jewish people and American Jewry." The physical safety of Israel and world Jewry are the epitome of survivalist concerns: "Israel's conflicts and the treatment of Jews in the Soviet Union should head the list of problems facing the American Jewish community" (124). Woocher details and ultimately celebrates a kind of secularized Jewish nationalism, twinned with Jewish nonsectarian dedication to humanitarian causes.

In contrast, Sklare's ruefully bemused tone in the Lakeville study two decades earlier carries a strong judgmental undertone of mourning that his

---

5   Charles S. Liebman, *The Ambivalent American Jew* (Philadelphia: Jewish Publication Society, 1973).

6   Charles S. Liebman, "Orthodox Judaism Today," *Midstream* 25, no. 7 (1979): 25.

7   Herbert J. Gans, "Symbolic Ethnicity: The Future of Ethnic Groups and Cultures in America," *Ethnic and Racial Studies* 2, no. 1 (January 1979): 435ff.

Lakeville Jewish respondents care little about Jewish learning, Jewish history and culture, and most traditional rituals; instead, "the actions and *mitzvot* which the Lakeville Jew esteems most highly are found in the general culture" and display a "lack of distinctiveness" which "is capable of eroding away group boundaries" (329). Scientific in his data collection, Sklare is hardly dispassionate about his findings that American Jewish suburban life is characterized by ethnoreligious impoverishment. In his conclusion, assessing the "meager Jewishness" of Lakeville's youth to be "the true *bete noire* of Jewish life in Lakeville," Sklare deliberately echoes the Rosh Hashanah liturgy and declares "assimilation" to be "an evil decree" which "threatens" Jewish "survival" (331–332).

All of these interpretive frameworks and assumptions were challenged by the findings of the 1990 National Jewish Population Survey (NJPS), which revealed a panorama of large patterns in American Jewish life. The 1990 NJPS and subsequent analyses surprised many and changed social scientific and policy discussions. Data showed that the social stratification which once motivated most Jews to befriend and marry Jews, for example, had given way to diverse friendship patterns and increasing intermarriage between Jews and non-Jews. The denominational framework which once provided scaffolding for Jewish associations and friendship circles lost membership. Issues crucial to Woocher's secular Jewish organizational leaders struck many young Jews as irrelevant, tribal, and sometimes alienating. America's hybridized younger Jews, most of them generations away from immigrant experiences, did not relate to images of Jewish vulnerability. As readings in this volume detail, some Jews rejected the concept of Jewish peoplehood, and some felt ambivalent about Israel or at least about Israeli policies. To be sure, studies revealed many indications of renewal and revitalization, new sources of engagement with and attachment to Jewish community, history, culture, and religion. But after 1990, the view that secularized survival alone could provide a sacred core for passionate attachments to Jewishness no longer seemed compelling.

4. Benny Morris, *The Birth of the Palestinian Refugee Problem, 1947–1949* and *The Birth of the Palestinian Refugee Problem Revisited*

Ari Shavit, "Survival of the Fittest? An Interview with Benny Morris" and "Lydda, 1948"

Benny Morris, *The Birth of the Palestinian Refugee Problem, 1947–1949*, Cambridge: Cambridge University Press, 1987 and *The Birth of the Palestinian Refugee Problem Revisited*, Cambridge: Cambridge University Press, 2004. The text below is from the 2004 edition.

Dr. Benny Morris (1948–) is a Middle East Studies faculty member at Ben-Gurion University in Beersheba, Israel. In addition to authoring several books on the Israeli-Palestinian conflict, he worked as a journalist at the *Jerusalem Post* and has written for various other news publications, including the *New York Times*, the *New Republic*, and the *New York Review of Books*.

In examining the causes of the Arab exodus from Palestine over 1947–1949, accurate quantification is impossible. I have tried to show that the exodus occurred in stages and that causation was multi-layered: A Haifa merchant did not leave only because of the weeks or months of sniping and bombings; or because business was getting bad; or because of intimidation and extortion by irregulars; or because he feared the collapse of law and order when the British left; or because he feared for his prospects and livelihood under Jewish rule. He left because of the accumulation of all these factors. And the mass of Haifaites who fled in his wake, at the end of April–early May 1948, did not flee only as a result of the Arab militia collapse and Haganah conquest of April 21–22. They fled because of the cumulative effect of the elite's departure, the snipings, and bombings, and material privations, unemployment and chaos during the previous months; and because of their local leaders' instructions to leave, issued on April 22; and because of the follow up orders by the AHC [Arab Higher Committee] to continue departing; and because of IZL [The Irgun—אצ״ל] and Haganah activities and pressures during the days after the conquest; and because of the prospect of life under Jewish rule. (598)

What happened in Palestine/Israel over 1947–1949 was so complex and varied, the situation radically changing from date to date and place to place, that a single-cause explanation of the exodus from most sites is untenable. At most, one can say that certain causes were important in certain areas at certain times, with a general shift in the spring of 1948 from precedence of cumulative internal Arab factors—lack of leadership, economic problems, breakdown of law and order—to a primacy of external, compulsive causes: Haganah/IDF [Israeli Defense Force] attacks and expulsions, fear of Jewish attacks and atrocities, lack of help from the Arab world and the AHC and a feeling of impotence and abandonment, and orders from Arab officials and commanders to leave. In general, throughout the war, the final and decisive precipitant to flight in most places was Haganah, IZL, LHI [Lehi], or IDF attack or the inhabitants' fear of imminent attack. During the second half of 1948, international concern about the refugee problem mounted. Concern translated into pressure. This pressure, initiated by [Folke] Bernadotte and the Arab states in the summer of 1948, increased as the months passed, as the number of refugees swelled, as their physical plight became more acute and as the discomfort of their Arab hosts grew. The problem moved to the forefront of every discussion of the Middle East crisis and the Arabs made their agreement to a settlement, nay, even to meaningful negotiations, with Israel contingent on a solution of the problem by repatriation. (599)

Ari Shavit, "Survival of the Fittest? An Interview with Benny Morris," *Haaretz*, January 08, 2004

Ari Shavit (1957–) has been a columnist for *Haaretz* since 1995. His work has also appeared in the *New Yorker*, the *New York Times*, and *Politico*.

You went through an interesting process. You went to research Ben-Gurion and the Zionist establishment critically, but in the end you actually identify with them. You are as tough in your words as they were in their deeds.

You may be right. Because I investigated the conflict in depth, I was forced to cope with the in-depth questions that those people coped with. I understood the problematic character of the situation they faced and maybe I adopted part of their universe of concepts. But I do not identify with Ben-Gurion. I think he made a serious historical mistake in 1948. Even though he understood the demographic issue and the need to establish a Jewish state without a large Arab minority, he got cold feet during the war. In the end, he faltered.

I'm not sure I understand. Are you saying that Ben-Gurion erred in expelling too few Arabs?

If he was already engaged in expulsion, maybe he should have done a complete job. I know that this stuns the Arabs and the liberals and the politically correct types. But my feeling is that this place would be quieter and know less suffering if the matter had been resolved once and for all. If Ben-Gurion had carried out a large expulsion and cleansed the whole country—the whole Land of Israel, as far as the Jordan River. It may yet turn out that this was his fatal mistake. If he had carried out a full expulsion—rather than a partial one—he would have stabilized the State of Israel for generations.

I find it hard to believe what I am hearing.

If the end of the story turns out to be a gloomy one for the Jews, it will be because Ben-Gurion did not complete the transfer in 1948. Because he left a large and volatile demographic reserve in the West Bank and Gaza and within Israel itself.

In his place, would you have expelled them all? All the Arabs in the country?

But I am not a statesman. I do not put myself in his place. But as an historian, I assert that a mistake was made here. Yes. The non-completion of the transfer was a mistake.

Ari Shavit, "Lydda, 1948," *New Yorker*, October 21, 2013

On July 11th, two platoons from the 3rd Battalion advanced from the conquered village of Daniyal toward the olive groves separating Ben Shemen from Lydda. The Arab militia defending the city held them off with machine-gun fire. In the meantime, the 89th Battalion, led by Moshe Dayan, had arrived in Ben Shemen. In the late afternoon, the battalion, consisting of a giant armored vehicle mounted with a cannon, menacing half-tracks, and machine-gun equipped jeeps, left Ben Shemen and stormed Lydda. In a forty-seven-minute-long blitz, dozens of Arabs were shot dead, including women, children, and old people. The 89th Battalion lost nine men. In the early evening, the two 3rd Battalion platoons were able to enter the city. Within hours, the soldiers held key positions in the city center and had confined thousands of Palestinian civilians in the Great Mosque.

The next day, according to "1948," by Benny Morris, two Jordanian armored vehicles entered the conquered city, setting off a new wave of violence. The Jordanian Army was miles to the east, and the two vehicles were of no military significance, but some of the Arab citizens of Lydda thought that they were harbingers of liberation. Soldiers of the 3rd Battalion feared that they were in imminent danger of Jordanian assault. Some Palestinians fired on Israeli soldiers near a small mosque. Among the young combatants taking cover in a ditch nearby were Ben Shemen graduates, now in uniform. The brigade commander was a Ben Shemen graduate, too. He gave the order to open fire. Some of the soldiers threw hand grenades into Arab houses. One fired an anti-tank shell into the small mosque. In thirty minutes, two hundred and fifty Palestinians were killed. Zionism had carried out a massacre in the city of Lydda.

When the news reached the headquarters of Operation Larlar, in the Palestinian village of Yazur, the military commander, General Yigal Allon, asked Ben-Gurion what to do with the Arabs. Ben-Gurion waved his hand: Deport them. Hours later, Yitzhak Rabin, the operations officer, issued a written order to the Yiftach Brigade: "The inhabitants of Lydda must be expelled quickly, without regard to age."

The next day, negotiations were held in the rectory of St. George's Church between Shmarya Gutman, the newly appointed military governor of Lydda, and the Arab dignitaries of the occupied city. When negotiations ended, in the late morning of July 13, 1948, it was agreed that the Arabs in Lydda and the refugees residing there would be expelled from the city immediately. By evening, approximately thirty-five thousand Palestinian Arabs had left Lydda in a long column, marching past the Ben Shemen youth village and disappearing into the east. Zionism had obliterated the city of Lydda.

Lydda is the black box of Zionism. The truth is that Zionism could not bear the Arab city of Lydda. From the very beginning, there was a substantial contradiction between Zionism and Lydda. If Zionism was to exist, Lydda could not exist. If Lydda was to exist, Zionism could not exist. In retrospect, it's all too clear. When Siegfried Lehmann arrived in the Lydda Valley, in 1927, he should have seen that if a Jewish state was to exist in Palestine an Arab Lydda could not exist at its center. He should have known that Lydda was an obstacle blocking the road to a Jewish state, and that one day Zionism would have to remove it. But Dr. Lehmann did not see, and Zionism chose not to know. For decades, Jews succeeded in hiding from themselves the contradiction between their national movement and

Lydda. For forty-five years, Zionism pretended to be the Atid factory and the olive groves and the Ben Shemen youth village living in peace with Lydda. Then, in three days in the cataclysmic summer of 1948, Lydda was no more.

COMMENTARY BY DANIEL KURTZER

As of 2018, the United Nations High Commissioner for Refugees reports that 44,400 people have been forced to leave their homes every day as a result of conflict and persecution. These people have taken refuge either in other parts of their countries or in neighboring states, and the UNHCR has taken on the responsibility to "protect refugees and resolve refugee problems worldwide[,] … to safeguard the rights and well-being of refugees[,] … to ensure that everyone can exercise the right to seek asylum and find safe refuge in another State, with the option to return home voluntarily, integrate locally or to resettle in a third country[,] … [and] to help stateless people." UNHCR currently has responsibility for 19.9 million refugees worldwide.

An additional 5.4 million refugees are registered with the United Nations Relief and Works Agency for Palestinian Refugees in the Near East. UNRWA, created by the UN in 1949, one year before UNHCR, is the only UN agency responsible for a single people. Initially assuming responsibility for about 750,000 refugees from the 1947–1949 Arab-Israeli war, the UNRWA rolls grew as it registered the children and grandchildren of the original refugees.

Everything about the Palestinian refugee issue and UNRWA is a source of deep and emotional controversy. Israelis and Palestinians differ sharply as to how and why the refugee situation came about—whether it resulted from the normal course of events in war when civilians flee their homes in search of safety and shelter; or whether Israel pursued a conscious policy of depopulating areas of the battlefield that it sought to integrate into the future State of Israel; or whether Arab leaders advised their people to move temporarily while Arab armies fought in Palestine.

This dispute over the origins of the problem has impacted the narratives of both Palestinians and the State of Israel. They dispute everything related to this issue. They dispute the number of refugees displaced and the definition of who is a refugee. They dispute whether the refugees should remain on the international agenda after so many years since the original displacement. And they dispute the core question of who was and is responsible for creating and resolving the problem. Palestinians want Israel to accept responsibility for causing the problem; Israel rejects this notion, believing that acceptance of any responsibility would be tantamount to agreeing that its state was born in sin.

Israel and the Palestinians also differ fundamentally about what to do to resolve the refugee issue. Israel says that the refugees should be absorbed into a future Palestinian state or offered resettlement in place or elsewhere. Israel fears that a refugee influx into Israel would threaten the Jewish majority in the country. Israel also argues for the rehabilitation of existing refugee camps, arguing that the refugees should not be consigned to live in miserable conditions while awaiting a political solution. The Palestinians believe that United Nations General Assembly resolution 194 (1948) confers a "right of return" for the refugees to regain the homes they left in Palestine. Palestinians reject resettlement and typically oppose the rehabilitation of refugee camps, believing this is a backdoor method for resolving the refugee problem *in situ*.

The two sides also have divergent views about the role of UNRWA and the international community. Israel charges that UNRWA has perpetuated the refugee problem, rather than having worked to resolve it; Israel also objects to the refusal of the Palestinians and the failure of UNRWA to rehabilitate the refugee camps. Palestinians cling to UNRWA as the international confirmation of their status and rely upon UNRWA to meet the basic needs of the refugees.

Palestinian scholars have never challenged the prevailing Palestinian narrative. They are constrained, in the first instance, by the deep national emotions attached to this issue and the likelihood of ostracism if their research admitted any fault lines in the Palestinian narrative. They are also constrained by the relatively poor state of Palestinian archives. There is no central national archive, and much material has been lost over time as a result of war.

Israeli scholars, on the other hand, started researching this issue in the 1980s, as the state archives began declassifying relevant material that could be assessed against British and private holdings. The first scholar to mine the archives was Benny Morris, who published *The Birth of the Palestinian Refugee Problem, 1947–1949* (Cambridge University Press, 1987). Morris acknowledged that the archives were incomplete, but his study was the first detailed account of Zionist/Israeli policy and actions that contributed to the refugee problem in the period of independence. Morris also provided details on Israeli military actions during that period, notably rapes and murders.

As would be expected, Morris's book was greeted with outrage by the Israeli establishment. He was accused of being an anti-Zionist and of harming state security; and other academics, notably Ephraim Karsh, attacked his scholarship, claiming that he had been selective in utilizing his sources and plain wrong in assessing Israeli statements, policies and actions. Morris and Karsh engaged in a war of words that, as usual in these cases, shed more heat than light on the problem. Several years after the original work was published, Morris published a revised version of the book, drawing on some additional sources and adding a new chapter on the idea of "transfer" in Zionist thinking. This revised edition did little to quiet the storm he had raised. (The excerpt above is from the revised edition.)

Over the next twenty-five years, additional scholarly work added to the debate by creating a more nuanced narrative of mixed responsibility, that is, a combination of the fog of war, Israeli proactive measures, decisions by Arab leaders to advise people to leave their homes, fear, and confusion, which all contributed to the Palestinian refugee problem. Once Palestinians had left their homes, politics, obstinacy, poor leadership, and diplomatic stalemate condemned the refugees to seventy years of statelessness.

More than twenty years of negotiations between Israelis and Palestinians failed to advance this issue very much. The 1991 Madrid Peace Conference paved the way for multilateral talks on the refugee issue, but no breakthroughs occurred. The refugee problem contributed to the failure of the Camp David II Summit in 2000, and it played a role in torpedoing every other effort to resolve the underlying dispute.

Recently, two factors have come into play to raise the public's consciousness about this issue. First, Benny Morris stunned the academic and political communities by revealing that, his own scholarship notwithstanding, he believed Israel had been justified in expelling the Palestinians during the war of independence: in his own words, "There are cases in which the overall, final good justifies harsh and cruel acts that are committed in the course of history."[1] Without the expulsions, Morris rued, the State of Israel would not have come into being.

Morris did not stop there, but argued further that Israel should have expelled all the Palestinians. Expressing the view that those Arabs who remained in Israel and became Israeli citizens were "a potential fifth column," Morris said: "If [Ben Gurion] was already engaged in expulsion, maybe he should have done a complete job. ... The non-completion of the transfer was a mistake."

And then along came Ari Shavit, at the time one of Israel's most respected journalists, who published "Lydda, 1948" in the *New Yorker* on October 21, 2013, a chapter from what was to become a popular book about the promise

---

1   Benny Morris, "Survival of the Fittest (Cont.)," *Haaretz*, January 8, 2004.

and challenges of contemporary Israel. Shavit, clearly conflicted in writing about events and Israeli actions that he knows were wrong, chronicles the ethnic cleansing of the Arab town of Lydda during the 1948 fighting. It was, he shows, a conscious act undertaken by Israeli commanders—notably among them future prime minister Yitzhak Rabin—who understood what their political leaders—notably David Ben Gurion—wanted done. In something of an echo of Morris, Shavit wrote: "From the very beginning, there was a substantial contradiction between Zionism and Lydda. If Zionism was to exist, Lydda could not exist."

For those, like me, who have been immersed in the search for peace for many decades, it has always seemed possible to bridge differences and thus avoid the stark choices that morality versus politics sometimes asks us to make. In the case of the Palestinian refugee issue, it was thought possible to preserve the Palestinians' "right of return" by offering them automatic citizenship and the right to settle in the Palestinian state that would one day be established. In this way, the refugees would satisfy their right to live in Palestine without asserting that right in the State of Israel. Under terms of a negotiated agreement, the international community would offer generous terms of financial compensation, both to those who chose to move to Palestine as well as those who decided to live elsewhere. Refugee-receiving countries would open their doors to a certain number of Palestinians. And language would be found to deal with the clash of narratives, so as to provide the refugees with some sense that their long wait for a resolution of their status was not for nothing, while exonerating Israel from any suggestion that the state was born in sin.

As the search for peace progressed over the years, there were some voices within each community ready to venture into these areas of compromise. In December 2000, President Bill Clinton offered "parameters" for negotiations that sought to narrow differences and provide a pathway for resolving outstanding problems. In those parameters, Clinton addressed all of the issues, starting his analysis with a striking declaration: "I believe that Israel is prepared to acknowledge the moral and material suffering caused to the Palestinian people as a result of the 1948 war and the need to assist the international community in addressing the problem." After offering American and international assistance to resolve the problem, Clinton addressed the core issue, the Palestinian claim of a "right of return":

> I know the history of the issue and how hard it will be for the Palestinian leadership to appear to be abandoning this principle. The Israeli side could

not accept any reference to a right of return that would imply a right to immigrate to Israel in defiance of Israel's sovereign policies and admission or that would threaten the Jewish character of the state. Any solution must address both needs.

Keeping his focus on the goal of a two-state solution to the Palestinian-Israeli conflict, Clinton argued that "the guiding principle should be that the Palestinian state would be the focal point for Palestinians who choose to return to the area without ruling out that Israel will accept some of these refugees. I believe that we need to adopt a formulation on the right of return that will make clear that there is no specific right of return to Israel itself but that does not negate the aspiration of the Palestinian people to return to the area." Clinton went on to propose multiple options for solving the problem, offering refugees a menu of choices where they could settle.

Neither side accepted the parameters, and Clinton withdrew them. However, right after Clinton left the presidency, the Israelis and Palestinians restarted negotiations in Taba, Egypt, and according to the European Union observer at the talks, they engaged in a substantive discussion of the refugee problem, in which they exchanged papers and ideas for the first time. The Taba talks ended without success, however, and the peace process went into hibernation until the 2008 talks between Israeli Prime Minister Ehud Olmert and Palestinian President Mahmoud Abbas. At that time, Olmert made a stunning offer to the Palestinians.

According to a report by Bernard Avishai in the *New York Times*, Olmert offered to accept into Israel 1,000 Palestinians a year for five years, and that the process of repatriation would be in the spirit of the Arab League peace plan of 2002, the first time an Israeli leader was prepared to accord some importance to that Arab plan. Olmert also offered wording that would address the Palestinian narrative of suffering. In return for these gestures, Olmert expected written confirmation that the agreement would represent the end of all claims and the end of conflict. Abbas reportedly demanded a much larger number of returnees to Israel, but in general did not respond to Olmert's overall peace initiative.

Since 2008, there have been no formal or official talks between Israel and the Palestinians on the refugee issue, and only occasional contacts at all on the peace process, including several efforts undertaken during the Obama administration. Meanwhile, think tanks and academics continue to develop formulas to try to bridge differences and offer tools for policy makers to try to fix this problem.

These diplomatic activities, however interesting and in some cases promising, have not addressed the underlying moral and ethical issues in relation to political imperatives. The selections from Morris and Shavit expose some of the thinking and arguments that Israelis grapple with when considering the Palestinian refugee issue. Palestinian writers have addressed the refugee question in detail, but their approach has been focused on advocacy, to demonstrate the legitimacy of the Palestinian position, without much self-reflection. The divergent Israeli views that follow, therefore, will reflect anguish and anger, offering a glimpse into what is arguably the most contentious issue in the Israeli-Palestinian conflict.

5. Irving Greenberg vs. Meir Kahane, Public Debate at the Hebrew Institute of Riverdale

Irving (Yitz) Greenberg vs. Meir Kahane, Public Debate at the Hebrew Institute of Riverdale, 1988[1]

Rabbi Dr. Irving (Yitz) Greenberg (1933–) served as President of the Jewish Life Network/Steinhardt Foundation and the National Jewish Center for Learning and Leadership (CLAL).

Rabbi Meir Kahane (1932–1990) founded the Jewish Defense League in 1968. In 1971, Rabbi Kahane emigrated to Israel, founded the Kach party, and, in 1984, became a member of Knesset. He was assassinated in Manhattan in 1990.

Kahane:
Halakhah. I'm a man of Halakhah. The Halakhah is clear that the non-Jew does not have a status of a Jew. Democracy is not Judaism. It may be painful to the Modern Orthodox. Of course it's painful. It's too bad. But it's Halakhah. Should I read to you the Rambam? The Halakhah is clear. …

But more important, long before the Arabs are a majority, what happens when they become a third of the population and they join together in a coalition government with the extreme left? Is that what you want? Is that what you want? Who is a Jew? Decided by one third of an Arab Knesset. And above all there is Halakhah here and if there is one Arab in the country who is not willing to accept the status that was given to him by the Halakhah, that Arab must go too. And we bow our heads to Halakhah, or are we not ordained rabbis? …

The Palestinians believe that there should be no Israel. That is the problem. We sit and play games and games with them, and worse, with ourselves. The Arabs are not, I repeat for the second time, are not, leaving the Territories. They are coming back in droves. Unemployment now is rife in Kuwait, in Saudi, in Oman, and in Abu Dhabi. They are returning. They never left. They left their families behind and send them checks constantly. There are Arabs from America

---

1   "Rabbi Kahane debates Prof. Greenberg," https://www.youtube.com/watch?v=ZefkNmO5ins. Accessed 2019.

who are not coming back. I saw them when I was on reserve duty for a month. Now, to live in this delusion, "if we give this back and we give that back," that somehow we will realize that time is not on our side. Time is on their side. As long as we have Jews who split the community. As long as we have Jews who condemn the policy of the government of Israel. As long as we have Jews who march with the Palestinians, then time is on their side. I'm not afraid of the Arabs. I'm afraid of such Jews and this one here who with no meaning is a danger to the existence of Israel.

Greenberg:
In short, the overwhelming consensus of responsible rabbis of any halakhic standing, or learning, or *menshlikhkeit,* is that these laws do not apply to Arabs or to Christians or non-Jews who are not idolaters and therefore [Kahane] is using this totally out of context in order to make the Halakhah appear to be cruel, atrocity ridden, antagonistic to gentiles. The truth is, I would say, the opposite, that there should be no limits to Arab rights because in fact democracy gives them a chance to grow and become integrated into society and to commit themselves to that society. Democracy is the best fulfillment of the vision of the Jewish covenant. ...

There is an indigenous Arab population on the West Bank and Gaza. It's 1,342,000 and growing. If we add them to the Israeli Arab population that changes ... the balance from 82/16 to 65/35. The highest birthrates in the Arab world are in the West Bank and Gaza because the women there are in rural situations and are in poverty and their absolute births would make Arab births outnumber the Jews. And for that reason alone because that is the only potential plausible theory of imbalance demographically. But the deeper reason is even deeper than that. Our dream is realized. We came back to the land of Israel, we paid in full for it. But there is a population there; and they are human beings. It's true they are neglected by their own Arabs, other Arabs, it's true they are exploited by the PLO and Israel. But they have roots, attachments, hopes, and lives. They didn't have a Palestinian nationalism twenty-five years ago but now they do. In part because of exposure of Israel and our model of self-respect and dignity and self-rule. If I can make room for them, I should. If I can make room for their dignity, the answer is yes. And the greatest respect and greatest peace chance come when there is self-rule and self-responsibility. Now our commitment to their dignity and their freedom cannot be to commit suicide. It is no *mitzvah* to destroy ourselves and therefore we will long for peace and if there is a new leadership that is prepared to make peace they are going to change. It's up to them to convince, to convince us the Jewish people.

COMMENTARY BY SHAUL MAGID

Debates are often entertaining but painful to watch, as they give us a sense of the pulse of opinion and sentiment in particular communities. Sometimes, as in the 1263 disputation between Moses Nahmanides and the apostate Pablo Christiani, they become canonical. More often they remain snapshots frozen in time that can tell us about one particular moment rather than signposts to the future.

1988 was a year that presaged the coming of a storm in Israel and thus a year of anxiety for many American Jews. It was more than ten years since Likud first came to power in 1977, making settlements in the West Bank and Gaza government policy. Peace Now, founded in 1978, was beginning to gain traction in the Israeli left. The shock and surprise of the First Intifada was two years away and yet many felt that Israel's tenuous control over its Palestinian population could not hold. Tensions with the Palestinians were running high and the election of Rabbi Meir Kahane to the Knesset in 1984, after two failed attempts, was a wake-up call for both the establishment right and the pragmatic left. In some way, Kahane's political ascendency made the political establishment realize something had gone terribly wrong in Israeli society.

In the winter of 1988 Kahane and Rabbi Irving (Yitz) Greenberg, former high school friends, debated at the Hebrew Institute of Riverdale in the Bronx. The debate was moderated by Rabbi Avi Weiss, who adeptly framed the debate around four pertinent issues: three dealing with contemporary political realities in Israel, especially regarding the Palestinians, and one about the status of non-Orthodox rabbis and Jews in Israel. Like most debates, the venue and context are significant. The Hebrew Institute of Riverdale was (and is) a Modern Orthodox synagogue in New York City. The audience was likely comprised mostly of Orthodox Jews who, in the late 1980s were strongly supportive of Israel but in many instances wary of Kahane's militarism and yet also nervous about the call for land compromise made by Peace Now.

Weiss was the synagogue's respected rabbi who had made his name as a leading voice in the movement for Soviet Jewry in the 60s and early 70s and was known to be center-right on Israel, and thus in some way closer to Kahane than Greenberg. He was also a strong believer in religious pluralism, and thus closer to Greenberg than Kahane. Weiss's questions were crisp, critical, and probing.

Debates are not usually won on merit; they are usually won on performance and persuasion. In this case, Kahane was much better suited for the task even as Greenberg was much better prepared. Greenberg was professorial and came prepared with statistics and facts, combined with a clear commitment to Israeli security and belief in Jewish pluralism. Each time he approached the podium he did so with seriousness and resolve even as he unfortunately often did little more than read a laundry list of facts with little emotion. The facts, Greenberg believed, would make his case.

Kahane, on the other hand, approached the podium with a swagger, each time glancing at a wrinkled piece of paper he took from his coat pocket, looked at the audience and spoke with passion, conviction, and verve, even if it was openly apparent he was exaggerating beyond the facts.

Greenberg argued that we have to take risks for peace. Kahane claimed there is, and can be, no peace, and that after the Holocaust Jews could not afford to take a risk for anything. Ironically, Greenberg looked like an ideologue while Kahane portrayed himself as a pragmatist.

We can point to three points of contention in the debate. The first is the use of Halakhah as a justification for policy in the State of Israel. A main issue on the table was the proposal Kahane had made in the Knesset for what was known then as "transfer," forcibly transferring the Palestinians in the West Bank to the Jordanian side of the river and then annexing the West Bank as part of Israel. It was a proposal that had been soundly rejected by the Knesset. Kahane argued that Arabs in Israel were the enemy and that coexistence could only happen if they were reconciled to Jewish hegemony. He repeated a comment he often noted that "the Arabs" were as fervently nationalist as Jews and thinking that they would compromise their national aspirations was an illusion. Palestinians, he claimed, would never abandon their national aspirations for indoor plumbing and a washing machine and should not be expected to do so.

Kahane cited Maimonides's description of how the biblical Israelites dealt with the seven nations in the land of Canaan as a mandate for his zero-sum tolerance for non-Jews in Israel. More precisely, he pointed to the *Mishneh Torah* for halakhic support as he stated: to the Arab individual, full civil rights if they bow to Jewish hegemony, to the Arab collectivity, nothing. (This, of course, is eerily similar to the Napoleonic equation for Jewish emancipation in France in the first decade of the nineteenth century.)

Greenberg responded with a list of rabbinic authorities who do not consider gentiles, especially Christians, to be idolaters, thus claiming that Kahane's halakhic justification for transfer was irrelevant. Security, for Greenberg, was only possible by taking a risk that included cultivating a trustworthy Palestinian leadership and working toward a two-state solution. Kahane, echoing a strong sentiment in Israeli and American Jewish society at the time countered that there is no Palestinian "people" and thus any national aspirations are founded on a myth.

Once Halakhah was evoked as both a rhetorical and substantive device, the debate became a battle for authenticity with Kahane at a significant advantage. In an Orthodox setting, the use of Halakhah was viewed as a legitimate approach to adjudicate these issues. What was missing was that Israel, the subject of the debate, is a secular state where Halakhah's authority in the public sphere is limited to a very narrow set of issues (marriage, divorce, conversion, and burial). Greenberg could have deflected the halakhic conversation by claiming that Kahane's idea of transfer was an attempt to transform the state into a theocracy, which was antithetical to the entire Zionist project. He did not make that argument, and I think he missed an important, even crucial, opportunity.

Indeed, Kahane openly stated that he supported democracy in Israel only for Jews and not for Arabs. Again, Greenberg could have exposed Kahane's revolutionary and subversive agenda by stressing the secular nature of the state and that by definition, democracy for some and not others is not democracy. But Greenberg, himself an Orthodox Jew and a Religious Zionist, chose to make a halakhic argument instead. The problem was that Greenberg did not make a strong enough case for the morality of Halakhah regarding the non-Jew in the Land of Israel. Kahane, armed with his simplistic and out-of-context reading of Maimonides's *Mishneh Torah*, sounded to the Orthodox audience more like a traditional rabbi.

A second issue emerged with Kahane's insistence that Zionism and the State must be focused on Jewish survival over peace, which he relegated to messianic times. As he put it, "In my plan there will be no peace. When Messiah comes there will be peace. Until then, survival, survival, survival." In contrast, Greenberg argued that the state had moral responsibilities and spoke in somewhat lofty terms about morality as a vehicle for redemption, even without the presence of the Messiah. He sounded like a Peace Now advocate using religious language.

The deflection of all messianic references in Kahane's Zionism went uncontested. The irony of his position was that after making a halakhic case for excluding Arabs from Israeli democracy, he was arguing that Israel is a completely secular nation-state with no moral or redemptive responsibilities beyond the survival of the Jewish people. The debate illustrates more broadly how much the Orthodox community in America was naïve in its understanding of Israel's political reality as a secular state with the responsibility of being part of the community of nations.

The third central issue of the debate emerged in the final segment, which addressed the status of non-Orthodox rabbis in the State. This was a perfect opportunity for Greenberg to regain his footing as the audience would likely be receptive to arguments for this type of pluralism in Israel as many may have had non-Orthodox parents, children, or other relatives. Citing Kahane's own words from a recent *Jewish Press* article about the illegitimacy of non-Orthodox rabbis, Greenberg tried to paint Kahane as an enemy to non-Orthodox Jews, by insinuating that once the "Arab problem" was solved Kahane would come after his fellow Jews.

It was a clever tactic, but it failed. Kahane claimed to be "outraged" that his childhood friend should even suggest that he would ever pit Jew against Jew. He noted that as a Knesset member he worked daily with mostly non-observant Jews for the security of Israel. Hearkening back again to the Napoleonic compromise of emancipation, he asserted that the individual Jew in Israel is equal no matter what he or she believes or how they choose to live. Non-Orthodox *Judaism*, however, is not acceptable because it is not committed to Halakhah. He asserted that giving Reform (and other non-Orthodox) Judaism legitimacy in Israel would invalidate Halakhah entirely and empower a liberal agenda that would put Israel's security, and thus its existence, at risk. Greenberg did not have a good response to this beyond restating his commitment to pluralism. He continued to insinuate that for Kahane the non-Orthodox *Jew* was equal to the Arab, while Kahane returned fire by ceding the point only in regards to non-Orthodox *Judaism*. It was difficult for Greenberg to make his case without aligning himself, at least to some extent, with non-Orthodox Judaism, which he did not want to do. Kahane thus turned Greenberg's strongest points against him. The audience was sympathetic to Greenberg here, but in the end, their own anxiety about a liberal solution in Israel turned them largely back to Kahane.

Finally, the date of this debate, winter 1988, is also very significant. Within a matter of months, the Israel Supreme Court would uphold the Knesset's "Racism Law" that would make Kahane's Kach party illegal and remove Kahane from the Knesset. In subsequent writing, Kahane became increasingly negative and desperate about the entire Zionist project, more apocalyptic, and more frightening. This debate was one of the last times Kahane would speak in America as a Knesset member, with the implicit authority of the state behind him. By the spring of 1988, he would be an outcast and increasingly defensive in his public appearances.

Kahane and Greenberg never appeared together again.

6. Yeshayahu Leibowitz, *Judaism, Human Values, and the Jewish State*

Yeshayahu Leibowitz, Eliezer Goldman (ed.), *Judaism, Human Values, and the Jewish* State, Cambridge: Harvard University Press, 1992

Dr. Yeshayahu Leibowitz (1903–1994) served as Professor of Biochemistry, Neurophysiology, Philosophy, and the History of Science at the Hebrew University in Jerusalem.

If the present situation continues (and here the emphasis must be on "if"), the growing savagery of Israeli society will be as inevitable as the severance of the state from the Jews of the world. The policy of a government of [Ariel] Sharon, Raful [Eitan], and [Haim] Druckman (or their counterparts), which in such circumstances also seems unavoidable, will begin with suppression of reliable information, elimination of free speech, the setting up of concentration camps for "traitors" (like myself and perhaps like you), and end in mass expulsion and slaughter of the Arab population. All this will lead to a decisive war between Israel and the Arab world. In that war the sympathy and backing of the entire world will be for the Arabs. Already today, the state of Israel, to which most of the world's nations were once sympathetic, has earned contempt and hatred throughout the world. Its very existence has come to depend on a thin life-line stretching out to it from the White House. Above all, the state, which was to have been the pride and glory of the Jewish people, is rapidly becoming an embarrassment to it. (245)

[P]artition will return Israel to us, in a portion of the land, as a Jewish state, in the true sense of these two terms:

"State"—in the sense of democratic, well-ordered system of governance which deploys the means at its disposal to fulfill necessary functions which only the political organ of society is capable of performing;

"Jewish"—in the sense that the efforts of the state are directed primarily toward dealing with the problems of the Jewish people in the state and in the Diaspora. These comprise social, axiological, educational, and economic problems as well as issues of the relations of the state with the Diaspora and with the Jewish heritage.

In its present condition, as the political authority over "the Undivided Land of Israel," the state of Israel is incapable of functioning as a Jewish state in these terms, because all its efforts and resources are devoted to the maintenance of its rule over the occupied territories and their population, a goal foreign to its authentic ends. On this aim the state squanders all its physical and mental resources, while neglecting the functions incumbent upon it. (245–246)

Even if the ruling establishment in Israel fails to appreciate the necessity of disengaging from the occupied territories, and even without a mass movement to force the government into taking such steps, it is plausible to assume that the country will eventually be repartitioned, however difficult it is to imagine that this will be done with the willing consent of Israel and the PLO (whose position in the matter remains vague). It is most probable that both we and the Palestinians will be coerced into such an arrangement by the world powers; by the United States, perhaps in conjunction with the Soviet Union and the United Nations. If we do not withdraw from the territories of our own free will, we may be compelled to relinquish them and thus be saved from corruption by fascism and from all-out war. It may well be the irony of history that the Gentiles will save the state of Israel from the Jews who are bent on its destruction. (248)

COMMENTARY BY JOSHUA SHANES

Utter the name "Leibowitz" in American Jewish circles and you will likely hear about the pioneering educator Nehama Leibowitz (1905–1997), an Israeli scholar whose weekly Torah studies remain standard texts in Religious Zionist circles to this day. Yet in Israel, it is, instead, her brother Yeshayahu (1903–1994) who is more well known. Over his life, he became one of the country's most divisive and influential public intellectuals, a beloved and hated curmudgeon whose prophetic insights and demeanor led to the rise of a popular mantra among the surviving Zionist Left, "*Leibowitz tzadak*"—Leibowitz was right.

A chemistry professor at Hebrew University, Leibowitz achieved his real fame teaching Jewish thought in countless public and private settings, including on television and radio; his teaching integrated sharp political criticism often at odds with mainstream Israeli thought, especially among the Orthodox. Many of his then shocking insights and predictions—particularly the need to withdraw from the West Bank in order to save Israel as a Jewish and democratic state, and the inevitable corruption and violence that would result should they fail to do so—have since grown normative, even tame. Yet arguably no one today matches either the erudition or the fiery passion with which he delivered his messages. These polemics were not digressions from his theological discourses, but rather natural extensions flowing directly from them. His works appeared nearly exclusively in Hebrew, contributing to his relative obscurity in the United States, until Eliezer Goodman's edited volume of Leibowitz's essays in English translation appeared in 1992, just two years before Leibowitz's death. For the first time, English-language readers could taste the full range of Leibowitz's religio-political philosophy.

Goodman organized the book not chronologically but thematically, dividing it between essays on "Faith," "Religion, People, State," "The Political Scene," and "Judaism and Christianity." In reality, these divisions are somewhat artificial as Leibowitz's theological *Weltanschauung* on the one hand and his political analyses and prescriptions on the other hand are manifest throughout all the sections. At the same time, this chronological and thematic disorder serves the editor, who argues in his introductory essay that Leibowitz remained politically and religiously consistent throughout his long life, despite some apparent contradictions.

The centerpiece of Leibowitz's theology—elaborated especially in the opening section on "Faith"—is a transcendent God to whom we owe fealty for no reason other than the covenant itself and our decision to accept its obligations. "The acceptance of the yoke of Torah and Mitzvoth is the love of God, and it is this that constitutes faith in God. ... True devotion to religious value is totalitarian" (44, 160). For Leibowitz, any theology—Jewish or otherwise—that ascribes self-serving motives to Divine service, or sacredness to the material world, is nothing less than idolatry. Any expression of Judaism that violates this dictum—whether Reform, Kabbalistic, or Zionist—is for Leibowitz a religious perversion.

Leibowitz argues that in contrast to Christianity, reward plays no role in Judaism. There must be no focus on salvation or redemption—especially national redemption, a messianic delusion that inevitably leads to heresy—but merely the observing of Torah commandments for their own sake.[1] Even spontaneous prayer is not a religious act for him! Only prayer that seeks to fulfill

---

1   Leibowitz has no problem with traditional messianism focused on the *eschaton*—the Messiah is he who perpetually *will* come—but messianic hopes focused on today inevitably overtake Divine service and sever themselves from Judaism. Such "sincere" longing for redemption, he states, led to Christianity, Sabbatianism, and now Gush Emunim, a triple pairing that appears often in these essays.

the exact requirements of Halakhah—not for one's needs, but because of the obligation—constitutes a true religious act. New liturgy, he writes, "composed to lend a religious halo to personal or collective interests" such as the state or its military forces, is "ludicrous and insipid ... [with] nothing to do with religious consciousness" (34).

This refusal to ascribe holiness to the material world extends even, and especially, to the Jewish people themselves and to the land of Israel. Indeed, "exalting the land itself to the rank of holiness is idolatry *par excellence*," he writes, "[for] idolatry is simply the representation of things profane as sacred, as possessing supreme and absolute worth" (87, 25). It is precisely the worship of ourselves and our land as Divine that made possible the massacre in Kibiyeh in 1953, when Israeli soldiers slaughtered dozens of Palestinian civilians in response to a terrorist attack that killed three Israelis (190). Those who argue for the inherent sanctity of the Jewish people turn the concept of Jewish chosenness into "an expression of racist chauvinism," even "fascism," worshiping a "trinity of land-nation-state with a coating of religious terminology" (65). This, he concludes, was the religion of Korach, the perversion of those who worshiped the Golden Calf, and the idolatry of the priests of the Baal whom Elijah destroyed on Mt. Carmel (227). It recalls for him Isaiah's attack on the Israelites for perverting his focus on Jerusalem, which he had hoped would direct them towards God but instead led to idolizing Jerusalem and the Temple (101).

The integration of his religious and political views—ironically expressed through an insistence on the radical separation of these categories—is especially clear when Leibowitz thunders against both secular and Religious Zionists for their heretical assignment of godliness to the mundane. While Leibowitz conceded the legitimacy of Kant's secular anthropocentric morality, in contrast to his own theocentric one, he reserved true vitriol for the "vicious and despicable" ethnocentric view that judged man from the perspective of a "deified collective." In this sense, even "religious" nationalists constitute antireligious heretics, for whom the Torah becomes a handmaiden serving the interests of the nation and the state (209). Citing Franz Grillparzer, who witnessed the early explosion of nationalism in 1848, Leibowitz attacked nationalism—whether in secular or religious garb—as a path that led "from humanity through nationality to bestiality" (247).

Nevertheless, Leibowitz remained a committed Zionist until his last day. His Zionism was a wholly secular movement for Jews to achieve and preserve full political sovereignty after centuries of powerlessness. Though briefly flirting with a call to develop new Halakhah to fit the unprecedented secular Jewish state (158–173), he thereafter remained a staunch opponent of any integration of religion and the state, viewing the official state rabbinate as a handmaiden of heretics (174–184ff). He likewise carefully avoided assigning any ontological substance to either the state or even the nation itself. He anticipated by decades a turn in nationalist theory popularized by Benedict Anderson and many others, who describe the nation as an "imagined community," or a "constructed" identity. As such, no nation has any "right" to a land, or a state. Moreover, in the case of Israel/Palestine, since two competing nations were forged on the same land, claiming the superiority of either one's exclusive right to the land is meaningless (230–232, 241).

Leibowitz's most political essays appear in the third section, including prophetic pronouncements about the consequences of Israel's remaining in the Occupied Territories. Leibowitz famously called for Israeli withdrawal from the West Bank and Gaza almost immediately following their capture in the 1967 war. He did so not because he worried about Palestinian rights—he explicitly denied this—but rather because of the pernicious effects on Israel of a "colonial" occupation of a foreign people (192, 238, 244ff). A colonial regime inevitably engenders violent resistance, he wrote, regardless of how it treats its disenfranchised subjects. This, in turn, will necessitate an apparatus of spiraling state violence against Palestinians and an apparatus of surveillance and oppression against domestic "traitors." Israel will cease to represent the Jewish people, he predicted, as Diaspora Jews increasingly refuses to identify with it, while the Israeli-Arab minority grows closer to other Palestinians (225).

Meanwhile, Jewish settlement in the Territories will grow, "adding fuel to the flames and making amelioration more and more difficult." Israel will cease to be a democracy or cease to be a Jewish state. "There is no way out of this situation," he concluded, "except withdrawal from the territories." He admitted that unilateral withdrawal would not achieve peace, but rather insisted that it was vital to Israel's security regardless of the success of negotiation. In any event, he wrote, "honest dialogue is not possible between rulers and ruled," but only between equals. Unilateral withdrawal might at least save the Zionist project from its self-inflicted doom (238–241).

Leibowitz always framed his prophetic fear of long-term colonial rule on the security and moral fiber of Israel within his religious condemnation of the theology of "greater Israel" and its "pseudo-religious" justifications for maintaining rule over the West Bank. He often cited Ezekiel's admonition against the "national religious fools" who expected to spill blood and worship idols and yet still possess the land (Ezekiel 33:25–26). "The Jewish people has legitimate claims to this country," he wrote, "but these claims have no 'religious cover.' To speak of the divine promise to Abraham and his issue as a gratuitous gift, to ignore the conditions of the promise, and to disregard the obligations it confers on the receivers is a degradation and desecration of the religious faith" (236).

The short final section on "Judaism and Christianity" seems almost gratuitous, particularly in its overt hostility towards Christianity, which will trouble many liberal readers otherwise attracted to his politics. Leibowitz celebrated the rise of women as Jewish leaders and educational equality (128–131), but he was no pluralist, an aspect of his worldview many of his liberal devotees often overlook. His rejection of denominational pluralism was driven by the same religious certainty that drove his political message. Reform Judaism was heresy no less than Gush Emunim or Labor Zionists, although he reserved particular vitriol for the latter, and particularly for the ideology of "greater Israel," which he labeled a "latter-day Sabbatianism, a prostitution of the Jewish religion in the interest of chauvinism and lust for power" (203).

Leibowitz spoke in a deliberately provocative manner, both in content and tone, such that one reviewer quipped that even just reading him felt like he was yelling at you. His moral and political certainty—and absolute focus on God's transcendent authority—certainly added to his prophetic aura, particular in light of his apocalyptic predictions should his warnings be ignored. At the same time, Leibowitz was not missionizing but rather speaking to those who chose to enter the conversation, whether to fight or to follow him. And he was no "cold intellectual," as Goldman put it. His passion, erudition, and brilliant oration were legendary, and come through brilliantly in Goldman's collection.

One year after the book's appearance, Leibowitz was offered the Israel Prize, the country's highest honor. Before the award ceremony, he gave a speech in which he repeated his call for Israelis to refuse orders to serve in the Occupied Territories, comparing Israeli soldiers to Nazis. Following a public outcry, and a threat by Prime Minister Rabin to boycott the ceremony, Leibowitz withdrew from consideration. He passed away just one year later. A generation on, his vision grows ever more relevant, his prophetic voice ever more missed.

7. Israeli Knesset Basic Law: Human Dignity and Liberty

Aharon Barak, "A Judge on Judging: The Role of a Supreme Court in a Democracy"

Israeli Knesset Basic Law: Human Dignity and Liberty, March 1992

1. Fundamental human rights in Israel are founded upon recognition of the value of the human being, the sanctity of human life, and the principle that all persons are free; these rights shall be upheld in the spirit of the principles set forth in the Declaration of the Establishment of the State of Israel.

1a. The purpose of this Basic Law is to protect human dignity and liberty, in order to establish in a Basic Law the values of the State of Israel as a Jewish and democratic state.

8. There shall be no violation of rights under this Basic Law except by a law befitting the values of the State of Israel, enacted for a proper purpose, and to an extent no greater than is required.

12. This Basic Law cannot be varied, suspended or made subject to conditions by emergency regulations; notwithstanding, when a state of emergency exists, by virtue of a declaration under section 9 of the Law and Administration Ordinance, 5708–1948, emergency regulations may be enacted by virtue of said section to deny or restrict rights under this Basic Law, provided the denial or restriction shall be for a proper purpose and for a period and extent no greater than is required.

Aharon Barak, "A Judge on Judging: The Role of a Supreme Court in a Democracy," *Yale Law School Faculty Scholarship Series*, January 2002

Aharon Barak (1936–) was President of the Supreme Court of Israel. He is currently Professor of Law at the Interdisciplinary Center in Herzliya.

Since the Holocaust, all of us have learned that human rights are the core of substantive democracy. ...

The protection of human rights—the rights of every individual and every minority group—cannot be left only in the hands of the legislature and the executive, which, by their nature, reflect majority opinion. Consequently, the question of the judicial branch's role in a democracy arises. ...

In present times democracy faces the emergent threat of terrorism. Passive democracy has transformed into defensive democracy. All of us are concerned that it not become uncontrollable democracy. As judges, we are aware of the tension between the need to protect the state and the rights of the individual.

Human rights are not the rights of a person on a desert island. Robinson Crusoe does not need human rights. Human rights are the rights of a human being as part of society. The rights of the individual must conform to the existence of society, the existence of a government, and the existence of national goals. The power of the state is essential to the existence of the state and the existence of human rights themselves. Therefore, limitations on human rights reflect a national compromise between the needs of the state and the rights of the individual. This compromise is a product of the recognition that human rights should be upheld without disabling the political infrastructure. This balance is intended to prevent the sacrifice of the state on the altar of human rights. As I once stated:

> A constitution is not a prescription for suicide, and civil rights are not an altar for national destruction. ... The laws of a people should be interpreted on the basis of the assumption that it wants to continue to exist. Civil rights derive from the existence of the State, and they should not be made into a spade with which to bury it.

Similarly, human rights should not be sacrificed on the altar of the state. After all, human rights are natural rights that precede the state. Indeed, human rights protections require preservation of the sociopolitical framework, which in turn is based on recognition of the need to protect human right. Both the needs of the state and human rights are part of one constitutional structure, which simultaneously provides for human rights and allows them to be limited. ...

This is the constitutional dialectic. Human rights and the limitations on them derive from the same source, and they reflect the same values. Human rights can be limited, but there are limits to the limitations. The role of the judge in a democracy is to determine and protect the integrity of the proper balance.

COMMENTARY BY YIGAL MERSEL

In his long tenure as justice and then President of the Israeli Supreme Court, and as a law professor, Aharon Barak produced an expansive legal doctrine premised on a theory of purposive interpretation that has been immensely impactful in Israeli law and society and has been recognized and cited as precedent across the globe. His approach has become the main method of interpretation in the Israeli legal system in matters of constitutional interpretation; interpretation of primary legislation; interpretation of regulations and government directives; and interpretation of administrative and military authority. Barak put into practice the general principles of the role of the court in democratic society that he developed over the years in his academic publications and in his judicial decisions. Together, they express a broad and substantive application of the principle of the rule of law: the rule of law over all of the state powers as adjudicated by the judiciary, and through the judiciary the demand for accountability, due process, and the protection of the individual's fundamental rights.

Many of Barak's judgements over the years entrenched the principle of "the rule of law over the rulers," meaning, that all of the state's bodies are equal before the law, that they are subject to the law, that they must act in accordance with constitutional standards, and that if they fail to do so, they will be held accountable. In this context, for example, Barak reinforced the principle that public servants must act as "public trustees" for the sake of the public as a whole, and that they must not act in situations of conflict of interest. He also established workable standards for the requirement that all state authorities must exercise their discretion within the authority granted by law, in a reasonable manner and in good faith and fairness. This includes the requirement to weigh all the relevant considerations, and only relevant considerations; to disregard any extraneous considerations; to act with fairness and in good faith; and not to act arbitrarily. Through many of his judgements, Barak also established the requirement that state authorities exercise due process, including granting a hearing to those who may be adversely affected by a decision; being fastidious regarding the lawful authorization to undertake a given action and the legal requirement to consult with the relevant bodies; the requirement that decisions be explained and justified; the requirement that decisions only be made after reviewing all of the relevant facts; the right of legal representation; and more.

Barak also manifested this doctrine of accountability of state authority before the law in his writing on proportionality. The logic of proportionality in this context means that state authorities cannot limit individual rights any more than is necessary. The "necessity" of any limitation on rights is assessed through the three criteria for establishing proportionality: the chosen means must fit the purpose; the chosen means must be the least restrictive means available for achieving that purpose; and there must be a proportional balance between the benefit derived from the chosen means and the injury to individuals' rights. In particular, Barak frequently focused on the idea of human dignity as an expression of the rights of individuals, which he treated as a critical variable in evaluating the proportionality of state power.

Barak's general worldview, as expressed in his judgements and academic writing, sees the judge and the court in democratic societies as the bulwark of individual rights against the power of the state. Thus, Barak issued dozens of judgements entrenching the protection of prisoners from invasive body searches; the protection of freedom of expression, including racist or otherwise offensive expressions, and enabling its limitation only when there is near certainty that the expression will lead to a significant limitation of an opposing public interest; to significant harm to public security; or significant harm to public sensibilities that "cannot be sustained." Barak stressed in his judgements that even in these cases, the limitation of constitutional rights must be for a proper purpose and must be done only to the extent that is necessary, according to the principle of proportionality.

Barak's decision in the *Mizrahi Bank* case is one of his most important, the Israeli equivalent to the American case of *Marbury v. Madison*.[1] Beginning

---

1   See C.A. 6821/93 *United Mizrahi Bank Ltd. v. Migdal Cooperative Village*, [1995] IsrSC 49(4) 221.

in 1958, following the failure to establish a constitutional consensus, the Knesset had passed over time a series of Basic Laws intended to serve a semiconstitutional function. In *Mizrahi*, the Supreme Court determined that the Basic Laws have a supreme normative position over regular legislation and that the courts have the authority to exercise judicial review over the Knesset's legislation. This decision, and several others in Barak's tenure, initiated an era of judicial review over the constitutionality of Israel's laws and also led to a reinterpretation—in light of the Basic Laws—of laws that preceded the Basic Laws. In a few instances, the Supreme Court even declared that certain laws passed by the Knesset contradict the Basic Laws, and as such are void. These decisions express a fundamental change in the Israeli legal system and strengthened the state's case to see itself as a true constitutional democracy wherein the legislature is subject to the Supreme Court's judicial review over its primary legislation, as part of the rule of law over the legislature. This legal legacy, however, also had the adverse effect of Barak courting controversy. His critics viewed the Barak court as an activist court.

As part of this "Constitutional Revolution," catalyzed legislatively by the 1992 Basic Law on Human Dignity and Liberty and judicially in the Barak court, Barak implemented the concept of a "dialogue" between the legislature and the judiciary, including a theory of constitutional remedies for instances wherein a law contradicts a Basic Law. In parallel, Justice Barak advanced the role of the legislature, and strengthened its position in relation with the government. This was all undertaken in an attempt to limit the concentration of power in the hands of the government at the expense of the legislature—the representative of the people in the parliamentary system. The legislature is supposed to check the power of the government, and the government is bound to operate within the confines of the authority granted to it by the legislature in primary legislation. This led Barak to develop the theory of "primary arrangements," which requires that certain fundamental issues be regulated by the legislature in clear primary legislation, rather than through general executive authority. Certain topics are so fundamentally important, especially when they involve limitations of individual rights, that the legislature must be the power that decides how to regulate them. In these topics, the legislature is not permitted to delegate its discretion to the executive.

Another example of Justice Barak's decisions subjecting the executive power to the rule of law is found in a case regarding methods of physical interrogation for terror suspects, one of a set of issues raised by the war on terror and more generally the need for balance between human rights and state security in times of crisis. Barak held that "absent express legal authority to infringe upon a person's right, it must not be done despite the importance of protecting state security. The individual's liberty not to be an object for an investigation is a fundamental right in our constitutional system. This right must not be infringed upon without a statutory provision that fulfills the constitutional requirements."[2] Barak held that without express authority in primary legislation, there is no legal basis for torture or other interrogation methods involving physical pressure, despite the possible importance of these methods for the war on terror. President Barak was fully aware of the possible dangers to state security. He closed his opinion with the now-famous determination that:

> This decision opened with a description of the difficult reality in which Israel finds itself. We conclude this judgment by revisiting that harsh reality. We are aware that this decision does not make it easier to deal with that reality. This is the destiny of a democracy—it does not see all means as acceptable, and the ways of its enemies are not always open before it. A democracy must sometimes fight with one hand tied behind its back. Even so, a democracy has the upper hand. The rule of law and the liberty of the individual constitute important components in its understanding of security. At the end of the day, they fortify its spirit and its strength, and this allows it to overcome its difficulties.[3]

Another issue that was raised repeatedly before the Israeli Supreme Court during Barak's tenure is the applicability of international humanitarian law to the West Bank and the Gaza Strip through the laws of belligerent occupation. In this context, Barak delineated the military commanders' obligation to act in accordance with both customary and treaty-based international law. Additionally, Barak imposed the obligation that military commanders act in accordance with Israeli administrative law, as the military commander is a "civil servant," filling a public position by law. As he wrote, "In his kit, every Israeli soldier carries both the rules of international law, and the fundamental rules of Israeli administrative law that apply to the situation

---

2   See H.C. 5100/94 *Public Committee Against Torture v. Prime Minister*, [1999] IsrSC 53(4) 817, para. 19 to the opinion of President Barak.

3   See H.C. 5100/94 *Public Committee Against Torture, supra* note 22, at para. 39 to the opinion of President Barak.

at hand."[4] As such, the military must operate in the Administrated Territories reasonably and proportionally, appropriately balancing personal freedoms with general needs.[5] This development, alongside the expansion of standing rights and the limitation of the justiciability claims, enabled the Supreme Court to exercise judicial review over decisions made by military commanders in the Administrated Territories and to hold both them and the military as a whole accountable to the demands of international law and administrative law when operating in the Territories. Judicial review is applied to military operations and to claims of limitation of the individual freedoms of the Territories' residents. This decision contributed immensely to the applicability of rule of law in the Administrated Territories, despite the fact that they are not under Israeli sovereignty.

In another instance, Barak discussed the limitations that international law and the Fourth Geneva Convention impose on methods of combat in the war on terror. The Court set limits on the military's ability to expel residents of the Territories and held that expulsion was a measure that could only be employed to prevent terrorism, but not as a punitive measure; that it could only be imposed on someone who personally posed a serious terrorism threat, but not on family members who do not pose a personal threat; that there must be a full and convincing evidentiary basis, with clear and convincing evidence of the serious threat posed; and that this measure must be imposed proportionally.[6] As *obiter dictum* aside from his opinion, Barak noted the difficulty inherent in the Geneva Convention's wording, and the necessity of a dynamic approach to its interpretation that is able to apply the Convention's provisions to the modern war on terror. Regarding the unique and complex task of the courts in the war on terror he added the following:

> The State of Israel is undergoing a difficult period. Terror is hurting its residents. Human life is trampled upon. Hundreds have been killed. Thousands have been injured. The Arab population in Judaea and Samaria and the Gaza Strip is also suffering unbearably. All of this is because of acts of murder, killing, and destruction perpetrated by terrorists. ... The

---

4   See H.C. 7015/02 *Ajuri v. Commander of the IDF Forces in the West Bank*, [2002] IsrSC 56(6) 352, at para. 13 to the opinion of President Barak.

5   See H.C. 3278/02 *The Center for the Defense of the Individual v. The Commander of the IDF Forces in the West Bank*, [2003] IsrSC 57(1) 385, at para. 23 to the opinion of President Barak, found in Annex D-b.

6   See H.C. 7015/02 *Ajuri, supra* note 26.

State is doing all that it can in order to protect its citizens and ensure the security of the region. These measures are limited. The restrictions are, first and foremost, military-operational ones. It is difficult to fight against persons who are prepared to turn themselves into living bombs. These restrictions are also normative. The State of Israel is a freedom-seeking democracy. It is a defensive democracy acting within the framework of its right to self-defence—a right recognized by the charter of the United Nations. The State seeks to act within the framework of the lawful possibilities available to it under the international law to which it is subject and in accordance with its internal law. As a result, not every effective measure is also a lawful measure. Indeed, the State of Israel is fighting a difficult war against terror. It is a war carried out within the law and with the tools that the law makes available. The well-known saying that "In battle laws are silent" ... does not reflect the law as it is, nor as it should be. ... Indeed, "even when the cannons speak, the military commander must uphold the law. The power of society to stand against its enemies is based on its recognition that it is fighting for values that deserve protection. The rule of law is one of these values." ... Indeed, the position of the State of Israel is a difficult one. Our role as judges is not easy either. We are doing all we can to balance properly between human rights and the security of the area. In this balance, human rights cannot receive complete protection, as if there were no terror, and state security cannot receive complete protection, as if there were no human rights. A delicate and sensitive balance is required. This is the price of democracy. It is expensive, but worthwhile. It strengthens the State. It provides a reason for its struggle. Our work as judges is difficult. But we cannot escape this difficulty, nor do we wish to do so.[7]

In another instance, and again on the basis of international law, Barak imposed rules and limitations on the conditions in which detainees may be held during operations aimed at preventing terror. Barak ruled:

Indeed, the nature of detention necessitates the denial of liberty. Even so, this does not justify the violation of human dignity. It is possible to detain persons in a manner which preserves their human dignity, even as national security and public safety are protected. Prisoners should not

---

7   See H.C. 7015/02 *Ajuri, supra* note 26, at para. 41 to the opinion of President Barak.

be crammed like animals into inadequate spaces. Even those suspected of terrorist activity of the worst kind are entitled to conditions of detention which satisfy minimal standards of humane treatment and ensure basic human necessities. How could we consider ourselves civilized if we do not guarantee civilized standards to those in our custody? Such is the duty of the commander of the Territory under international law, and such is his duty under our administrative law. Such is the duty of the Israeli government, in accordance with its fundamental characters: Jewish, democratic, and humane.[8]

In later rulings, Barak imposed rules and limitations regarding the rights to due process of detainees during military operations in the war on terror and the rights of prisoners to meet with a lawyer.[9] In his judgements, Barak ruled, for example, that it is impermissible to use civilians in administrated territories to warn the inhabitants of a home before security forces enter, as such behavior contradicts the principles of international law.[10]

Another important development regarding the application of international law and the limitations it imposes on the military commander during the war on terror came from rulings regarding the route of the security fence that was built in part on expropriated land, in territory subject to the laws of belligerent occupation. Barak ruled that the military commander can only use his authority to expropriate land for military reasons and not for political reasons. Regarding the commander's discretion when exercising his authority, Barak held that the rules of proportionality apply, based both on international and Israeli law. As such, the commander must assess the proportionality of the measures employed when limiting civilians' fundamental rights, including property rights and the right to freedom of movement, and must limit these rights only insofar as it is proportionate. The measures employed by the military commander must have a rational connection with their goal; the measures must be the least restrictive to the civilians' human rights while still achieving the goal; and the limitations must be proportionate to the direct military benefit gained.[11]

---

8   See H.C. 3278/02 *The Center for the Defense of the Individual, supra* note 27, at para. 24 to the opinion of President Barak.

9   See H.C. 3239/02 *Marab v. Commander of the IDF Forces in the West Bank*, [2003] IsrSC 57(2) 349.

10 See H.C. 3799/02 *Adalah Legal Center for Arab Minority Rights in Israel v. IDF Central Commander*, [2005] IsrSC 60(3) 67.

11 See H.C. 2056/04 *Beit Sourik Village Council v. Government of Israel*, [2004] IsrSC 58(5) 807.

Barak also used the principle of proportionality during judicial review of the constitutionality of primary legislation. One judgement involved a security policy of not granting citizenship or residency status to spouses of Israeli residents only because the spouses were residents of the Occupied Territories. In his minority opinion, Barak held that the policy involved a disproportionate limitation of the Israeli spouses' rights to family life and to equality, both daughter-rights of the constitutional right to human dignity.[12] In another case, Barak held that a law which limited state liability in torts for military operations in the Occupied Territories, despite the operations not amounting to "acts of war," was unconstitutional, as it limited constitutional rights, including the right to property, disproportionately.[13] President Barak's final judgement on the Supreme Court also involved judicial review of decisions made during the war on terror. Barak established limits on the military's ability to carry out "targeted killings" on terrorists. Chief among these limitations was the requirement to act proportionately, especially as regards the concern of collateral damage to innocent civilians.[14]

Barak also made a significant contribution through his writings about the role of judges in democracies. He began his work on this topic in his article, "Foreword: A Judge on Judging,"[15] and continued it in his book *The Judge in a Democracy* (2004). In these publications, Barak expanded his theories on the role of the judge and the court and developed them into a coherent thesis. According to Barak, the judge has two primary tasks: bridging the gap between law and reality, and defending the constitution and its values. Barak repeats the general principles of his theory on judicial discretion, but clarifies that insofar as there exists judicial discretion, that is, room for choosing between multiple lawful solutions, the judge must choose the solution that optimally bridges the gap between law and reality while defending the constitution and its values. He also clarifies that there must be preconditions for the fulfillment of the judge's role. For example, judicial discretion must be applied objectively and not on the basis of personal opinions. The judge is also a member of a given society, and must consider the needs of the society as a whole and its unique characteristics.

---

12 See H.C. 7052/03 *Adalah Legal Center for Arab Minority Rights in Israel v. Minister of Interior*, [2006] IsrSC 61(2) 202.

13 See H.C. 8276/05 *Adalah Legal Center for Arab Minority Rights in Israel v. Minister of Defence*, [2006] IsrSC 62(1) 1.

14 See H.C. 769/02 *Public Committee against Torture in Israel v. Government of Israel*, [2006] IsrSC 62(1) 507. For further review see Owen Fiss, *Law is Everywhere—Tribute*, 117 Yale L. J. 257 (2007).

15 Aharon Barak, *Foreword: A Judge on Judging: The Role of a Supreme Court in a Democracy*, 116 Harv. L. Rev. 16 (2002).

He must consider social consensus. It is imperative that the judge enjoy public confidence in his office, which does not refer to his popularity but rather to public confidence in his judicial professionalism, fairness, and neutrality.

Regarding the role of the judge in bridging the gap between law and reality, Barak explains that the law is constantly called upon to solve problems arising from changes in society that the original norm did not foresee. Thus, societal changes naturally bring about legal changes. Legal history is therefore the history of adapting law to meet reality's changing demands. The legislator bears the primary responsibility for initiating the necessary legal changes. He is the senior partner. The judge has a limited role. His role is interpretive. The judge must be dynamic in adopting the interpretation that best bridges the gap between law and life's changing realities. Barak continues by discussing the attributes of this "bridging" interpretation, and its limitations. At the same time, Barak argues for the role of the judge in defending the constitution and its values. Each country's formal and substantive constitution defines its democratic values and the characteristics of its government. The judicial review entrusted to the courts is the only way to ensure the supremacy of the constitution. As part of this role, the judge must realize values and principles, such as the separation of powers; judicial independence; human rights; and fundamental values.

In an era of terror, mass immigration, and political instability, Barak's legal theories attempted to provide crucial tools for Israeli democracy to maintain a moral compass as it confronted new threats and challenges. Purposive interpretation meant to allow the courts to fill old norms with the content necessary to cope with new realities that show themselves on a daily basis. It sought not only to allow the courts to remain relevant in this new reality, but also demanded the reinforcement of the status of the court and the judge in the face of attempts to weaken them. Barak's theories and judgements regarding the independent judge, the independent court and their relationship to other state powers sought to strengthen the democratic system and its internal balances against challenges posed by technological and scientific advances, enabling sustainable development while preserving the rule of law and the principles of justice and ethics. This remains his enduring—if still controversial—legacy in Israeli society and jurisprudence.

8. Aharon Lichtenstein, "On the Murder of Prime Minister Yitzchak Rabin z"l"

Aharon Lichtenstein, "On the Murder of Prime Minister Yitzchak Rabin z"l," November 13, 1995

Rabbi Dr. Aharon Lichtenstein (1933–2015) served as *Rosh Yeshiva* and *Rosh Kollel* at Yeshiva University and then as *Rosh Yeshiva* at Yeshivat Har Etzion in Gush Etzion.

This shame, that our state, our people, should have fallen to such a level, should be felt by everyone—religious, secular, right and left. For to the extent that we feel any sense of unity within Am Yisrael, to the extent that we feel like a single body, then the entire body should feel shamed and pained no matter which limb is responsible for this tragedy. We should feel deep shame that this method of supposedly solving conflicts has become part of our culture. ...

There are some of us who rejoice at every chance to point out the drugs, the prostitution, or the violence in the wider community, so we can say, "Look at the difference between US and THEM,"—look at the statistics, look at Dizengoff, look at their family lives. But remember—the people on Dizengoff aren't foreigners; they are our flesh and blood. It is our city and it should hurt; it cannot be a source of joy, of satisfaction, of self-congratulation and gloating. We should cry over the lack of values. And if, indeed, part of what has happened is the result of the culture of the city—and I think this is undoubtedly so—we are also part of the city, and we too must take part in the city's *egla arufa*.[1]

The self-confidence that arises from commitment and devotion to a world of values and eternal truths—whether in terms of Torat Yisrael or Eretz Yisrael—sometimes has led to frightening levels of self-certainty and ultimately to arrogance. This arrogance has sometimes led us to act without sufficient responsibility towards other people, and at times even without responsibility to other values. "We are good, we have values, and they are

---

1   Eds.: *egla arufa* refers to a ceremony of decapitating a heifer as described in Deuteronomy 21, a rite to be performed by priests in the surrounding towns to atone for the discovery of a corpse in no man's land.

worthless,"—this attitude has seeped deeper and deeper into our con-sciousness. ... Because we wanted our youth to strive, to run up the altar, we not only promoted simplistic slogans, but also a simplistic lifestyle. Once, shocked to my core, I walked out of a meeting of religious educators where a teacher said that although we know that the Ramban and the Rambam disagree about the nature of the *mitzvah* to settle the Land of Israel, we must keep this information to ourselves, lest we lower the enthusiasm of our youth and dampen their fervor. Here we aren't delegitimating Dizengoff; we are del-egitimating the Rambam! ...

The challenge is, can we continue to inspire the yearning for sanctity, shake people out of complacency, get them to face the great call of the hour—to understand the importance of the Medina [state], to understand the historical process in which we live—without losing a sense of morality, of proportion, of right, of spirituality? Do we have to choose between *azarot* and morality? *Chas ve-shalom!* But we must purify our hearts and our camp in order to serve Him in truth.

COMMENTARY BY DAVID WOLKENFELD

I. From a distance of twenty years, Rabbi Aharon Lichtenstein's remarks to his yeshiva following the assassination of Prime Minister Yitzchak Rabin stand out as an enduring legacy of one of modern Judaism's most brilliant and humane rabbis, as a provocative advertisement for a model of rabbinic authority that has since been partially eclipsed, and as a window into a political worldview that, for all of its decency and appeal, may by now have succumbed to its own internal contradictions and naïveté.

By November 1995, Lichtenstein had emerged as one of the most credible heirs to the mantle of the recently deceased Rabbi Joseph Soloveitchik. Lichten-stein had built his reputation as a brilliant young Talmudist whose Harvard PhD bolstered his ability to exemplify the Modern Orthodox "*Torah uMadda*" ethos in which Torah scholarship and general culture, revelation and reason, are both the worthy objects of human scrutiny and intellectual devotion. In 1971, Licht-enstein moved to Israel, where he accepted the offer of Rabbi Yehuda Amital to become *rosh yeshiva* at the new Yeshivat Har Etzion, that had been founded by Amital a few years earlier in the small West Bank community of Alon Shvut.

In an act of uncommon modesty, Lichtenstein insisted that Amital serve beside him as co-*rosh yeshiva*, an arrangement that worked harmoniously and productively until Amital's death in 2010.

II. Talmudic scholarship as it was distilled and developed at the great Lithuanian yeshivot and their daughter institutions in America and Israel is arguably the most refined and rarified product of Jewish civilization. As Talmudic scholarship was practiced in the "Brisker School," the method championed by Soloveitchik and Lichtenstein, the goal of Talmud study is the development of *chiddushim*, new creative insights into the deeper meaning of Talmudic concepts. Lichtenstein's remarks following the assassination of Prime Minister Rabin display the fluency and creativity of his Talmudic brilliance and show how Torah scholarship can be illuminating and morally uplifting. The intellectual core of Lichtenstein's discourse is an analysis of a Talmudic story concerning a murder that occurred in the Temple. The Talmud itself connects this episode to the biblical *eglah arufah* ceremony described in Deuteronomy 21 as a means of resolving the guilt associated with an unsolved murder, but Lichtenstein, with devastating insight, understood that the Talmudic discussion implicates the religious and social environment within which a murder happens without mitigating any portion of responsibility from the murderer himself. This is a Talmudic *chiddush* which sheds light on the nature of moral responsibility.

III. A generation later, we can read these powerful words, contemplate the grandeur of this thundering demand for introspection and self-criticism, and marvel at the awesome spectacle of a religious leader, at the peak of his vigor and the height of his intellectual and moral leadership, demanding that his community absorb the tragic sadness of the moment and embark on a full moral accounting for its share of responsibility for the murder. I can think of few similarly compelling moments of religious leadership in the twenty years since. On the contrary, the Modern Orthodox community has spent much of the past twenty years engaged in an internal polemic. The authority of *rashei yeshiva* such as Lichtenstein has been one of the points of contention in this polemic. Liberal Orthodox rabbis and activists have championed the right of congregational rabbis "on the ground" to render independent halakhic decisions for their communities, and activists have chafed at the perceived interference of "out-of-touch" *rashei yeshiva* who have allegedly arrogated communal influence and power for themselves beyond what is appropriate for ivory tower intellectuals and educators.

Pushing back against the authority of *rashei yeshiva* was part and parcel of the liberal Orthodox agenda of the last few decades, including Rabbi Saul Berman's "Edah" organization (1998–2006) and Rabbi Avi Weiss's "Open Orthodoxy" (since 2000). The link between religious liberalism, personal autonomy, and a more circumscribed concept of rabbinic authority has become so strong that reading Lichtenstein deploying the full measure of his rabbinic authority on behalf of a liberal and humane agenda is somewhat shocking. For those who, like me, hail from the "modern wing of Modern Orthodoxy" and yearn for more liberal expressions of Orthodox Judaism, it is important to remember what can be lost when rabbinic authority is undermined.

Yes, there are rabbis from the ivory tower who are disconnected from the concerns and values of the Jewish masses and who are beholden to a narrow set of concerns that are shared within the confines of their professional network. But Lichtenstein brought the full measure of his charisma, institutional authority, and scholarly reputation to the service of decency and religious humanism. Those causes too can be championed by figures representing institutional authority.

A breakdown in institutional authority can allow for a flowering of ideological creativity and protect society from institutional corruption. But, the anarchic absence of intact authority figures can put vulnerable populations at risk and make it more difficult to instigate systemic reform.

IV. Lichtenstein's reaction to the murder of Rabin is part of a genre of public Torah scholarship that he promulgated in opposition to political extremism within Israeli Religious Zionism. On at least three other occasions, Lichtenstein advocated for political moderation within Israeli Religious Zionism.

In 1994, Lichtenstein initiated and later published an exchange of letters with Rabbi Dov Lior on the appropriateness of Lior's eulogizing Baruch Goldstein, who was killed as he murdered twenty-nine Palestinian worshippers in Hebron in 1994.

In 2005, Lichtenstein publicly responded to a public statement calling upon Israeli soldiers to refuse orders to take part in the evacuation of Jewish settlements in Gaza. Rabbi Avraham Shapira, a former chief rabbi of Israel and a revered figure within Religious Zionism, had issued that call to disobedience, and Lichtenstein took great umbrage at the dangerous implications of calling upon soldiers to refuse orders as well as Shapira's unwillingness to countenance alternative halakhic positions, including that of Soloveitchik, who had emphatically permitted territorial compromise in the Land of Israel.

In 2010, Lichtenstein responded, again through a public letter, to a campaign that was initiated by Tzfat Chief Rabbi Shmuel Eliyahu calling for Jews to refuse to rent or sell homes to Arabs. Eliyahu's letter was endorsed by several dozen Religious Zionist rabbis, even as it earned scorn from across the religious and political spectra. Lichtenstein's public letter to Eliyahu questions his judgment: how could he have expected such a letter to be received? But it also criticizes Eliyahu's superficial presentation of the pertinent halakhic issues. To be a rabbi and to exercise leadership through one's Torah scholarship requires one to convey the full diversity and complexity of every issue, even at the expense of a short-term victory.

V. Lichtenstein's consistent record of defending decency and political moderation within Religious Zionism is now a cherished part of the legacy he left to his students upon his death in 2015. This moderate political stance may be rare among the religious ideological core of the West Bank settlement movement, but is thoroughly at home in Gush Etzion. Indeed, it is no coincidence that the students and neighbors of Lichtenstein comprise the heart of the "moderate settlement movement." One can hear echoes of Lichtenstein's American background in his support for civic decency, pragmatism, and political moderation. And a significant number of Gush Etzion residents share an American background.

Residents of Gush Etzion are proud to be on the avant-garde of Zionism as they settle the Land of Israel, even as they enjoy a patina of mainstream respectability from living within "the consensus," a region of the West Bank almost certainly slated for annexation to Israel in the context of a future peace agreement. Some residents of Gush Etzion even go so far as to state that they would willingly leave their homes and communities in the context of a peace agreement with the Palestinians.

Rabbi Mosheh Lichtenstein, one of Lichtenstein's sons, publicly wrote in 2006 of his own willingness to leave his home for the sake of peace, which is something almost unheard of among other West Bank settlers.

The decency and humanity of this moderate political stance is apparent in 2015 just as it was in 1995. But with the passage of twenty years, the blind spots of this perspective are also apparent. How could a political worldview shaped by the legacy of Madison, Jefferson, and Lincoln ever reconcile itself to the status quo in the West Bank, where Jewish settlers enjoy the rights of citizenship in a Western-style democracy while their Palestinian neighbors are disenfranchised? What does it mean for Gush Etzion to be part of an Israeli "consensus" that excludes Israel's purported negotiating partner?

It is not just settlers who did not pay attention to Palestinians and their political aspirations. Israeli society as a whole did not see Palestinians. During the years of the Oslo Peace Process of the 1990s Israel and the global Jewish community undertook a heated debate about the wisdom of "land for peace" and whether Yasser Arafat's PLO was a trustworthy partner for peace. Left, right, and centrist positions emerged in the Israeli political spectrum (represented by the Labor, Likud, and Center Party respectively) and a vigorous debate ensued. And yet, this debate took place without any reference to longstanding and clearly articulated Palestinian aspirations. The segment of Palestinian society that is prepared to live in peace with Israel has been quite consistent in its political demands since its emergence in 1988. Their demand has been, and remains, an independent Palestinian State comprising all or most of the West Bank, East Jerusalem, and Gaza. It can be hard to believe in 2015, when even politicians of the political right endorse (however grudgingly) the "two-state solution," that not a single credible candidate for prime minister during the years of the Oslo Peace Process ever ran for office on a platform that included an independent Palestinian state.

Lichtenstein mourned for the murdered Rabin in 1995 and hoped that his words could divert Israel from a dark and foreboding future. Compared to 1995, there is more bloodshed, more brutality, and more extremism afoot in the Israeli-Palestinian conflict today. But, perhaps, there is also a more sober assessment of the reality and the fears and aspirations of both Israelis and Palestinians. This sober assessment of reality seems to be a *sine qua non* of eventual peace. But peace is no more certain to come in this generation than it was a generation ago.

9. Aviezer Ravitzky, *Messianism, Zionism, and Jewish Religious Radicalism*

Aviezer Ravitzky, *Messianism, Zionism, and Jewish Religious Radicalism*, Chicago: University of Chicago Press, 1996

Dr. Aviezer Ravitzky (1945–) is Professor Emeritus of Jewish Thought at the Hebrew University of Jerusalem. He was awarded the Israel Prize in Jewish Thought in 2001.

Furthermore, in seeking the normalization of the Jewish people on a purely mundane, historical level, the national movement deliberately called into question the transcendent law that had governed all of Jewish history: the ahistorical law of divine reward and punishment, exile and redemption; the Divine Providence which had delivered Israel from the rule of physical casualty prevailing in nature and "normal" human affairs. The covenant between Israel and the Creator had placed Jewish destiny on a purely religious plane. The catastrophes that had befallen the people had resulted, not from the aggressive intentions of its enemies, but, as the Prayer Book puts it, "because of our sins." Similarly, the future restoration of Jewish life would not be a matter of mere bricks and mortar; rather, in Maimonides'[s] words, "Israel is to be redeemed by penitence alone." The political attempt to bring the Eternal People into the history of the nations is blasphemy, brazen defiance of Divine Providence. (61)

The closer Zionism came to realizing its goals, the more sharply focused became the ideology and historiosophy of Jewish passivity in opposition to it. Inactivity regarding mundane political matters was turned into the essential feature of Jewishness in the premessianic era. It is the Jews' patient expectation of complete, utopian redemption, a miraculous occurrence unconnected with any worldly effort on their part, that captures the fundamental nature of Judaism itself: acknowledgement of divine rule, of prophetic destiny, of the chosenness of Israel, and of the special laws governing Israel's fate. It is no longer just the Jews' unique way of life that has religious significance; the very fact that they live in exile becomes a declaration of faith. Their very passivity represents a heroic decision that must daily be reaffirmed.

The Zionist claim that it can bring about salvation and national rebirth in advance of the messianic age expresses the exact opposite. Any attempt to realize messianic expectations by human means—the conquest of the land, political liberation, the ingathering of the exiles—is tantamount to blasphemy. A sovereign Jewish state would thus be a new tower of Babel, an insolent human attempt to usurp the prerogative of the Creator Himself. It is antimessianic hubris, "absolute apostasy, brazen arrogance, dreadful heresy that shakes the foundations of the world and hacks at the very root of the covenant linking [the children of] Israel and their Father in heaven." (62–63)

The establishment of the State of Israel and the reclaiming of the Land of Israel thus stand at the very heart of a decisively messianic process. This being the case, the Jewish state can no longer be portrayed as a merely historical or social phenomenon; its very existence is fraught with religious meaning, and in the final analysis it appears to embody something quite metaphysical. "Zionism is a heavenly matter," Kook went so far as to say. "The State of Israel is a divine entity, our holy and exalted state!" In other words, the tidings of the redemption of Israel, the consciousness of present messianic realization, have not only toppled "the wall separating us from our land"; they have eliminated at one stroke the formidable barrier between the theological and the political, the heavenly and the earthly.

Indeed, some thirty years prior to the founding of the state, Zvi Yehudah Kook's distinguished father, Rabbi Abraham Isaac Kook, the Chief Rabbi of Eretz Israel, already envisioned "our state, the State of Israel, the pedestal of God's throne in this world". ... But what for the father had been merely a utopian hope was manifest to the son and his followers as a concrete reality. The apparently eschatological laurels bestowed by Rabbi Kook on the future messianic state—"an ideal state, whose only aim should be that the Lord be acknowledged as one and His name one, which is truly the highest happiness"—were now to be bestowed upon a given political-historical entity, in the here and now. The latent holiness that had so long awaited its appointed hour now burst forth into the full light or day, in all of its authenticity, in the shape of the state of the redeemed people of Israel. To be sure, the Jewish state is to be judged, not just by its outward appearance, but by its "inner hidden essence." We are asked to strip away its outer shell and, with a spiritual eye, gaze into its metaphysical core. In the words of a eulogy of Zvi Yehudah Kook delivered by one of his core disciples, Rabbi Hayyim Druckman, dean of the Or Etzion Yeshivah and former member of the Knesset: "He was one of the few in his generation—I dare say the only one—to grasp fully the messianic revelation the State of Israel represents, to see the light of the Messiah shining forth from the State of Israel. ... He was the only one who taught us how to embrace wholeheartedly the truth that this state, with all of its problems, is a divine one." The point was made even more strongly by Rabbi Eliezer Waldman, dean of the Kiryat Arba Yeshivah, likewise a former Knesset member, in response to a debate that raged in Israel following the [First] Lebanon War: "'Our state, the State of Israel, the pedestal of God's throne in the world'—this has, in fact, been the purpose of the Jewish state ever since it was founded. Its purpose is to reveal the unity between the most exalted divine values and their manifestation by Israel in the world." Here we have the image of the Jewish state as an integral theopolitical whole, the very existence of which aims at the realization of a Jewish "City of God" here on earth. Borrowing for a moment the rhetoric of the sociologists of religion, we may say that in this concept religious faith sanctifies the sociopolitical structure, transferring it to the real, of the absolute and thereby bestowing upon it a transcendent validity.

Inevitably, the concrete actions of the Jewish state too become hallowed. "The holiness of the divine service [*avodah*, literally, work], the service of the Temple, is extended to the work of the state as a whole, both practical and spiritual, both public and private," wrote Zvi Yehudah Kook. By the same token, Israel's wars, too, come to be seen not merely in terms of national survival (in halakhic terms, "rescuing Israel from the enemy") or reclaiming ancestral land. They are portrayed in ethical and theological terms, as a mighty struggle to uproot evil and achieve universal rectification. (82–83)

COMMENTARY BY YEHUDA MAGID

On the night of July 31, 2015 the Dawabsheh family returned to their home in the central West Bank village of Duma from a visit with relatives and went to bed. Between 2:00 and 4:00 A.M., a masked Israeli settler by the name of Amiram Ben-Uliel smashed a bedroom window and threw a Molotov cocktail through it. Both parents emerged from their home enveloped in flames and both would succumb to their injuries within weeks. Their eighteen-month old son, Ali Sa'ed Muhammad Dawabsheh, did not escape and was killed at the scene. Within weeks Ben-Uliel was arrested and tried both for the crime and for his membership in a terrorist network.

On February 21, 2017, Iran held the sixth iteration of its International Conference in Support of the Palestinian Intifada. The anti-Zionist conference was replete with anti-Israel rhetoric and support for Palestinian resistance against the State of Israel. While the event was standard fare in Iran, the presence of black-clad Chasidim from the Neturei Karta sect sitting attentively in the audience was jarring. While diametrically opposed in their support or rejection of Zionism, the behavior of radical Religious Zionists and ultra-Orthodox anti-Zionist behavior may be explained, according to Aviezer Ravitzky, by the modern "crisis of messianism."

Ravitzky's book *Messianism, Zionism, and Jewish Religious Radicalism* is a seminal work in the study of modern Jewish religious extremism. An impressive and important piece of scholarship, the book explores numerous theological responses to the formation of a Jewish nation state. According to Ravitzky, "The Zionist national revolution confronted traditional Jewry with a unique, unforeseen historical situation: a Jewish political sovereignty in the heart of the Holy Land prior to messianic times, under the leadership of nonpracticing, rebellious Jews" (207). Traditionally, Orthodox Jewry had maintained that Jewish sovereignty could only be established in the messianic age. Attempting to preempt this process by establishing a secular Jewish nation-state risks undermining the process of redemption (74). Given the importance of messianic beliefs in the Jewish religious tradition and the traditional link between messianism and Jewish sovereignty, Orthodox Jewry was unable to conceptualize messianism and Zionism as two concurrent but separate phenomena. The establishment of the Jewish state required Orthodox Jewry to consider how this new reality affected their understanding of exile and redemption. Their responses have been highly variable, ranging from a radical rejection of Zionism to a feverish support for the Zionist project.

Ravitzky examines four ways in which Orthodox Jewry responded to the success of the Zionist movement. First, groups such as the Neturei Karta and Satmar Chasidim have adopted ardently anti-Zionist positions, viewing Israel as an abomination, even the work of Satan. These groups reject the secular nature of the Israeli state and also vociferously reject the notion of Jewish sovereignty prior to redemption. According to this view, a premessianic Jewish theocracy is just as heretical as a democratic and secular state. Second, the leaders of the Agudat Israel movement have taken a more moderate and pragmatic stance. While they reject the notion that Israel's founding heralded redemption and that Jews are living in a post-exilic era, they are willing to cooperate with and even participate in the institutional framework of the state in the name of protecting "Jews in exile." Third, messianic Religious Zionists represented by the teachings of Abraham Isaac Kook and his son Zvi Yehudah Kook, adopt an ardently Zionist position which is founded on the belief that the Zionist project is an integral part of the process of redemption. Finally, Chabad Chasidism believes, consistent with the teachings of the seventh Lubavitcher Rebbe, Rabbi Menachem Mendel Schneerson, that Orthodox Jewry should actively work to increase the religiosity of Israel's Jewish population and bring Israel's institutions and policies in line with Jewish law and tradition. Chabad demands that the Israeli government take a "radically hawkish stance" on the relations between Jews and non-Jews in Israel-Palestine, stridently supporting the extension of Jewish sovereignty to all of *Eretz Yisrael*, yet without identifying as Zionists. Overall, what *Messianism, Zionism, and Jewish Religious Radicalism* makes clear is that the tension between messianism and Zionism has produced highly divergent responses from the Orthodox community and that it is one of the central challenges of Jewish modernity.

In his book, Ravitzky speaks to an important tension in the existing scholarship: whether Jewish radicalism is driven by ideology or by practical considerations. On the one hand, social scientists have attempted to show that Israel is not *sui generis*; it is, in fact, a nation among nations. Events in Israel can largely be explained, according to this view, by way of a careful analysis of the political and social dynamics in Israel-Palestine. While ideas are important, they are largely epiphenomenal. On the other hand, those who study the development and history of Zionism tend to conceptualize Israel as a unique case. They ascribe the majority of causal weight to specific ideas rather than to social and political conditions. This is not to say that real-world events do not matter, but socio-political conditions play second fiddle to ideology and theology.

While each chapter of Ravitzky's book has been relevant to specialists who work on the relevant streams of Judaism, his chapter on messianic Religious Zionism is particularly consequential for understanding contemporary conflict in Israel-Palestine. Literature on the settler movement can loosely be divided into historical/social scientific and ideational approaches. Social scientific scholarship on the settler movement has primarily focused on the behavior of Israeli settlers and their navigation of Israel's political system. While the majority of these studies describe the basic tenets of the messianic religious ideology of Zvi Yehudah Kook and Meir Kahane, the primary focus is on the political machinations, mobilization strategies, and non-institutionalized behavior of the Israeli settler movement. In these studies, ideas, while important, largely play a tertiary role. In fact, ideas tend to be viewed as largely ad-hoc, developed to legitimate the behavior and goals of the settlement movement.

Messianism, Zionism, and Jewish Religious Radicalism directly challenges this approach by offering a far more detailed examination of the ideas underlying the Religious Zionist movement. Whereas previous intellectual histories had focused primarily on the development of mainstream Zionism, Ravitzky shines a light on the fringes of Jewish thinking on the subject. He seeks not only to describe the Religious Zionist ideological framework, but also to explain the behavior of Israel's radical religious right. For example, Ravitzky believes that Israeli settler violence against the Palestinian population can be explained by the gap between expectations created by theological orientation and the political realities on the ground (139). In other words, the belief that the extension of Jewish sovereignty into the territories Israel captured in 1967 was part of the ongoing process of redemption, could not cope with the political realities inhibiting this expansion. Failing to push this process forward was not only frustrating for Kookists, it was a direct challenge to their understanding of the relationship between the secular Zionist project and redemption. As a result, many Israeli settlers supported radical activities, such as civil disobedience and even violence, in order to further the expansion of Jewish sovereignty and thus preserve their convictions regarding the ongoing process of redemption.

Arguably, the most significant implication of Ravitzky's study is the highly fluid and contingent nature of ideological and theological development it reveals amongst Orthodox Jewry over the last century. Faced with the theological and practical crisis of Zionism's success, Orthodox Jewry fractured. While Ravitzky skillfully explores various ways in which Orthodox Jewry dealt with this crisis, the implication of his study is equally significant. Just as religious leaders reevaluated and modified their theological frameworks to account for the establishment of a sovereign secular Jewish state, they have continued to do so in response to Israel's particular constellation of sociopolitical challenges. This has happened both by diffusion and amalgamation. For example, Kahanism has diffused throughout parts of the Israeli settler movement and radical right in Israel, while the new Hardal [Nationalist–Ultra-Orthodox] movement has blended elements of ultra-Orthodoxy and Religious Zionism. The latter, it should be noted, has become increasingly popular with antistatist elements, such as the Hilltop Youth, within the larger settler movement. These trends are affected both by circumstances such as the Palestinian Intifadas, ongoing Palestinian terrorism, and the Israeli-Palestinian peace process as well as by charismatic leaders such as Meir Kahane and Yitzhak Ginsburg. In this way, Ravitzky not only provides valuable information about radical religious reactions to Zionism's success. He also provides a framework for understanding radical religious reactions to the fluid sociopolitical context in Israel-Palestine. More specifically, Ravitzky shows that while conceptions of the relationship between messianism and Zionism are dynamic, they require careful theological adjustment, the contours of which help to shape and reshape the sometimes volatile relationship between Orthodox Jewry and the State of Israel. Given that, *Messianism, Zionism, and Jewish Religious Radicalism* will certainly remain relevant in its scope, its scholarship, and its claims about contemporary Jewish society.

10. The Israeli Supreme Court sitting as the High Court of Justice: Horev v. Minister of Transportation, 1997

The Israeli Supreme Court sitting as the High Court of Justice: Baruch Marzel v. Jerusalem District Police Commander, Mr. Aharon Franco, 2002

The Israeli Supreme Court sitting as the High Court of Justice: Horev v. Minister of Transportation, 1997

B ar-Ilan Street has ceased to be just a road in the Israeli public discourse. It has instead become a social issue. It reflects the deep political divide between the ultra-Orthodox and the secular. This isn't a debate on the freedom of movement on Friday and Shabbat on Bar-Ilan Street. It is, in essence, a difficult debate about the relationship between religion and state in Israel; it's a poignant debate on the character of Israel as a Jewish state or as a democratic state; it's a bitter debate on the character of Jerusalem. ...

The values of the State of Israel are its values as a "Jewish and democratic state." It appears beyond dispute that consideration of religious sensibilities is commensurate with the values of the State of Israel as a Jewish state. This is true, a fortiori, when these feelings are connected to the Sabbath itself. Sabbath observance is a central value in Judaism. The fourth of the Ten Commandments, the Sabbath constitutes an original and significant Jewish contribution to the culture of mankind. It is a cornerstone of the Jewish tradition and a symbol, an expression of the Jewish message and the character of the Jewish people. Deprive Judaism of the Sabbath, and you have deprived it of its soul, for the Sabbath comprises the very essence of Judaism's nature. Over the generations, throughout its blood-soaked history, our nation has sacrificed many of its children in the name of the Sabbath.

Is it consistent with democratic values to restrict human rights for the purpose of protecting religious feelings? The answer to this question is quite complex.

On the one hand, protecting human feelings is natural to the democratic system, for society exists in order to give expression to these. This is the principle of tolerance, a basic tenet of democratic theory, vital to a pluralistic democracy.

A democratic society, which is prepared to restrict rights in order to prevent physical injury, must be equally sensitive to the potential need for restricting rights in order to prevent emotional harm, which, at times, may be even more severe than physical injury. A democratic society seeking to protect life, physical integrity and property, must also strive to protect feelings.

On the other hand, a democratic system prioritizes human rights above all else. Clearly, communal life in a democratic society, by its very nature, requires some openness to offense in order to realize human rights. The principle of tolerance, by virtue of which consideration for feelings arises, itself gives rise to the requirement that one whose feelings are offended be tolerant. This is the other side of mutual tolerance, necessary in a pluralistic society. ...

The "Israeli style" solution to this is that consideration of people's sensitivities as grounds for overriding human rights is allowed if the following three conditions are met: First, that this consideration [of people's sensibilities] is consistent with the special purpose of the legislation [on human freedom and dignity], which is what gives authority to legislating such a consideration; Second, that this consideration of religious sensibilities is allowed only insofar as it does not constitute religious coercion; Third, this consideration of sensitivities is allowed only to the extent that: A) the harm done to religion and the sensibilities of religious people is severe, grave and serious; B) the probability that this harm will occur is at a level close to certainty; C) there is an essential social interest in protecting, in this instance, religious sensibilities and people who lead religious lives; D) of the harmful measures, we must choose the option that generates the least harm; the harm to the freedom of movement needs to be proportionate to the benefits incurred from such a restriction.

The Israeli Supreme Court sitting as the High Court of Justice: Baruch Marzel v. Jerusalem District Police Commander, Mr. Aharon Franco, 2002

As part of the basic right to freedom of expression, members of the gay-lesbian community, like all citizens of the state, are guaranteed the right to express their unique identity as they see fit, subject to and within the framework of the law. Assembling and holding a procession through city streets are an accepted and natural means of exercising the constitutional right to freedom of expression, which is one of the most important human rights.

The gay-lesbian community's constitutional right to self-expression by means of a procession and rally is objected to on the grounds of a possible offense to the sensibilities of a broad section of both the religious and secular public in Jerusalem. The opponents maintain that holding the Gay Pride Parade in the center of the city offends deep-seated religious and moral sensibilities and deeply contradicts the values unifying the city's residents. The possibility of serious harm to sensibilities is a relevant concern that cannot be overlooked when considering the constitutionality of the scope of the protection given to the community's members to exercise their right to freedom of expression in the context of the parade.

The broad scope of the right to freedom of expression, from which the right to hold a parade and rally is derived, does not mean that the protection accorded to this right is absolute and that it necessarily coincides with the full extent of that right. The clash between the constitutional right and the conflicting public interest—in this case, protection against serious harm to public sensibilities—requires striking a balance between the conflicting interests in a way that might lead to a certain narrowing of the protection accorded to the freedom to hold a parade or procession.

We have already ruled that although holding the Gay Pride Parade is likely to offend public sensibilities; nevertheless, the anticipated offense does not cross the high threshold of public tolerance that would justify curbing personal and collective freedom of expression. It follows that there is no legal justification under constitutional principles for completely banning the parade. Nonetheless, by the very nature of the required balance, the community's right of expression does not enjoy absolute protection and it can be restricted. Such restrictions are an outcome of the proper balance between the constitutional right to exercise freedom of expression and the protection afforded against serious harm to public sensibilities, which is a public interest recognized by law.

Hence, on one hand, the Gay Pride Parade should not be prevented from taking place, but, at the same time, public sensibilities should be taken into account and the harm to them should be mitigated as much as possible in various relevant aspects, including timing, venue, route length, event duration and content, and the manner in which the event participants are expected to behave and conduct themselves. It appears to us that, in this case, controlling these aspects serves to maintain the required balance between the conflicting values which should be accorded their appropriate proportional weight.

COMMENTARY BY DONNIEL HARTMAN

The framers of the Israeli Declaration of Independence believed that the Jewishness of Israel should be principally expressed not in its fidelity to Jewish law, but in the fact that it would be the nation-state of the Jewish people. As such, it would give priority and preference to Jewish immigration over that of other national groups, and would "be based on freedom, justice, and peace, as envisaged by the Prophets of Israel." Judaism, as a religion, would enter into the machinery of the State only as the cultural language with which Israel expresses its commitment to the universal values of freedom, justice, and peace.

The Declaration is clear: the State of Israel is not based on all of the teachings of the Prophets. It is based on the teachings of the Prophets which reflect a commitment to the principles of freedom, justice, and peace. All other teachings of the Prophets are inconsequential.

The choice of the Prophets was also intentional. There are teachings in the Torah and in rabbinic literature which also advocate for freedom, justice, and peace. The preference for the Prophets is a result of the fact that under Jewish law, prophetic teachings have no legal authority. In Jewish law, it is only Moses, and afterward the rabbis of the Oral Torah, who have the authority to frame Jewish legal obligations. A prophet who legislates has the status of a false prophet. "The teachings of the Prophets" are thus not meant as a source of law, but as a Jewish cultural language with which to express Israel's universal commitments.

The hope of the founders of Israel was that the Jewish people would build a secular, democratic state for the Jews. Hebrew would be the principal language of the country, the national holidays would follow the Jewish calendar, and universal humanistic values would receive a Jewish hue. To them, this was all that a Jewish State meant.

For the sake of greater political ends and coalition politics, the State's founders allowed compromises on this vision of a secular nation-state of the Jews. To enable leaders of the Orthodox community to sign on, the framers closed the Declaration of Independence by stating they were "placing our trust in the Rock of Israel," indirectly referencing God. On issues of personal status, the Ottoman Millet legal system was incorporated into the laws of the country, giving the Rabbinate—an Orthodox institution from the beginning—sole jurisdiction over Jews in the areas of marriage, divorce, and conversion. Coalition politics forced the implementation of limitations on public transportation on Shabbat, as well as some areas of commerce. These were justified as preservation of a mythic "status quo," which was allowed to exceed the guidelines of the secular, democratic state of the Jews.

All in all, these compromises were tolerated, because the secular, Ashkenazi founders of the country expected that they would be temporary. They believed that they could "Ashkenize" immigrants from Arab and Northern African countries and that the assimilation of Orthodoxy into enlightened, secular Judaism was imminent and inevitable. In addition, secular Judaism had not developed its own Rabbinate or clearly defined a Torah of secular Judaism. Consequently, their primary agenda was freedom *from* religion, as distinct from freedom *of* religion. If Orthodoxy wanted to control some areas of the State, so be it, as long as the areas of coercion were kept to a minimum and the coalition remained stable.

Over the decades, contrary to the founders' expectations, Orthodox Judaism did not disappear but thrived. Sephardic Judaism did not undergo a secular, Ashkenazic conversion, but instead reasserted both its Sephardic heritage and its traditional approach to Judaism. By the end of the twentieth century, the majority of Jews in Israel no longer saw their Jewish identity in purely secular terms, and the Declaration of Independence's vision of a secular democracy of Jews was no longer adequate. A new approach to thinking about issues of state and religion was necessary in order to reflect a broader sense of Judaism in the Jewish state and to enable coexistence among the different Jewish tribes of Israel. Using the Basic Law of Human Freedom and Dignity of 1992, together with its amendment establishing Israel as both a Jewish and democratic state, Chief Justice Aharon Barak attempted to redraw the relationship between state and religion in Israel.

In a radical departure from the vision of the Declaration of Independence, Barak argues that a Jewish state is not merely a secular, democratic state of the Jews, but also a place where Judaism must be allowed to shape the public sphere. Interpreting the Basic Law of Human Dignity and Freedom, he argues that the right to dignity entails the right to have one's religious feelings taken into account by the State. By this he means that the public sphere must reflect the religious feelings and sensibilities of its citizens, and in certain circumstances these must outweigh considerations of human rights. For example, by virtue of Israel being a Jewish state, committed to the dignity of all its citizens, it is legally coherent to consider limiting freedom of travel on streets in an Orthodox neighborhood, limiting the freedom of speech of the gay and lesbian community in Jerusalem, and limiting access to liberal prayer groups at the Kotel, and the like.

He posits that democracy, being founded on the principle of tolerance of difference, requires a willingness to limit human rights not only in instances of potential danger to life, but also when feelings are harmed. In doing so, Barak is combining the notion of Israel as a Jewish state with the notion of Israel as the homeland of the Jewish people. In a home, we ought to consider each other's feelings. Outside our national homeland, Jews can be Jewish in their homes. The meaning of Israel as a Jewish homeland is that here Jews must be able to be Jewish in their public home, as well.

According to the Basic Law of Human Freedom and Dignity, however, Israel is not merely a Jewish state, but also a democratic one. Barak argues that democracy does not merely require tolerance of feelings, but also the willingness of citizens to limit the weight of their hurt feelings for the sake of protecting human rights and the feelings of others. How one balances the two, according to Barak, cannot be answered in theory, but is conditional on the cultural reality of each country.

For Israel, he offers the following compromise. As stated, religious feelings have legal weight. Consequently, the feelings of an Orthodox Jew who wants to walk to synagogue on Shabbat without seeing traffic, need to be taken into account. So too, the feelings of Orthodox Jews who do not want a gay rights parade near their neighborhood. Similarly, the feelings of Orthodox Jews about women reading the Torah and mixed-gender prayer at the Kotel. The commitment to Israel as a democracy, however, limits the extent and circumstances wherein these feelings of hurt must be given legal consideration.

First and most significantly, Barak argues that religious feelings may be taken into consideration only if in doing so, one does not engage in counter-religious coercion, for then, someone else's religious feelings are being hurt. Religious feelings about Shabbat can limit the right to freedom of travel in a predominantly Orthodox neighborhood but cannot limit a citizen's ability to observe Shabbat in whichever way they see fit. Consequently, Barak was willing to close roads in Orthodox neighborhoods to through-traffic, but not to secular Jews who resided in the neighborhood itself, for whom travel to and from their homes was an integral part of their Shabbat observance.

Following this reasoning, in a later case involving the petition of the Women of the Wall to conduct a women's prayer group and Torah reading at the Kotel on the first day of the new month, their petition could not be rejected on ground that doing so would hurt the feelings of the Orthodox community. Such a sensitivity would violate the religious feelings and rights of the Women of the Wall, and as such would violate the requirements of democracy. Consequently,

Supreme Court Justice Michael Cheshin accepted the petition. He subsequently suspended its implementations in order to allow the government time to arrange for an alternate Kotel experience near Robinson's Arch. A failure to do so, he ruled, would result in the granting of permission for Women of the Wall to worship at any part of the Kotel.

Secondly, religious feelings may eclipse human rights only when the hurt is certain and extensive, and thus it is the civil courts of Israel who have the jurisdiction to adjudicate this issue. Consequently, the Court recognizes that given the centrality of Shabbat, hurt feelings in this area are legitimate.

Far more significantly, Barak distinguishes between the religious sensibilities of encountering traffic on Shabbat, when one is traditionally outside one's home and going to prayer services, from feelings of hurt at seeing cars going by while one is in one's home eating meals or resting. He argues that it is only in the former situation that the hurt feeling is certain and extensive, while in the latter, the onus on the Orthodox citizen is to overcome their feelings of hurt. Consequently, Barak is only willing to consider street closure to through-traffic during those specific hours of prayer services on Friday evening, Shabbat morning, and Shabbat afternoon.

Following Barak's reasoning, in the case of the Gay Pride Parade in Jerusalem, it is only the feeling regarding its proximity to the Orthodox neighborhood of Mea Shearim that Justice Ayala Prokacha was willing to consider. Once the location of the parade was moved to the southern part of the city, the Court assessed the degree of hurt to be diminished, in which case it could no longer transcend the right of freedom of speech.

Within these latter considerations lies a more radical vision for Israeli society. The only instances in which "Jewish" outweighs "democratic" are when the individual's religious feelings are directly harmed. When my travel on Shabbat meets your walking to synagogue in your predominantly Orthodox neighborhood, or when I parade about something you believe to be religiously offensive in your neighborhood, then the weight of Israel as a Jewish state can prevail. If, however, your religious feelings are hurt by the fact that in Israel, Shabbat is being violated, or that the gay and lesbian community are marching somewhere within "your" entire Jerusalem, your feelings must be ignored.

The founders of Israel envisioned a secular democracy of Jews. Barak suggests that we cease seeing all spaces as monolithic. In a sense, Barak is arguing for Jewish neighborhoods in a democratic state. You cannot separate state from religion in people's homes. And these homes are not merely their private ones, but also the public neighborhoods in which they live. Depending on the specific population in question, Israel must be prepared to accommodate religious feelings, and in so doing give expression to citizens' desire to live within a Jewish state. That said, the State must also be democratic. Religious sensibilities may be allowed to govern one's own neighborhood, but they cannot dictate what happens in other peoples' neighborhoods. Most significantly, tolerance toward one side's religious feeling cannot be grounds for intolerance toward others, even if one has greater political power.

For Barak, a Jewish democratic state that is the homeland of the Jewish people does not allow for simple, binary distinctions or divisions. We have come home, and a home is messy. Judaism does not unite us; it divides us. Yet at the same time, we want to create one state which can serve as the home for all Jews. Barak's revolution was to put a complex system of considerations into play which would guide the uniquely Israeli balance between Judaism and democracy: a new status quo which will be given life and meaning by the legislature and the courts.

11. Samuel G. Freedman, *Jew vs. Jew: The Struggle for the Soul of American Jewry*

Samuel G. Freedman, *Jew vs. Jew: The Struggle for the Soul of American Jewry*, New York: Simon and Schuster, 2000

Samuel G. Freedman (1955–) is Professor at the Columbia University Graduate School of Journalism.

The present struggle sets two archetypes against one another. One is unity and the other is pluralism, and both are innocuous euphemisms for more controversial agendas. As invoked by America's Orthodox Jews, "unity" means unity if all Jews act and think as we do, accepting the inerrancy of Torah and the yoke of 613 commandments, the mitzvot. As invoked by America's non-Orthodox Jews, "pluralism" means that any variation of Judaism must be accepted by everyone, no obligations required and no questions asked. The sociologist Steven M. Cohen had described the vying camps as "transformationalists" and "survivalists," with one faction seeing Jewish identity enriched by the influence of polyglot America and the other fearing that identity's erosion for precisely the same reason. Put another way, the dueling models might be expressed as "I am what I feel" versus "I feel what I am." I am what I feel: I define the terms of my Jewish identity. I feel what I am: Judaism defines the terms of my Jewish identity. I feel what I am: Jewish ethnicity exists independent of Jewish religion. I am what I feel: Jewish ethnicity arises from Jewish religion.

To recognize how irreconcilable are these versions of Jewish identity is to understand why the civil war promises only to deepen and worsen. The Modern Orthodox rabbi Irving (Yitz) Greenberg asked in a 1986 essay, "Will there be one Jewish People by the year 2000?" He predicted, "Within decades, the Jewish people will split apart into two mutually divided, hostile groups who are unable or unwilling to marry each other." And he continued, "In the past anti-Semites built their plans on the expectation and hope that Jews will disappear. We have come to the tragic situation where good and committed Jews are predicting their survival strategies on the disappearance of other Jews."

For more than four thousand years of slavery, exile, oppression, persecution, and genocide, the Jewish people endured out of a nearly sacred devotion to the concept of *Klal Yisrael*, the community of Jews. Indeed, whatever shatters Jewish community is described as a *chillul Hashem*, a desecration of God's name. At the most practical level, a succession of gentile enemies from Pharaoh to Hitler threatened Jews as an undifferentiated mass. The Marxist, the boulevardier, and the shtetl rabbi died alike in the gas chambers, and the lesson, as the renowned American Orthodox rabbi Joseph Soloveitchik expressed it, was that in a hostile world all Jews were joined by a *brit goral*, a covenant of common fate.

Why is it, then, that the ancient bond no longer holds in modern America? Why is it that the most comfortable, secure, and prosperous Jewish community in history is also one of the most fractious? (26–27)

COMMENTARY BY NOAM PIANKO

Samuel Freedman's *Jew vs. Jew*, published in 2000, brought in the new millennium with a troubling claim for American Jews: the American Jewish community long celebrated as unified by a set of shared values and commitments faced unprecedented polarization across fundamental issues from definitions of Judaism to relationship with Israel. The book challenged decades of efforts by American Jewish leaders and organizations to emphasize American Jewish solidarity. Reading the book in hindsight from 2018, Freedman's prophecy of American Jewish polarization correctly forecasted many trends in American Jewish life. As Freedman predicted, the American Jewish relationship with Israel has continued to shift from great unifier to divider. While Freedman identified this trend, however, he did not fully anticipate how deeply this issue would emerge, even perhaps becoming the fundamental axis of American Jewish fragmentation. At the same time, tensions around religious practice have mitigated in response to a greater acceptance of religious hybridity and a culture of syncretism in American Jewish practice and belief.

Freedman's book presented a significant critique given the backdrop of the largely unchallenged rhetoric of American Jewish unity during the sixties, seventies, and eighties. The 1967 war solidified the centrality of Zionism across religious and political boundaries, the Soviet Jewry movement in the 1970s and 1980s brought Jews together from across the religious spectrum to advocate for the right to practice Judaism freely, and the continuity crisis of the 1990s offered the threat of assimilation as the motivation for a collective mission of survival. *Jew vs. Jew* shattered the comfortable assumptions that "we are one" by underscoring the tremendous internal disagreements and conflicts between various Jewish groups in the United States.

Jew vs. Jew focused largely on differences in religious beliefs, practice, and identities. As Freedman framed the debates in American Jewish life, "I have witnessed the struggle for the soul of American Jewry. It is a struggle that pits secularist against believer, denomination against denomination, gender against gender, liberal against conservative, traditionalist against modernist even within each branch" (23). Freedman understood the battlegrounds of American Jewry in 2000 as dividing the community along mutually opposed foundational beliefs. No doubt, these rifts, especially around gender and traditionalist Orthodoxy and modernist liberal Jewish denominations, continue to separate American Jewish streams.

Yet the trend over the last two decades toward hybridity and religious pluralism in the United States have mitigated these defining poles as the primary cause of Jew vs. Jew struggles. The changing American and American Jewish landscape of religious identity construction more closely reflects a path outlined in another volume published in the same year, *The Jew Within: Self, Family, and Community*. Authors Steven Cohen and Arnold Eisen offered a less binary way of framing changing Jewish identities and explaining how Jews reconcile conflicting religious claims. Instead of viewing individual and Jewish categories as mutually exclusive, *The Jew Within* describes Jewish identity as a personal, malleable, and flexible set of experiences. Unlike Freedman's *Jew vs. Jew* protagonists, the subjects of *The Jew Within* portrayed Jewish identity as far less about ideological commitments requiring careful boundary preservation and far more about evolving and fluid personal narratives that seek meaning rather than philosophical consistency. It is interesting from this historical vantage point to look back and see how deeply postmodern notions of hybridity and multiculturalism have mitigated some of the denominational and religious division in American Jewish life described by Freedman. Freedman failed to see the how the non-Orthodox American Jewish community would accommodate and welcome individuals and families that blur historically fixed boundaries between religious, ethnic, and racial communities.

The relationship between American Jews and Israel, on the other hand, has emerged as the most divisive debate in the American Jewish community over the last decade. Freedman presciently argued that the disagreements over the Oslo peace process, especially following the murder of Prime Minister Rabin, would have a transformative impact on American Jewish life. Freedman observes,

> For American Jews who had grown up dropping coins into the tins of the
> Jewish National Fund or donating dollars for trees to be planted in the
> reborn Zion, Israel had become and would remain the cause of communal

tension, not the antidote to it. Instead of bridging the gaps between denominations, or between secularist and fervent believers, Israel deepened them. (25)

Since Freedman flagged Israel as an emerging area of contention, the centrality of Israel as a fragmenting force of American Jewry has accelerated. Israel has shifted from one of the most important areas of debate and discussion to *the* primary issue that potentially could disqualify full membership in most communal organizations. In order to promote the idea of continued unity around Israel as a consensus issue, Jewish organizations have increasingly referred to a "big tent" (generally when referring to Israel policies) as the language for articulating a broad spectrum of normative consensus.

Yet, this claim is misleading. The "big tent" claim, in reality, creates a rigid boundary between acceptable and unacceptable attitudes toward Israel. This constructs a justification to discredit organizations or individuals for positions outside the tent, which are then perceived as "anti-Israel." For example, in 2014 the Conference of Presidents of Major Jewish Organizations voted against including J Street in the organization partially on the grounds that the organization's position on Israel went beyond the big tent litmus test. This move toward placing Israel politics as the only significant area of enforced communal consensus has introduced an unprecedented level and scale of boundary policing among Jews. The conflicts between secular and religious and within religious denominations which Freedman reported and which continue to create friction, never generated broadly accepted litmus tests for denying inclusion within mainstream Jewish organizations. Of course, individual rabbis or leaders might decide whether or not to appear with other leaders. However, communal Jewish organizations, from Hillel to Federations, never instituted guidelines around religious practices. Eating *treyf*, violating Shabbat, proclaiming oneself an atheist, and even the decision to marry a non-Jew, would not disqualify individuals from full participation in mainstream Jewish organizations.

The Jew vs. Jew tensions around Israel have created an even deeper rift that Freedman, like so many other observers of American Jewish life in the early 2000s, could not have anticipated. The polarization of American politics has increasingly shifted Israel from an issue pitting Jew vs. Jew to American vs. American. American support for Israel during the Obama and Trump administrations has increasingly emerged as one dividing America along party lines. Prime Minister Netanyahu's open criticism of President Obama's Iran policy, which gained support from American Jewish organizations like AIPAC, put a

position presented as "pro-Israel" in direct conflict with the Democratic administration's foreign policy. Similarly, President Trump's 2018 decision to move the
US embassy to Jerusalem and refusal to specifically endorse a two-state solution
further split Republicans and Democrats on the issue and tied Israel politics
into a series of deeper questions about nationalism, immigration, and minority
rights. As many American Jews continue to identity with the Democratic side
of the political spectrum, they will increasingly associate a "pro-Israel" stance as
a policy aligned with Republicans. For Jews galvanized to challenge American
nationalist politics represented by the Trump administration, American political activism will take precedence and only deepen the ambivalence around
Israel as it is increasingly associated with the political right in the United States.

Were Freedman's book to be written today, far more emphasis would need
to be given to the politicization of Israel in American politics and the implications of this shift. The struggle for the soul of American Jewry qualitatively
changes when issues dividing Jews internally become aligned with issues polarizing American politics. Internal debates about Jewish issues can be set aside or
played down because most American Jews do not see them as central to their
day-to-day experiences. However, American political alignments create frac-
tures far more difficult to bridge in the name of Jewish unity. Once the struggle
over what it means to be an American Jew is linked so intimately with what it
means to be an American, Jew vs. Jew tensions will enter a far more publicly
contentious and internally divisive stage.

Jew vs. Jew is just as much of a reality today as it was in 2000 when Freedman coined the term. Yet, the key areas of contention have shifted in the last two
decades—Israel has emerged as a far clearer ideological boundary than religious
differences, which have been mitigated by an increasing comfort with hybrid
and personalized integration of various aspects of Judaism from across traditional denominational or ideological barrier lines. Cheeseburger-eating atheist
Jews who study Talmud are far more common in organized Jewish spaces than
members of J Street, Jewish Voice for Peace, IfNotNow, New Israel Fund, and
other Jewish groups committed to changing Israel's policies. Israel's increasingly
central position has brought communities with opposing theologies into partnership and created far deeper rifts between Jews of similar religious practice
who have different political approaches to Israel. Whether or not the new Jew
vs. Jew disagreements can, or should, be bridged is a question that will shape the
future of the American Jewish community.

12. *Breaking the Silence Testimonies*

Breaking the Silence Testimonies, https://www.breakingthesilence.org.il/testimonies/database, Founded in March 2004

"Shoot, shoot everywhere"
Unit: Infantry
Area: Northern Gaza strip
Period: 2014

But the more time that passed [since the operation started], the more immediate authorizations became. The rules of engagement for soldiers advancing on the ground were open fire, open fire everywhere, first thing as you go in. The assumption being that the moment we went in [to the Gaza Strip], anyone who dared poke his head out was a terrorist. And it pretty much stayed that way throughout the operation.

———

"Good Morning al-Bureij"
Rank: First Sergeant
Unit: Armored Corps
Area: Deir al-Balah area
Period: 2014

I remember it, all the tanks were standing in a row, and me myself, I asked my commander: "Where are we firing at?" He told me: "Pick wherever you feel like it." And later, also, during talks with the other guys—each one chose his own target, and the commander, on the two-way radio, called it "Good Morning al-Bureij."

———

"They wanted to find some Palestinian and kill him"
Rank: First Sergeant
Unit: Nahal, 932nd Battalion
Area: Hebron
Period: 2014

We were called traitors, [told] that we're Nazis, that we hate Jews and hate Israel because we're protecting innocent Palestinians.

———

"Little girls"
Rank: First Sergeant
Unit: Nahal Haredi
Area: Jericho and the Jordan valley
Period: 2002–2003

I arrived one morning and a bus passed by full of girls from the [Jordan] Valley area who studied in the villages inside. The girls need to get off the bus; a soldier gets on the bus, searches it, and then they get back on. One day I saw them standing in rows of three, and I asked what happened. I was told that the morning before the commander was there and he taught them to stand in rows of three and shout "attention, sir."

———

"I'm not going to make such racial segregation"
Unit: Nahal, 932nd Battalion
Area: Hebron
Period: 2014

There's the Abraham Spring in which many Jews like to swim. … Soldiers got the impression from somewhere, as did the squad commanders and everyone else, that Arabs aren't allowed to swim in that spring. They're prohibited from going to a spring that's in their own neighborhood.

———

"The checkpoint commander called himself 'the doctor'"
Rank: First Sergeant
Unit: Golani Brigade

He really liked looking at people who came with X-rays. … He'd look at the X-ray, peer at it as if he were deciding to do some kind of physical inspection. It was all a joke.

———

"They pissed their pants with fright, of course"
Rank: First Sergeant
Unit: Reserves
Area: Ramallah and al-Bireh area
Period: 2006

I remember we were in the outskirts of some village, we walked and heard some voices and saw some father with two kids making a bonfire, a campfire of sorts, outside their house in the yard. Without provocation or anything like that, just to scare them, we threw stun grenades at them.

COMMENTARY BY SARAH ANNE MINKIN

It is July 2004, and a handful of young men, all soldiers in the Israeli reserves, are gathered outside a small building near Tel Aviv, waiting for the visitors they will guide through their brand-new, temporary exhibit. The reservists will personally explain every object. In a different exhibit, a few sentences on the wall might have sufficed for explanation, but not here.

This collection's photos are mostly of Hebron, one of the four classical holy Jewish cities and the largest city in the West Bank. It is home to more than 200,000 Palestinians, who live under Israeli military occupation, and several hundred Jews, who live as Israeli citizens with the full protection of their state and its military.

Photos show Hebrew graffiti on Palestinian homes and stores with slogans like "Arabs to the gas chambers" and "death to Arabs." One photo shows a young Palestinian man with hands bound and eyes covered, perched uncomfortably on a chair while soldiers lounge around him. Another features an Orthodox Jewish man, a settler, with a long beard and side curls, a guitar in one hand and an automatic weapon in the other; he smiles as he leans towards a helmeted soldier, also holding an automatic weapon, finger on the trigger, smiling and leaning back. The guide tells the viewers that settlers are "partners" to the Israel Defense Forces (IDF) and help the soldiers maintain military rule over Palestinian civilians.

One frame displays many sets of keys, dangling from hooks. The guide explains that in many instances, IDF soldiers force Palestinian drivers and their passengers to exit their cars, park them on the side of the road, and leave the keys with the soldiers. "The IDF spokesman says that the IDF does not collect keys," the soldier says, pointing at the display of hundreds of keys. Each key illustrates inconvenience and loss to the driver, and also the wide gap between the military narrative and the lived experience of soldiers and Palestinians. The guide said, "There are hundreds more 'keys the IDF says we didn't collect' from where these came."

This exhibit marked the launch of Breaking the Silence, an organization that collects and publishes testimonies from soldiers about their military experiences in the Occupied Palestinian Territories. Breaking the Silence (BTS) seeks to end Israel's fifty-plus-year-old occupation of Palestinian Territories, and uses soldiers' testimonies to demand "accountability regarding Israel's military actions in the Occupied Territories, which are perpetrated by its citizens and in their names."[1]

---

1 Breaking the Silence, *Our Harsh Logic: Israeli Soldiers' Testimonies from the Occupied Territories 2000–2010* (New York: Metropolitan Books, 2012), xvi.

As former combatants who have served on Israel's front lines, their voices carry significant weight in the hierarchy of Israel's militarized society. Since their 2004 founding, the group has collected and published testimonies from more than 1,000 former IDF soldiers who have maintained Israel's occupation of the West Bank and Gaza Strip and also participated in major combat operations in Gaza, including Cast Lead (2008–2009) and Defensive Shield (2014). BTS says they have a "civil obligation"[2] to share the information they collect, arguing that "the facts are clear and accessible; the testimonies oblige us to look directly at Israel's actions and ask whether they reflect the values of a humane, democratic society."[3]

Men and women from nearly all the units that serve in the Occupied Territories, including officers, medics, infantry, and pilots, have given testimonies. They volunteer their experiences, adding their voices and critical views in an attempt to stimulate public discussion of the Occupation. Through a multistep verification process that includes corroboration of testimony, BTS has thus far proven themselves as conveyors of accurate information. Not one of their testimonies has been disproven. In order to prevent the exposure of classified material, BTS submits their testimonies to the Israeli Military Censor for approval before publication. BTS disseminates the testimonies through publications, a searchable Internet-based archive, public lectures and house meetings, tours of Hebron and the South Hebron Hills, and media campaigns.

The testimonies describe the daily operations of Israel's military occupation of the West Bank and Gaza Strip, detailing the policies, acts, and orders that maintain the Occupation as "a reality in which young soldiers face a civilian population on a daily basis, and are engaged in the control of that population's everyday life."[4] The testimonies describe the widespread view that every Palestinian poses a potential threat to Israel and, consequently, that each tactic the Israeli military uses against them—from the proliferation of checkpoints to the confiscation of property, from collective punishment to annexation of land—is necessary for the protection of Israel and its citizens. BTS disputes the presumption that security is what drives Israel's military actions. BTS writes:

---

2   *This is How We Fought in Gaza: Soldiers' testimonies and photographs from Operation "Protective Edge" (2014)*, accessed July 8, 2019, Breaking the Silence, https://www.breakingthesilence.org.il/pdf/ProtectiveEdge.pdf.

3   *Our Harsh Logic*, 6.

4   "About organization," *Breaking the Silence*, accessed February 1, 2019, https://www.breakingthesilence.org.il/about/organization.

The testimonies left no room for doubt: while the security apparatus has indeed had to respond to concrete threats during the past decade, including terrorist attacks on citizens, Israel's actions are not solely defensive. Rather, they have systematically led to the de facto annexation of large sections of the West Bank through the dispossession of Palestinian residents and by tightening control over the civilian population and instilling fear. The widespread notion in Israeli society that control of the Territories is exclusively aimed at protecting citizens is incompatible with the information conveyed by hundreds of IDF soldiers.[5]

In *This is How We Fought in Gaza (2014)*, a collection of testimonies from soldiers who fought in Operation Protective Edge, BTS points to systematic policies, particularly the open-fire policy, that led to widespread destruction of human lives and infrastructure over that seven week campaign (of the 2200 Palestinians killed, more than 500 were children and several hundred more were civilians,[6] and more than 100,000 people were made homeless as more than 18,000 homes were destroyed or badly damaged[7]). Detailing the policies and practices of the IDF according to more than 100 testimonies, BTS argues that the operation casts grave doubt on the IDF's ethical norms.[8]

As the number of soldiers who have shared testimony with BTS has grown, so too has the challenge that this organization poses to the IDF's claims to moral authority and truth-telling. BTS sees themselves as acting out of loyalty to and love for their society. Yet they are accused of being enemies of the state and subjected to increasing hostility and fierce opposition from state authorities, the Jewish Israeli public, and Israel advocates abroad. Incitement and denunciations against BTS take many forms, including forced cancellation of events, periodic barring of their tours from entering Hebron, and the occasional detaining of their leadership. Israel has pressured European countries to not engage with BTS, turning these soldiers' testimonies into international diplomatic

---

5   *Our Harsh Logic*, 1–2.
6   "50 Days: More than 500 Children: Facts and figures on fatalities in Gaza, Summer 2014," BTselem, accessed February 1, 2019, https://www.btselem.org/press_releases/20160720_ fatalities_in_gaza_conflict_2014.
7   "Black Flag: The legal and moral implications of the policy of attacking residential buildings in the Gaza Strip, Summer 2014," BTselem, accessed February 1, 2019, https://www.btselem.org/publications/summaries/201501_black_flag.
8   "Background," Breaking the Silence, accessed March 14, 2018, http://www.breakingthesilence.org.il/protective-edge/background.

controversy. BTS has faced physical threats, and sometimes assault, from settlers and their supporters in Hebron. In 2016, a group affiliated with an extremist settler organization infiltrated the organization in an attempt to plant false testimonies, aiming to delegitimize the organization's work. BTS discovered and averted the attempted sabotage.

Ominously, leading public figures and policymakers, including Prime Minister Benjamin Netanyahu, regularly denounce BTS as "traitors" who spew "lies" and "slander" Israeli soldiers and "defame" the state.[9] Authorities deploy state power against them: a 2018 law codified an already-existing ban on BTS speaking in Israeli schools; former Defense Minister Moshe Ya'alon barred them from engaging with active-duty soldiers; Justice Minister Ayelet Shaked initiated an investigation (later closed) against their spokesperson; and the State Prosecutor demanded they reveal the identities of several soldiers who provided testimonies (they refused). And over the last several years, members of Knesset have targeted the Israeli civil and human rights sector, including BTS, seeking to weaken it by threatening access to funding and imposing legal and financial repercussions for acting against the Occupation or in solidarity with Palestinian civil society. These efforts reflect a growing intolerance in Israel for dissent.

BTS has also been a lightning rod in Jewish communities across North America, illuminating the struggles over what is acceptable public discourse regarding Israel. They are a welcome voice among the growing segment of American Jews whose opposition to the Occupation is part of their engagement with Jewish life. At the same time, some dominant Jewish institutions and influential Israel advocates have denounced BTS or excluded them from Jewish spaces, in the name of protecting Israel. Controversy often breaks out when students invite BTS to speak at their universities.[10]

The efforts to silence, marginalize, and undermine BTS point to the tremendous importance of their project. The soldiers who chose to "break the silence" make public information that many people—from IDF commanders to Israeli politicians to American Jewish advocates—do not want exposed.

9   Joshua Leifer, "'You are all traitors': The political persecution of Breaking the Silence," *972mag*, November 19, 2017; Or Kahti, "Education Minister Bennett Bars Breaking the Silence From Schools," *Haaretz*, December 15, 2015; Almog Ben Zikri, "Education Minister Bennett Bars Breaking the Silence From Schools," *Haaretz*, March 02, 2017.

10   Barred from Princeton University and Washington University in St. Louis. Allowed in Hillel after contentious struggles at Columbia University, Harvard University, University of California-Berkeley, and University of Pennsylvania.

Attempts to undermine BTS suggest that its opponents see danger in the impact BTS has on Israelis' views of themselves and their public image abroad. That threat, to them, outweighs the harsh realities of Palestinian lives under Israeli occupation, the struggles of Israeli soldiers forced to compromise themselves in the course of their military duty, and the devastation that the absence of real security brings to both Israelis and Palestinians.

13. Steven M. Cohen and Jack Wertheimer, "Whatever Happened to the Jewish People?"

Steven M. Cohen and Jack Wertheimer, "Whatever Happened to the Jewish People?," *Commentary*, June 1, 2006

Dr. Steven M. Cohen (1950–) served as Research Professor of Jewish Social Policy at Hebrew Union College-Jewish Institute of Religion and Director of the Berman Jewish Policy Archive at Stanford University.

Dr. Jack Wertheimer (1948–) is the Joseph and Martha Mendelson Professor of American Jewish History at the Jewish Theological Seminary.

Does any of this matter? What exactly is lost by a redefinition of Jewry in terms of individuals rather than in terms of a single people, and of Judaism in terms of personal and private identity?

Our own answer is unabashedly "essentialist": seeing Jews as a global extended family, exhibiting concern on these grounds for one's fellow Jews, are authentic expressions of what, from biblical times forward, it has meant to be Jewish, and to act responsibly for the sake of the Jewish future. Jews are not solely the agglomeration of adherents of a particular faith, each seeking personal meaning; they are a people whose primary mark has been the conviction of a unique corporate role in history—the mark, to use classical theological language, of chosenness. To retreat from peoplehood is to repudiate what has been at the core. ... In the end, the decline of Jewish peoplehood is symptomatic of a decline of morale, of national self-respect. A people no longer proud of what and who it is, no longer dedicated to caring for its own, cannot long expect to be held in high regard by others, or to move the world by its message.

COMMENTARY BY YEHUDA KURTZER

Steven M. Cohen and Jack Wertheimer's "Whatever Happened to the Jewish People?" is a sweeping criticism of the American Jewish community and its priorities. It is a brutal assessment of a community by two of its most prominent scholars, calling the community to account for its social and communal behaviors that had developed over the preceding decades. But the article is not merely an argument: it is a window into a huge set of questions facing the American

Jewish community at the time about power, priorities, and the business of "thought-leadership."

In the article, Cohen and Wertheimer argue that a large-scale collapse was taking place in American Jewish life. They claim that American Jews of the time were exhibiting "weakened identification with their fellow Jews abroad, as well as a waning sense of communal responsibility at home." Drawing a contrast between the capacity of the Jewish community to organize on behalf of Soviet Jewry back in the 1980s—which they see as evidence of still-strong attachments to Jewish peoplehood—and what they call the "soft-pedaled" rhetoric of their own time, the authors deride the fact that American Jews could not or would not mount meaningful campaigns for their fellow Jews but focus instead on addressing issues facing humanity more broadly, such as alleviating the suffering caused by Hurricane Katrina and genocide in Darfur, or domestic (non-Jewish) poverty.

Cohen and Wertheimer offer multiple supports for their critique of American Jews and their behaviors. They argue that historically, a belief in peoplehood and a corresponding bond with other Jews was a more important anchor of Jewishness than faith in God. They argue that Jewish religion was meant to be practiced in community. They point to a wide swath of social and political trends—intermarriage, the trends towards individualization in American religious identity, the Second Intifada—as forces at work in diminishing Jewish collective consciousness. They ultimately claim that what was damning American Judaism was a collapse of self-respect. Cohen and Wertheimer thus connect the dots between what they perceived as a diminishment of Jewish identity and its consequences for collectivity and community. It was not just about individual Jews and what they might lose; it was about what was being lost for the Jewish people as a whole.

Cohen and Wertheimer came to this argument from different disciplines and orientations. Cohen's primary concern during this time was what he saw as the problem of intermarriage and, more specifically, that marriage between Jews and non-Jews would lead to a negative growth in the population of American Jews and diminished Jewish institutions for the committed core. Cohen was known to have referred to intermarriage as a "cancer," even in public fora. The 1990 National Jewish Population Survey's most famous statistic was its initial pegging of the Jewish intermarriage rate as over 50%, which catalyzed a wide set of community responses including a renewed Orthodox outreach campaign and some major programmatic interventions, like Birthright Israel, aimed at stemming the tide. In spite of these efforts, the 2001 NJPS suggested the rate of intermarriage had increased. By 2006, it was also clear that changes in the nature of Jewish identity and corresponding changes in the rates and nature of affiliation and belonging to key institutions were transforming the Jewish communal infrastructure. Cohen's expertise in statistical analysis positioned him to become the central voice of expertise in Jewish communal anxiety about demographic changes and their consequences. Indeed, he became the American Jewish community's pre-eminent sociologist, ubiquitous in the Jewish media commenting on the news of the day, responsible for dozens of community surveys, and vested in senior leadership positions in academe and in the community.

In fact, right around the time of the publication of this essay, Cohen produced the most extensive and thorough expression of his position on intermarriage, a lecture published under the auspices of the Jewish Life Network/Steinhardt Foundation.[1] Here as elsewhere, Cohen's research divided the small field of Jewish social scientists, inviting harsh criticism from those who advocated for acceptance of and outreach towards intermarried Jews, and praise from those who believed in "holding the line."[2] On this issue, Cohen and his research were already a lightning rod in Jewish communal discourse: often funded by the Jewish organizational establishment; and often arguing against the normative behavior of the overwhelming majority of American Jews.

Wertheimer's interests were slightly different. A historian of American Judaism, Wertheimer had become increasingly concerned with the decline of what he called the "center" of American Judaism. By the late 1990s, Conservative Judaism had lost principal status to Reform as the religious movement with which the plurality of American Jews identified.[3] At that time, Wertheimer collaborated with Cohen and Charles Liebman on "How To Save American Jews," an article arguing for a greater investment in the committed core: the minority of the community that already exhibited more intense intra-ethnic behavioral bonds and higher levels of affiliation and commitment. In their words, "For Jews on the margins who may be surfeited with rootlessness and looking for something authentic in their lives, the existence of an enthusiastic and fulfilled core population, a population offering a genuine alternative, can surely act as

---

1   "A Tale of Two Jewries: The 'Inconvenient Truth" for American Jews," November 2006, https://www.bjpa.org/search-results/publication/2908.
2   Sue Fishkoff, "Report: Outreach to Intermarried Not the Best Use of Community Resources," *J Weekly*, February 9, 2007.
3   Jack Wertheimer, "Conservative Synagogues and Their Members," https://www.bjpa.org/content/upload/bjpa/cons/Conservative%20Synagogues%20and%20their%20Members.pdf

a more powerful lure than the bland nostrums of an establishment that offers them, in effect, only another version of what already ails them."[4] On his own, Wertheimer would go on to become a consistent critic of Jewish communal efforts focusing on social justice, which he saw as compromising the need for particularistic institutions such as Jewish day schools and camps.[5]

This 2006 essay by Cohen and Wertheimer thus reflects the merger of two agendas: Cohen brought his opposition to intermarriage as revealing and then encouraging the weakening of ethnic bonds among Jews; and Wertheimer brought what he thought should be the priorities of Jewish communal and institutional life: support for Israel, support for Jewish peoplehood, and support for the core institutions of Jewish communal life. In short, Wertheimer and Cohen believed that the behavioral trends and institutions that had been instrumental to American Jewish thriving in the middle of the twentieth century were indispensable to American Jews living in the twenty-first.

This argument was reactionary, in the technical sense: it entailed an appeal to the image of a better (if imagined) past, a more ideal moment in American Jewish life. Here we see the confluence of Cohen's survey methodologies with Wertheimer's historical methods. The former's reliance on using consistent markers and metrics of identity were sourced from earlier patterns of behavior identified by the latter. Because they were measuring the present on the basis of markers drawn from the past, however, the data consistently demonstrated decline. In treating the evolving trends of American Jewish life—in the realms of identity, ideology, and infrastructure—as indicators of failure as opposed to indicators of change (much less progress) Cohen and Wertheimer were equating change with loss, with all the economic and political opposition that such a conclusion would inevitably engender.[6] And as a reactionary position, this approach also depended on a particular reading of history: that peoplehood, narrowly defined, was a once dominant reality in Jewish life, and was now in decline. This was a position that invited criticism on both moral fronts (the relationship between progress and nostalgia) and

---

4   Jack Wertheimer, Charles S. Leibman, and Steven M. Cohen, "How to Save American Jews," *Commentary,* January 1996.

5   Jack Wertheimer, "The High Cost of Jewish Living," *Commentary,* March 2010.

6   Michal Kravel-Tovi: "one could say that the continuity crisis was significantly augmented by a 'hyperbole of pessimism'"—"Wet Numbers: The Language of Continuity Crisis and the Work of Care among the Organized American Jewish Community" in Michal Kravel-Tovi and Deborah Dash Moore (eds.), *Taking Stock: Cultures of Enumeration in Contemporary Jewish Life* (Bloomington, Indiana University Press, 2016), 147.

on historical fronts (whether the portrayal of an earlier period of Jewish history was accurate, or representative.)[7]

In examining Cohen, Wertheimer, and their critics, we see that their debates are also about who has the expertise and power to shape the Jewish communal agenda. Since the 1970s sociology had become the dominant industry of ideas in the Jewish community,[8] even though Judaism and the Jewish people are invested in and with all sorts of knowledge and analytical tools, and it was not inevitable that this discipline should have become as hegemonic as it did. But to say that sociology became important is to underplay the economy of knowledge in the Jewish community. The study of Jewish history in America lives in the province of secular academia, and it is produced and judged by those standards. Sociological studies of American Jews are overwhelmingly produced under the auspices of the Jewish community and funded by Jewish philanthropy. This is in addition to the ideological biases often driving the collection of survey data, as noted above.

Recent trends in anthropology and sociology have problematized the gaze of the scholarly observer and invited us to understand the intimate and intertwined nature of the researcher and the researched. Accordingly, we must ask: when is it legitimate for scholarly research to take normative or prescriptive moral stands about its subjects? The same question applies regardless of ideological orientation: the Jewish Outreach Institute, later renamed Big Tent Judaism, which argued for greater inclusion and outreach to the intermarried (and ultimately against the very definitional scheme dividing between inmarried and intermarried) was also founded by a sociologist, Egon Mayer.

And how does the interconnection between that research and the capital that fuels it—often from the same Jewish community that is being studied—inform the value of the research itself? The funders who founded Birthright Israel, for instance, also underwrote the research conducted by sociologists at Brandeis University evaluating Birthright Israel; Birthright Israel in turn used

---

7   See in particular Noam Pianko, *Jewish Peoplehood: An American Innovation* (New Brunswick: Rutgers University Press, 2015), who argues that Cohen and Wertheimer's idealized presentation of Jewish collectivism from the middle of the twentieth century was really just an anomalous post-war "blip" in intra-Jewish loyalties, made urgent and possible by the Holocaust and the project of founding the State of Israel, and that the American Jewish retreat from collectivism was a reversion to the mean; also Shaul Magid, *American Post-Judaism: Identity and Renewal in a Postethnic Society* (Indiana: 2013).

8   Lila Corwin Berman: "An intimate affair between Jews and sociologists was consummated by the 1970s around their common interest in—and for some, deep fear of—Jewish intermarriage," in "Sociology, Jews, and Intermarriage in Twentieth-Century America," *Jewish Social Studies*, 14:2 (2008).

curated versions of that research for fundraising and other purposes. Where are the lines for the Jewish community between the patronage of scholarship, scholarship itself, and the communal policy agenda?

These questions of research and presentation take on a different urgency when we see the extent of the gap between Cohen and Wertheimer's prescriptions and the dominant social dynamic already underway within the Jewish community itself in 2006 and even more so today. Cohen and Wertheimer were swimming against an overwhelming tide of American Jewish behavior. No significant efforts to "reduce" intermarriage have ever succeeded; the counter-cultural posture that would require American Jews to gamble with their own social, political, economic, and ideological security through a commitment to endogamy is by definition a minority position. In other words, Cohen and Wertheimer represent minority positions supported by elites in the Jewish community; their critics represent majority positions that are oftentimes rejected by the elite infrastructure. Though Cohen and Wertheimer did not intend it in this way, this essay testifies to a growing conceptual irreconcilability between two Judaisms—the mid-twentieth century model portrayed by the authors as slipping away or already lost, and the Judaism lived or practiced by an overwhelming majority of American Jews.

Finally, we must note that conversations about intermarriage and continuity are inherently embodied and gendered; so too are communal conversations in Jewish life about whether the past is better than the present, and so are resource-allocation questions in Jewish life. Policy recommendations at the communal level inevitably implicate human beings and their autonomous personal choices. To "produce" more Jews requires Jewish bodies, through birth or through conversion; any regulation thereof runs counter to the deregulation of bodily choices, the commitment to personal autonomy, and the belief that "love is love," all of which shape the value system of the predominantly progressive American Jewish polity.

This might have been a sufficient summary of the legacy of these ideas by 2017. In July 2018, however, as the #metoo movement coursed through the Jewish community, Cohen was accused of sexual harassment and other misconduct by several women, including professional colleagues and subordinates, with allegations that spanned decades over the course of his illustrious career. Cohen resigned—or was removed—from his many senior positions and affiliations, and expressed remorse publicly.

While Cohen has largely disappeared from a Jewish communal conversation that he had dominated for decades, questions about the legacy of his work, about Jewish social science, and about the continuity agenda more broadly have now taken on a different level of urgency and ferocity. Some interpreters of Cohen's research argue that Cohen's pro-endogamy, pro-natalist positions are inseparable from his pattern of abusive conduct insofar as both suggest he was inherently interested in asserting control over women, both their bodies (through whom the call for more Jewish babies inevitably traveled), and their choices. At the same time, Wertheimer's good name—and the continued support for the intellectual and ideological arguments in Cohen and Wertheimer's writing by other scholars with good personal reputations—make it rightfully challenging to intertwine Cohen's personal failings with prima facie legitimate public policy positions about Jewish individual and communal behaviors.

Anxiety about and commitment to Jewish continuity antedate the writings of Steven M. Cohen and Jack Wertheimer at the end of the twentieth century—after all, Abraham is the first in our tradition to be anxious about whether he would be inherited by his own kin—and the conversation about Jewish collective responsibility and belonging is equally ancient. What we find chronicled here is a process by which such debates took on the scientific tone of statistical language and moved into the heart of communal policy, obscuring or ignoring or fighting against the realities of a community in flux amidst rapidly changing social norms; and the interweaving into that story of a protagonist in the public eye with serious personal failings. But even now, with the re-examination of this research—prodding for its biases, unmaking its hegemony—a new economy of Jewish knowledge and new industries of Jewish responsiveness are likely to emerge as well. American Judaism and its Jews are changing in their identities and choices faster than can be studied, and in ways that can vex both the business of description and the business of prescription. Cohen and Wertheimer and their writings—in rhetoric, in relationship to capital and power—represent the apex of these tensions.

14. Yitzhak Shapira and Yosef Elitzur, *Torat HaMelekh*

Yitzhak Shapira and Yosef Elitzur, *Torat HaMelekh*, Yitzhar: Od Yosef Chai Yeshiva, 2009[1]

Rabbi Yitzhak Shapira (1966–) heads Od Yosef Chai Yeshiva in the settlement of Yitzhar in the West Bank.

Rabbi Yosef Elitzur (birthdate unknown) teaches at the Od Yosef Chai Yeshiva in Yitzhar.

We conclude that the life of a fetus is superior to the life of a non-Jew. … For [saving] the life of a non-Jew, it is prohibited to desecrate the Sabbath. From this ruling it follows that his [the non-Jew's] life is not like the life of a Jew. Therefore, it is permitted exploit it for saving the life of a Jew. But a fetus—its life is so precious, so much that it is permitted to desecrate the Sabbath [in order to save it]—there is no permission to kill it to save others, only in a case in which its presence causes danger [to other lives]. (167)

And although the civilians were tied or imprisoned, and they have no choice rather than to stay in place and be hostages—it is permitted to run over them and to kill them if this is the way to be saved from the evil. … Young children are often in this situation: they block the rescue in their presence, and they do so unwillingly and unintentionally. Still, it is permitted to kill them as their presence assists the murdering. (198)

There are situations in which we would want, deliberately, to harm specifically the innocents. Their presence and their killing are actually beneficial and helpful for us. For example: harming young children of the evil king's family, though they are now innocent. Killing them helps us to hurt him so that he will stop fighting against us. (198)

If it is permissible for the king to kill his own citizens for the sake of war [by forcing them to risk their life by fighting on his behalf]—the same reasoning

---

1   Translated from the Hebrew by Bar Guzi.

applies as well to the citizens of the evil kingdom. In a war of righteousness against evil, we presume that eventually evil will harm us all if we let it raise its head, and the citizens of the evil kingdom will suffer from it as well. (215)

COMMENTARY BY HILLEL BEN-SASSON

Torat HaMelekh originates from a growing rabbinical circle in Israel whose work bears several distinct characteristics. These include: a strong nationally chauvinistic approach; overt anti-Arab tendencies; emphasis on Jewish supremacy; and novel halakhic discussions aimed at legally grounding the aforementioned positions. It is important to note at the very outset that neither theoretical nor hermeneutical considerations merit including *Torat HaMelekh* in this anthology. As a work in Jewish thought and law it is of little importance. Its significance rather lies in two other areas. First is the deplorable increase in Jewish terror that has occurred in recent years against innocent non-Jews, which correlates to the intellectual activity of this rabbinic circle. Second, it may serve as a yardstick for measuring a shift in the manner of engagement with issues of foreign policy and national security by nationalist rabbinic figures. We shall begin the discussion with this latter point and reach the first toward the end.

In a lengthy interview given after the expansive Israeli triumph in the 1967 Six Day War, Rabbi Joseph Soloveitchik, pro-Zionist leader of American Orthodox Jewry, firmly rejected the notion that rabbis can or ought to interfere with political matters. "The meddling of rabbis in the issue of which territories may be returned to the Arabs and which it is prohibited to return," he said, "seems to me absolutely unreasonable. The whole issue of territories belongs to experts of policy and security and not to rabbinical assemblies. I do not adjudicate what should be returned and what ought not. The government will act based on national security considerations and that will be the *pesak* [halakhic decision]."[2] As *Torat HaMelekh* demonstrates, a certain group of National Religious rabbis have shifted so considerably from Soloveitchik's position that they are at ease not only to prohibit any territorial compromise but also to adjudicate on the permissibility of taking the lives of innocent non-Jews, all in the name of Halakhah.[3] In order to understand this shift, one

---

2   Geulah Cohen, "Hagrid Soloveitchik: Shikulim bitchoniyim ve-midyaniyim yakhre'u be-'inyane ha-shtachim." *Hatsofeh*, October 20, 1967.

3   The exact socio-political boundaries of the National Religious sector in Israel is a matter of ongoing debate. Our working definition will take this group as Israeli Jews who commit to

needs to take a broader look at the informal yet pervasive integration of religion into state in Israel.

During the 1950s, the younger public intellectual and philosopher
Yeshayahu Leibowitz was the opposite of the vocal spokesperson for the separation of church and state he later became. Back then, Leibowitz believed
that traditional Halakhah, which was designed to regulate the lives of individuals and small communities only, should be thoroughly updated to
include collective laws (*halakhot tzibbur*, הלכות ציבור) so that it might serve
as a legal basis for the state law. Without such reform, argued Leibowitz,
Judaism would become a mere anecdote in the nascent state, a marginal set
of symbols in the highly secular newly founded Israel. Leibowitz's prediction
proved wrong. In the past two decades, Jewish religious sentiments and language have become increasingly dominant in Israeli public discourse, despite
the fact that Halakhah neither modernized nor became public through state
law. Rather, religious language has become increasingly dominant thanks to
the prominence of messianism in the public imagination, which combined
from its inception strong political engagement with mystical conviction and
a sense of urgency.[4]

In this form Halakhah proudly cultivated strong nationalistic priorities
that had largely been absent from halakhic discourse in earlier generations.
It has even become a means of justifying religiously motivated use of power
and even violence. Gradually, this kind of power has come to be carried out in
spite of state law, many times against it altogether. Torah has become an instrument, indeed even a weapon, to uphold a political outlook. From the 1960s
until his death in 1994, Leibowitz argued against this use of Halakhah, insisting
emphatically that integrating religious aspects into the Israeli regime structure
is a severe form of idolatry, as it endows divine, religious value to secular, man-
made political apparatus.

We now turn to our text, as well as the related *Barukh HaGever* by Rabbi
Yitzchak Ginsburgh (born 1944). Ginsburgh, strongly affiliated with Chabad
Lubavitch and considered one of the most prominent Jewish mystics alive
today, heads a cluster of *yeshivot* and other educational institutions. He has been
arrested and indicted more than once for his inflammatory political rhetoric and

---

full observance of Halakhah while at the same time define themselves as Zionists and partake
in various civic activities, above all military service. Surveys show that the overwhelming
majority of this group identifies as right-wing and pro-settlements.

4   Aviezer Ravitzky, *Messianism, Zionism, and Jewish Religious Radicalism* (Chicago: University
of Chicago Press, 1996), 80–144.

writing. In *Barukh HaGever*, Ginsburgh offers five legal principles that either justify Baruch Goldstein's massacre of dozens of Muslim worshippers at the Cave of the Patriarchs in Hebron (1994) or even deem it to have been an obligation. These are: 1) sanctification of the name of God (*kiddush Hashem*); 2) saving the lives of Jews at the expense of spilling non-Jewish blood (*hatzalat nefashot*); 3) blood feud (*ge'ulat dam ve-nekamah*); 4) extermination of Amalek and extermination of evil (*hashmadat Amalek u-veur ha-ra*); 5) taking the Promised Land by war (*milchamah le-kivush ha-'aretz*).

Rabbi Yitzhak Shapira, one of the authors of *Torat HaMelekh*, is one of Ginsburgh's senior students and heads the *yeshiva* at the settlement of Yitzhar. Together with Ginsburgh, he is a founding member of a movement dedicated to replacing current Israeli law with the Torah. *Torat HaMelekh* focuses on one particular issue, the killing of non-Jews, whether combatants or innocents, according to Halakhah. The authors invoke here as well the notion of revenge as a positive halakhic value. Both of these texts challenge the basic hesitance of modern *poskim* to adjudicate in state matters.[5] They provide a way in which halakhic tools par excellence could be utilized to set the norms of Israeli society. And this way is expansive, creative in harnessing values to override legal tradition, and, most important, showing total disregard for state law.

How innovative is *Torat HaMelekh* in respect to previous halakhic dealings with Arabs within the Zionist context? Ariel Picard demonstrates that after 1967 a shift occurred in halakhic discussions regarding non-Jews among National Religious rabbis. Pre-1967 Zionist *poskim* dealt with the non-Jew in traditional manners, that is, exclusively as a religious challenge. Post-1967 National Religious *poskim*, on the other hand, view the Arab as a national security threat. Conversely, pre-1967 Zionist rabbis aimed to mitigate tensions between democratic values of civic inclusion and halakhic approaches, which tend to be more exclusive, aiming to find halakhic justification for the civil rights of Israeli Arabs. Since 1967, however, the National Religious party has become the party of the settlement movement. When National Religious policy is in tension with international law and democratic values, the party's rabbis have chosen increasingly harsh halakhic categories for dealing with Arabs, deepening the cleavage between Halakhah and Israeli rule of law.[6]

---

5   Benjamin Brown, "The Da'at Torah Doctrine: Three Stages" [Hebrew], *Jerusalem Studies in Jewish Thought* 19 (2005): 537–600.
6   Ariel Picard, "Ma'amad ha-nokhri be-medinat yisrael be-psikat rabane ha-tziyonut ha-datit," *Re'shit* 1 (2009): 187–208.

There is a clear affinity between these post-1967 settler rabbis and the more recent text selected here, primarily in their harshness toward Arabs and the integration of national security considerations into halakhic discussions. Yet in spite of such lines of continuity, they are essentially different. National Religious views of the State of Israel as a manifestation of divine will and as an initial phase of the messianic redemption bestow great importance on Jewish collective public opinion. The latter was viewed as part of this divine manifestation, and termed by Rabbi Abraham Isaac Kook (1865–1935) and his followers as the holy "will of the nation" or "the nation's soul in its generality." Rabbis and leaders of the settler movement felt perpetually obligated to temper their revolutionary politics in order to adjust to the general Jewish public opinion. This tendency is clearly manifest in the internal critique raised in the 1980s against the Jewish underground movement that planned to take down the mosques on Temple Mount. Rather than criticizing the choice to act violently or the colossal results such an action would create, members of the underground were attacked by their rabbinical leaders for advancing redemption by means of weapons rather than patient persuasion of the Jewish Israeli masses.

Compared to the settler right's mainstream religious approach in the 70s and 80s and even the 90s, one can thus discern two major shifts in contemporary anti-Arab halakhic compositions such as *Torat HaMelekh*.[7] First, the break with both the state apparatus and the Jewish majority's public opinion as sources of authority and legitimacy. Contemporary hard-right *poskim* such as those brought here highlight the importance of individual initiative and show total disregard to notions of popular consensus or the rule of law. That is why *revenge* and *feud* become so prominent in their adjudication: they signify an extralegal principle that enables one to bypass normative law.

Second is the very topic and theme of contemporary discussions. With regard to non-Jews under Israeli control, earlier National Religious approaches—especially in the aftermath of 1967—attempted to formulate an alternative legal principle to that of liberal democratic laws. Their focus was accordingly on creating halakhic justification of discriminatory civic status for Palestinians. In contrast, *Torat HaMelekh*, as well as *Barukh HaGever*, largely ignore the question of civic status, for they see no legitimacy in state rule of

---

7   As already noted by some, the authors of the texts hereby draw less from messianic Religious Zionism and more from Chabad Lubavitch. Ariel Finkelstein, *Derekh Hamalekh: Racism and Discrimination against Gentiles in Halakha: An Alternative Halakha and Meta-Halakha to Torat ha-Melekh* (Netivot: Yeshivat Ahavat Yisrael, 2010), vol. 2, 10–17, shows that they derive mainly from Chabad Lubavitch.

law. It is the right of non-Jews to life that is called into question and ultimately negated by these texts, either conditionally or overall. As such, these voices represent a wholly different political theology than that of Gush Emunim and the traditional settler leadership. For them, the State of Israel is no longer a manifestation of divine will and not even "a nation's spirit" led astray. It is rather an obstacle against divinely sanctioned monarchy.

In 2005, the settler leadership abjectly failed to prevent the eviction of Gaza Strip settlements. In the aftermath of that failure, a growing circle of younger generation settlers have grown to become more and more alienated from the state as well as from their parents' wish to redeem Israeli society by persuasion. They choose violent revolution as their way, calling for a full-blown rebellion that will ultimately "undermine the foundations of the state."[8] Terror against innocent Palestinians is well anchored in their theological worldview.

8   Chaim Levinson, "Meet the Jewish Extremist Group That Seeks to Violently Topple the State," *Haaretz*, July 08, 2015.

15. Moshe Halbertal, "The Goldstone Illusion"

Moshe Halbertal, "The Goldstone Illusion," *The New Republic*, November 5, 2009

Dr. Moshe Halbertal (1958–) is Professor of Jewish Thought and Philosophy at the Hebrew University of Jerusalem and Gruss Professor at New York University Law School.

Faced with this unprecedented and deeply perplexing situation, two extreme positions have emerged in Israel. The radical left claims that, since such a struggle necessarily involves the killing of innocent civilians, there is no justifiable way of fighting it. Soldiers ought to refuse to engage in such a war, and the government has only one option, which is to end the occupation. This view is wrong, since Israel has the right and the obligation to protect its citizens, and without providing real security, it will fail also to achieve peace and to put an end to the occupation. The radical right claims that, since Hamas and Hezbollah initiated the targeting of Israeli civilians, and since they take refuge among their own civilians, the responsibility for harming Palestinian civilians during Israel's attempt to defend itself falls upon the Palestinians exclusively. This approach is also wrong. The killing of our civilians does not justify the killing of their civilians. Civilians do not lose their right to life when they are used as shields by Hamas and Hezbollah. In fighting the militants, Israel must do as much as it possibly can do to avoid and minimize harm to civilian life and property. ...

These are not simple issues. They are also not political issues. They are the occasions of deep moral struggle, because they are matters of life and death. If you are looking for an understanding of these issues, or for guidance about them, in the Goldstone Report, you will not find it. ...

If there is no time for moral reflection in battle, then moral reflection must be accomplished before battle, and drilled into the soldiers who will have to answer for their actions after battle. ... But in this new kind of micro-war, every soldier is a kind of commanding officer, a full moral and strategic agent.

COMMENTARY BY ELANA STEIN HAIN

Published in the *New Republic*, the *Goldstone Illusion* is a scathing rebuttal of the Goldstone Report, a document prepared for the UN and finding both the IDF and Hamas guilty of war crimes in the 2008–2009 Gaza War. In the *Goldstone Illusion*, Moshe Halbertal argues that the Report ignores the realities of asymmetrical warfare, which has, since the 1990s, become the norm in Israeli-Palestinian conflicts. In such engagements, the two sides have vastly different military capacities and tactics: in the case of the Israeli-Palestinian conflict, one side attacks in plainclothes from densely populated civilian areas, while the other side's military advantage is either stymied or necessarily results in collateral damage due to the impossibility of isolating combatants. Moreover, the Report neglects to mention the IDF Code of Ethics, which mandates that Israeli soldiers risk their lives to protect enemy civilians.

But the *Goldstone Illusion* is not only about the Goldstone Report. It asserts Israel's right to defend itself, within or despite the realities of asymmetric warfare. It is an articulation the very possibility of *jus in bello*, morality *in* war.[1] Before a world audience, the piece lays bare the dilemmas and debates internal to Israeli discourse on these issues. While this excerpt included here lays out the positions of the radical right and the radical left, Halbertal also eventually gets to the core of more nuanced debates about the principle of avoidance: what degree of risk need Israeli soldiers assume to protect the lives of enemy civilians? He believes that it is this question that Israel answered inconsistently in the Gaza War.

Halbertal's own position on avoidance represents one side of a debate between the shapers of the 1994 and the 2000 versions of *Ruach Tzahal* [IDF Spirit], the IDF ethical code. Halbertal was part of the group—composed of mostly moral philosophers like himself—responsible for the newer edition. They made substantive edits to the earlier version. Comparing the section called *Purity of Arms* [*tohar ha-neshek*] in the two versions is instructive:

> *IDF Spirit*, 1994:
>
> The soldier will use his weapon and his force only to the degree necessary to defeat the enemy and *will practice restraint to avoid unnecessary casualties to human life*, whether in body, dignity or possession.

---

1   This is distinct from *jus ad bellum*, morality *of* war, that is, whether the decision to wage a particular war is moral.

The purity of arms of IDF soldiers lies in their restrained use of their weapon and of their force, in accomplishing tasks using only necessary action without excessive casualties to human life, whether in body, dignity or possession—*be they combatants or non-combatants, and especially those who are defenseless*—during war as well as ongoing security operations in times of calm and peace.

In short: Israeli soldiers may not kill civilians *or soldiers* wantonly: sanctity of life obtains even for enemy soldiers. Moreover, sanctity of life obtains for IDF soldiers: thus, while the code requires restraint to avoid civilian casualties, it does not necessarily require that soldiers risk their own lives. Contrast this with the newer version:

IDF Spirit, 2000:
A soldier must use his weapons and force only for carrying out the task, only to the extent required for this, and he will safeguard humanity even in battle. A soldier must not use his weapons and force *to injure non-combatants or prisoners of war, and he should do all in his power* to prevent injury to their person, their dignity and their possessions.

In this version, the protection of enemy *soldiers* is absent. Moreover, protecting enemy *civilians* requires more than restraint: a soldier must "do all in his power," even risk his own life, to protect them.

These changes can be partially explained by the emergence of asymmetrical warfare in the late 1990s. Because of this, enemy combatants are no longer assumed to be conscripts representing a foreign entity but are viewed instead as terrorists waging war against civilians; as such, their lives are no longer to be protected. Simultaneously, enemy civilians are now more vulnerable and require more protection. On a deeper level, these differences signal a philosophical divergence regarding the rights of soldiers in comparison with the rights of civilians. In the newer edition of the code, the life of a civilian *by definition* takes precedence over the life of a soldier, whereas in the older version, this prioritization is not specified and may even be problematic.

The revision of the code heightened the debate about the relative weight of the lives of IDF soldiers and enemy civilians. Asa Kasher and General Amos Yadlin, members of the committee responsible for the 1994 version of the code, persisted in advocating for it in the *Journal of Military Ethics* in 2005:

According to the ordinary conception underlying the distinction between combatants and noncombatants, the former have a lighter package of state duties than the latter. ... We reject such conceptions, because we consider them to be immoral. A combatant is a citizen in uniform. In Israel, quite often he is a conscript or on reserve duty. His blood is as red and thick as that of citizens who are not in uniform. His life is as precious as the life of anyone else.[2]

Later in the same piece, they argue that:

Preference given by a state, under such circumstances, to the life of its citizens over the life of persons in the vicinity of a terrorist, is compatible with the moral duty of respecting human dignity. On the one hand, the state has the moral duty to respect the human dignity of those bystanders. On the other hand, the state has the moral duty to respect the human dignity of its citizens and the additional moral duty to protect their civil rights, including their right to have an effective state defense of their life.[3]

In short, they claim that soldiers and civilians are essentially the same and a state must protect its own first. As a result, Israeli soldiers need not risk their lives to protect enemy civilians.

In the wake of Operation Cast Lead (2008–2009), Professors Avishai Margalit and Michael Walzer entered the fray.[4] Walzer, a prominent American political theorist who authored a book on military ethics in the 1970s, and Margalit, a philosophy professor at Hebrew University, both close colleagues of Halbertal, advocated the logic of the later code: the rights of soldiers and civilians are distinct. Period. They wrote:

The most "significant and sensitive claim" of Kasher and Yadlin, as they term it, can be summed up as follows: that the safety of "our" soldiers precedes the safety of "their" civilians. This claim is mistaken and dangerous. ...

2 Asa Kasher and Amos Yadlin, "The Military Ethics of Fighting Terror," *Journal of Military Ethics* 4 (2005): 17.
3 Ibid., 20.
4 Avishai Margalit and Michael Walzer, "This is not how to conduct a just war," *Haaretz*, September 4, 2009. Both Margalit and Walzer's piece and a rebuttal by Kasher and Yadlin appeared in the May 14, 2009 issue of the *New York Review of Books*.

The decisive means of limiting the scope of warfare is marking a clear line between combatants and non-combatants. This is the only relevant distinction that all sides must agree to. Terror, in its essence, is an evil attempt to blur this distinction in that it turns civilians into a legitimate target. When fighting against terror, one must not imitate it. The ability to harm and to damage is what turns combatants into a legitimate target in times of war. Those who cannot harm and damage, i.e., non-combatants, are all presumed innocent.

What Kasher and Yadlin claim is immoral is, for Walzer and Margalit, the very heart of *jus in bello*. Soldiers are legitimate targets because they bear arms; civilians are not. Equating these two groups amounts to terrorism. Instead, they argue as follows:

> To what degree of danger is it permissible to expose Israel soldiers? The guideline, in our opinion, should be this: in an area where there are civilians, they should battle with the same level of concern and consideration as if the civilians on the other side were Israeli civilians.
> In other words: civilians are civilians are civilians.

This debate, and not only the claims of Goldstone Report, sits at the heart of the *Goldstone Illusion*. What is the effect of Halbertal bringing this moral discussion into the context of responding to a blatantly politicized report? First, it changes the register of the conversation: instead of focusing only on Goldstone's assertions, he illustrates the kind of elevated and ethically infused debate that the Israeli army is engaged in. Second, by asserting his side of the avoidance principles argument in this context, he positions the newer edition of the *IDF Spirit* as Israel's official public voice. He is not only a scholar or even military theorist in this piece, but also a defender of Israel, and he uses that authoritative voice in representing his version of the code. This also affords to possibility of winning broad international approval for the revised *IDF Spirit* to be the decisive guide for Israel's war on terror.

16. Peter Beinart, "The Failure of the American Jewish Establishment"

Peter Beinart, "The Failure of the American Jewish Establishment," *New York Review of Books*, June 10, 2010

Peter Beinart (1971–) is Editor-at-Large of *Jewish Currents* and Professor of Journalism and Political Science at the City University of New York. Beinart is also a contributor to *The Atlantic*.

Among American Jews today, there are a great many Zionists, especially in the Orthodox world, people deeply devoted to the State of Israel. And there are a great many liberals, especially in the secular Jewish world, people deeply devoted to human rights for all people, Palestinians included. But the two groups are increasingly distinct. Particularly in the younger generations, fewer and fewer American Jewish liberals are Zionists; fewer and fewer American Jewish Zionists are liberal. One reason is that the leading institutions of American Jewry have refused to foster—indeed, have actively opposed—a Zionism that challenges Israel's behavior in the West Bank and Gaza Strip and toward its own Arab citizens. For several decades, the Jewish establishment has asked American Jews to check their liberalism at Zionism's door, and now, to their horror, they are finding that many young Jews have checked their Zionism instead.

Morally, American Zionism is in a downward spiral. If the leaders of groups like AIPAC and the Conference of Presidents of Major American Jewish Organizations do not change course, they will wake up one day to find a younger, Orthodox-dominated, Zionist leadership whose naked hostility to Arabs and Palestinians scares even them, and a mass of secular American Jews who range from apathetic to appalled. Saving liberal Zionism in the United States—so that American Jews can help save liberal Zionism in Israel—is the great American Jewish challenge of our age. And it starts where [Frank] Luntz's students wanted it to start: by talking frankly about Israel's current government, by no longer averting our eyes.

COMMENTARY BY SARA YAEL HIRSCHHORN

Does this sound familiar?

> American Zionism is in a downward spiral. If the leaders of groups like
> AIPAC and the Conference of Presidents of Major American Jewish
> Organizations do not change course, they will wake up one day to find a
> younger, Orthodox-dominated, Zionist leadership whose naked hostility
> to Arabs and Palestinians scares even them, and a mass of secular Ameri-
> can Jews who range from apathetic to appalled. Saving liberal Zionism in
> the United State is the great American Jewish challenge of our age. And it
> starts ... by no longer averting our eyes.

When I agreed to write this reflection on an important contribution to
contemporary Jewish thought, I expected to re-encounter Peter Beinart's now
canonical essay "The Failure of the American Jewish Establishment" (*New York
Review of Books*, June 10, 2010) as an antiquated critique of contemporary
Jewish-American politics. I remembered how authoritative Beinart's formidable attack on the ruling elite of American Jewish institutional life and against the
status quo of Diaspora-Israel relations as well had seemed in its time. I expected
that its foretelling of a soon-to-come fundamental redrawing of the American
Jewish landscape would now read as a *fait accompli*. Yet, the initial paragraphs
chronicling the indifference of the average Jewish-American college student to
the Zionist cause, the inability of the organized American Jewish community
to engage in an open and pluralistic discourse on contemporary Judaism and
Israel, and the widening gap between American Jewish liberalism and attitudes
toward the State of Israel could have been ripped from the headlines of any 2018
Jewish periodical. Perhaps then, despite fulsome praise for what was once perceived as a kind of prophetic jeremiad for American Jewry, the invective failed
to inspire a fundamental change. Nevertheless, revisiting this treatise nearly a
decade on reveals that the American Jewish establishment has changed from
within and without and that Beinart's piece deserves to be reappraised today.

Beinart opens his blistering disputation by citing what he considered to be "the
most damning indictment of the American Jewish community I have ever seen,"
a report commissioned by major Jewish philanthropists to investigate the debate
over Israel on college campuses. While predating the entrenchment of the Boycott,
Divestment, and Sanctions (BDS) Movement at many universities worldwide, the
study reflected the anxieties of donors that millennials (using the now-common

parlance) were "distancing" themselves from Israel. Jewish-American students were seemingly unwilling to check their liberalism at the door of the Diaspora-Israel discourse and sought a more capacious and inclusive conversation on the Zionist cause. In essence, Beinart adduced that "the only kind of Zionism [these college students] found attractive was the kind that the American Jewish Establishment has been working against for most of their lives."

Surveying the Jewish hemispheres of Beinart's piece, we find a depressing description of an increasingly right-wing and racist government in Israel, a settler movement surpassing its own apocalyptic expectations for expansion, the two-state solution in open retreat, a stalled peace process (that generated only process and no peace), and radicalized generations of both Israelis and Palestinians rooted in their own narratives of and encounters with never-ending conflict. Liberal Zionism and Israel's discouraged and dying left were under siege, from within and without. Meanwhile, in the United States, the "terrible irony" that Beinart characterized in the widening gulf between the American Jewry's "liberal vision of Israel" and the "real Israel" could no longer be denied. The "establishment" (although who this represents is never truly specified apart from some Washington acronyms like American Israel Public Affairs Committee (AIPAC), the Anti-Defamation League (ADL), the Zionist Organization of American (ZOA), and the Conference of Presidents of Major American Jewish Organizations (CPMAJO)), in Beinart's view, steadfastly pursued a policy of "see no evil, hear no evil, speak no evil" when it came to Israel and silenced sharply critical voices opposed to both Israeli domestic and foreign policy (generally from the left), often finding strange political bedfellows in their uncritical support. "Unless they change course," Beinart warned with a sense of Delphian doom, this stance would "portend the future: an American Zionist movement that does not even feign concern for Palestinian dignity and a broader American Jewish population that does not even feign concern for Israel. ... Either prospect fills me with dread."

Beinart's column struck a chord at a moment of collective soul-searching amongst Diaspora Jewry, especially in the United States. Penned in the aftermath of 2008 Operation Cast Lead in Gaza (which saw serious Palestinian civilian casualties and global opprobrium against Israel), the Gaza Flotilla of 2010, the re-election of Prime Minister Benjamin Netanyahu's Likud government coalition, the middle of the first Obama presidency, the withdrawal of US forces from Iraq and Afghanistan, and tensions over the reanimation of the Israeli-Palestinian peace process under the new American administration, the piece was published at a kind of tipping point for American Jewish politics. Like the

First Lebanon War had been in 1982, the "Gaza War" was a watershed for young American Jews who were struggling to reconcile the Zionist idealism that had been instilled in them at Jewish schools, overnight camps, and synagogues with a country they perceived as committing war crimes. Meanwhile, Israel was increasingly becoming a wedge issue in US elections, leading to philanthropist Sheldon Adelson later quipping, seemingly on behalf of entire older generation of Jewish-Americans, that "I didn't leave the Democrats, they left me."[1] As Beinart points out (presciently articulating the findings of the Pew Research Center's "Portrait of Jewish Americans" survey in 2013), a major demographic shift that would profoundly impact American Jewish identity, religion, and politics as well as Diaspora-Israel relations was well underway, with the decline of the denominational Judaism and the dramatic boom in American ultra-Orthodoxy. Young American Jews (apart from the strictly devout) increasingly could not see eye-to-eye with their elders in the establishment, and the two camps were on a kind of collision-course.

Despite its full embrace by the liberal American Jewish intelligentsia and associated institutions, the "failure" of the essay was that this fateful encounter never really seemed to materialize. While Beinart essentialized the "us" and "them" of his essay, the predominantly white, Ashkenazi, wealthy, politically influential, and overwhelmingly male senior leadership of major Jewish organizations has carried on mostly unscathed, while the young, unaffiliated, and increasingly non- or anti-Zionist youth are progressively alienated. Occasionally, the two constituencies have collided over communal priorities—such as the rejection of the liberal Zionist group J Street from under the Conference of Presidents' umbrella in spring 2014, the second Gaza-Israel war of July-August 2014, and the election of President Trump in 2016—but for the most part, the two "sides" have pursued their own agendas with growing polarization.

Yet, time itself has wrought significant changes that bring Beinart's arguments into sharper definition. Evolution within the establishment itself softens some of the blows of the essay's critique. For example, the "changing of the guard" at some of the major communal Jewish organizations as a generation reached retirement age has yielded communal activism with a new face. (The lively riposte from Abraham Foxman, then National Director of the ADL published in the NYRB Letters to the Editor section now seems a bit quaint with the recruitment of Jonathan Greenblatt, an entrepreneur and former assistant in

---

1   Sheldon Adelson, "I Didn't Leave the Democrats. They Left Me," *Wall Street Journal*, November 4, 2012.

the Obama White House, to lead the organization after Foxman's retirement.) Further, although many of the institutional heads who, according to the Pew survey, failed an entire generation of America Jewry, continue to hold office, their like-minded donor pool is also aging and new allegiances and agendas are being adopted in a desire to reach out to younger financiers. Even at organizations where there has been little turnover or change in direction, current events have sometimes weakened their sway on the American Jewish imagination—notably, the unsuccessful lobbying of AIPAC against the Iran nuclear deal during the Obama presidency, leading some to claim that the lobbying organization had been reduced to a paper tiger.

On the left, however, the monopolization of a discourse of identity politics (especially on university campuses and in the political parties) has also magnified some of Beinart's admonitions. With BDS and the denial of the right of the State of Israel to exist becoming increasingly fashionable on the far left, and more young American Jews drawn to non- and anti-Zionist activism on its fringes, the divergence between liberalism and Zionism has been drawn into starker relief. While the "establishment" remains slow to react (and often does so badly in a way that millennials see as a kind of bullying behavior), the growing hand-wringing over "distancing" may finally produce new ideas and institutions. (It is most likely that these models may emerge from the middle, as it is moderates who feel most profoundly implicated by the orthodoxies of identity politics.) Last but not least, demographic change may soon overtake these questions, as the American Jewish millennial of tomorrow will most likely be ultra-Orthodox with a very different relationship to modernity and communal modalities.

While rereading Beinart's essay is a timely reminder of the polarization that persists in American Jewish politics, it misses the point that the distance between American Jewry and Israel is not between Democrat and Republican, liberal and conservative, Long Island and Long Beach, but between Teaneck and Tel Aviv. Jewish and Israeli identity have never been—and certainly are not—synonymous, and the interests that animate Diaspora Jewry about Israel are often religious and moral issues that speak to American Jewish principles and practices, rather than Israeli priorities. Those like Beinart who care deeply about the relationship between US Jewry and Israel may focus less on deconstructing the American Jewish establishment than developing a shared vocabulary and values between Diaspora and Israeli Jews in the future.

17. Daniel Gordis,
"When Balance Becomes Betrayal"

Sharon Brous, "Lowering the Bar"

Daniel Gordis, "When Balance Becomes Betrayal," *Times of Israel*, November 18, 2012

Dr. Daniel Gordis (1959–) is Senior Vice President and Koret Distinguished Fellow at Shalem College in Jerusalem. He writes a regular column for the *Jerusalem Post* and the *Bloomberg View*.

On weeks like this, with hundreds of thousands of Israelis sleeping in bomb shelters and many millions more unspeakably frightened, it's become clear that this universalized Judaism has rendered not only platitudinous Jews, but something worse. It bequeaths us a new Jew utterly incapable of feeling loyalty. The need for balance is so pervasive that even an expression of gut-level love for Israelis more than for their enemies is impossible. Balance has now bequeathed betrayal. ...

I knew, even before reading Rabbi Brous's missive, that we Israelis are surrounded by enemies. When I finished reading her, though, I understood that matters are much worse than that. Yes, we're surrounded, but increasingly, we are also truly alone, utterly abandoned by those who ought to be unabashedly at our side.

Sharon Brous, "Lowering the Bar," *Times of Israel*, November 19, 2012

Rabbi Sharon Brous (1973–) is the Founder and Senior Rabbi of IKAR in Los Angeles.

Gordis draws some terrifying new fault lines: he now redefines a traitor not only as someone who challenges Israel on any count (farewell, democracy), but also as anyone who recognizes the human tragedy of war while loving and supporting Israel. ...

It ought not be an act of courage in the American Jewish community to remind us that as Jews we are called to affirm our essential humanity even in the most trying of times. Indeed, many of us see that as a powerful expression of loyalty to Israel, a state built on the promise of freedom, justice and peace as envisaged by the prophets. One could even argue that these are the aspirations that have kept the Jewish people alive through a long and tumultuous history.

COMMENTARY BY YEHUDA KURTZER

In the midst of the outbreak of military hostilities in Gaza and the Israel Defense Forces' Operation Pillar of Cloud (also called Pillar of Defense) in November 2012, a contentious political debate broke out online between two major Jewish religious figures with eerily similar biographies. In a blog post at the *Times of Israel*, Daniel Gordis—a rabbi ordained in the Conservative Movement who had moved from Los Angeles to Israel in 1998 around age forty—sharply criticized Rabbi Sharon Brous—a forty-something rabbi ordained in the Conservative Movement and living in Los Angeles—for what he considered to be her equivocation on the morality of Israel's actions in Gaza, and for insufficient loyalty to and support for Israel in the midst of the conflict. Gordis's essay, "When Balance Becomes Betrayal," cited Brous's letter to her congregation—in which she had urged "empathy and grace" and had expressed support for immediate negotiations between Israel and the Palestinian authority—as indicative of the triumph of an ethics of universalism over those of particularism; and more damningly, of Brous's inability to draw hierarchical distinctions between good and evil.

Both Gordis's essay and the quick, vociferous responses it invited went viral. Responses included the historian David Myers who criticized Gordis's misrepresentation of the history of Zionist concerns for universal values, the philanthropist Adam Bronfman who rebuked Gordis's rejection of moral universalism, Rabbi Ed Feinstein (also a Los Angeles Conservative rabbi) who urged the two rabbis to reconcile, and finally Brous herself. In her stinging rejoinder, Brous accused Gordis of "lowering the bar" on debate on Israel by personalizing his attacks and by taking her comments out of context, and especially by failing to adhere to his own stated desire for a wider tent for debate on Israel. More pointedly, Brous cited the IDF's own code of ethics in warfare to demonstrate that concern and empathy for the deaths of Palestinian civilians is Israel's own aspiration, and therefore cannot be denounced as a naïve American Jewish universalistic moralism.

The debate between the two positions—and the many opinion pieces that attempted to advocate for one side or the other, or to mediate between the two positions—remained intense throughout the actual conflict, and left enormous bitterness and severed friendships in its wake. Brous received death threats as a result of the publication of the exchange. The Brous-Gordis debate was startling especially because of how well Brous and Gordis knew one another, and traveled in similar circles: ostensibly, liberal rabbis with similar biographies and aligned value-systems should identify with similar politics and a similar political tone. Indeed, Brous and Gordis are not generally political or ideological enemies, and in their other writings demonstrate a broad shared commitment to the same values as relates to Israel and to the Israeli-Palestinian conflict. That Gordis saw Brous as a stand-in for the larger moral and political failing of American Jews—from whom he was standing apart since moving to Israel—meant that the chasm between the two communities was yawning wider. Moreover, the debate illuminated the "small world" quality of internal Jewish polemics— these are two rabbis who know each other quite well, and travel in the same social and religious circles—and reading the hostility of their debate, now out in public, demonstrates the anxiety of a trembling and vulnerable Jewish communal core.

The debate also helps us understand the ways in which the personal, theoretical, and political often overlap in intra-Jewish conflict, especially as it relates to Israel. Israel invites not just hostility and anxiety in internecine debate, but also a deep personalization of political views and expressions. This can be seen in the context of Israel education, where the affective language of "love" and "hate" are widespread, if unlikely, indicators of success and failure in the business of teaching a complicated topic. Gordis takes pains in his essay to refer to Brous as a former babysitter to his children, which serves both to connect him to her and to demean her standing, as he uses his children's military service as the central axis of what is supposed to motivate her (apparently lost) love for him and by extension for the State of Israel. Brous, in turn, tosses Gordis aside as her "former" teacher and friend, suggesting she has gone beyond what he was able to teach her and now knows more than he. These relationships matter enormously in the business of public polemic.

Gordis's reference to his children is also substantively meaningful in helping us to understand his relationship to Jewish peoplehood. For Gordis, Jewish peoplehood constitutes essentially an extension of the idea of family. The obligations incumbent on other Jews, therefore, are comparable to the commitments we should have to family: we don't have to agree, but when we are under attack, we expect family to come to our aid and defense. Brous does not contest this argument, and in fact in her response she acquits herself of the accusation of disloyalty by arguing that in her approach she is, in fact, "standing with" Israel in the ways that Gordis demands. In contrast to Gordis, she offers an understanding of Jewish peoplehood that extends, or possibly rejects, the family metaphor, by arguing that loyalty to Israel entails a recommitment to Israel's own vision of the prophetic promise of "freedom, justice, and peace." Peoplehood does not merely entail support of one's people, but of the people's aspirations. And sometimes those two come into conflict.

But beyond the personal vitriol, the debate offers witness to one of the central themes of organized Jewish life since the Second Intifada, and that is the deteriorated, hostile, and deeply intransigent nature of intra-Jewish debate about Israel and the conflict with the Palestinians. A further casualty of the Israeli-Palestinian conflict has been the nature of Jewish communal life in its debates *about* the conflict.

Implicit in this exchange, then, are two referenda on Jewish peoplehood. Does peoplehood mean that we must temper our criticisms of one another—especially the people we know and/or especially in public? And does peoplehood demand merely that we support each other in moments of conflict, or are we responsible to counsel (or criticize) each other in those moments as well? These questions define and shape an uneasy Jewish public conversation about Israel in America, and continue to hobble the relationships between Israeli Jews and American Jews who seem increasingly uncertain about the nature of their obligations to one another. Brous and Gordis—who should understand one another more than most—are evidence of an increasingly unbridgeable moral and temperamental chasm.

But perhaps the most enduring legacy of the Brous-Gordis debate was invisible to its own readers, even as their shares and reposts defined the story. The *Times of Israel* site where Gordis's original post appeared had been launched just six months earlier. It represented a bold attempt by its editors and publishers to enter into and take over the English-language market for news, information, and especially opinion about Israel. Its most appealing feature to many people was also its qualitative liability, the wide-open platform it offered anyone to become a blogger and an opinion writer, which meant that it was cultivating a readership by attracting the loyalty of those who saw themselves as its base of writers. The *Times of Israel* built a successful platform quite quickly, which meant that accomplished opinion authors like Gordis moved over to its site to increase their readership. And the Brous-Gordis debate was very good for the *Times of Israel* at this nascent moment in its history. The debate continued to attract more opinion pieces not just on the merits of the two positions, but because of the invisible hand of a site that benefited enormously from the contentiousness of the exchange.

With this background, the Brous-Gordis debate emerges as a moment not just in growing Jewish divides about Israel, but in the transformation of the venues and the nature of how Jews write and how they publicly disagree. The moving of Jewish public debate online intertwines Jewish ideas with the commodification of "web traffic," which incentivizes incendiary rhetoric and a combative approach, and the platforms reward primarily those ideas and their expressions which animate the reader and inspire loyalty or loathing. An effective blog post has to engage the reader immediately to differentiate itself in the clutter, it is unrewarded for subtlety and nuance, and it is aided by the popularity of its author and the popularity of the object under attack. It is likely that—substance aside—the Brous-Gordis debate will serve as an enduring template of tone and style for the future of Jewish political debate as it will live online, for better or worse.

18. Matti Friedman, "An Insider's Guide to the Most Important Story on Earth"

Matti Friedman, "An Insider's Guide to the Most Important Story on Earth," *Tablet*, August 26, 2014

Matti Friedman (1977–) is a writer and journalist. He is a former Associated Press correspondent, and his writing has also appeared in the *New York Times*, the *Wall Street Journal*, and the *Washington Post*.

A reporter working in the international press corps here understands quickly that what is important in the Israel-Palestinian story is Israel. If you follow mainstream coverage, you will find nearly no real analysis of Palestinian society or ideologies, profiles of armed Palestinian groups, or investigation of Palestinian government. Palestinians are not taken seriously as agents of their own fate. The West has decided that Palestinians should want a state alongside Israel, so that opinion is attributed to them as fact, though anyone who has spent time with actual Palestinians understands that things are (understandably, in my opinion) more complicated. Who they are and what they want is not important: The story mandates that they exist as passive victims of the party that matters.

Israel is not an idea, a symbol of good or evil, or a litmus test for liberal opinion at dinner parties. It is a small country in a scary part of the world that is getting scarier. It should be reported as critically as any other place, and understood in context and in proportion. Israel is not one of the most important stories in the world, or even in the Middle East; whatever the outcome in this region in the next decade, it will have as much to do with Israel as World War II had to do with Spain. Israel is a speck on the map—a sideshow that happens to carry an unusual emotional charge.

COMMENTARY BY RACHEL FISH

In August 2014, conflict erupted between Israel and the Hamas-controlled Gaza Strip. Rockets were fired daily from Gaza across the Green Line, the pre-1967 borders of the State of Israel. Israel responded first by activating its defensive Iron Dome technology and eventually with airstrikes and infantry. These events were not a surprise in the sense that the relationship between Palestinians living in Gaza and Israelis in the southern region of Israel was regularly in an ebb and flow of hostility and conflict.

In 2005, under Prime Minister Ariel Sharon's direction, Israel had unilaterally pulled out of Gaza, which it had captured in the 1967 war and occupied since then. Sharon's hope was that by removing the Israeli presence from the Gaza Strip and permitting Palestinians to control the territory, Israel freed itself of the burden of protecting the Israeli Jews living there. The settlers of Gaza were compensated and relocated to homes within Israel proper, and some chose to settle in the West Bank. Shortly after the unilateral withdrawal, the Palestinian residents of Gaza elected Hamas as the leadership responsible for administering the territory. Hamas faced two challenges: providing for a basic level of social services in the territory of Gaza—picking up garbage, ensuring roads and other infrastructure were sound, providing food and water—and differentiating itself from the secular, nationalist Fatah party, which it had defeated in the election. Unlike Fatah, Hamas shares intellectual and religious roots with the Muslim Brotherhood of Egypt. In line with these roots, Hamas's doctrine is a theological-political framework that imagines Jews purely as a religious community void of any nationalistic aspirations as a people. The Hamas leadership thus understands the State of Israel as existing within *dar al-harb*, the realm or territory of war or conflict. As Israel controls territory that was once under Islamic control, Hamas considers it imperative to engage in *jihad*, struggle, by whatever means necessary, to restore the territory they call *Filistinia* to the realm of *dar al-Islam*, the realm of peace. This is the justification used by Hamas's religious and political leadership for engaging in military strife with Israel and aiming to dismantle the Jewish nation-state.

Matti Friedman's essay "An Insider's Guide to the Most Important Story on Earth," appeared in *Tablet* shortly after the conflict in Gaza broke out in the summer of 2014. Friedman's essay highlighted AP journalists' obsession with Israeli military actions and behaviors in comparison with all other countries in the Middle East, let alone other parts of the world. He wrote as an insider, an experienced journalist who was part of the Associated Press agency from 2006–2011. He saw firsthand the AP's policies and decision making in action, recognizing the disparity between an over-emphasis on Israel and a general lack of emphasis on countries in the region that were controlled by dictators, lacked democratic practices and rule, and allowed—sometimes perpetrated—human rights violations against their own citizens. As Friedman notes, more AP news staff covered the "Israel story," whether focused on the conflict or some other aspect, than covered either China, India, or all of the fifty or so countries that comprise sub-Saharan Africa combined. Friedman asks why the Palestinians and Israelis have become *the* symbol of conflict between strong and weak, powerful and powerless, victimizer and victim, and not the Turks and Kurds; Iraqi Muslims and Iraqi Christians; Syrian Alawites, Syrian Sunnis, and Syrian Christians; Saudi Sheikhs and Saudi women; or Han Chinese and Tibetans.[1] Friedman highlights for his readers the way journalism has projected the ills of the world at large only onto one people, the Jewish people, at the expense of engaging fully with the complexity of relations and historical record of interactions between Israel and her Arab neighbors, and in particular, the Palestinian people: "Having rehabilitated themselves against considerable odds in a minute corner of the earth, the descendants of powerless people who were pushed out of Europe and the Islamic Middle East have become what their grandparents were—the pool into which the world spits."

Friedman extended his analysis beyond the essay in *Tablet* magazine, addressing the British Israel Communications and Research Center (BICOM) annual dinner in January 2015. His essay based on that talk, "The Ideological Roots of Media Bias against Israel,"[2] was published in the *Fathom Journal*. Here, he openly questions why the media dissect every move Israel makes and spotlight Israel's flaws while ignoring challenges in neighboring countries. "How have the doings in a country that constitutes 0.01 per cent of the world's surface become the focus of angst, loathing and condemnation more than any other?"[3] He emphasizes that Israel is situated in a region largely characterized by intense conflicts, religious zeal, nationalist fervor, and dictatorial demands amidst democratic aspirations. While Friedman does believe that Israel's control of the West Bank deserves critique and concern, he also questions the Western world's obsession with it and portrayal of its existence as a moral sin. He suggests that this "Cult of the Occupation" is an attack on all of Israel for multiple "sins": nationalism, militarism, racism, imperialism, colonialism, and the "original sin" of its creation in 1948. Israel's control over the West Bank and the Palestinians who reside there is merely a symptom of a larger phenomenon, and those who critique it are asking Israel to dismantle itself for the sake of an imagined utopia.

---

1   Matti Friedman, "The Ideological Roots of Media Bias against Israel," *Fathom*, January 26, 2015.
2   Ibid.
3   Ibid.

Why does Israel face this broad-reaching criticism? Friedman's expanded analysis suggests that the answer lies in the media's distorted portrayal of the Jews as the root of the problem, namely, Jews holding power as Israelis. In the media, there is one standard set of images for Israeli Jews: the soldier, of European descent, using a highly specialized weapon against a darker-skinned child with only a rock in his hand in a Palestinian village; the Israeli Jewish Prime Minister's coalition government's policy increasing settlement construction; the religious Jewish settler living in the West Bank and bent on denying Palestinian national consciousness. These unidimensional caricatures of Israeli Jews fit neatly into a predetermined journalistic framing that ignores any complexities in fear of dissonance. There are no images of the Jew who feels threatened by regular terrorist attacks and an unnerving sense of persistent anti-Semitism emanating from the surrounding Middle East region and parts of Europe; the dark-skinned Jew from an Arab country who speaks fluent Arabic; the left-wing secular Israeli Jew calling for an end to settlement construction and demanding greater equality for all Israeli citizens and collective and individual rights for the Palestinian minority.

Friedman argues that journalists do not readily accept a view of Jews having agency, returning to history as actors, no longer subjects to be acted upon within the host societies in which they lived. His analysis suggests that this tendency among journalists is the latest transmutation of hatred toward the Jews over time. This time Jews are despised not because of their religion or their race, but because of their nation-state and desire for national sovereignty, even as other peoples seek self-determination.

Friedman argues that the international press has become less an observer of the conflict and more a player in it. "It had moved away from careful explanation and toward a kind of political character assassination on behalf of the side it identified as being right. It valued a kind of ideological uniformity from which you were not allowed to stray."[4] Friedman asserts further that editors refuse to print stories that offer a counter viewpoint portraying Israel with complexity and nuance, let alone in a positive light.

Those who are willing to embrace complexity at the expense of advancing simple narratives with particular agendas will find that the region of the Middle East, the Arab-Israeli conflict, and the Palestinian-Israeli conflict deserve much more serious journalistic work. They should be producing sophisticated analysis and expanding of readers' literacy on a complicated subject matter, not

---

4   Ibid.

offering a premeditated outcome based on fantasies and confusions. Journalists who share a sense of journalistic integrity would be wise to heed Friedman's message and see reality as it is rather than as imagined. Only then can journalists, and thus global citizenry, fully frame the Israel story, the Palestinian story, and the Arab stories with all their triumphs and failures, harnessing the necessary tools to enhance knowledge, recognize biases, and impart empathy.

II

History, Memory, and Narrative

1. David Hartman, "Auschwitz or Sinai?"

David Hartman, "Auschwitz or Sinai?," *Jerusalem Post*, December 12, 1982

Rabbi Dr. David Hartman (1931–2013) was the Founding President of the Shalom Hartman Institute in Jerusalem and also served as Professor of Jewish Thought at Hebrew University.

One of the fundamental issues facing the new spirit of maturity in Israel is: should Auschwitz or Sinai be the orienting category shaping our understanding of the rebirth of the State of Israel? There are important differences resulting from the relative emphasis we place on these two models.

In the twentieth century we have again become a traumatized nation. The ugly demonic forces of anti-Semitism have horrified our sensibilities. We can never forget the destruction of millions of Jews in World War II. Many, therefore, justify and interpret the significance of our rebirth in terms of Jewish suffering and persecution.

One often hears in speeches in the Knesset and at the UJA fundraising dinners phrases such as: "Never again will we be vulnerable. Never again will we expose our lives to the ugly political forces in the world. Our powerful army has eliminated the need to beg for pity and compassion from the nations of the world."

While I respect and share in the anguish expressed in these sentiments, I believe it is destructive to make the Holocaust the dominant organizing category of modern Jewish history and of our national renewal and rebirth. It is both politically and morally dangerous for our nation to perceive itself essentially as the suffering remnant of the Holocaust. It is childish and often vulgar to attempt to demonstrate how the Jewish people's suffering is unique in history.

Our bodies have painfully tasted man's indifference and inhumanity to his fellow man. We have witnessed in our own flesh the moral evil present in human society. But this should not tempt us to become morally arrogant. Our suffering should not lead us to self-righteous postures, but to an increased sensitivity about all human suffering.

Nonetheless, there are individuals obsessed with the trauma of the Holocaust who proclaim that no one can judge the Jewish people. "No nation has the right to call us to moral judgment. We need not take the moral criticism of the world seriously because the uniqueness of our suffering places us above the moral judgment of an immoral world".

Those who make such statements judge others, but refuse to be judged. In so doing, a basic Judaic principle is violated: no one may judge if he refuses to be judged himself.

Although it is right to appreciate the dignity that comes with power and statehood, with freedom from the inconsistent and fragile goodwill of the nations of the world, it is a serious mistake to allow the trauma of Jewish suffering to be the exclusive frame of reference for understanding our national renaissance.

COMMENTARY BY RACHEL SABATH BEIT-HALACHMI

Very rarely does a short essay challenge such foundational ideas and generate such penetrating debate that it echoes for decades and only increases in relevance. David Hartman's essay "Auschwitz or Sinai?" raised precisely the kind of theological and political dilemmas that would continue to be at the center of Jewish religious and political discourse for the next thirty-five plus years. Among the foundations examined by Hartman's essay are: 1) the role of the Holocaust in the Israeli and Jewish collective consciousness; 2) the challenges of Zionism, the sovereign State of Israel, and its unprecedented military power; and 3) the necessary centrality of universal ethics in Jewish life and thought. Hartman not only raised these dilemmas but also asked radical questions about the political and moral underpinnings of Israeli society and made a dramatic theological argument to reframe Israel's existence.

In 1982, Hartman was largely alone and in many ways a renegade in publically challenging the meaning of the Holocaust for Israeli society in an age of both increasing Israeli military power and ongoing conflicts on several fronts as well as with the Palestinians. Israelis felt increasingly isolated while the powerlessness and suffering of Jews during the Holocaust was regularly proclaimed to be a proof of the necessity of Israel's military strength that also rendered it beyond reproach. After all, the narrative held, the world stood idly by while more than six million Jews were murdered; who are "they" now to criticize Israel's use of power in self-defense?

Rosh Hashanah began on the evening of September 17. During the holiday, the front pages of newspapers in Israel and worldwide pictured Israeli tanks, soldiers and flags in Lebanon, not far from Sabra and Shatila, two refugee camps outside of Beirut. The photographs also showed streets of the refugee camps lined with dead bodies following a massacre led by a right-wing Lebanese militia which entered the two Palestinian refugee camps. During a three-day rampage, the militia, linked to the Maronite Christian Phalange Party, raped, killed, and dismembered at least 800 civilians, according to some reports, and left at least 800—and some say nearly 3,000— innocent people dead. Over thirty-five years later, the massacre at the Sabra and Shatila camps is remembered as a defining moment in modern Middle Eastern history, anchoring contemporary Palestinian anti-Zionism and perhaps still influencing the relationships among Israel, the United States, Lebanon, and the Palestinians.[1]

The massacre at Sabra and Shatila thrust the State of Israel and World Jewry onto an international stage of judgement and moral questioning. Hartman sought to respond to the horror, the moral challenge, and the theological urgency of the moment.

As the news media and leaders throughout the world began to question and critique Israel's alleged responsibility in allowing for the conditions of the massacre, Hartman argued that Israel must first and foremost question and criticize itself and take responsibility for the "unintended consequences" of its actions. But it wasn't just the particulars of the massacre that troubled Hartman, it was the pervasive culture and narrative of the IDF and Israeli society as a whole that must be examined. In "Auschwitz or Sinai?" Hartman asked whether Israeli Jews should continue to see themselves as eternal victims of the Nazis, remnants of the Holocaust and thus beyond moral reproach. Or, alternatively, could Israeli society absorb the horrors of the Holocaust into its "normative" collective memory but transcend those horrors to deepen its sensitivity and moral commitment to all those who suffer? Could Israel be founded not on a narrative of Auschwitz but on the ideals of a new ethical society based on the biblical revelation of morality at Sinai?

Hartman presents a powerful dichotomy: Israel must choose either Auschwitz or Sinai as its "orienting category." Each choice bears profound implications. Emphasizing Auschwitz as the core narrative for Israel's existence "is both politically and morally dangerous" wrote Hartman, because those who are "obsessed with the trauma of the Holocaust" are often those "who proclaim that no one can judge the Jewish people." Despite Jewish experiences of unimaginable evil, insisted Hartman, such experiences "should not tempt us to become morally arrogant. Our suffering should not lead us to self-righteous postures,

---

1   Seth Anziska, "A Preventable Massacre," *New York Times*, September 16, 2012.

but to an increased sensitivity about all human suffering." In contrast, taught Hartman in this essay and in many essays to follow, emphasizing the narrative of Sinai "awakens the Jewish people to the awesome responsibility of becoming a holy people."

Creating such a powerful dialectic between the culturally sacred narratives of Auschwitz and the narrative of Sinai was both politically and theologically radical. Hartman posited several narratives of modern Jewish life (the Holocaust, Zionism, and biblical revelation) and posed them starkly—and perhaps in a false dichotomy—against each other, essentially uprooting core beliefs of much of the organized Jewish community.

Challenging the sacred narrative of Auschwitz and suggesting that it often leads to a problematic moral stance was considered not only heretical, but deeply offensive. Hartman also called within the essay for a kind of universal ethics to emerge from the experience of Auschwitz. Some critics dismissed this call as the radical expressions of a displaced Orthodox rabbi. Others later argued that this essay demonstrated the extent to which Hartman was a prophet before his time. The country simply wasn't yet ready for the deep self-critique that Hartman knew it needed.

The Israeli government's Kahan Commission investigated the events at Sabra and Shatila in the months following, and in a report made public in February 1983 concluded that Israeli leaders were "indirectly responsible" for the killings and that Ariel Sharon, then the defense minister and later prime minister, had "personal responsibility" for failing to prevent them. The Kahan Commission report remarkably cited a biblical text which insists that leaders do bear responsibility for that which happens in their domain (Deuteronomy 21:6–7). For Hartman and many others concerned about Israeli military power and restraint, the report was a significant judicial confirmation of the meaning of the events, what must be learned from them, and the relevance of ancient Jewish values for contemporary Israeli morality. The report also gave more credence to the heretical questions that Hartman had asked in his essay "Auschwitz or Sinai?" For many thought leaders, Hartman's questioning of the state's narratives and values—which definitions of identity and ethical standards are prioritized— were the questions that needed to be asked and answered in order to prevent such a massacre in the future. These were the issues that needed to be grappled with in order to ensure the morality of the IDF and the society as a whole.

Hartman's "heretical imperative" opened the possibility for other rabbis and leaders from across the denominational spectrum in Israel and North America to be cautious about a pedagogic emphasis on Israel as a response to the

Holocaust. Even more dramatically, Hartman emboldened many of them to be publically critical of the ways in which Israeli military power was not always used only to protect the Israeli citizens but was also indirectly responsible for "unintended consequences" against non-enemy populations in Lebanon during the war and directly responsible for maintaining the occupation (and oppression) of Palestinians in Israeli administered territories on a daily basis. The profound and urgent relevance of these questions would only increase in the years to come, years which included the First Intifada, the Second Intifada, the Second Lebanon War, and Operation Protective Edge. At the height of each of these conflicts, educators, rabbis, and communal leaders returned to Hartman's "Auschwitz or Sinai?" for its cautionary rebuke and for the hope it offers of a better Israel.

By rooting his questioning in the theme of the religious value of *cheshbon ha-nefesh*, self-critique, Hartman offered the concept as a necessary national stance. He argued that "breakthroughs in the human spirit are facilitated by the courage to admit to moral failures." When Hartman passed away in February 2013, hundreds of obituaries, sermons, and articles attempted to ascertain the impact of his leadership and his writings on Israel, on North American Jewry, on philosophy. A single article, more than any of his books or many lectures, is mentioned most often: "Auschwitz or Sinai?"

As Israeli society has become more diverse and generationally more distant from the Holocaust, the questions of morality on the battlefield and the State's responsibilities as an occupying force have become even more profound and urgent. Outside of Israel there is a growing criticism of Israeli policies among American Jewish leadership and younger North American Jews. Many leaders today are now loudly echoing Hartman's demand that Israel build a healthy society based on the ethical demands of Sinai while still remembering Auschwitz. Whether or not they embrace the particularism of the theological aspect of Hartman's call, they almost certainly echo his demand for Jewish as well as universal humanistic ethics.

2. Yosef Hayim Yerushalmi, *Zakhor: Jewish History and Jewish Memory*

Yosef Hayim Yerushalmi, *Zakhor: Jewish History and Jewish Memory*, Seattle: University of Washington Press, 1982

Rabbi Dr. Yosef Hayim Yerushalmi (1932–2009) was Salo Wittmayer Baron Professor of Jewish History, Culture, and Society at Columbia University.

As for the sages themselves—they salvaged what they felt to be relevant to them, and that meant, in effect, what was relevant to the ongoing religious and communal (hence also the "national") life of the Jewish people. ... True, they also ignored the battles of the Maccabees in favor of the cruse of oil that burned for eight days, but their recognition of this particular miracle should not be passed over lightly. Hanukkah alone, be it noted, was a post-biblical Jewish holiday, and the miracle, unlike others, did not have behind it the weight of biblical authority. The very acceptance of such a miracle was therefore a reaffirmation of faith in the continuing intervention of God in history. Indeed, we may well ponder the audacity with which the rabbis fixed the formal Hanukkah benediction as: "Blessed be Thou O Lord our God ... who has commanded us to kindle the Hanukkah light."

I suspect, of course, that many moderns would rather have the Maccabees than the miracle. If so, that is assuredly a modern problem, and not that of the rabbis. They obviously felt they had all the history they required, and it will help us neither to applaud nor to deplore this. To continue to ask why they did not write post-biblical history or, as we shall yet see, why medieval Jews wrote so little, is somewhat reminiscent of those "educated" Indians who, westernized under the benevolent auspices of the British Raj, are embarrassed by the absence of historiography in their own traditions and cannot reconcile themselves to it.

We, I think, can afford to be less troubled. We can acknowledge serenely that in rabbinic Judaism, which was to permeate Jewish life the world over, historiography came to a long halt even while belief in the meaning of history remained. We can freely concede, moreover, that much in the rabbinic (and even the biblical) heritage inculcated patterns and habits of thought in later generations that were, from a modern point of view, if not antihistorical, then at least ahistorical. Yet these factors did not inhibit the transmission of a vital Jewish past from one generation to the next, and Judaism neither lost its link to history nor its fundamentally historical orientation. The difficulty in grasping this apparent incongruity lies in a poverty of language that forces us, faute de mieux, to apply the term "history" both to the sort of past with which we are concerned, and to that of Jewish tradition. (25–26)

COMMENTARY BY ALEXANDER KAYE

Yosef Hayim Yerushalmi's *Zakhor* is the rare work of scholarship that enjoys as much esteem from a general readership as from its author's fellow historians. A generation of readers has recognized that this little book offers profound insights relevant to Jews today. The metaphysical and historical assumptions underpinning the structures of Jewish identity have been thrown into question by intellectual and political developments of the past two centuries. *Zakhor* offers a framework to articulate what may have been gained and what might have been lost with these changes, and how to think purposively about Jewish identity in the future.

The main contribution of the book is to distinguish between Jewish history and Jewish memory. History, in Yerushalmi's definition, is a record of things that happened and presupposes both contingency and human agency in its account of the world. Memory, by contrast, is an understanding of events through the lens of mythical narratives and, (at least in the Jewish case,) prophetic portent. Whereas history seeks facts, memory asserts meaning. Whereas history is found in the archives and preserved in works of scholarship, memory is transmitted by the liturgy and ritual of holy communities.

Before the modern period, Yerushalmi argued, few Jews were interested in history. The Hebrew Bible does contain historical narratives—alongside many other literary forms—but the force of those narratives is to focus the attention on "God's acts of intervention in history" (11) rather than merely to chronicle past events. So the Jews, Yerushalmi posited, were the "fathers of meaning in history" (8) but they were not historians. By the second century CE, he claimed, the Jews abandoned mundane history altogether. Other than during a brief blip in the seventeenth century (for reasons elaborated in Chapter 3 of *Zakhor*), Yerushalmi argued that for nearly two millennia Jews interpreted events around them exclusively in terms of the mythical patterns of divine intervention and particularly in terms of the typology of sin-exile-repentance-punishment that had been firmly established by the Bible. New events were folded into existing memory: every oppressor was Haman, every Jew who intervened with Gentile powers was Mordechai (36). Every catastrophe echoed the Ninth of Av, every redemption the Exodus from Egypt.

And so it was until the beginning of the nineteenth century. Then, for reasons having to do with civic emancipation, religious reform, and the *Haskalah* movement, a small group of scholars committed themselves to the writing of Jewish history, forging a new mode in which to interpret the Jewish past. By contrast to the lens of traditional Jewish memory, the new Jewish historians assumed no special relationship between God and the Jewish people. Indeed, they believed the study of the history of the Jews should be exactly the history of any other people. They raised up events ignored by ancient chronicles and questioned those that formed the foundation of Jewish myth. In Jewish memory, the Exodus is the archetypal event. In Jewish history, it may never have happened.

Zakhor made a substantial impact among scholars when it was first published in 1982. It received a glowing review by the famous literary critic Harold Bloom, who later wrote a Foreword to the Second Edition, and it was translated into many languages.[1] Yerushalmi's choice to write about memory as a historian was particularly prescient in the early 1980s. *Zakhor* was one of the works that launched an entire academic field around the historical study of memory. It therefore had global impact on the scholarly community, far beyond its immediate field of Jewish history.

To be sure, not all of Yerushalmi's arguments were accepted without challenge. Some scholars questioned his account of the absence of Jewish historical thinking in the Middle Ages.[2] Others wondered whether Yerushalmi was right in his assessment of Jewish histories of the early modern period, of the intentions of *Wissenschaft* historians, or of the place of memory in contemporary Judaism.[3] Even its critics, though, acknowledged the brilliance of the work. On the twenty-fifth anniversary of its publication, a special forum on the book was published in the journal *Jewish Quarterly Review*. The forum's convener,

---

1   Harold Bloom, "Memory and Its Discontents," *New York Review of Books*, February 17, 1983.
2   Amos Funkenstein, "Collective Memory and Historical Consciousness," *History and Memory* 1, no. 1 (1989): 5–26.
3   Bonfil, Robert, "How Golden Was the Age of the Renaissance in Jewish Historiography?," *History and Theory* 27, no. 4 (1988): 78–102; David N. Myers and Amos Funkenstein, "Remembering 'Zakhor': A Super-Commentary [with Response]," *History and Memory* 4, no. 2 (1992): 129–48; Gavriel D. Rosenfeld, "A Flawed Prophecy? 'Zakhor', the Memory Boom, and the Holocaust," *The Jewish Quarterly Review* 97, no. 4 (2007): 508–20.

David N. Myers, asserted that *"Zakhor* can surely take its place as one of the most important and consequential books to be published in Jewish Studies in the last twenty-five years."[4]

The impact of *Zakhor* on the scholarly community does not alone explain its enduring popularity among such a wide readership. Many works of similar academic prominence are all but ignored by readers outside of their specialized field. *Zakhor* has special resonance because it is fundamentally a meditation on how it is possible for a Jew, or for any person, to maintain a sense of connection to the past without denying the ruptures of the modern age.

Part of the attraction of *Zakhor* is that it is a deeply personal book. Yerushalmi described it as "part history, part confession and credo" (xxxii). He believed that scholarly objectivity does not preclude personal investment.[5] Indeed, Yerushalmi urged historians to eschew "antiquarianism" and rejected the idea that a "conscious responsibility toward the living concerns of the group" (100) somehow tars the credibility of the scholar.

Zakhor is so personal because it is Yerushalmi's attempt to make sense of himself as "a new creature in Jewish history." Ostensibly, Yerushalmi's "new creature" is the professional Jewish historian. One does not have to read too deeply, though, to see that this appellation could apply equally to any modern Jew. No Jew alive today—and this includes the ultra-Orthodox as much as the atheist, the Israeli as much as the American—can avoid historical consciousness altogether. A question faced by all Jews today is how to balance history with memory, scientific observation of evidence with the power of collective myth.

Critically, Yerushalmi, the archetypal historian, did not tip the balance unequivocally to the side of history. In *Zakhor*, he wrote with some lament about the "decay of Jewish memory" (93). Elsewhere, he expressed undisguised nostalgia about his childhood as a Hebrew- and Yiddish-speaking child of Russian immigrants to the Bronx in New York. He wrote that "It is almost impossible for me to describe the culture and society in which I was raised, because that world has disappeared."[6] Yerushalmi dedicated his professional life to describing lost worlds (the seventeenth-century world of the *conversos*,

---

4   David N. Myers, "Introduction," *The Jewish Quarterly Review* 97, no. 4 (2007): 487–90.

5   Elsewhere, Yerushalmi endorsed Thomas Haskell's distinction between objectivity and neutrality. Thomas L. Haskell, "Objectivity Is Not Neutrality: Rhetoric vs. Practice in Peter Novick's *That Noble Dream,*" *History and Theory* 29 (1990): 129–57.

6   Yosef Hayim Yerushalmi, "To the Russian Reader," in *The Faith of Fallen Jews: Yosef Hayim Yerushalmi and the Writing of Jewish History*, ed. David N. Myers and Alexander Kaye (Lebannon, NH: UPNE, 2013), 26.

the Vienna of Freud's childhood, and so on), so his failure to describe his own youth is quite poignant. It seems not to have been a lapse in literary ability but a recognition that sometimes the tools of history fall short and only memory suffices.

Yerushalmi diagnosed the "decay of memory" as "a symptom of the unraveling of that common network of belief and praxis through whose mechanisms ... the past was once made present" (94). This "unraveling" is experienced by many Jews today as a mixed blessing. Even those who celebrate the boons of modernity often feel the loss of existential grounding that comes along with them. Indeed, some would argue that this "unraveled" state describes an experience beyond the Jewish community, common to all people who embrace the progress of modern life but mourn the loneliness of its individualism and atomization.

If the loss of memory has a cost, so too does ignorance of history. Yerushalmi pointed out that, even today, Jews tend to explain their lives through myths. This is not always a good thing. Ideologies about the State of Israel (as sin or as salvation), about Jewish assimilation (as blessing or as curse), or about the meaning of Judaism today (as vehicle for social justice or as fulfillment of divine command) are all myths of a sort. But of what sort? Yerushalmi noted that "There are myths that are life-sustaining and deserve to be reinterpreted for our age. There are some that lead astray and must be redefined. Others are dangerous and must be exposed" (99–100). Determining which myth is which, and developing the ability to think critically about the collective memory upon which competing myths depend, may be one of the most urgent tasks for Jews today. *Zakhor* does not offer a conclusive solution to these conundrums but it explains their origins and describes their character in a way that few other works have been able to do. That is why the book has enticed decades of readers and lives up to Yerushalmi's exhortation that even if history is not memory, it must still be memorable (101).

3. Emil Fackenheim, *To Mend the World*

Emil Fackenheim, *To Mend the World*, New York: Schocken Books, 1982

Rabbi Dr. Emil Fackenheim (1916–2003) was Professor of Philosophy at the University of Toronto.

The limit of philosophical *intelligibility*, however, is not quite yet the end of philosophical *thought*. The circular thought-movement that fails produces a result in its very failure, for it grasps, to the extent possible, a *whole*. The grasp of a whole by a circular thought is no novelty in philosophy. It is abundantly present in Hegelian thinking, nowhere as profoundly as in Hegel himself. For Hegel, however, to grasp a whole in a circular thought is to comprehend it, to transcend it, and, from a higher standpoint, perceive the meaning of the whole by placing it into a perspective. On our part, in contrast, we confront in the Holocaust world a *whole of horror*. We cannot comprehend it but only comprehend its incomprehensibility. We cannot transcend it but only be struck by the brutal truth that it cannot be transcended. Here the very attempt to see a meaning, or do a placing-in-perspective, would *already* constitute a dissipation, not only blasphemous but also untruthful and hence unphilosophical, of either the *whole* of horror—the fact that it was not random, piecemeal, accidental, but rather integrated into *a world*—or else *of the horror* of the whole—the fact that the whole possessed no rational, let alone redeeming purpose subserved by the horror, but that the horror was starkly ultimate.

The philosopher may feel—he believes that nothing human is alien to him—that this whole is not unintelligible after all. He wants to understand Eichmann and Himmler, for he wants to understand Auschwitz. And he wants to understand Auschwitz, for he wants to understand Eichmann and Himmler. Thus his understanding *gets inside* them and their world, bold enough not to be stopped even by Eichmann's smirk and Himmler's gloves. To get inside them is to get inside the ideas behind the smirk and the gloves; and whereas this is not necessarily to accept these ideas it is in any case to obtain a kind of empathy. And thus it comes to pass, little by little, that a philosopher's *comprehension* of the Holocaust whole-of-horror turns into a *surrender*, for which the horror has vanished from the whole and the *Unwelt* has become a *Welt* like any other. In this way, one obtains a glimpse of the Ph.D.s among the murderers, and shudders.

The truth disclosed in this shudder is that to grasp the Holocaust whole-of-horror is not to comprehend or transcend it, but rather *to say no to it, or resist it.* The Holocaust whole-of-horror is (for it *has been*); but it *ought not* to be (and *not* to have been). It ought *not* to be (and have been), but it *is* (for it has been). Thought would lapse in escapism if it held fast to the "ought not" alone; and it would lapse into paralyzed impotence if it confronted, nakedly, the devastating "is" alone. *Only by holding fast at once to the "is" and "ought not" can thought achieve an authentic survival. Thought, that is, must take the form of resistance.*

This resistance-of-thought, however, cannot remain self-enclosed in thought. The tension between the "is" and the "ought not"—the more unendurable to philosophical thought, the deeper, the more rational, the more philosophical it is—would lose all depth and seriousness if the resulting no were confined to thought alone. Having reached a limit, *resisting thought must point beyond the sphere of thought altogether, to a resistance which is not in "mere" thought but rather in overt, flesh-and-blood action and life.* (238–239)

COMMENTARY BY BENJAMIN POLLOCK

In the spring of 1967, philosopher and rabbi Emil Fackenheim articulated the anguish and perplexity of a generation struggling to come to terms with the Holocaust when he asked, "can we confront the Holocaust and yet not despair?" Alongside and in tension with the vivid sense of duty Jews felt, in those first decades after the Holocaust, to remember the victims of the Nazi atrocities, they were struck at once by a kind of existential paralysis in the face of the unfathomable horrors that had been systematically perpetrated. Fackenheim suggested contemporary Jews were left with a choice that was no choice: either "to affirm present and future life, at the price of forgetting Auschwitz," or "to turn present and future life into death, as the price of remembering death at Auschwitz." But in the midst of this struggle, Fackenheim at once bore witness to the beginnings of what he saw as a profound Jewish response. The commitments of his contemporary Jews to continue to live as Jews and to honor the memory of the victims, while despairing neither of God nor of humanity after the Holocaust, should be recognized, Fackenheim argued, not as the consequences of a mere drive to communal survival, but rather as nothing less than a response to a *command.* More specifically, it was a response to what Fackenheim identified as "the

614th commandment": "the authentic Jew of today is forbidden to hand Hitler yet another, posthumous victory."[1]

The 614th commandment marked a revolution in Fackenheim's thought, and the beginning of a philosophical struggle with the Holocaust which he engaged in for the rest of his life. A *revolution*: the 614th commandment expressed Fackenheim's newly crystalized conviction that neither philosophy nor Judaism were "immune" to the events of history. Thus, while the 614th commandment grounded the contemporary response to the Holocaust in the language of Torah, identifying a *commandment* as issuing out of the Holocaust—the first addition to the traditional 613 commandments—Fackenheim was claiming that the unprecedented events of the Holocaust had changed Judaism irreversibly, placing a new normative claim upon the Jews of his time to which Jews of earlier historical periods had not been subject. The uniqueness of the Holocaust was also indicated in the very specificity of the commandment. As much as Fackenheim would have liked nothing more than to avoid speaking Hitler's name, he claimed that only by thus insisting on the utter particularity of the Holocaust, could the 614th commandment resist dissolving into the universal moral call to fight inhumanity which, however important, would amount to escapism in the face of the specific evils perpetrated at Auschwitz.

The 614th commandment was also a *beginning*: although Fackenheim never retracted the 614th commandment, in the years that followed he came to view it as philosophically insufficient. How, Fackenheim wondered, was obedience to such a commandment so much as possible? Fackenheim's magnum opus, *To Mend the World: Foundations of Post-Holocaust Jewish Thought*, sought to answer this question. *To Mend the World* presents a starkly honest philosophical struggle with the horrors perpetrated by the Nazis, in their details and as a totality. Here Fackenheim draws together historical accounts and theoretical studies to detail not only the ways in which degradation, torture, and murder became ends in themselves, conceptualized by idealists and carried out as if they were ordinary tasks by perpetrators who often otherwise sought to be decent human beings; but especially the ways these all came together to form an unprecedented whole, a *world*, with its own structure and internal logic, its own horizon and language. As an attempt at comprehension this philosophical struggle with the Holocaust fails: Fackenheim arrives again and again at the conclusion that the Holocaust world of horror is unfathomable, that "where the Holocaust is, no

---

1   Emil Fackenheim, "Jewish Values in the Post-Holocaust Future," *Judaism* 18, no. 3 (Summer 1967): 271–72.

thought can be," that the Holocaust as a totality paralyzes the understanding in unprecedented ways. But in Part IV, section 8 of *To Mend the World*, Fackenheim also begins to trace examples of resistance to Nazi atrocities from within the Holocaust world. Fackenheim is astounded by such cases of resistance; moreover, based on careful readings of reports of resistance, he posits at their root a unique form of understanding of the Holocaust world on the part of some of its victims. Crucial to Fackenheim's account is the testimony of Auschwitz prisoner Pelagia Lewinska: "They wished to abase us, to destroy our human dignity, to efface every vestige of humanity[,] … to fill us with horror and contempt toward ourselves and our fellows. … But from the instant that I grasped the motivating principle … it was as if I had been awakened from a dream. … I felt under orders to live. … I was not going to become the contemptible, disgusting brute my enemy wished me to be. … And a terrible struggle began which went on day and night."[2]

According to Fackenheim, Lewinska's is a "historic statement." It describes an existential resistance to the Holocaust world that is rooted in a unique grasp of that world from within ("I grasped the motivating principle"), a grasp that immediately yields normative consequences ("I felt under orders to live"). Precisely in the context of the Holocaust world of horror, Fackenheim asserts, resistance is revealed as "an ontological category," "a way of being" grounded in an awareness of being commanded to resist. The possibility of shaping one's life as a response to the 614th commandment in the wake of the Holocaust, Fackenheim concludes, is grounded in the actuality of such resistance *during the Holocaust* itself.

The passage selected for this volume is the culmination of Fackenheim's analysis of resistance in Part IV, sections 8 and 9, of *To Mend the World*. The passage reiterates Fackenheim's conclusions to the effect that the horrors perpetrated by the Nazis were both ultimate, ends in themselves, and at once parts of an integrated whole, a *world*. Insofar as this Holocaust world of horror is unfathomable, Fackenheim now asserts, attempts to comprehend it are destined to be "not only blasphemous"—that is, a failure to recognize the extremity of what the victims of Auschwitz endured bordering on profanity—"but also untruthful and hence unphilosophical." To attempt to grasp the Holocaust through traditional categories of thought; through a systematic ordering of its workings; through comparison, say, with other genocides; or by

2 Pelagia Lewinska, *Twenty Months at Auschwitz*, cited in Emil Fackenheim, *To Mend the World: Foundations of Post-Holocaust Jewish Thought* (New York: Schocken Books, 1982), 217.

trying to get inside the heads of its perpetrators and victims; leads not to the understanding of the Holocaust "whole of horror" in its truth, but rather to an *escape from that truth*. Thus, the only authentic way to philosophize in the face of the Holocaust, the only way to think the Holocaust truthfully, Fackenheim claims, is to do so *resistingly*, that is, to give one's thinking the very same form of resistance which defined the way of being of those victims who resisted the Holocaust world from within. "To grasp the Holocaust whole-of-horror is not to comprehend or transcend it, but rather *to say no to it, or resist it*," Fackenheim writes; and he proceeds to offer a striking analysis of such resistance thinking. In conversation with both Kantian and Hegelian accounts of the relationship between what "is" and what "ought to be," Fackenheim defines resistance thinking as a thinking that faces the Holocaust whole of horrors as *what it was* while at the same time pointing to it in its singularity as that which *ought not to have been*. Only such thinking that resists by "holding fast at once to the 'is' and 'ought not,'" Fackenheim asserts, amounts to authentically philosophical thinking in the face of the Holocaust. And just as the victim's grasp of the Holocaust world from within came in the form of a command to resist, so too Fackenheim concludes that resisting thought must make possible resistance in post-Holocaust life, that is, a life that takes up the 614th commandment.

The discussion of resistance thinking in the face of the Holocaust in *To Mend the World* is the culmination of the philosophical response to the Holocaust which Fackenheim first articulated in the 614th commandment. In later years, Fackenheim came to question whether this response might not itself amount to an escape from the very whole of horrors which it aimed to think philosophically. Did not the privileging of those capable of resistance to the Holocaust world avoid confronting those most dehumanized among the victims, precisely those who most vividly embodied the unprecedented horror of the Holocaust? Fackenheim was increasingly troubled by Primo Levi's descriptions of "the *Muselmänner*, the drowned," those death camp prisoners whose living dignity had been taken from them even before death itself, and by Levi's suggestion, in *The Drowned and the Saved*, that these victims alone were the true witnesses to the horrors of the Holocaust world. Fackenheim's late reflections leave it wholly unclear whether, in the end, he was prepared to give a positive answer to that question he first posed in 1967: "Can we confront the Holocaust and not despair?"

Fackenheim often wondered whether it might not be too early, whether he might not stand in too close a historical proximity to the Holocaust to comprehend its philosophical and theological significance. But in a late note he asked whether perhaps it was both "too late and too early" for such comprehension. In a short time, the last of the generation of survivors will have left us. The Holocaust has, indeed, become a staple of Jewish consciousness, but cynicism abounds regarding the use to which the Holocaust has been put to strengthen Jewish identity, on the one hand, and to justify various Israeli and Diaspora political agendas, on the other. Recognizing that Jewish philosophy may not be immune to historical events may also require recognizing that Jewish philosophy is not immune to the passing of such events, to their receding into the newly distant past.

Can we confront the Holocaust, today, and still despair?

4. Robert M. Cover, "The Supreme Court, 1982 Term—Foreword: Nomos and Narrative"

Robert M. Cover, "The Supreme Court, 1982 Term—Foreword: Nomos and Narrative," *Harvard Law Review* 97 (1983)

Robert M. Cover (1943–1986) was Professor at Yale University Law School.

A legal tradition is hence part and parcel of a complex normative world. The tradition includes not only a corpus juris, but also a language and a mythos—narratives in which the corpus juris is located by those whose wills act upon it. These myths establish the paradigms for behavior. They build relations between the normative and the material universe, between the constraints of reality and the demands of an ethic. These myths establish a repertoire of moves —a lexicon of normative action—that may be combined into meaningful patterns culled from the meaningful patterns of the past. The normative meaning that has inhered in the patterns of the past will be found in the history of ordinary legal doctrine at work in mundane affairs; in utopian and messianic yearnings, imaginary shapes given to a less resistant reality; in apologies for power and privilege and in the critiques that may be leveled at the justificatory enterprises of law.

Law may be viewed as a system of tension or a bridge linking a concept of a reality to an imagined alternative—that is, as a connective between two states of affairs, both of which can be represented in their normative significance only through the devices of narrative. Thus, one constitutive element of a *nomos* is the phenomenon George Steiner has labeled "alternity": "the 'other than the case,' the counter-factual propositions, images, shapes of will and evasion, with which we charge our mental being and by means of which we build the changing, largely fictive milieu for our somatic and our social existence."

But the concept of a *nomos* is not exhausted by its "alternity"; it is neither utopia nor pure vision. A *nomos*, as a world of law, entails the application of human will to an extant state of affairs as well as toward our visions of alternative futures. A *nomos* is a present world constituted by a system of tension between reality and vision.

Our visions hold our reality up to us as unredeemed. By themselves the alternative worlds of our visions—the lion lying down with the lamb, the creditor forgiving debts each seventh year, the state all shriveled and withered away—dictate no particular set of transformations or efforts at transformation. But law gives a vision depth of field, by placing one part of it in the highlight of insistent and immediate demand while casting another part in the shadow of the millennium. Law is that which licenses in blood certain transformations while authorizing others only by unanimous consent. Law is a force, like gravity, through which our worlds exercise an influence upon one another, a force that affects the courses of these worlds through normative space. And law is that which holds our reality apart from our visions and rescues us from the eschatology that is the collision in this material social world of the constructions of our minds.

The codes that relate our normative system to our social constructions of reality and to our visions of what the world might be are narrative. The very imposition of a normative force upon a state of affairs, real or imagined, is the act of creating narrative. The various genres of narrative—history, fiction, tragedy, comedy—are alike in their being the account of states of affairs affected by a normative force field. To live in a legal world requires that one know not only the precepts, but also their connections to possible and plausible states of affairs. It requires that one integrate not only the "is" and the "ought," but the "is," the "ought," and the "what might be." Narrative so integrates these domains. Narratives are models through which we study and experience transformations that result when a given simplified state of affairs is made to pass through the force field of a similarly simplified set of norms.

The intelligibility of normative behavior inheres in the communal character of the narratives that provide the context of that behavior. Any person who lived an entirely idiosyncratic normative life would be quite mad. The part that you or I choose to play may be singular, but the fact that we can locate it in a common "script" renders it "sane"—a warrant that we share a *nomos*.

COMMENTARY BY CHRISTINE HAYES

For centuries, law has been an essential mode of Jewish religious expression. Accordingly, halakhic observance (in all its varying definitions and degrees of adherence) has long been a constitutive element of Jewish identity. Not even the separation of law and religion in the Enlightenment unseated the belief that commandedness lies at the heart of Jewish tradition, Jewish identity, and the Jewish conception of the divine-human relationship. But it troubled this belief, and two centuries later, in postwar America, some Jews struggled anew to make sense of the centrality of law to Jewish tradition and identity.

At stake was the very idea of Judaism on the one hand and the very idea of America on the other. The centrality of law in Judaism raised a fundamental question about Judaism itself: can a religion be "reduced" to law when law is no more than a system of rules that serve as mechanisms of social control? The centrality of law in Judaism also raised a fundamental question about America: does a group's adherence to religious law jeopardize the tolerance, not to mention the civic integration and flourishing, that is America's great promise to insular minority communities?

Robert Cover addressed these twin questions in his brilliant 1983 essay "The Supreme Court, 1982 Term—Foreword: *Nomos* and Narrative." To the question of Judaism's "reduction" to a system of rules, Cover responded with an expanded and enriched conception of law, inspired by his reading of biblical and Talmudic sources, as a system of *meaning* rather than a system of social control. To the question of America's ability to deliver on its promise to insular minority communities, Cover responded with a prescient admonition to the Supreme Court: the court must overcome its customary caution in order to provide a robust delineation of the state's guarantee of protection for insular communities and, conversely, an honest articulation of the principles that might demand the curtailment of such protection.

Cover's expanded concept of law views law as an entire world. "We inhabit a *nomos*—a normative universe" (4) that consists of not only a *corpus juris* (a body of legal precepts or rules) but also communal narratives. The narratives of law serve three central purposes: they imbue legal precepts with meaning, they articulate aspirational alternatives, and they create obligation.

The biblical inspiration for Cover's expanded view of law, in which narratives situate a community's legal norms and give them *meaning*, is evident in the following iconic line: "For every constitution there is an epic, for each decalogue a scripture" (4). The narratives of the Bible convey the interpretive commitments that imbue its laws with meaning, and actions with communicative significance. Thus, resting from labor may be a mundane act, but when performed by Jews committed to a narrative of redemption from slavery for a life in covenant with the universal creator, it becomes a holy and identity-conferring act of *imitatio dei*. Cover notes, however, that legal narratives not only authorize and enrich a community's legal precepts; they can contradict and subvert them, resulting in a complex and multivocal *nomos*.

The narratives that endow law and actions with meaning serve a second function. They project a vision of what we hope might be, an imagined ideal towards which we might strive. In the light of that ideal, we critically evaluate and transform our existing norms, so that they might lead us from the reality in which we find ourselves to the ideal alternative we craft in our narratives. The vision of racial equality projected by the narrative of the civil rights community provided a trenchant critique of legal segregation, prompting lunch counter sit-ins and other actions that transformed existing laws. For Cover, then, law can serve as a bridge between that which is and that which ought to be, between who we are and who we ought to be.

By themselves, utopian visions of a better world are only dreams and yearnings that dictate no particular action. But the alternative visions of *legal* narratives create an *obligation* to pursue them. This, then, is the third function of legal narratives—to obligate us towards our aspirations. For in law, Cover says, there is no vision without obligation. Indeed, law *is* nothing but vision plus obligation. To live in a legal world or *nomos*, therefore, is to know not just the norms of that *nomos*, but the narratives that imbue them with *meaning* and the *vision* that those narratives *obligate* us to pursue.

How does a community motivate fidelity to its *nomos* if its norms are not objectively real or true, but the subjective creation of the community? Cover argues that it is the human capacity for metaphor which enables us to treat our subjective creations as objective realities. He explains that the community dedicates itself not to the genuine *objectivity* of its laws but to an objectified *understanding* of its laws, by employing a "metaphor of separation" that "permits the allegory of objectification" (45). This metaphorical disowning of the communally generated law that makes possible its re-adoption as an objective reality is achieved through narrative—the stories the community tells about the genesis of its laws and their vital role in the creation and maintenance of the community's identity and ongoing life. Narrative, writes Cover, is the "literary genre for the objectification of value."

In one simple stroke, Cover brings hope to a disenchanted generation. Fidelity to a particularistic *nomos* does not require a *literal* belief in a myth of divine revelation, or the genuine objectivity of one's *nomos* or even its superiority over every other *nomos*. It requires only a communally constructed narrative with the power to nourish a sense of legal meaning and value in "the absence of a single 'objective' truth" and "despite the destruction of any pretense of superiority of one *nomos* over another" (44).

In short, normative worlds and the narratives that animate them do not fall from the sky; nor are they universal in scope. They are the culturally specific creations of *particularistic* communities that Cover refers to as *paideic* communities—committed groups in which law is a system of meaning rather than a system of power. Religious communities are prime examples of *paideic* communities, whose members are educated into the community's *nomos*—a common body of precept, narrative, and interpersonal commitment that provides personal and communal direction. Their bond is strengthened by shared rituals, prayers, and a common literary corpus that is believed to have normative force.

In contrast to the *paideic* mode of *nomos* creation (or *jurisgenesis*) is the *imperial* mode of the state in which law is first and foremost a system of power. In the imperial mode, norms are universal rather than particularistic, and enforced by institutions that require obedience and a minimal obligation to non-violence. While the imperial mode of the state creates weak interpersonal commitments, as compared to the strong bonds that bind the members of *paideic* communities, it performs an indispensable "world-maintaining" function in two ways:

First, in any given society, multiple committed groups with their multiple narrative universes must co-exist peacefully. The state establishes coercively the minimum conditions for maintaining the peaceful coexistence of multiple communities and their diverse normative worlds. But the imperial, or "law as power" mode, is also necessary because *paideic* communities are radically unstable. Owing to the "too fertile forces of jurisgenesis," dissent inevitably arises in *paideic* communities. In the struggle for domination—whether within or between committed groups—communities and their normative worlds may be threatened and consumed by competing communities and their normative worlds, necessitating coercive mechanisms that ensure the maintenance and peaceful coexistence of all worlds. Resolving conflicts between normative worlds, courts must resort to the imperial mode, selecting one law and silencing the rest. This is a *jurispathic* act in which a judge "kills" rather than "creates" law, but it is occasionally required to put an end to violence and maintain a harmonious coexistence of multiple lawful *paideic* communities.

Thus, law as meaning can be protected only by law as power. This principle is a fundamental strand in the braided story of America. Enshrining freedom of association in the First Amendment, the founders of the nation acknowledged the reality of nomian separation (32) and guaranteed to *paideic* communities not merely freedom from persecution but "associational self-realization in nomian terms" (31). In America, *paideic* communities—whether Mennonite or Chasidic, Mormon or Pavee—may create and inhabit particularistic normative universes.

Cover describes two kinds of *paideic* communities: insular communities, that exist as autonomous enclaves, and "redemptive" communities, that seek not only a measure of integration with the larger social order but an opportunity to transform it. To the extent that an insular community does not breach the peace or infringe the basic rights of its members or fellow citizens it must be accommodated (Cover's exemplar is the Mennonite community); to the extent that the transformative politics of a redemptive community may be aligned with the larger society's deepest aspirations, it too can be accommodated (Cover's exemplar here is the redemptive interpretation of the Constitution offered by some abolitionists). But what is to be done when the norms elaborated by an insular community breach the peace or infringe individual rights? What is to be done when a redemptive community works to displace the state's *nomos* with totalitarian norms? Such cancerous mutations of the legitimate process of *jurisgenesis* must be regulated or excised by the *jurispathic* action of the judge. But like the surgeon's knife, the judge's tools can both heal and harm. And there's the rub: how to navigate the dangers of both inadequate and inordinate judicial action.

In his article, Cover urged the Supreme Court to provide a more explicit account of the limits of nomic insularity and the state's duty to regulate *paideic* communities. Should the state curtail the autonomy of a committed group when its norms violate the health, welfare, and civic rights of its members or other citizens? Should it act when an evangelical university discriminates against non-whites? When a parent's religious convictions prohibit the use of life-saving medicine, and a child suffers and dies? When a *charedi* school's curriculum deprives its graduates of the secular knowledge and basic literacy essential to financial independence and civic life?

These are the questions that troubled Robert Cover. These are the questions that should trouble twenty-first-century American Jews, as insular communities of all stripes successfully invoke First Amendment guarantees of freedom of conscience and association to create islands of racial discrimination, misogyny, and illiberalism in the very society whose liberalism is the condition for those communities' existence. America's insular communities deserve to know the extent of their protections so as to rest secure in the state's guarantee of freedom from persecution. At the same time, all of America's citizens need to know the limits to those same protections so as to rest secure in the state's guarantee of freedom from discrimination, harassment, and violence by committed groups. In "*Nomos* and Narrative," Cover called upon the Supreme Court to summon the courage to adjudicate these competing claims; to exercise, in the face of *jurisgenesis* run amok, the *jurispathic* function essential to both the preservation of individual rights and the maintenance of the diverse *paideic* communities that are—to paraphrase Moses Mendelssohn—the evident plan and purpose of Providence.

A dense and erudite article, "*Nomos* and Narrative" was addressed to the justices of the United States Supreme Court and the larger guild of American legal scholars. And yet, its enriched conception of law, based on a deep familiarity with biblical and rabbinic sources, inspired American Jews to view their religious communities as *paideic* communities educating their members into a community *nomos*. It enabled them to (re-)embrace Halakhah as a normative universe of both commitment and obligation, in which narratives rooted in memory and tradition imbue legal precepts with meaning, project an ideal vision of what might be, and sustain a community faithful to the pursuit of that vision.

5. Kahan Commission

Kahan Commission (Report of the Commission of Inquiry into the Events at the Refugee Camps in Beirut), February 8, 1983

Even if these legal norms are invalid regarding the situation in which the Israeli government and the forces operating at its instructions found themselves at the time of the events, still, as far as the obligations applying to every civilized nation and the ethical rules accepted by civilized peoples go, the problem of indirect responsibility cannot be disregarded. A basis for such responsibility may be found in the outlook of our ancestors, which was expressed in things that were said about the moral significance of the biblical portion concerning the "beheaded heifer" (Deuteronomy 21:1–9). It is said in Deuteronomy (21:6–7) that the elders of the city who were near the slain victim who has been found (and it is not known who struck him down) "will wash their hands over the beheaded heifer in the valley and reply: our hands did not shed this blood and our eyes did not see." Rabbi Yehoshua ben Levi says of this verse (Babylonian Talmud, Tractate Sota 38b): "The necessity for the heifer whose neck is to be broken only arises on account of the niggard-liness of spirit, as it is said, 'Our hands have not shed this blood.' But can it enter our minds that the elders of a Court of Justice are shedders of blood?! The meaning is, [the man found dead] did not come to us for help and we dismissed him, we did not see him and let him go—that is, he did not come to us for help and we dismissed him without supplying him with food, we did not see him and let him go without escort." (Rashi explains that escort means a group that would accompany them; Sforno, a commentator from a later period, says in his commentary on Deuteronomy, "that there should not be spectators at the place, for if there were spectators there, they would protest and speak out.")

When we are dealing with the issue of indirect responsibility, it should also not be forgotten that the Jews in various lands of exile, and also in the Land of Israel when it was under foreign rule, suffered greatly from pogroms perpetrated by various hooligans; and the danger of disturbances against Jews in various lands, it seems evident, has not yet passed. The Jewish public's stand has always been that the responsibility for such deeds falls not only on those who rioted and committed the atrocities, but also on those who were responsible for safety and public order, who could have prevented the disturbances and did not fulfill their obligations in this respect. It is true that the regimes of various countries, among them even enlightened countries, have side-stepped such responsibility on more than one occasion and have not established inquiry commissions to investigate the issue of indirect responsibility, such as that about which we are speaking; but the development of ethical norms in the world public requires that the approach to this issue be universally shared, and that the responsibility be placed not just on the perpetrators, but also on those who could and should have prevented the commission of those deeds which must be condemned.

COMMENTARY BY YEHUDA KURTZER

The Commission of Inquiry into the Events at the Refugee Camps in Beirut—chaired by Israeli Supreme Court President Yitzhak Kahan, and thus colloquially known as the Kahan Commission—represented an effort by the State of Israel to investigate and hold accountable its political and military leaders in the wake of the massacre of Palestinian civilians in the Sabra and Shatilla refugee camp in the midst of the Lebanon War in September of 1982. The Israeli government authorized the commission, which operated independently but roughly contemporaneously to a UN investigation, just weeks after the massacre. The two commissions produced different conclusions in their reports: whereas the UN commission found Israel—as the occupying power—directly responsible for the massacre perpetrated under their authority by the Lebanese Phalange militia, the Kahan Commission held the Israeli military leadership only "indirectly responsible." The Commission's enduring legacy for Israel, however, transcends questions of its accuracy and even its significant political aftermath of forced resignations and a shake-up in the military establishment: it tells a story of Israel's attempts to navigate its moral aspirations and the standards to which it seeks to hold itself in the midst of its prolonged conflicts, it represents a significant pivot in the use of the Jewish tradition in the Israeli legal system, and it constitutes a turning point in Israel's concern and regard for its international reputation.

The bulk of the lengthy Commission report is devoted to a detailed analysis of the perpetration of the massacre itself, based on the Commission's interviews and research methodology (which is explicated at length in the report, including a sharp rebuke of Thomas Friedman and the *New York Times* for their failure to comply with its requests to supply information from their reportage to the investigation). This analysis can be best summarized as the question of what Israeli leaders knew, and when they knew it. Although the Commission ultimately distinguishes between direct responsibility for the massacre—which it assigns to the Phalange—and the indirect responsibility which it assigns to Israel, the Commission was still unsparing in its criticism of Israel's leaders:

> In our view, everyone who had anything to do with events in Lebanon should have felt apprehension about a massacre in the camps, if armed Phalangist forces were to be moved into them without the I.D.F. exercising concrete and effective supervision and scrutiny of them.

In sum, the combination of Israel's knowledge about the inferior "combat morality" of the Phalange under their control, the deep enmity of the Phalange for the Palestinians, and the immediate precipitating and shocking assassination of the Lebanese President, Phalange leader Bashir Gemayel, just a week earlier, should have led Israeli leaders to supervise the actions of the Phalange militia much more closely.

Nevertheless, the Commission did not believe that this failing rose to the level of direct responsibility, but rather assigns them "indirect responsibility." To make this case, the Commission first reviewed the ambiguities that complicate the legal clarity of the case—including the question of the legal nature of Israel's occupation at the time—but then posits that the indirect responsibility charge rests first, and rather curiously, on a provocative argument:

> Even if these legal norms are invalid regarding the situation in which the Israeli government and the forces operating at its instructions found themselves at the time of the events, still, as far as the obligations applying to every civilized nation and the ethical rules accepted by civilized peoples go, the problem of indirect responsibility cannot be disregarded.

Indirect responsibility, in other words, stems from "ethical rules accepted by civilized peoples." This language—imputing to Israel a responsibility due to its desire to belong to the family of civilized nations—is morally aspirational in trying to hold Israel to a higher moral standard than merely the letter of the law. But it also echoes the bigotry of low expectations that we saw earlier in the reference to the inferior Lebanese "combat morality," that Israeli leaders should have known about the Lebanese "belittling" of life compared to the values of "civilized peoples." Israel is responsible, in other words, because it wants to see itself as part of a family of nations that should be committed to transcending the barbarism of both the people they occupy and the forces adjacent to and subordinate to its own. This argument is a troubling but perhaps inevitable consequence of a nation trying to situate its claims to self-determination through positioning itself as a member of the family of nations and also by insisting that it operates by a different moral standard. The Commission differentiates between the civilized and the barbarian—accepting the responsibility of *noblesse oblige* in its conduct even as it deeply disparages its own allies.

The Commission then shifts to a second key argument in making the case for indirect responsibility, which is through analogy to precedent in Jewish tradition. Here, and without citing it, the Commission roots its claim in the Israeli "Foundations of Jurisprudence Law" passed just a few years prior in 1980, which had stipulated that "Where the court, faced with a legal question requiring decision, finds no answer to it in statute law or case-law or by analogy, it shall decide it in the light of the principles of freedom, justice, equity and peace of Israel's heritage." The Commission does exactly this, using the case of the beheaded heifer in Deuteronomy 21 as an example of how biblical tradition apportions some responsibility to Israelite elders who fail to prevent acts of violence in territories under their political control. The analogy is not perfect, but is aided by the use of the rabbinic commentaries on the verse which expand the Deuteronomic case beyond its limited meaning to include a principle of indirect responsibility.

Here, again, the Kahan Commission predicates its argument on a double-edged sword. While the supporters of the Commission tend to take pride in the novelty and bravery of the Commission holding the Jewish state accountable for its actions through recourse to Jewish tradition, it relies on a law that others—especially Palestinian civil rights organization—have criticized as inherently antidemocratic in its privileging of the Jewish tradition as legally instructive for a state that includes non-Jewish citizens. The law amplifies the earlier language in Israel's Declaration of Independence, that the state "will be based on freedom, justice and peace as envisaged by the prophets of Israel" and transforms what might have been a conceptual ethic into an argument for the legitimacy of Jewish "principles" as legal precedent. While the Commission is careful not to use Deuteronomy and the rabbinic tradition explicitly in the language of law, it does marshal these principles for the purpose of a legally-instructive argument. This is an extraordinary navigation of a fine line that will invite critics on either end—those who do not want Israel to hold itself accountable more than is legally necessary, and those who believe that Israel is crossing over in its legal code towards an antidemocratic preferential particularism. These positions are likely to correlate with broader support or criticism of the actions of the IDF regardless of the findings of the Commission! As a result, the use of this rhetorical strategy creates the risk of undermining the integrity of the argument in either direction.

The Commission then offers a third argument for indirect responsibility, beyond the legal ambiguity of the case and the voice from Jewish tradition, and that is the voice of Jewish history. The Commission argues that in Diaspora, vulnerable Jewish communities never tolerated the argument that it was only the "hooligans" who perpetrated pogroms and incited violence against Jews, but wanted to also hold accountable "those who were responsible for safety and public order, who could have prevented the disturbances and did not fulfill their obligations in this respect." This is not a purely moral argument; it appears as a kind of challenge to Israel to start taking seriously its own pivot from Jewish history, as the political expression of a people that has shifted from an identity as a vulnerable minority to a powerful majority. Will it act now in the ways that it always sought from others?

It is easy to detect here again in the Commission's language an eagerness to classify Israel among the enlightened and civilized nations—in many ways, one of the express interests of the national and political leaders of the State of Israel since its founding. The Commission seems content with the trade-off of accepting some measure of responsibility for the State's actions in exchange for this language of legitimacy; a generous reading would tie this instinct to a desire for Israel to hold itself to a moral standard for its behaviors that should be more concerned with right than might, and that would look to different standards than merely realpolitik and comparison with the neighbors to establish Israel's moral credibility.

A cynical read, however, might argue that the Commission simply offered manageable and politically savvy sacrifices without exacting any real deep reflection on Israeli policy or any long-term consequences for Israeli society. The Commission called for Ariel Sharon's job and those of other military officials, and its indictments sacrificed some measure of Israel's moral reputation, and in return it received praise from members of the international community for its candor, and the larger prize of experiencing a sense of belonging in the family of nations. Did Israel let itself off the hook too easily? In his roughly contemporaneous sketch of Israeli society, *In the Land of Israel*, Amos Oz quotes a cynical Israeli hawk (widely believed to be Rehavam Ze'evi), arguing that Israel should continue to act violently in its own interest, and then make whatever apologies necessary, and through this process of conquest and repentance to emerge as clean on the other side as the nations to which it so wishes to endear itself:

> What's so terrible about being a civilized people, respectable, with a slight criminal past? It happens in the best of families. And I've already told you that I'm willing to take the criminal record on myself, together with Sharon and Begin and General Eitan. And I'm willing for you to be the future— rosy, pure, gutless. Write books of atonement for my crimes. And you'll be forgiven. Oh, boy, will you be forgiven! The international audience will adore your conscientiousness.

This haunting prose probes deeper than the scope of the Commission's report: can moral conscientiousness ever fully restrain the nationalist ethos in its desire for self-preservation?

And the anonymous hawk's wish, of course, happened. The international audience applauded the Kahan Commission; then in 2012, Sharon's son Gilad called for Israel to "flatten" Gaza. Were the lessons of indirect, or even direct responsibility, for Sabra and Shatilla ever fully internalized? Or was it all theater?

The historical record of the Sabra and Shatilla massacre, and the accuracy of the Kahan Commission, continued to be litigated after the release of the Commission, and continues to be litigated today. Sharon briefly contested his own firing, and then filed libel lawsuits against various news media outlets in America and Israel about their characterization of his role in the war and the massacre. And of course, his image was not sullied enough to create any meaningful caesura in his political career. Within two decades, he ascended to the role of Prime Minister, the history of allegations of war crimes not a significant enough liability to attenuate his political popularity. And in the past several years, the official story what actually transpired in the massacre has been challenged with the release of previously sealed or undisclosed evidence and testimony, including a heretofore "secret" appendix to the Commission report, and especially through the research of Seth Anziska, among others, resulting in arguments that the Commission either failed to understand, or underplayed, the depths of Israeli— and American—responsibility and what they knew or should have known.[1]

The story of the Commission may indeed require revision, both for the historical record as well as for the families of the victims and for an Israeli

---

1 Seth Anziska, "Sabra and Shatila: New Revelations," *New York Review of Books*, September 17, 2018.

society that may have elided some of the responsibility that should have fallen more squarely than the official story represents. But the larger legacy of the Commission may be in the ways it preserves a moment in Israeli history likely never to replicated. Israel's place in the international community has so dramatically shifted since the early 1980s as to engender mutual distrust and disdain; the likelihood that Israel would submit to, and produce, as candid a report as the Kahan Commission today is very low. The more common instinct, as happened after the release of the 2009 Goldstone Report, was to search for the means to dismantle claims of accountability (as happened rather successfully in the response by Moshe Halbertal to which Goldstone himself later significantly capitulated). The Kahan Commission showcases a moment of Israeli self-awareness as to its evolving role in the family of nations, and an effort to negotiate its own moral character in relationship to the world in which it wished to live. Today, those indexes of moral character—Israel in relationship to itself, and the international community in relationship to Israel—are deeply misaligned. The future of the search for truth and accountability, as a result, will be indefinitely compromised.

6. Amos Oz, *In the Land of Israel*

Amos Oz, *In the Land of Israel*, New York: Harcourt Brace Jovanovich, 1983

Amos Oz (1939–2018) was a writer, novelist, and Professor of Literature at Ben-Gurion University in Beersheba.

This is the place to make my first shocking confession—others will follow. I think that the nation-state is a tool, an instrument, that is necessary for a return to Zion, but I am not enamored of this instrument. The idea of the nation-state is, in my eyes, "goyim naches"—a gentiles' delight. I would be more than happy to live in a world composed of dozens of civilizations, each developing in accordance with its own internal rhythm, all cross-pollinating one another, without any one emerging as a nation-state: no flags, no emblems, no passport, no anthem. No nothing. Only spiritual civilizations tied somehow to their lands, without the tools of statehood and without the instruments of war.

But the Jewish people have already staged a long running one-man show of that sort. The international audience sometimes applauded, sometimes threw stones, and occasionally slaughtered the actor. No one joined us; no one copied the model the Jews were forced to sustain for two thousand years, the model of a civilization without the "tools of statehood." For me this drama ended with the murder of Europe's Jews by Hitler. And so I am forced to take it upon myself to play the "game of nations," with all the tools of statehood, even though it causes me to feel (as George Steiner put it) like an old man in a kindergarten. To play the game with an emblem, and a flag and a passport and an army, and even war, provided that such a war is an absolute existential necessity. I accept those rules of the game because existence without the tools of statehood is a matter of mortal danger, but I accept them only up to this point. To take pride in these tools of statehood? To worship these toys? To crow about them? Not I. If we must maintain these tools, including the instruments of death, it must be not only with glee but with wisdom as well. I would say no glee at all, only with wisdom—and with caution. Nationalism itself is, in my eyes, the curse of mankind.

COMMENTARY BY WENDY ZIERLER

In the fall of 1982, shortly after the Sabra and Shatila massacre in which a Pha-
langes militia, allied with the IDF, claimed the lives of some 800 Palestinians
under the nose of Israeli forces, novelist Amos Oz set out to speak to people
and find out what they were thinking in this country of his, which seemed to
be moving in a very different direction than he had hoped. What ensued was
a series of controversial articles that were published between December 1982
and January 1983 in the leftist paper *Davar*. These articles, together with an
additional, previously unpublished final chapter, came to comprise *Po ve-sham
be-'Eretz Yisrael* (1982), later published in English translation as *In the Land of
Israel* (1983), a now-classic work that continues to speak to the current Israeli
political condition some thirty-five years after its original publication.

At the time, the book was something of a departure for Oz. To be sure, by
1982 Oz was no stranger to political discourse. Only two months after the Six
Day War, he began publishing articles warning against the intoxicating effects of
military victory and occupation, including what he considered the many dangerous comparisons being made to the victories of Joshua in the Bible. Already then,
Oz was insisting that Israelis acknowledge that "the right to self definition and
national sovereignty needs to be reserved 'even' for the Arabs."[1] By 1976, Oz's
political articles and speeches had been collected and published in book form
under the title in *Be-'or ha-tkheilet ha-'azah* (*Under This Blazing Azure Light*).

In marked contrast to this early collection, however, *In the Land of Israel*
was not so much an opportunity for Oz to polemicize and press a leftist, pro-
peace agenda but to listen to others and bear witness to their fervent positions.
In most of the chapters, in fact, Oz speaks very little, choosing instead to curate
particularly potent, and some cases, shockingly extremist voices and comments
from the *charedi*, settler, and Mizrahi communities. In this sense the book is the
very opposite of an essay, a piece in which one "essays" or mounts one particular
argument. Instead, Oz permits his interview subjects to talk uncensored and say
things that we know, from his previous essay writing, he considers very dangerous and problematic. In a certain sense, this strategy anticipates, in a more
serious, less over-the-top vein, the method employed by Sasha Baron Cohen
in the satirical film, *Borat* (2006), creating a context for people to express and
"out" their prejudices while leaving it to the reader or viewer to judge. The hope

---

1 Amos Oz, "Sar ha-bitachon u-merchav ha-mihyah," *Davar*, August 22, 1967. Reprinted in
   Be-'or ha-tkheilet ha-'azah (Tel Aviv: Sifriyat Po'alim, 1976), 70.

in giving airtime to this kind of speech and thinking is not so much to legitimize or shore it up, but to shock readers into an awareness of legitimate grievances as well as disturbing ideas and trends.

A lot of people at the time were very unhappy about this strategy of letting Israeli extremists speak without offering immediate rebuttal or balancing these opinions with more middle-of-the-road or mainstream views. Oz's choice, for example, to provide an extended forum to a self-professed Judeo-Nazi (named in the book as "Z") and to allow space for extremist *charedi* and settler voices alongside a number of very mild, compromise-oriented Palestinians, provoked charges of treachery on the part of more than a few readers.

This is not to say that Oz entirely omitted moderate voices. One of the last chapters in the book, "A Cosmic Jew," profiles an eminently sane, elderly farmer from Zichron Ya'akov, who served as a mounted police officer during the British Mandate, and recognized early on the necessary but corrosive effects on the Israeli spirit of "living by the sword." To live without power, says this elderly farmer, ironically named Tzvi Bahour (young man), is tragic but living by this power is equally tragic. But while Bahour models sobriety and wisdom, born of experience and hard work farming the land, the chapter communicates a sad sense, pervasive in Oz's fiction as well, that the younger generation of Israelis has not inherited the elder generation's commitment or work ethic. (The figure of Yoni Lifschutz, in *A Perfect Peace,* the son of the kibbutz secretary who runs away from the kibbutz is a case in point.)

In addition to the voice of Bahour, Oz includes a last chapter, not originally included in the Davar articles, that addresses some of the imbalance of the book by giving voice to the objections on the part of a member of Oz's own Kibbutz Hulda that Oz failed to offer a proper representative sampling, especially from the Labor and the Kibbutz sectors of Israel (*In The Land of Israel*, 236). Yet Oz makes clear in his prefatory "Author's Note" that he "does not believe in representative pictures or typical cross-sections. Every place is an entire world and every man is a world in himself." Indeed, one of the overarching arguments made by the book is the importance of listening to these fringe voices if one really wants to understand what Israel is facing. Rather than striving to present some sort of representative, bland, and balanced sampling, one must dare to reckon with the uncomfortable, even reprehensible things that people in Israel believe and are hankering to express. Doing this is itself is form of pluralism and a mark of a free society.

To be sure, one can detect in Oz's choices of voices for the book his long-standing novelist's interest in peculiar, unusual characters whose non-mainstream, non-representative behaviors nevertheless may come to stand for certain, specific unacknowledged truths. Characters such Geula in his early story "Nomad and Viper" (1965), or Hava, Yonatan, Rimona, and Azariah in *A Perfect Peace* (*Menuhah nekhonah*, 1982), are not meant to be seen as exemplifying kibbutz life or as part of a balanced sampling of Israeli society. Interestingly enough, the mantle of moderation or balance is often reserved in Oz's fiction to the figure of the kibbutz general secretary. Unlike the more moderate figure of Srulik in *A Perfect Peace*, however, the other odder, more fringe characters are the ones that propel the action and compel a crisis. For this reason, they are the ones to watch.

All this said, *In the Land of Israel* Oz does not entirely cede the floor to the cast of characters he assembles. The second part of the section devoted to the West Bank settlement of Ofra is comprised of a speech Oz gave to the residents of the settlement in the fall of 1982 and makes clear exactly what he believes. The speech reiterates many of the arguments Oz made in his earlier essay collection and anticipates the arguments that he makes in his more recent short book, *Eikh lerapeh kanai?* (*How to Cure a Fanatic*, 2006). Though Oz speaks of Zionism as a surname for a family divided, he makes a plea for the values of spiritual pluralism and humanism. He insists upon an awareness of the state as a means, not as an idolatrous end in and of itself. Recalling his earliest post-Six Day War article, Oz tells the people of Ofra, that in "the ecstasy of military victories and messianic intoxication, our arrogance swelled, our sense of reality dwindled, and the feverish attempt to create facts all over the face of the territories we occupied brought about the collapse of Zionism's legitimacy, a collapse for which I fear we have yet to pay" (*In The Land of Israel*, 142).

In the afterword included in the 2009 reprint of the book with its Hebrew title *Po ve-sham be-'Eretz Yisrael*, novelist David Grossman refers to the potent, almost paralyzing effect the book had on him when he first read it.

> Every time I finished a chapter, I would have to put the book aside and take a deep breath. Over and over again I thought to myself, "Enough, it cannot work. There is no chance we can live normal lives here. With terrors of this sort and hatred of this sort, we shall never make it out free." Would that I could say that now, 26 years later, I feel otherwise.

To be sure, the intervening years have brought much cause for worry. Two Intifadas have come and gone, and some speak of the outbreaks of violence in 2015–2016 as a harbinger of a third. The land-for peace negotiations that Oz advocated for in the Ofra chapter of the book, have long since ended and efforts on behalf of a two-state solution have reached an impasse. Extremism and messianic fervor on all sides seems more rather than less prevalent.

Oz's answer to this kind of extremism in *In the Land of Israel* is the image of Ashdod: a pretty city, a good city, with no great historical importance, and therefore, no outsized, biblical, or messianic pretensions. Ashdod stands for normalcy and non-exceptionalism, for a Zionism emptied out of the fanatic, religious, ideological energies without which the State of Israel could never have come to be. For some, Oz's desire to flee rather than to draw on mythic energies to shore up the State of Israel might appear flat—uninspiring and counter-intuitive. But it remains a potent counter-model to the dangers and potential excesses of Zionist myth-making and extremism of all varieties.

7. David Biale, *Power and Powerlessness in Jewish History*

David Biale, *Power and Powerlessness in Jewish History*, New York: Schocken Books, 1986

Dr. David Biale (1949–) is Emanuel Ringelblum Professor of Jewish History and Director of the Jewish Studies Program at the University of California, Davis.

The Jews have chosen the modern nation-state, whether in the form of the state of Israel or American democracy, as the best guarantee for their survival. That they have identified with the nation-state is no surprise, for they have always demonstrated a shrewd understanding of the political forms of each age, from partial sovereignty in imperial antiquity to corporate power in the Middle Ages. Identification with the state is the modern version of Jewish politics; different strategies pertained in the past. To suggest that modern Jews should adopt some other strategy for survival—to argue that nationalism or democratic pluralism are foreign to Judaism—is to ignore the political legacy of Jewish history, a persistent tradition of political imitation and accommodation, but never of passivity or retreat from politics. Zionism and Diaspora nationalism in their modern forms may be new in Jewish history, but they represent no more and no less than the latest incarnation of this political tradition.

These contemporary strategies for survival, for all their limitations and failures to fulfill messianic expectations, have still proven to be largely successful. The Jews of Israel and the Western Diaspora face less of a threat to their physical survival than at any other time since the end of the Holocaust and certainly less in comparison to the Jews of Europe before the Holocaust. To say that these Jews are secure would be foolhardy in the light of Jewish history, but they are certainly more secure than they allow themselves to believe.

The discrepancy between contemporary Jewish power and the insecurity many Jews feel owes much to the inverted image that modern anti-Semites have of Jewish power. If Jews typically see themselves as less powerful than they really are, anti-Semites, since the nineteenth century, portray them as much more powerful: a secret cabal in control of the world. The state of

Israel has not diminished this paranoia; on the contrary, anti-Semites now see Zionism as a force equal to twentieth-century imperialism. Afraid of feeding these bizarre delusions, many Jews shrink from acknowledging the actual power they possess. The reality, as I have argued throughout this book, lies somewhere between Jewish fear and anti-Semitic fantasy.

Traumatic historical memories play as great a role in the Jews' misperception of their contemporary power. Every nation labors under the burden of its own history, caught in the tensions between its understanding of history and current political realities; these tensions are often the cause of misguided political decisions. The United States, torn between conflicting legacies of isolationism and interventionism, and fearful of being perceived as a "paper tiger," became entangled in Vietnam. The Soviet Union, invaded repeatedly by the West, holds tenaciously to the countries of Eastern Europe as a buffer against imagined Western threats. The Germans, fearful of their neighbors and obsessed with national unification, repeatedly launched wars against the rest of Europe, only to find themselves after World War II permanently divided between East and West; by succumbing to paranoid fears and messianic appetites, the Germans brought down on themselves exactly the situation they most dreaded. (206–207)

COMMENTARY BY JUDAH M. BERNSTEIN

Before embarking on what would become his award-winning *Power and Powerlessness in Jewish History*, historian David Biale had intended to write a sequel to Arthur Hertzberg's popular anthology, *The Zionist Idea*. First published in 1959, *The Zionist Idea* had emerged in the United States as the chief textbook of the history of the Zionist movement, enjoying multiple printings over the next two decades. Hertzberg construed the Jewish return to political power in 1948 as the climax of two interrelated developments. The founding of a Jewish state, Hertzberg reasoned, capped European Jewry's long struggle to secure the grand promise of Emancipation as an end to anti-Jewish sentiment and the Jews' political alienation. At the same time, Hertzberg contended, the Jewish state would conserve the Jews' special sense of "destiny," fending back the forces of secularization and the creeping assimilation it engendered.[1]

In making this argument, Hertzberg had adopted a distinctively Zionist division of Jewish history. On one side stood the vast pre-1948 era of exilic

---

1   Arthur Hertzberg, *The Zionist Idea* (Philadelphia: Jewish Publication Society, 1997), 21–22, 32.

vulnerability, and on other a post-1948 return to political power and the glorious sustainability of Jewish life. Biale quickly realized, however, that the Zionist ideology that recommended such a neat historical dichotomy was in a state of crisis. In view of the First Lebanon War, Biale claimed to identify a marked dissonance between the political realities of Jewish life in Israel and America and the ways in which Jews thought about power and influence. Though Jews in these countries enjoyed unprecedented degrees of both, Biale felt, they seemed to obsess over the plight of Jewish powerlessness in a world dominated by forces hostile to the Jewish people. Biale wished to understand the origins and the current permutations of this phenomenon.[2]

Thus, what began for Biale as an essay on the enfolding of Zionist ideology after 1948 turned into an extended meditation on the place of political power in Jewish history, from the Bible, through the medieval period, and into the modern era. In situating the relationship between Jews and power in the foreground of his study, *Power and Powerlessness,* published in 1986, would go on to influence an array of scholars, activists, and journalists seeking to comprehend Jewish identity through the lens of how Jews conceived of power. Moreover, in utilizing contemporary questions to investigate the past, and in carefully applying some of the lessons he drew from his historical analysis to the topic of Jewish power in the present, Biale advanced piercing observations about Zionism and American Jewry still relevant today.

To understand the influence of *Power and Powerlessness,* one must consider the book's synoptic scope as well as the substance of its argument, both inspired by Biale's doctoral advisor and the person to whom the book was dedicated, Amos Funkenstein. Published at a time when academic conventions were shifting towards narrower chronologies and away from broad historical surveys, the expansive timeframe of *Power and Powerlessness* paid homage to Funkenstein's approach to history. To truly comprehend an idea, Funkenstein surmised, one had to trace that idea back to its historical antecedents. No concept, no matter how modern it may appear, constituted a *novum* in intellectual history, but rather had its origins in medieval and ancient intellectual traditions. Biale contended similarly in *Power and Powerlessness* that one could not fully understand Jewish politics in the twentieth century without taking into account the legacies and myths of earlier eras. In extending *Power and Powerlessness* from the Bible to the present, Biale was able to intervene in numerous

---

2   David Biale, *Power and Powerlessness in Jewish History* (New York: Schocken Books, 1986), ix, 3–4.

subfields of Jewish Studies, thus lending the book a far-reaching influence in scholarly circles (x, 6).

It was Biale's thesis, also inspired by Funkenstein, which proved especially important. In much of his scholarly oeuvre, Funkenstein had attempted to put to rest the old canard of Jewish political passivity and powerlessness in the Diaspora. *Power and Powerlessness* advanced Funkenstein's agenda in two ways. It catalogued a plethora of historical examples of the Jews' use of power in the absence of state sovereignty. It argued, furthermore, that one cannot fully understand Jewish power in any given time period without contextualizing power within that period itself. As an example, Biale revealed how Jews in medieval Europe skillfully manipulated their mercantile role in a feudal economy in order to obtain charters of protection from local sovereigns. But Biale also pointed out that, in the medieval period, power did not signify autonomy vested in the nation state, as it does today. Instead, medieval power meant the possession of privileges and protections in a deeply hierarchical society and anarchic political world. Thus, by the standards of the medieval era, many medieval Jewish communities proved remarkably adroit at accruing an impressive degree of power (x, 6, 40, 62–64).

According to Biale, the misreading of Jewish political power in the past animated the myths of Jewish powerlessness perpetuated in Israel and America in the present. Where classical Zionism had argued that only state power could eradicate anti-Semitism and normalize the Jewish condition, Biale maintained that Israeli policymakers, most notably Menachem Begin, had come to replace that vision with one of a mystical survivalism. Obsessing over specters of the Holocaust, and warning of an enduring global anti-Semitism that condemned Israel as the eternal pariah state, Begin and his acolytes mobilized nightmares of powerlessness to justify the execution of lavish displays of military force. Though by no means rejecting the necessity of Jewish sovereignty, Biale argued that the actions taken by the Begin administration during the First Lebanon War pointed up the ways in which the acquisition of power, the special dream of the Zionist movement, had failed to fully resolve, and had sometimes even exacerbated, fundamental questions of Jewish security (156–173).

The survivalism that seemed to exercise Israeli officials, Biale averred, found parallels in American Jewish self-perceptions. In *Power and Powerlessness* Biale maintained that guilt over the Holocaust and unwavering support for Israel had come to constitute the two pillars of contemporary American Jewish identity. Dismay over the former frequently bolstered an unquestioning commitment to the latter. The near-obsession of a remarkably powerful diasporic community such as America with Holocaust remembrance and Israel advocacy revealed a mismatch between perceptions of powerlessness and the realities of American Jewish power that mirrored the gap between Israel's actual military might and its gnawing fears of utter annihilation (198–205).

Biale's reading of Jewish history and his critiques of contemporary Jewish affairs resonated among a wide circle of readers, both academic and lay. For one, *Power and Powerlessness* helped herald a burgeoning interdisciplinary field of Jewish Political Studies. Take, for instance, political philosopher Michael Walzer's introductory essay to the anthology *The Jewish Political Tradition*, a voluminous project to collate the diverse expressions of Jewish political thought published in 2003. In acknowledging that "politics is pervasive without state sovereignty" and that Jewish texts serve as a prime example of this fact, Walzer channeled Biale's thesis in *Power and Powerlessness* regarding the thriving political traditions of Diaspora Jewry in ancient, medieval, and modern times.[3]

Yet, beyond the study of history, Biale's reconsideration of Zionism in *Power and Powerlessness* was an important step in a larger American Jewish shift away from a pro-Israel consensus then taking place on heels of the First Lebanon War. The critique Biale offered, for instance, inspired the guiding question of journalist and activist Leonard Fein's 1989 *cri de coeur*, *Where Are We? The Inner Life of America's Jews*. Fein began by asking what Israeli and American Jews risked in exercising power, in becoming, in Fein's terminology, the "hunter" instead of the "hunted." A central premise of *Where Are We?* is the gap between the ideal Israel of the diasporic imagination and the real Israel of the 1980s, a gap brought into stark relief, Fein contended, by the realization among American Jews that, unlike previous military campaigns, the First Lebanon War was one of choice that wreaked havoc on civilian populations. Fein advocated for the teaching of a realistic and ordinary Israel, not a magical state that could never measure up to the harsh realities of the Middle East. In this, he followed Biale's recommendation that Zionists think in more clear-eyed terms about the solemn limitations and pitfalls, as well as the seemingly miraculous benefits, of state sovereignty.[4]

In *Where Are We?*, Fein also echoed Biale's scrutiny of American Jewry's survival complex, or "survival as vocation" as Fein called it. Fein argued that

3   Michael Walzer, Menachem Lorberbaum, Noam J. Zohar, and Yair Lorberbaum (eds.), *The Jewish Political Tradition*, vol. 1: *Authority* (New Haven, CT: Yale University Press, 2003), xxi.
4   Leonard Fein, *Where Are We? The Inner Life of America's Jews* (New York: Harper & Row, 1988), xv, 77–82, 89, 99–100, 216.

American Jews had transformed the quest for survival into an end in itself, in the process absolving American Jews of the difficult task of cultivating values informed by Jewish tradition. A few years later, Biale's analysis of the chasm between myths of powerlessness and realities of immense political influence served as the framework for another popular study of American Jewish affairs, journalist J. J. Goldberg's *Jewish Power: Inside the American Jewish Establishment*, published in 1996. Examining the rather extraordinary political power American Jews had developed in the postwar period, Goldberg too identified as a central theme of his work the "gap between the Jews' self-image of vulnerability and the reality of Jewish power."[5]

In placing Jewish conceptions of power at the center of his inquiry, in examining the ways in which Jews wielded power prior to Zionism, and in dwelling extensively on the crisis of Zionist ideology, Biale's *Power and Powerlessness* departed from Hertzberg's *The Zionist Idea*. Yet, Biale shared with Hertzberg a willingness to apply his scholarship to the pressing matters of his own day. A primary goal of *The Zionist Idea* was to locate the origins of mid-twentieth-century debates between Israelis and Americans over the nature of Zionism. In the same vein, Biale began *Power and Powerlessness* with the conviction that the crisis of Zionism in the 1980s necessitated an examination of the historical relationship between Jews and power, one that, Biale felt, would "liberate us from the burden of a mythical past, while at the same time presenting us with a new past we may not have considered."[6] Both Hertzberg and Biale, then, set out to place the past in conversation with the present, and to untangle history from memory in the process.

---

5   Ibid., 128, 149. J. J. Goldberg, *Jewish Power: Inside the American Jewish Establishment* (Boston: Addison Wesley Publishing Co., Inc., 1996), 6–7.
6   Cf. Hertzberg, *The Zionist Idea*, 91–100, and Biale, *Power and Powerlessness*, ix–x, 8–9.

8. Elie Wiesel, Nobel Peace Prize Acceptance Speech

Elie Wiesel, Nobel Peace Prize Acceptance Speech, December 10, 1986

Elie Wiesel (1928–2016) was a noted Holocaust survivor, award winning novelist, journalist, human rights activist, and winner of the Novel Peace Prize.

And now the boy is turning to me: "Tell me," he asks. "What have you done with my future? What have you done with your life?"

And I tell him that I have tried. That I have tried to keep memory alive, that I have tried to fight those who would forget. Because if we forget, we are guilty, we are accomplices.

And then I explained to him how naive we were, that the world did know and remain silent. And that is why I swore never to be silent whenever and wherever human beings endure suffering and humiliation. We must always take sides. Neutrality helps the oppressor, never the victim. Silence encourages the tormentor, never the tormented. Sometimes we must interfere. When human lives are endangered, when human dignity is in jeopardy, national borders and sensitivities become irrelevant. Wherever men or women are persecuted because of their race, religion, or political views, that place must—at that moment—become the center of the universe.

Of course, since I am a Jew profoundly rooted in my people's memory and tradition, my first response is to Jewish fears, Jewish needs, Jewish crises. For I belong to a traumatized generation, one that experienced the abandonment and solitude of our people. It would be unnatural for me not to make Jewish priorities my own: Israel, Soviet Jewry, Jews in Arab lands … But there are others as important to me. Apartheid is, in my view, as abhorrent as anti-Semitism. To me, Andrei Sakharov's isolation is as much of a disgrace as Josef Biegun's imprisonment. As is the denial of Solidarity and its leader Lech Walesa's right to dissent. And Nelson Mandela's interminable imprisonment.

There is so much injustice and suffering crying out for our attention: victims of hunger, of racism, and political persecution, writers and poets, prisoners in so many lands governed by the Left and by the Right. Human rights are being violated on every continent. More people are oppressed than free. And then, too, there are the Palestinians to whose plight I am sensitive but whose methods I deplore. Violence and terrorism are not the answer. Something must be done about their suffering, and soon. I trust Israel, for I have faith in the Jewish people. Let Israel be given a chance, let hatred and danger be removed from her horizons, and there will be peace in and around the Holy Land.

COMMENTARY BY CLAIRE E. SUFRIN

In November 1989, two Holocaust deniers attempted to interrupt the keynote address at a conference on the Holocaust held at Northwestern University in Evanston, Illinois. Once their intentions became clear, they were quickly escorted out by one of the conference organizers, a Holocaust survivor and educator, and then arrested.

The following day, the front page of the student newspaper reported on the event, including a quote from one of the Holocaust-deniers, who claimed that he was "rushed" by "Holocaust survivor Elie Wiesel." While this account bears little resemblance to what actually happened (and the article also provided the accurate information), the incident has greater significance than most cases of misrecognition. Just three years after Wiesel had won the Nobel Peace Prize, this Holocaust denier unwittingly demonstrated that the Peace Prize had cemented Wiesel's career as spokesperson for the six million Jews murdered by the Nazis. In the eyes of many, Wiesel was no longer *a* survivor, he was now *the* survivor, a symbol of every Jew who had somehow made it through the horrors of the Holocaust.

Indeed, in beginning his Nobel acceptance speech, Wiesel told the gathered dignitaries that the honor bestowed upon him "belongs to all the survivors and their children, and through us, to the Jewish people with whose destiny I have always identified." As Wiesel accepted the mantle of representing all survivors, he also claimed that the survivors collectively represent the entirety of the Jewish people. By naming survivors to the role of representing world Jewry, Wiesel placed the Holocaust at the center of collective Jewish identity. It is the lens through which he viewed the world, and he expected that Jews around the world would join him.

In the speech's next section, Wiesel stated his commitment to fighting injustice wherever it occurs: after the Holocaust, he explained, "I swore never to be silent whenever and wherever human beings endure suffering and humiliation. We must always take sides. Neutrality helps the oppressor, never the victim." One must always become involved, on the side of the victim and against the oppressor.

Wiesel continued by explaining his priorities when it comes to the prevention of human suffering and the recognition of human dignity. He was unapologetic in stating that the well-being of the Jewish people is his top priority. He believed that his destiny was inextricably wound up in theirs. He found security in the strength of the State of Israel and its promise to defend the Jewish people but also fretted about the anti-Semitism of the Soviet Union.

Wiesel called it natural that, as a Jew, he would care most about Jews. Regardless, the statement points to a tension inherent in the very idea of giving a prize for peace. On the one hand, the award is given for specific work that the recipient has done toward peace. This work will, by definition, be located in some particular place and target some particular need. It would be impossible for anyone to prevent all acts of injustice; in order to accomplish anything an activist for justice must target certain injustices. Thus, Wiesel was honored for his work to commemorate the victims of the Holocaust and against further specific violations of human dignity.

On the other hand, in its very name, the Peace Prize gestures toward something broader than any one cause and toward a goal that remains ever elusive. The concept of peace suggests something universal and redemptive, a new world order in which everyone will share. This is why Wiesel began by stating his general commitment to all who are suffering before focusing on the needs of the Jewish people as his top commitment. Nevertheless, there is something jarring about the straightforwardness with which he stated this priority, even as it is practical and realistic.

The dissonance between the aspiration of a universal peace and the particularities through which it will be accomplished is only underscored by Wiesel's commenting, after he assessed the relative well-being of Jews around the world, that there are other cases of injustice about which he cared deeply: apartheid in South Africa, the denial of Lech Walesa's right to dissent in Poland, and a few others.

The two lists—first of injustices against Jews and then of injustices against others—underscore Wiesel's claim that Jews must care for one another before they cared for anyone else in need. It is his interpretation of the classic Hebrew idiom, *kol Yisrael 'aravim zeh b'zeh*: the people Israel are responsible one for the other. It is a message that resonated in the wake of the Holocaust, coming as it did from a survivor who pointed a finger at the world and accused them of failing to prevent the murder of six million Jews.

But as the Holocaust recedes into the past, as Jews are accepted more and more fully into American society, his reference to a shared Jewish destiny now registers as ethnocentrism, which can be of questionable value when it comes to getting along in a multicultural society. Sudden flares of anti-Semitism renew the debate, however temporarily: can Jews count unequivocally on anyone but one another?

There is a second question to ask: what of non-Jewish victims of the Nazis, of which there were several million? Where do the memories of these victims fit in, whether they were killed for being political dissidents, for being homosexuals, for being members of the Roma or Sinta peoples, or Jehovah's Witnesses? What, in short, is the meaning of the Holocaust or the lessons we should take from it?

In the 1980s, Wiesel chaired the United Holocaust Memorial Council, responsible for the establishment of the United States Holocaust Memorial Museum, which opened in Washington, DC in 1993. Today the museum's mission statement identifies the Jews as having been the "primary victims" of the Nazis but then lists other groups that "suffered grievous oppression and death under Nazi tyranny."[1] The statement points to the underlying question: should we understand it as an event of the most extreme anti-Semitism? Or is it meaning more universal, about a universal human capacity for hate of the other?

Wiesel concluded his Nobel speech by addressing the despair of Palestinians living under Israeli occupation in the West Bank and Gaza. He derided the Palestinians for using terrorism and violence to resist Israel. At the same time, he also said that "Something must be done about their suffering, and soon," insisting that if Palestinians and others in the region stop hating Israel, it will be possible for Israel to make peace and thus to alleviate the suffering of Palestinians.

Wiesel did not know then that the First Intifada would break out just a few months later or that the conflict would remain ongoing, with periods of relative calm and others of outright war, for the rest of his life. Throughout, Wiesel's strident Zionism kept him from addressing the suffering of Palestinians perpetrated by the State of Israel beyond statements similar to the one he made in Stockholm. Whenever Israel asserted itself against Palestinians in particularly egregious ways, there were voices calling upon Wiesel to use his platform to condemn the Jewish state or to speak out on behalf of more peaceful resolutions to the conflict. But Wiesel never did so. After his death in 2016, assessments of

---

1   United States Holocaust Memorial Museum, "Mission and History," accessed July 9, 2019, https://www.ushmm.org/information/about-the-museum/mission-and-history.

his life were filled with praise for the tremendous humanitarian work he did as a writer and speaker somewhat tempered by a resurgence of this criticism.

Ultimately, Wiesel's unapologetic refusal to criticize the State of Israel or to promote policies that the State might enact toward finding a solution to the suffering of the Palestinians serves as a reminder of yet one more aspect of the Nobel Peace Prize. In accepting the award, Wiesel climbed the final step onto an invisible pedestal, and it was from there that he spoke to the world for the rest of his life. We, his audience, looked to him as a moral compass. That he had a blind spot, so to speak, is a reminder that he was, after all, still human. His determination to protect Jews and then all others facing genocide brought him the Nobel Prize; the Prize in turn enabled him to do more good for humanity. But that very same determination became, for some, the source of his most significant limitation.

Wiesel's humanity is underscored by a moment from the ceremony that is not captured in the text of his speech but can be seen in the video recording of the ceremony. Just before he formally began his speech, Wiesel placed a black kippah on his head and recited the *she-hecheyanu*, the blessing thanking God for sustaining us until that particular moment. The blessing is a statement of gratitude; it is also a statement of bewilderment: how could it be, God, that I am here? Wiesel took off the kippah before he began his official words and accepted the mantle of speaking on behalf of the Jewish people.

9. Primo Levi, *The Drowned and the Saved*

Primo Levi, *The Drowned and the Saved*, New York: Summit Books, 1986
Primo Levi (1919–1987) was a chemist, writer, and a Holocaust survivor.

Every victim is to be mourned, and every survivor is to be helped and pitied, but not all their acts should be set forth as examples. The inside of the Lager [German for (concentration) "camp"] was an intricate and stratified microcosm; the "gray zone" of which I shall speak later, that of the prisoners who in some measure, perhaps with good intentions, collaborated with the authority, was not negligible. Indeed, it constituted a phenomenon of fundamental importance for the historian, the psychologist, and the sociologist. There is not a prisoner who does not remember this and who does not remember his amazement at the time: the first threats, the first insults, the first blows came not from the SS but from other prisoners, from "colleagues," from those mysterious personages who nevertheless wore the same striped tunic that they, the new arrivals, had just put on. This book means to contribute to the clarification of some aspects of the Lager phenomenon which still appear obscure. It also sets itself a more ambitious goal, to try to answer the most urgent question, the question which torments all those who have happened to read our accounts: How much of the concentration camp world is dead and will not return, like slavery and the dueling code? How much is back or is coming back? What can each of us do so that in this world pregnant with threats at least this threat will be nullified? (20–21)

The ascent of the privileged, not only in the Lager but in all human coexistence, is an anguishing but unfailing phenomenon: only in utopias is it absent. It is the duty of righteous men to make war on all undeserved privilege, but one must not forget that this is a war without end. Where power is exercised by few or only one against many, privilege is born and proliferates, even against the will of the power itself. On the other hand, it is normal for power to tolerate and encourage privilege. Let us confine ourselves to the Lager, which (even in its Soviet version) can be considered an excellent "laboratory": the hybrid class of the prisoner-functionary constitutes its armature and at the same time its most disquieting feature. This *gray zone* possessed an incredibly complicated internal structure and contains within itself enough to confuse our need to judge. (42)

The harsher the oppression, the more widespread among the oppressed is the willingness, with all its infinite nuances and motivations, to collaborate: terror, ideological seduction, servile imitation of the victor, myopic desire for any power whatsoever, even though ridiculously circumscribed in space and time, cowardice, and, finally, lucid calculation aimed at eluding the imposed orders and order. All these motives, singly or combined, have come into play in the creation of this gray zone, whose components are bonded together by the wish to preserve and consolidate established privilege vis-à-vis those without privilege. (43)

COMMENTARY BY SARAH CUSHMAN

The "gray zone" is arguably Primo Levi's most important conceptual contribution to Holocaust studies. Levi's chapter on the Gray Zone is the second in his book *The Drowned and the Saved*, published in 1986 (1988 in English). Many regard it, his final book, as a condensation of all his writings about the Holocaust. Fundamentally, the Gray Zone underscores the complexity of the Holocaust as a historical event. Even as Levi tries to explain his concept, his discussion demonstrates just how difficult it is to unpack. In the course of his short essay, an array of issues, challenges, and debates that continue to animate the field of Holocaust Studies come to the fore. Levi warns about simplification and the glorification of survivors; cautions against judgement of privileged Jews during the Holocaust and analyzes privilege itself; delves into the uniqueness of the Holocaust and its continuity with history more broadly; and in so doing identifies potential "lessons" of the Holocaust. The result is a brilliant chapter characterized not only by great insight, but also by inconsistency—an inconsistency that, perhaps inadvertently, emphasizes his point. The Gray Zone idea has fostered explorations of many aspects of the Holocaust—regarding the *Sonderkommando* (see below) and the Jewish Councils, but also: complicity among German business leaders; social dynamics among children in hiding; uses of gender and sexuality by Nazis and those they targeted; deployment of humor during the Holocaust; representation, justice, restitution, and commemoration in the aftermath of the Holocaust; and even the behavior of members of the German Army. In short, Levi's model has enriched the field immeasurably.

Levi first applied the Gray Zone idea to prisoners in the Nazi camp system who had become functionaries and had collaborated (in Levi's characterization) with the camp SS in exchange for privilege—privilege that gave them, if not actual power, at least a sense of power vis-à-vis other prisoners. He noted that while "privileged prisoners were a minority within the Lager population; nevertheless they represent a potent majority among survivors." Perhaps portending the future or observing a tendency around him, Levi warned about mistaking survivors for saints. He asserted that "it is naïve, absurd, and historically false to believe that an infernal system such as National Socialism sanctifies its victims: on the contrary, it degrades them, it makes them resemble itself." The Holocaust was not a character-building experience for survivors or anyone else. Survivors speak from experience, but it was a negative experience, not to be heard and absorbed uncritically, but rather to serve as a cautionary tale. Levi thus calls us to listen survivor testimony not only with open hearts, but also with questioning minds. Scholars' training prepares them to work amid this tension, but the broader public has more difficulty. Educators and scholars must help people understand that memory is fragile, that survivors have constrained perspectives, that they inadvertently omit from or add to their stories, especially when they are ethically opaque. Ruth Franklin, a literary critic, takes Levi's admonition a step further. She asserted in her book *A Thousand Darknesses: Lies and Truth in Holocaust Fiction* (Oxford: Oxford University Press, 2010) that the unfettered admiration and adulation bestowed on survivors and the uncritical reading of their testimony feeds Holocaust denial. Reading uncritically creates space in which imposters can proffer falsehoods with impunity.

The Gray Zone Levi described encompasses a convergence and divergence of "masters and servants," and Levi admitted that conceptually the Gray Zone could apply to some perpetrators of the Holocaust. But "to confuse them with their victims is a moral disease or an aesthetic affectation or a sinister sign of complicity: above all, it is a precious service rendered (intentionally or not) to the negators of truth." The worst pangs of conscience did not relegate perpetrators to victim status and the iniquities of any prisoner, privileged or otherwise, could not place them in the category of perpetrator. Yet Levi often seems to heap acrimony on privileged prisoners, confusing some with perpetrators when, for example, he characterized them as having become like those who ran the camps. Levi argued that "it is illogical to demand—and rhetorical and false to maintain—that [prisoners] all and always followed the behavior expected of saints and stoic philosophers." In the very next paragraph, however, Levi turned to the group he most closely associated with the Gray Zone, the

Sonderkommando [special work commando, SK]. The SK was a group of Jewish men whose forced labor involved operating the gas chambers and crematoria in Auschwitz-Birkenau, where massive numbers of Jews were murdered and their remains destroyed. Their tasks included calming prisoners and herding them into the gas chambers, transporting bodies from the gas chambers to the crematoria, burning bodies, and sorting goods stolen from those murdered. In exchange, the SK had access to items considered luxurious in the setting of a death camp. Levi termed members of the SK "collaborators," a designation that infers choice on the part of SK members to work with the perpetration.

Levi called for a suspension of judgment, but scholars, survivors, and others have found it very difficult to do so. The Gray Zone is dirty and few entered and remained unsullied by the experience. Levi himself seemed unable to withhold judgment. Among the motivations he ascribed to those in privileged positions were: "terror, ideological seduction, servile imitation[,] … myopic desire for any power[,] … cowardice, and … lucid calculation." Hardly a judgment-free assessment. These very contradictions have spurred scholarship. Adam Brown, a professor of Media Studies, for example, dedicated an entire book (*Judging "Privileged" Jews*, Berghahn Books, 2013) to analyzing how many of those attempting to represent the Holocaust, beginning with Levi, have judged privileged Jews during the Holocaust. Navigating the Gray Zone and its many shades has proved a difficult, but worthwhile task that while not necessarily achieving freedom from judgements has certainly expanded our general understanding of what transpired in Nazi-occupied Europe and how Jews responded to it.

Levi did not see the Gray Zone as confined to the camps. He saw it in other parts of Nazi-occupied Europe, particularly among the Jewish Councils that oversaw eastern European ghettos. He also saw it throughout history in various locations and eras, and in a variety of organizations, including the mafia. In fact, he saw it anywhere "undeserved privilege" existed; everywhere, that is, except utopias. This idea that something inside the camps might inform experiences or phenomena outside the camps points to a debate that once raged among Holocaust scholars, but now simmers and bubbles: whether the Holocaust was unique or connected to other historical events. For Levi, "arrival in the Lager was indeed a shock because of the surprise it entailed. The world into which one was precipitated was terrible, yes, but also indecipherable; it did not conform to any model." The universe of the camps was unlike any other. Those who entered were unequipped to counter its assault because it was so different from what lay outside. Nothing was familiar. Adding to the shock: other prisoners—privileged prisoners—carried out the initial assault. Levi argued that the Lager replicated the hierarchy of the totalitarian state, and that even outside the camps there were numerous people ready to compromise themselves in order to gain privilege. He emphasized that those who study the Lager experience not only can, but "must make war on all undeserved privileged, but one must not forget that this is a war without end."

One goal of Levi's book was to answer the questions of how much of the camp world is with us and what each of us can do to make sure its threat never becomes manifest again. For decades, scholars contended that the Holocaust was beyond comprehension, inexplicable, unique, incomparable, and impossible to describe or even talk about. All along the way, however, scholars and artists have tried to understand and explain, describe and represent, and even as efforts have fallen short, they remain imperative. The Holocaust often serves as the paradigmatic episode of genocide—it becomes a point of comparison. To compare or not to compare the Holocaust with other genocides remains a simmering question—a gray zone itself. Each genocide is unique—a topic of study in its own right, but trying to decipher what genocides have in common is the key to prevention. Levi would concur.

Levi ends his essay with a discussion of Chaim Rumkowski, the senior Jewish leader in the Lodz ghetto. Rumkowski was a complicated figure, who ruled the ghetto with an authoritarianism that seemed to ghetto denizens and historians alike altogether similar to that of the Nazis. His power and position could alleviate some of his suffering, but because he was Jewish, it could not save him. Levi saw Rumkowski not as a monster, but as a human being navigating the Gray Zone. "We are all mirrored in Rumkowski, his ambiguity is ours, it is our second nature, we hybrids molded from clay and spirit. ... [W]e too are dazzled by power and prestige as to forget our essential fragility. Willingly or not we come to terms with power, forgetting that we are all in the ghetto, that the ghetto is walled in, that outside the ghetto reign the lords of death, and that close by the train is waiting." Levi urged us to stay vigilant and counter undeserved privilege; engage with the complexity of reality, which must confound an "us versus them" perspective; and resist the intoxication of power, which produces a syndrome characterized by "a distorted view of the world, dogmatic arrogance, the need for adulation, convulsive clinging to the levers of command, and contempt for the law." The walls and trains of our historical moment may not be those of the Holocaust. The most difficult challenge may not be to denounce the privilege of others, but rather to recognize and renounce our own.

10. Irving (Yitz) Greenberg, "The Third Great Cycle of Jewish History"

Irving (Yitz) Greenberg, "The Third Great Cycle of Jewish History," in *Perspectives*, CLAL: The National Jewish Center for Learning and Leadership, 1987

Rabbi Dr. Irving (Yitz) Greenberg (1933–) served as President of the Jewish Life Network/Steinhardt Foundation and The National Jewish Center for Learning and Leadership (CLAL).

In retrospect, we can see that in all of Jewish history, there have been two grand fusions of basic condition, theological message, institutional performance and leadership group. Despite continuing shifts in local situations, institutions, practices and self-understanding, these four elements were so coherent that one may characterize the overall era as a unity. In each case, it took a fundamental change in condition to motivate the kind of transformation which led to a new synthesis. Yet the resolution was seen as a continuation of the previous pattern and the new Jewish equilibrium that emerged was perceived as a station on the way to the final goal. These two historical syntheses correspond to the Biblical and the Rabbinic eras. Each era oriented the Jewish way in the light of a major event. In the Biblical Age, the event was one of great redemption, the Exodus; in the Rabbinic Age, it was an event of great tragedy, the Destruction of the Temple. Remarkably enough, in this age the emergence of a new synthesis is taking place before our very eyes. The third era is beginning under the sign of a great event of destruction, the Holocaust, and a great event of redemption, the rebirth of the State of Israel.

Elsewhere I have suggested that "no statement, theological or otherwise, should be made that would not be credible in the presence of burning children." This suggests that we are entering a period of silence in theology—a silence that corresponds to profound hiddenness. The fundamental religious act is the reaffirmation of faith, redemption and meaningfulness through acts of love and life giving. Indeed, creating life is only possible out of enormous faith in ultimate redemption and a willingness to risk the worst suffering to keep the covenantal chain going. In an age when one is ashamed or embarrassed to talk about God in the presence of burning children, the creation of an image of God—viz., a human being of infinite value, equality and uniqueness—is an act that speaks even louder than words. This image points beyond itself to transcendence. The human vessel imprinted with the image of God testifies by its very existence to the source of that image. Perhaps this testimony is the only statement about God we can make.

COMMENTARY BY JOSHUA FEIGELSON

In a dispatch from the 1977 General Assembly of Jewish Federations for the *New York Jewish Week*, columnist Bernard Postal noted something rather remarkable. Former Israeli Prime Minister Golda Meir, just three years out of office, was in attendance for the first time in nearly thirty years. On Friday evening, Postal reported, "Seven hundred people eager to hear Meir stood jammed together like a rush-hour subway crowd for over an hour outside a part of the hotel ballroom, waiting more or less patiently and good-naturedly to be admitted." But, Postal continued, "the larger segment of the ballroom was filled with some 1,800 people listening to Rabbi Irving Greenberg lead an Oneg Shabbat on the Holocaust."[1] Such was the influence of Yitz Greenberg: he could outdraw even Golda Meir.

Beginning in the late 1960s, and continuing for the next half-century, Greenberg was one of the most influential interpreters, teachers, and institution-builders in American Jewish life. As a young professor of history at Yeshiva University, and later at CUNY, Greenberg traveled the country to deliver lectures on the challenges, opportunity, and meaning of contemporary Jewish experience. By 1974 he had founded the National Jewish Conference Center, later renamed CLAL (National Jewish Center for Leadership and Learning), to serve as a think-tank, convener, and laboratory for his many ideas. Through NJCC, Greenberg convened scores of retreats for young adult Jewish lay leaders, in an effort to deepen their Jewish educations. He published hundreds of articles in Jewish and general newspapers and magazines, ranging from the *New York Times* to the *Jewish Press* to *Redbook*. He built new institutions, created new forms of engagement, and theorized new ways of understanding and enacting Jewish life.

A 1959 PhD graduate in history from Harvard who had been reared and yeshiva-educated in Orthodox Borough Park, Brooklyn, Greenberg could speak with equal facility about a passage of Talmud or Bible, contemporary philosophy, the latest scientific discoveries, and popular culture. A half-century later,

---

1   Bernard Postal, "Postalcard from Dallas," *The New York Jewish Week*, November 20, 1977.

when people would ask me about my doctoral dissertation and I would tell them I was writing about Yitz Greenberg, the nearly uniform response from those of a certain age was: "I can vividly remember the first time I heard him speak."

Central to Greenberg's teaching were several key elements, all of which appear in "The Third Great Cycle of Jewish History." These include: the idea of Judaism as a "midrash on history"; human beings created in the image of God as a *clal gadol*, or orienting principle, of Judaism; the notion that the Holocaust and the establishment of the State of Israel represent shattering events in Jewish history that demanded new paradigms and institutions; the concept of "voluntary covenant"; and the notion of "holy secularity." I will briefly discuss each of these concepts.

In many ways, the first four paragraphs of "The Third Great Cycle" encapsulate the essence of Greenberg's ideas. "Judaism is a midrash on history," he begins. For Greenberg, Judaism is distinguished by its focus on this world and on a belief that it can be perfected: "Judaism affirms that this incredible perfection will be attained in this world, in actual human history." That, in turn, means the stakes are high: either the claims made by the tradition are reflected in the realities of life on Earth, or they are not. And if they are not, then God is not credible. The endpoint of this perfection is that "every human will attain his or her fullest expression as a creature created in the image of God."

The teaching that "human beings are created *be-tzelem Elohim*, in the image of God" has become an aphorism in contemporary Jewish life. And while many have espoused the idea, Greenberg would seem to claim the lion's share of the credit for popularizing it. Beginning in the late 1960s, Greenberg began articulating a basic religious framework built on the notion articulated in Genesis 1:26: if human beings are created in God's image, then they bear three fundamental dignities, all of which are mentioned in the first paragraph of "The Third Great Cycle": 1) like God, each human is unique; 2) because we are all images of God, humans are fundamentally equal; and 3) just as God is infinite, each human is infinitely valuable. As such, the destination of human history is that these dignities will be upheld: "there will be no oppression or exploitation; there will be adequate resources to take care of every single life appropriately. The physical, emotional and relational aspects of the individual's life will be perfected."

This claim sets up the architecture of history that Greenberg then outlines. Judaism endured crises of credibility previously, most particularly with the destruction of the Second Temple. That event was so cataclysmic that, in

Greenberg's narrative, it demanded a new approach to Jewish life. As a result, the Biblical Era came to an end, and the Rabbinic Era began. The Rabbinic Era lasted nearly 2,000 years, according to Greenberg. And while the European Enlightenment and Jewish emancipation represented a first step toward a third era, it was ultimately the twentieth-century events of the Holocaust and the formation of Israel that ushered it in.

It is essential to emphasize that, for Greenberg, it is not one or the other that is important: the Holocaust and Israel *together* constitute the shattering event. "The Holocaust and the rebirth of Israel are profoundly linked yet dialectically opposed to each other," he writes. "Does the Holocaust disprove the classic Jewish teaching of redemption? Does Israel validate it? ... How should we understand the covenant after such a devastating and isolating experience? Can the Jewish condition be the same after sovereignty is regained?" Greenberg understands a need for these questions to be asked simultaneously. In many respects this distinguishes him from Holocaust theologians like Emil Fackenheim and Richard Rubenstein, on the one hand, or Israeli theologian-philosophers like David Hartman or Yeshayahu Leibowitz on the other, who tend to treat one event much more than the other. Greenberg's formulation of the Holocaust and Israel as deeply intertwined—not from a causal point of view, but from a theological one—is unique.

As a result of both the Holocaust and the establishment of Israel, Greenberg taught that the relationship of humans and God is fundamentally changed. The divine was not manifest only in things traditionally considered sacred, like rituals and services. Rather, in the modern world, even those things we might think of as secular were moments to encounter God. Greenberg termed this notion "Holy Secularity." Advances in medicine, agriculture, economics, and human rights are all manifestations of God's presence in the world. For Greenberg, this represents a radical move: after the Holocaust, God should not be understood as absent, but more hidden. "The divine is more present than ever, in street and factory, media and stage," he writes, "but the catch is that one must look and be open to the encounter." (In this, Greenberg echoes thinkers like Rabbi Abraham Isaac Kook and German theologian Dietrich Bonhoeffer.)

Concomitantly, God needs to be understood as continuing on a path begun with the transition from the Biblical to the Rabbinic Era: making ever-greater room for humans to take responsibility. Where the Rabbinic Era replaced prophecy with the notion that God "is not in heaven" (Babylonian Talmud Bava Metzia 59a), in the Third Era humans must take even greater responsibility for the world: "If God did not stop the murder and the torture, then what was the statement made by the infinitely suffering Divine Presence in Auschwitz? It was a cry for action, a call to humans to stop the Holocaust, a call to the people Israel to rise to a new, unprecedented level of covenantal responsibility."

From here flowed an idea that proved controversial in Greenberg's native Orthodox circles: if God had fundamentally broken the covenant through the Holocaust, then any Jew who decided to live a Jewish life, or even to have Jewish children, expressed a voluntary commitment to uphold the covenant. And since it no longer came from a place of requirement or imposition, acting on the covenant voluntarily thus reflected a higher degree of agency and maturity on the part of the Jewish people. Greenberg elaborated this idea more fully in the companion essay published with "The Third Great Cycle" entitled "Voluntary Covenant."

Taken together, these elements established an approach to Jewish life that claimed unusual purchase on a generation of Jewish leadership that was college-educated, professionally successful, and thirsty for an approach to Jewish living that was academically credible, historically attuned, and felt traditional and authentic. With a dialectical approach that allowed him to stake out competing positions—on tradition and innovation, power and powerlessness, the holy and the secular—Greenberg provided his listeners and readers with a combination they devoured.

On the basis of this approach, Greenberg would establish many of the projects and institutions he discussed in the essay: Jewish education programs through Federations and Jewish foundations; pluralist retreat centers; projects in media; synagogue renewal programs; the Association for Jewish Studies. Most singularly, perhaps, Greenberg, working with Elie Wiesel, led a movement to create Holocaust memorials in cities across the country. And as a result of one of his 1970s retreats, he eventually led the development of the President's Commission on the Holocaust, which created the United States Holocaust Memorial Museum, which Greenberg chaired from 2000–2002.

11. Deborah Lipstadt, *Denying the Holocaust*

Yaffa Eliach, *There Once Was a World: A 900-Year Chronicle of the Shtetl of Eishyshok*

Deborah Lipstadt, *Denying the Holocaust*, New York: Free Press, 1993

Dr. Deborah Lipstadt (1947–) is Dorot Professor of Modern Jewish History at Emory University.

I rving is one of the most dangerous spokespersons for Holocaust denial. Familiar with historical evidence, he bends it until it conforms with his ideological leanings and political agenda. A man who is convinced that Britain's great decline was accelerated by its decision to go to war with Germany, he is facile at taking accurate information and shaping it to confirm his conclusions. A review of his recent book, *Churchill's War*, which appeared in *New York Review of Books*, accurately analyzed his practice of applying a double standard to evidence. He demands "absolute documentary proof" when it comes to proving the Germans guilty, but he relies on highly circumstantial evidence to condemn the Allies. This is an accurate description not only of Irving's tactics, but those of deniers in general. (181)

Others have argued that the best tactic is just to ignore the deniers because what they crave is publicity, and attacks on them will provide it. I have encountered this view repeatedly while writing this book. I have been asked if I am giving them what they want and enhancing their credibility by deigning to respond to them. Deny them what they so desperately desire and need, and, critics claim, they will wither on the vine. It is true that publicity is what the deniers need to survive, hence their media-sensitive tactics—such as ads in college papers, challenges to debate "exterminationists," pseudoscientific reports, and truth tours of death-camp sites. I once was an ardent advocate of ignoring them. In fact, when I first began this book I was beset by the fear that I would inadvertently enhance their credibility by responding to their fantasies. But having immersed myself in their activities for too long a time, I am now convinced that ignoring them is no longer an option. The time to hope that of their own accord they will blow away like dust is gone. Too many of my students have come to me and asked, "How do we know there were really gas chambers?" "Was the *Diary of Anne Frank* a hoax?" "Are there actual documents attesting to a Nazi plan to annihilate the Jews?" Some of these students are aware that their questions have been informed by deniers. Others are not; they just know that they have heard these charges and are troubled by them.

Not ignoring the deniers does not mean engaging them in discussion or debate. In fact, it means *not* doing that. We cannot debate them for two reasons, one strategic and the other tactical. As we have repeatedly seen, the deniers long to be considered the "other" side. Engaging them in discussion makes them exactly that. Second, they are contemptuous of the very tools that shape any honest debate: truth and reason. Debating them would be like trying to nail a glob of jelly to the wall.

Though we cannot directly engage them, there is something we can do. Those who care not just about Jewish history or the history of the Holocaust but about truth in all its forms, must function as canaries in the mine once did, to guard against the spread of noxious fumes. We must vigilantly stand watch against an increasingly nimble enemy. But unlike the canary, we must not sit silently by waiting to expire so that others will be warned of the danger. When we witness assaults on the truth, our response must be strong, thought neither polemical nor emotional. We must educate the broader public and academe about this threat and its historical and ideological roots. We must expose these people for what they are.

The effort will not be pleasant. Those who take on this task sometimes feel—as I often did in the course of writing this work—as if they are being forced to prove what they know to be fact. Those of us who make scholarship our vocation and avocation dream of spending our time charting new paths, opening new vistas, and offering new perspectives on some aspect of the truth. We seek to discover, not to defend. We did not train in our respective fields in order to stand like watchmen and women on the Rhine. Yet this is what we must do. We do so in order to expose falsehood and hate. We will remain ever vigilant so that the most precious tools of our trade and society—truth and reason—can prevail. The still, small voices of millions cry out from the ground demanding that we do no less. (221–222)

Yaffa Eliach, *There Once Was a World: A 900-Year Chronicle of the Shtetl of Eishyshok*, Boston: Little, Brown, and Company, 1998

Dr. Yaffa Eliach (1935–2016) was a Holocaust survivor and Professor of History and Literature in the Department of Judaic Studies at Brooklyn College.

The years 1935–1937 saw a number of anti-Jewish pogroms in Poland, such as the ones in Grodno in 1935, Przytyk and Minsk-Mazowieck in 1936, Czestochowa and Bszesc nad Bugiem in 1937. Zalman Lubetski happened to be in Przytyk in 1936, and heard eyewitness accounts of that pogrom. But when he tried to tell people at home what he had heard, or described his own experiences of anti-Semitism in the army, most of his townsmen turned a deaf ear. Surely nothing like what he was talking about would happen in Eishyshok: The business ties between the Eishyshkian Jews and their Polish neighbors were so strong that the Poles needed the Jews for their livelihood.

Zalman's visit to Eishyshok coincided with an anti-Semitic attack on his relative Israel Yekutiel, who lived in the nearby villiage of Poshitva. Polish thugs beat him with an iron bar, crushing the bones of his skull. Though Dr. Lehr operated on him at the hospital in Eishyshok and was able to save his life, after which he had further surgery in Vilna, he lived in constant pain for his few remaining years. Stull, Eishyshkians reassured themselves that Eishyshok was not Poshitva.

Among the older people, there was considerable annoyance with what they regarded as the alarmism of their sons and daughters. They discounted the similarities the young people pointed out between the Nuremberg Laws in Germany and the various official actions of anti-Semitism in Poland (such as the Janina Prystor bill and the "ghetto benches" that had been introduced into academic institutes). They viewed the rising tide of anti-Semitism in their own country, as in Germany, as nothing more than a passing phase. And some of the young people agreed with them, or at least hoped they were right. Szeina Blacharowicz, writing to her best friend Malka Matikanski in Palestine in October 1936, told her: "At the present no changes have taken place in Eishyshok. It is the same Eishyshok. The only noticeable alteration is anti-Semitism. It has finally reached us, but I hope that we will outlive our enemies." (562–563)

As had happened after the Big Fire of 1895, people who had suffered losses in the various fires of the 1930s took stock of their lives and considered whether to rebuild or emigrate—but now, due to all the restrictions on emigration, their options were limited. Mordekhai Munesh Kaleko was one of the lucky ones. After his house on Vilna Street burned down, he decided to leave. Shortly after receiving the highly coveted certificates of emigration from their children in 1935, he and his wife Mina made aliyah. For years, Mordekhai had been quoting the dire warnings of his children in Germany and Palestine, and the speeches of Yitzhak Gruenbaum and Vladimir Jabotinsky, who were rivals in many areas but agreed on one thing: the necessity of large-scale Jewish emigration from Poland. Now at last Mordekhai was following his own advice.

The Dubczanski family, who also lost a house to the Vilna Street fire, were less fortunate. Their daughter Vela Portnoy was not able to get them a certificate to join her in Palestine, and their daughter Gale Laufer was unable to get them emigration papers to join her in America. They rebuilt their house on Vilna Street. Leibke Sonenson, whose house had burned in 1936 in a padpalshchiki [Jewish arsonist] fire on Radun Street, also rebuilt. Though his brothers Moshe and Shepske pleaded with him not to do so, quoting Mordekhai Gebirtig's prophetic lines, "It burns, brothers dear, it burns! / Our poor little shtetl is on fire!" Leibke responded, "You may be pleased to raise your children in a rented house, but not me and Geneshe." Soon a beautiful new house was going up on the site of the old one, where Radun Street met the market square. Moshe Sonenson and his family continued to reside in the house he rented from Eliezer Remz. Moshe also took the precaution of converting a substantial portion of his income into gold, always considered a reliable currency in times of trouble. Later he would be burying part of his gold in the ground.

On the end of the abyss, the shtetl continued to go on with its life as normally as possible. In 1934 a fund-raiser for Vaad ha-Yeshivot, the umbrella organization for the yeshivot of Eastern Europe, successfully solicited donations from a number of Eishyshkians, including, of course, the always dedicated Rabbi Szymen Rozowski, who was active as both the local campaign organizer in Eishyshok and as a contributor. By 1939, however, a similar fund-raiser was proving less successful. Thus a 1939 letter to Vaad ha-Yeshivot from Rabbi Zusha Lichtig, the head of Eishyshok's yeshivah ketanah [elementary school], regretfully announced: "We have not as yet collected all the pledges. Those who are usually active in community work did not want to be involved with this, and we have had to find new people to do the collecting." Attached to the letter was a list of those who had contributed thus far, mainly balebatim [heads of households] in their forties or older. The younger people in the shtetl felt that in such hard times money collected in the shtetl should remain there, since its own yeshivah was underfunded.

The younger people were also continuing to monitor the events of the world with ever-increasing intensity, scanning the headlines for any relevant information they could glean. In a May 26, 1939, letter to his friend Fishke Shlanski (son of Zelig), in New York, Moshe "Deutch" Ginunski (so nicknamed because his father had been a POW in Germany) expressed their hunger for news, and for some understanding of how these global matters would affect them:

> Dear Fishke,
>
> The Eishyshkian news you know. All is as usual; here nothing ever changes. In the world things sound bad. Black clouds are gathering, with the latest instance being the quarrel over Danzig. Who knows what tomorrow will bring as a result? Surely we can anticipate some very unpleasant surprises. As for me, not so far in the future my turn as a soldier will come up.
>
> Dear friend, write to me how in your part of the world they are assessing the situation. Here in the local press there is not a thing about the situation in Poland. We are unable to find out anything about it. This is why I am asking you to write me what the American press is saying about it.

Moshe would be murdered in Eishyshok, along with his father, on September 25, 1941. (563–565)

COMMENTARY BY YEHUDA KURTZER

The specter of the loss of the memory of the Holocaust, with the passing on of the survivor generation, has loomed over Jewish communal life since the immediate aftermath of the Holocaust. This fear has inspired a remarkable industry of cultural production, the building of memorials, and genres of literature meant to capture the memories of the survivors for the benefit of those without those memories: to enshrine as fact, in monument and on paper, what might otherwise disappear as the vicissitudes of forgotten personal experience.

In the spring of 1993, the American (and American Jewish) commitment to the preservation of Holocaust memory took on new heft with the opening of the United States Holocaust Memorial Museum on the National Mall in Washington, D.C., the result of over a decade of intense politicking, fundraising, and no small amount of controversy about the question of how the tragedy would be commemorated, which other victims would be included, and how the story of the Holocaust could be "justified" as being of enough national concern to the American people to merit such a prominent place in the American preservationist pantheon. In the same year, Deborah Lipstadt's *Denying the Holocaust* was published, and it is easy to connect the two events: in both monumental architecture, and in the production of scholarship, American Jews—leaders and scholars—were crafting the counterclaim to an insurgent culture of Holocaust denial whether in its passive form of forgetting or in the active forms of revisionist and pseudo-history.

Lipstadt's book was the first and most systematic analysis of Holocaust denial (and profile of the most significant Holocaust deniers) at the time that it was published, and in retrospect served as a valuable manual to understand a phenomenon that would only intensify as the internet changed the nature of communications and networking among what had previously been a marginal community of deniers and revisionists. More significant, however, was the book's implicit juxtaposition of the agendas of understanding and documenting Holocaust denial together with mounting a response to it. And in many respects, the legal and political afterlife of the book has become its primary legacy. In the book Lipstadt had identified David Irving as a Holocaust denier and debunked his claims. Irving famously sued Lipstadt in British court for libel, which put the burden on the defense to support the merit of the original claim—in other words, to defend the historicity of the Holocaust. Lipstadt set aside much of her academic work for two decades to the case, in which she—and more importantly, the historical case—were vindicated.

Five years after the publication of *Denying the Holocaust*, Yaffa Eliach published *There Once Was a World*, what was to become the popular master-work connected to the ongoing archival work of the Center for Advanced Holocaust Studies at the museum. (The more comprehensive magisterial *Encyclopedia of Camps and Ghettos* continues to be produced, and already offers an indispensable resource to researchers and scholars.) Eliach's work chronicled the destroyed shtetl of Eishyshok over a 900-year period, and was twinned to "The Tower of Life"—a vertical spiral of 1,500 photographs of Eishyshok residents at the Museum. Together, the projects blur the line between the rigor of historical scholarship—which includes documenting what happened, and what was lost—and the memory-preservation culture that drives the building of museums and the affective, experiential elements of how memory is formed through image and pilgrimage.

Eliach's work also constitutes a late re-awakening of the genre of *yizker bikher* that had prevailed in earlier decades of Holocaust memory but since become dormant. The *yizker bikher* were independently produced, highly idiosyncratic collections of stories, maps, names, and remembered histories of shtetls and Jewish communities that were compiled by small groups of survivors in the first two decades after the war, and were usually published in small numbers for the survivors themselves. They defy classification in a single genre, though they share certain qualities of lyricism and urgency in trying to codify the fleeting memories of people in something firm that would endure past the time of their own infirmities. Eliach's book is, in essence, a *yizker bukh*—the story of a particular set of families in a particular place, organized towards memory more than rigid history—but its heft, its depth, and most importantly, its accessibility, makes it a *yizker bukh* that could transcend the idiosyncrasies that made the previous generations of such books inaccessible to the children and grandchildren of those that had produced them, and now leave them lining the shelves of used bookstores in Israel.

Both Lipstadt and Eliach's contributions to the literature of Jewish memory, however, surface a paradox inherent in Holocaust preservation. Memory, and especially Jewish memory, thrives in mimesis and in narrative transmission, which are vulnerable to the passage of time and to "mistakes" but are secure in the ways that they connect catalytic events to a transformed consciousness. Acts of codification, meanwhile, which attempt to preserve the authentic history of what happened, makes the official record of the events more secure, but it also inadvertently shifts the theater in which the legitimacy of memory is adjudicated from the consciousness to the public record. This, in turn, invites their litigation: sometimes by charlatans in court, like the Holocaust deniers whom Lipstadt indicts; and sometimes simply by the difficulty of trying to obligate people to take possession of a story that is meant to be their own, but is actually a piece of the past that does not correlate to their own lived experience. Commanding stories have moral meanings, and their facts are flexible; canonized history may be more accurate, but it can be depersonalized. Paradoxically, the activities that respond to the fear of the loss of the past create new risks.

Lipstadt and Eliach and their work is the generation-long bridge between those who remember the Shoah and those that are bidden to become the custodians of memory with no personal access to the stories except that which they have received. And Lipstadt and Eliach constitute bookends of sorts to the normative framework of the inheritance of memory as has shaped American Jewish memorial culture: between efforts to preserve the richness and complexity of what was lost, as Eliach tries to do; and the necessity to stave off the nitpickers and naysayers of the historical record, at which Lipstadt proves to be so adept.

But these are primary documents about memory themselves, and the lingering images from Lipstadt and Eliach's contributions make their own claim on the immutability of memory. Lipstadt's work transformed her life from scholar to dramatis personae in the preservation of the story of the Holocaust, yielding her subsequent book about the libel trial to which she was subjected in which she triumphantly—and tragically—proved the truth of the Holocaust in a British court. This first serious book on Holocaust denial bred her second, a personal chronicle of Holocaust denial that was also meant as cautionary tale, and then a feature film of the whole experience which enshrines the act of trying to preserve the past as a usable story for generations who would follow. And Eliach's book ends not with the usual catalog of catastrophe that ends most such *yizker bikher*, the tragic teleology that leaves its inheritors burdened with figuring out the future, but with the striking image of her survivor father dancing with Eliach's daughter—his granddaughter—at her wedding. The survivors—and their memories, and their future—endure in the lives of the custodians of memory.

12. Haym Soloveitchik, "Rupture and Reconstruction"

Haym Soloveitchik, "Rupture and Reconstruction," *Tradition* 28, No. 4 (Summer 1994)

Dr. Haym Soloveitchik (1937–) is Merkin Family Research Professor of Jewish History and Literature at Yeshiva University.

If I were asked to characterize in a phrase the change that religious Jewry has undergone in the past generation, I would say that it was the new and controlling role that texts now play in contemporary religious life. And in saying that, I open myself to an obvious question: What is new in this role? Has not traditional Jewish society always been regulated by the normative written word, the Halakhah? Have not scholars, for well over a millennium, pored over the Talmud and its codes to provide Jews with guidance in their daily round of observances? Is not Jewish religiosity proudly legalistic and isn't exegesis its classic mode of expression? Was not "their portable homeland," their indwelling in their sacred texts, what sustained the Jewish people throughout its long exile?

The answer is, of course, yes. However, as the Halakhah is a sweepingly comprehensive regula of daily life—covering not only prayer and divine service, but equally food, drink, dress, sexual relations between man and wife, the rhythms of work and patterns of rest—it constitutes a way of life. And a way of life is not learned but rather absorbed. Its transmission is mimetic, imbibed from parents and friends, and patterned on conduct regularly observed in home and street, synagogue and school.

Did these mimetic norms—the culturally prescriptive—conform with the legal ones? The answer is, at times, yes; at times, no. And the significance of the no may best be brought home by an example with which all are familiar—the kosher kitchen, with its rigid separation of milk and meat—separate dishes, sinks, dish racks, towels, tablecloths, even separate cupboards. Actually little of this has a basis in Halakhah. Strictly speaking, there is no need for separate sinks, for separate dishtowels or cupboards. In fact, if the food is served cold, there is no need for separate dishware altogether. The simple fact is that the traditional Jewish kitchen, transmitted from mother to daughter over generations, has been immeasurably and unrecognizably amplified beyond all halakhic requirements. Its classic contours are the product not of legal exegesis, but of the housewife's religious intuition imparted in kitchen apprenticeship. ...

Losing confidence in one's own authenticity means losing confidence in one's entitlement to power, that is, delegitimation, and a monopoly on authenticity swiftly becomes a monopoly on governance.

COMMENTARY BY YEHUDA KURTZER

The publication of Haym Soloveitchik's genre-bending essay "Rupture and Reconstruction" was an event in contemporary Modern Orthodoxy. The essay—first published in *Tradition*—circulated quickly through yeshivot and among the educational and intellectual elite, catalyzing several critical conversations. It remains a conceptual lightning rod in trying to understand the soul and the mind of Modern Orthodoxy, a subdenomination with an influence in American Judaism far greater than its size.

"Rupture and Reconstruction" is a work that is difficult to classify. It reflects an attempt by a historian and philosopher of Jewish law to understand the shifting dynamics around popular piety and the observance of Jewish law as they have changed in his lifetime in a community that he considers his own, in relationship to historical and social events through which he has lived; as a result the scholarship and tone of the article alternate between dispassionate analysis of intellectual and social history, anecdotal observation, the invested critique of an insider, and deeply personal lament.

The central idea of the essay is a distinction Soloveitchik draws between mimetic traditions—those passed along from parents to children through the modeling and imitation of lived behaviors—and scholastic traditions, especially in the form of books and responsa, in which the tradition is transmitted through codification and study. Soloveitchik argues, with reference to both memories of his own upbringing as well as to the history of the practice of Jewish law, that the mimetic has lost its central role in shaping Orthodox religiosity in light of a series of ruptures in the nineteenth and twentieth century that have remade traditional systems of authority and knowledge and replaced them with what Soloveitchik decries as structures of stricture and stringency. These in turn serve the narrowing of authority into the hands of the few, but also diminishes Jewish spirituality from the striving for and possibility of success to the constant fear of failure. In a system that privileges "maximum compliance," and makes possible such compliance in the form of detailed handbooks and manuals, Soloveitchik bears witness to a transformation of both the religious sensibilities and the power structures of contemporary Orthodoxy.

What Soloveitchik is seeking, conspicuous in its absence even as it is hard to define, is "authenticity," which is a keyword recurring frequently throughout the essay. Soloveitchik sees a loss of authenticity in the yielding of "traditional conduct," learned primarily in the home, to demands set by the performance of or acquiescence to strictures imposed in theoretical literature; in the shifting from home to school as the primary site for the imprinting of knowledge and identity; in granting knowledge of the text not just scholarly credibility but religious value; and then, ultimately, in attaching to the masters-of-the-text—the rabbinic leaders— actual political and social authority over the lives of their adherents. Soloveitchik draws a contrast between the premodern enclave, sealed from the outside but diffusing religious authority—and thus authenticity—among its members on the inside; and the modern open society, with its processes of acculturation, which compromise the community's ideas and ideals and require centralized authority structures to police the boundaries. Those in pursuit of knowledge became subject to the controllers of text, and yielded authority to them accordingly.

This fixation on an authenticity lost and the urgency to regain it betrays a powerful irony in Soloveitchik's argument. The very quest for authenticity itself is a quintessentially modern and American story, especially when it marshals nostalgia for a lost (or imagined) past as an instrument in its service. As demonstrated by both Stuart Charme and Arnold Eisen, this sort of nostalgia for a past—real or imagined—and its instrumentalization into the quest for a contemporary identity superior in the face of the debilitations invited by modernity is deeply characteristic of the modern American Jewish experience.[1] Soloveitchik criticizes his own milieux even as his essay represents the ideal type produced by it. The principal difference between Soloveitchik and other American Jewish elegiasts of the hallowed past is that for Soloveitchik it is his owned lived memory that he is describing as lost (even as most of the historical transformations that Soloveitchik describes as bringing about the fraying of traditional society long predate his own birth). Unlike the desire for the retrieval of an imagined past or a second naïveté, Soloveitchik wants to restore a grandeur he once experienced. Still, his very efforts constitutes a *case* of modern Judaism more than it does an indictment of it.

---

1   Arnold Eisen, *Rethinking Modern Judaism* (Chicago: University of Chicago Press, 1998); Stuart Z. Charme, "Varieties of Authenticity in Contemporary Jewish Identity," *Jewish Social Studies* 6, no. 20 (2000): 133–155.

Soloveitchik also elides the question of whether the gains of modernity and the fraying of traditional bonds may outweigh all that he sees as lost. Perhaps this is not his principal concern, but inasmuch as he quickly translates the loss of the traditional past into a set of political and moral indictments of the present, it forces the question of gains. A feminist lens provides the best window into this question. Soloveitchik repeatedly invokes the pedagogy and authority of the "home," and in one of the more famous formulations in the piece, locates powerful authenticity in what he calls "the housewife's religious intuition imparted in kitchen apprenticeship." This is Soloveitchik's highest testament of approval: it is through mimesis, mother through daughter, that the laws of kashrut were not just remembered and transmitted, but even legally *understood*. That it would become more religiously authentic and sincere to enact a new culture of strictures based on books becomes scandalous.

To the feminist reader, this particular example is the perfect site for negotiating the question of moral costs. I think Soloveitchik prides himself on this example because he knows that there is no greater way to indict the new traditionalists whom he sees as interlopers in his tradition than to discredit them through the housewife, and to hold up the housewife as the authentic transmitter of the tradition. But the cost is not merely that Soloveitchik has entirely domesticated women into the kitchen as the only site of their authority and authenticity; his argument also undermines the very possibility of women becoming authoritative in ways that depart from the kitchen. The rise of feminist Orthodoxy has long had to contend with the accusations by its critics that women cannot become authority figures or serve in rabbinic roles until they become fully learned in the tradition. If the rabbi's authority stems from his learning, the (slow) route towards the empowerment of women has to happen through the mastery of the texts. This may be oppressive and onerous, but it is also fundamentally more democratic. By the logic of the critics, if and when women do become masters of the tradition, opportunities for leadership and authority can follow. And indeed, the map of Orthodox institutions committed to teaching Torah to women—either oriented towards, or agnostic about, the eventual question of ordination—has flourished. Soloveitchik offers no such pathway. His skepticism about the correlation between book-knowledge and authority ultimately leaves women in the kitchen. They may have authority in that domain, but no power beyond it. When it comes to the question of whether there was more or less democracy in traditional power structures, we have to ask: democracy for whom?

And then there is the question, as is always the case with the construction of the past as a tool for the future, of whether the past in question is real or imagined. One of the great strengths of the piece is its emotional core, the evocative images that Soloveitchik conjures of the moments of piety of his youth, and by extension those of his premodern forebears. These indict the learned legalism of contemporary leaders, and the spiritual chasm that such learned authority perpetuates between the elites and Soloveitchik's imagined *erliche Yid*, the pious simple Jew. But this strength is also the tragedy of the essay. At the end of the essay, it emerges that Soloveitchik's deepest concern is for a loss of intimacy and immediacy with the Divine. This theological argument that comes at the end of what reads as a historical and sociological analysis, is at the end of the day the most important point. But it is the historical and sociological analysis—and the critique thereof—that has come to define the main legacy of the essay. We might phrase it this way: if for contemporary Orthodoxy, sincerity has been replaced with structures, it is the analysis of those structures—and not the seeking of that sincerity—that has defined the legacy of the reception of the essay identifying the shift.

Orthodox Jews will continue reading "Rupture and Reconstruction" for a long time. The essay has been described as "the most widely discussed" article in thirty years of *Tradition*. A commemorative twenty-fifth anniversary issue of *Tradition* devoted to the essay was published in 2019. And with good reason: Soloveitchik articulates with great drama Orthodoxy's version of "the Jewish problem," a yawning sensibility that the business of political emancipation and spiritual survival ultimately fall short of the larger theological and existential questions that a religious Jew was supposed to engage with, and that modernity has as yet failed to solve for these questions. And he offers a familiar but elusive postmodern response, a grasping for the past, whose mystique always offers some security in the face of discomforts about the present and anxieties about the future. Left unsaid and unknown, however, is that Orthodox Judaism continues to be ascendant in America and Israel, both as a percentage of the overall Jewish population but also increasingly in halls of Jewish leadership and where the agenda and identity of American Jewry are set and defined. It may be that the very technologies that Soloveitchik sees corrupting the spiritual core of Orthodoxy are essential to its actual thriving. Whether retrieval and rehabilitation—what Soloveitchik really means by "reconstruction"—are possible in response to the ruptures, without a crisis of numbers, remains to be seen.

13. Naomi Seidman,
"Elie Wiesel and the Scandal of Jewish Rage"

Naomi Seidman, "Elie Wiesel and the Scandal of Jewish Rage," *Jewish Social Studies*, New Series 3, No. 1 (1996)

Dr. Naomi Seidman (1960–) is Chancellor Jackman Professor in the Arts in the Department of Religion and the Centre for Diaspora and Transnational Studies at the University of Toronto.

The question I would put to the 1954 interview, then, is this one: What happened between these two men to explain the transformation of *Un di velt hot geshvign* into *La Nuit*, the survivor's political rage into his existentialist doubt? The encounter, it seems to me, could be described as a series of delicate negotiations, in which the survivor's first concession was to relinquish all talk (if not thought) of Jewish revenge—and why not? As an author whose audience crossed ethnic borders, it made sense for Wiesel to suppress an impossible fantasy whose clearest effect would be to alienate Christians. It is only in later writings that Wiesel makes the further move of seeing this failure to take revenge as a sign of Jewish moral triumph—a nearly Christian turning of the other cheek—rather than the unfortunate result of cowardice or realism. In an open letter "To a Young Palestinian Arab," Wiesel compares the Jewish response to their victimization with that of the Palestinians:

> We [survivors] consistently evoked our trials only to remind man of his need to be human—not of his right to punish. On behalf of the dead, we sought consolation, not retribution. In truth, the lack of violence among these survivors warrants examination. Why deny it? There were numerous victims who, before dying, ordered him or her who would survive to avenge their death. ... And yet ... with rare exceptions, the survivors forced themselves to sublimate their mandate for revenge. Whereas you ...

There is something disingenuous, it seems to me, about Wiesel's description of the Jews as having "sublimate[d] their mandate for revenge." This sublimation, after all, was Wiesel's ticket into the literature of non-Jewish Europe.

A final question, and one that echoes and reverses the question that ends *Un di velt hot geshvign*: Was it worth it? Was it worth translating the Holocaust out of the language of the largest portion of its victims and into the language of those who were, at best, absent, and at worst, complicitous in the genocide? Was it worth "unshattering" the mirror the Yiddish Elie breaks, reviving the image of the Jew as the Nazis wished him to be, as the Christian is prepared to accept him, the emblem of suffering silence rather than living rage? In the complex negotiations that resulted in the manuscript of *Night*, did the astonishing gains make good the tremendous losses? It is over this unspoken question that the culture of Holocaust discourse has arisen and taken shape.

COMMENTARY BY ERIN LEIB SMOKLER

In 1996, Professor Naomi Seidman took a risk. She pried open a work of canonical importance, penned by a man of iconic significance. *Night*, by Elie Wiesel, had been translated into thirty languages and would sell (ironically) more than six million copies in the United States alone. It had become *the* Holocaust tale and Wiesel had become *the* Survivor, the voice from the ashes of Auschwitz. His eye-witness testimony was invaluable and "beyond criticism" to most.[1] His moral conscience inspired a generation and a 1986 Nobel Peace prize. "Auschwitz is as important as Sinai," he famously said.[2] A dim revelation took place during the time of the Holocaust, and Wiesel was the Moses who both heard and transmitted its message.

Seidman's essay, "Elie Wiesel and the Scandal of Jewish Rage," removed *Night* from its sacred perch. It asked readers to consider Wiesel's book as not only a constructed work of art, but as a deliberate act of memory-making, even of survivor-making. In telling the complex history of its writing—from the Yiddish version, *Un di velt hot geshvign* (*And the World Kept Silent*), published in 1956 in Buenos Aires, to the French version, *La Nuit* (*Night*), published in 1958 (to say nothing of the English and Hebrew versions, which add their own complexities)—Seidman showed how the book was condensed and subtly yet radically

1   Ruth Franklin, *A Thousand Darknesses: Lies and Truth in Holocaust Fiction* (New York: Oxford University Press, 2011), 69.
2   Naomi Seidman, "Elie Wiesel and the Scandal of Jewish Rage," *Jewish Social Studies* 3, no. 1 (1996): 2.

transformed over time. From Yiddish to French, it moved from an act of detailed reportage, full of anger and calls for vengeance, to a more sanitized, sacralized work; from a piece of testimony and political outrage to one of existential and theological reflection; from an insider's grappling with Jewish disappointment in the world to a more universal, arguably Christological, engagement with divine silence. "There are two survivors, then," she concludes, "a Yiddish and a French" (8). There is one survivor, largely lost to history, alive with Jewish rage—against the world, against God, and against a self consumed by suffering and victimhood. And then there is the survivor who survived, helped along by his French Catholic writer-friend, François Mauriac. That survivor is meek, haunted by death, overwhelmed by silence. That survivor "is no longer the enraged seeker of revenge but rather a religiously potent emblem of martyrdom" (16). And it is that survivor, insinuates Seidman, indeed that Jew, who can live on, for that survivor is palatable to the world: he is less threatening, less angry, less empowered. *The* Survivor, it turns out, is actually a character of cultivated quietism.

In light of this evolution, Seidman ends her essay with a devastating question: "Was it worth it? … [Was it worth] reviving the image of the Jew as the Nazis wished him to be, as the Christian is prepared to accept him, the emblem of suffering silence rather than living rage?" It seems that her answer is likely no. And yet, as scholars would argue in the years following, there is more than one way to understand editorial choices over time, more than one way to account for shifts between languages, and more than one way to contend with the formation of memory.

"Elie Wiesel and the Scandal of Jewish Rage" invited a fair share of Jewish rage upon publication. Seidman was accused of a "brand of Holocaust revisionism [that] is more deadly than Holocaust denial. … [I]t is a corrosive poison that destroys from within."[3] Having disrupted the integrity of Wiesel's oeuvre, she was branded a traitor by some. To turn a critical lens on the voice of the Holocaust was to undermine the Holocaust itself. Though other scholars came to Seidman's defense, and called for the decoupling of source-criticism from historical revisionism, it must be noted that this article has indeed come to be used as evidence for it. In its most extreme expression, Seidman has been cited by Holocaust deniers as proof of Wiesel's unreliability as a witness to an altogether exaggerated event. If he can tell his story in multiple ways, it must be because the story itself, and therefore the Holocaust itself, is fabricated. Less extreme

---

3   Peter Manseau, "Revising Night: Elie Wiesel and the Hazards of Holocaust Theology," *Crosscurrents* 56, no. 3 (2006): 387–399.

expressions of this kind of "gotcha" thinking make a sport of the source criticism, comparing the Yiddish, French, Hebrew, and English versions for notes of inconsistency and thus inaccuracy. Seidman's article opened up a thirst to question the facticity of the Holocaust memoir.

Here is where Seidman's long-standing contribution lays, however. *Night* is not a memoir in the strictest sense. It is a work of art. Or, as Ruth Franklin notes in *A Thousand Darknesses*, a hybrid genre variously called a "novel/autobiography," "non-fictional novel," "semi-fictional memoir," "fictional-autobiographical memoir," "fictionalized autobiographical memoir," or "memoir-novel."[4] The deliberate craft that Seidman exposed, the process of revision and redirection that clearly gave rise to the product, was one of artistic construction. The ability to see that and not to shy away from it lest the sacred text be corrupted: that was what Seidman offered. The willingness to appreciate the creation of memory and the persona of the survivor: that is the true scandal of the "Scandal of Jewish Rage." Seidman charted the development of Wiesel from raw observer to self-conscious witness and in so doing rendered him, and Holocaust literature more broadly, no longer "beyond criticism" and ever so much richer.

Seidman also provoked one more kind of rage, aimed not at the book, but at the man. With her portrayal of the "sad, sad" survivor, she unleashed a sharp critique of the tenor of the witness Wiesel offered, the quiet, dignified, restrained grief that he embodied.[5] Ron Rosenbaum, for example, citing Seidman, accused Wiesel of "gentrifying the Holocaust."[6] With his gentle comportment and his refusal to rage, Wiesel made Jewish anger unseemly, says Rosenbaum, for other Jews and for a world interacting with Jews. With his emphasis on silence and the impossibility of representing the Holocaust, Wiesel silenced others and perverted in perpetuity the image of the survivor and the Jew.

Though this kind of ad hominem attack is brutally harsh, it points to the continuing power that Seidman's essay holds over those who think about the literature of the Holocaust and its legacy. Rosenbaum might be unforgiving, but his essential claim—that the way that the survivor is cast informs the way that we understand his trauma and tell his story (and our own)—stands. This too is part of what Seidman unlocked. She called attention to the grand implications of storytelling on our own self-understanding. Storytellers cannot be separated

---

4   Franklin, *A Thousand Darknesses*, 72.

5   Ron Rosenbaum, "Elie Wiesel's Secret," *Tablet*, September 29, 2017.

6   Ibid.

from the stories they tell, the events to which they bear witness, and the identities and theologies to which they give rise.

Elie Wiesel called the Holocaust "the ultimate event, the ultimate mystery, never to be comprehended or transmitted."[7] He wrote: "Auschwitz is something else, always something else. It is a universe outside the universe, a creation that exists parallel to creation. Auschwitz lies on the other side of life and on the other side of death."[8] Naomi Seidman helped bring the Holocaust back to this side of life and Elie Wiesel out from the specter of death.

---

7   Ibid, 85.
8   Elie Wiesel, "Art and the Holocaust: Trivializing Memory," *New York Times,* June 11, 1989.

14. *Dabru Emet*

Dabru Emet, New York Times, September 10, 2000

In recent years, there has been a dramatic and unprecedented shift in Jewish and Christian relations. Throughout the nearly two millennia of Jewish exile, Christians have tended to characterize Judaism as a failed religion or, at best, a religion that prepared the way for, and is completed in, Christianity. In the decades since the Holocaust, however, Christianity has changed dramatically. An increasing number of official Church bodies, both Roman Catholic and Protestant, have made public statements of their remorse about Christian mistreatment of Jews and Judaism. These statements have declared, furthermore, that Christian teaching and preaching can and must be reformed so that they acknowledge God's enduring covenant with the Jewish people and celebrate the contribution of Judaism to world civilization and to Christian faith itself.

Christians can respect the claim of the Jewish people upon the land of Israel

The most important event for Jews since the Holocaust has been the reestablishment of a Jewish state in the Promised Land. As members of a biblically based religion, Christians appreciate that Israel was promised—and given—to Jews as the physical center of the covenant between them and God. Many Christians support the State of Israel for reasons far more profound than mere politics. As Jews, we applaud this support. We also recognize that Jewish tradition mandates justice for all non-Jews who reside in a Jewish state.

COMMENTARY BY MARCIE LENK

In the mid-1960s three of the most influential rabbis in the United States published public statements indicating what each felt to be the proper attitude of Jews with regards to Christians and Christianity. Rabbi Joseph Soloveitchik delivered a paper entitled "Confrontation" at a 1964 conference of the Rabbinical Council of America.[1] Rabbi Abraham Joshua Heschel published an article entitled "No

---

1   Joseph B. Soloveitchik, "Confrontation," *Tradition: A Journal of Orthodox Jewish Thought* 6, no. 2 (1964): 5–29.

Religion is an Island" in 1966.[2] Rabbi Moshe Feinstein wrote two responsa in 1967 including "Concerning the Prohibition Against Attendance at a Meeting with Christians on Matters of Rapprochement in Faith and Association with Them." Soloveitchik acknowledged that Jews and Christians must encounter each other in day-to-day life, "In the secular sphere, we may discuss positions to be taken, ideas to be evolved and plans to be formulated."[3] Discussions of theology, however, were off-limits. Heschel insisted that Jews and Christians need to work together as people of faith and as human beings in our shared universe, "The religions of the world are no more self-sufficient, no more independent, no more isolated than individuals or nations."[4] Feinstein rejected both of these approaches, considering any Jewish dialogue with Christians fraught with the danger of evangelism. In the words of Rav Moshe, "a plague has now broken out in many locales on account of the initiative of the new pope, whose only intent is to cause all the Jews to abandon their pure and holy faith so that they will accept Christianity."[5]

Feinstein's reference to the "initiative of the new pope" was an acknowledgement of *Nostra Aetate*, a ground-breaking and theology-shaking statement about Judaism which emerged from the Second Vatican Council, and famously proclaimed that "what happened in [Jesus's] passion cannot be charged against all the Jews, without distinction, then alive, nor against the Jews of today" and warned against "hatred, persecutions, displays of anti-Semitism, directed against Jews at any time and by anyone."[6] The biggest and most authoritative church body in the world was beginning a process of

---

2   Abraham Joshua Heschel, "No Religion is an Island," *Union Seminary Quarterly Review* 21, no. 2 (1966), 117–134.

3   Soloveitchik, "Confrontation," 24.

4   Heschel, "No Religion is an Island," 119.

5   *Iggerot Moshe, Yoreh Deah* 3:43, translated by David Ellenson in his "A Jewish Legal Authority Addresses Jewish-Christian Dialogue: Two Responsa of Rabbi Moshe Feinstein," *The American Jewish Archives Journal* 52, nos. 1–2 (2000): 113–128.

6   *Nostra Aetate* is the "Declaration on the Relation of the Church to Non-Christian Religions," which emerged as part of the move of the Catholic Church towards *aggiornamento* [bringing things up to date]. The brief 1965 declaration was followed by Catholic and Catholic-Jewish committees which considered the issues raised by *Nostra Aetate* and have published many statements in its spirit since on a variety of theological and spiritual issues up until the present. These decades also saw statements by the Lutheran World Federation (1964, 1982), the United Methodist Church (1972), the Presbyterian Church USA, the United Church of Christ, the Mennonite European Regional conference (1977), the Synod of the Protestant Church of the Rhineland (1980)—all decrying anti-Semitism and calling for a constructive engagement with Jews and Judaism. All of these statements (and more) can be found on the denominational websites. They have also been gathered together in the *Dialogika* project of the Council of Centers on Jewish-Christian Relations: http://www.ccjr.us/dialogika-resources.

acknowledging the wrongs in creed and in deed of the Church towards the Jewish people. What was to be the Jewish response? Would Jews trust that this was a real change in Church attitude? Would Jews really be accepted and respected *as Jews* by Christians? Should Jews pay any attention at all to internal Christian statements?

In addition to the three rabbis cited above, a number of individual Jewish leaders and scholars—Eugene Borowitz, Irving Greenberg, and Jacob Neusner among others—did respond to *Nostra Aetate* in the years after its publication, but their writings, as well as the 1965 Catholic statement, others from the Catholic, Protestant, and Orthodox Churches, as well as from interfaith organizations, remained (and remain) little known among Jews. *Dabru Emet* was the first American Jewish communal response to *Nostra Aetate* and the change of attitude towards Judaism from most Christian denominations. *Dabru Emet* appeared as a two-page spread in the *New York Times* on September 10, 2000. By then most Christian denominations had issued statements, changed liturgy, and added courses on the Shoah and Judaism in their schools and seminaries. Respecting and taking seriously this work of Christians, the writers and signers of *Dabru Emet* were ready to publicly challenge the common assumption that Jews either had little to learn from Christians or that engagement with Christians and Christianity remains a danger to Jews. As Christians have reassessed their ideas and theology about Jews and Judaism, there was a sense among these scholars that the time had come for Jews to reassess their ideas and theology about Christians and Christianity. According to one author, "Dabru Emet is not a definitive statement. It is the beginning of a discussion first among Jews themselves."[7]

Dabru Emet was developed from eight years of discussions of "The Jewish Scholars Group on Christianity," originally sponsored by the Institute for Christian and Jewish Studies in Baltimore, and authored by Tikva Frymer-Kensky, Peter Ochs, David Novak, and Michael A. Signer. The signatories were rabbis (mostly liberal) and academics. The statement did not emerge from the organized Jewish community—official organizations (AJC, ADL, or Jewish Federation) or denominational organizations. *Dabru Emet* appeared in the *New York Times* and the *Baltimore Sun*, where it was widely seen, in coordination with the publication of a companion volume, *Christianity in Jewish Terms*.[8]

---

7   Michael A. Signer, "*Dabru Emet*: A Contextual Analysis," *Théologiques* 11, nos. 1–2 (2003): 187–202.

8   Tikva Frymer-Kensky, David Novak, Peter Ochs, David Fox Sandmel, Michael A. Signer (eds.), *Christianity in Jewish Terms* (Boulder, CO: Westview Press, 2000).

The appearance of *Dabru Emet* elicited much support,[9] but also strong critique. The official Orthodox response, authored by Dr. David Berger, declared that the call to reconsider Jewish theology was "fraught with danger," insisting that Christianity is *avodah zarah* (idolatry), and summarizing *Dabru Emet* as "relativistic."[10] A. James Rudin of the AJC argued that *Dabru Emet* was too uncritical of Christian responsibilities for Nazi anti-Semitism.[11] The strongest and most specific critique came in a series of articles by Jon D. Levenson who argued that imprecision in many statements in *Dabru Emet* led to falsehoods.[12] Levenson felt that the statement ignored or obscured differences between Christianity and Judaism which remain important to both Christians and Jews. He declared that *Dabru Emet* showed "the disturbing tendency to hide from inconvenient differences." Authors and supporters of *Dabru Emet* published responses, acknowledging that any short statement about something so complex will obscure and lack depth and pointing to the companion volume, *Christianity in Jewish Terms*, to further explore the issues raised in the statement.

Since *Dabru Emet*, many Jewish academics and spiritual leaders have embraced changes in Jewish-Christian relations and are considering the implications of these changes for intergroup cooperation and for Jewish self-understanding. If *Dabru Emet* oversimplified or obfuscated, it did succeed in challenging Jews to consider the meanings for Jews of Christian changes in theology and attitude about Judaism. Since the initial responses, many more articles and books on related themes have been published, as well as a commentary on the New Testament, *The Jewish Annotated New Testament*, written entirely by Jewish scholars. Recent decades have seen growth in Jewish Studies courses in universities, including in Christian universities and departments of theology. Jewish, Christian, and interfaith organizations have published more developed statements, and the half-century anniversary of *Nostra Aetate* even

---

9   David Rosen, "'Dabru Emet': Its Significance for the Jewish-Christian Dialogue," Dutch Council of Christians and Jews (OJEC) at Tilburg, The Netherlands, November 6, 2001.

10 David Berger, "Statement by Dr. David Berger regarding the New York Times ad by Dabru Emet," September 14, 2000, accessed July 9, 2019, https://advocacy.ou.org/statement_by_dr_david_berger_regarding_the_new_york_times_ad_by_dabru_emet/.

11 A. James Rudin, "Dabru Emet: A Jewish Dissent," accessed July 9, 2019, http://www.jcrelations.net/Dabru+Emet%27%3A+A+Jewish+Dissent.2349.0.html?L=3.

12 Jon D. Levenson, "How Not to Conduct Jewish–Christian Dialogue," *Commentary* 112, no. 5 (December 2001): 31–37, with a reply to correspondents in "Controversy: Jewish–Christian Dialogue, Jon D. Levenson & Critics," *Commentary* 113, no. 4 (April 2002): 17–21; Jon D. Levenson, "The Agenda of Dabru Emet," *Review of Rabbinic Judaism* 7 (2004): 1–26.

brought two statements by Orthodox rabbis showing willingness and desire to consider Christianity as an expression of God's will.[13]

Public statements like *Dabru Emet* have provoked study, conversation, and a deeper understanding of the other. Still, challenges remain:

- Most statements, including *Dabru Emet,* are composed and consumed by professional interfaith representatives. How much trickles down to the average Jew?
- Jewish institutions use their limited time to educate Jews about Judaism, leaving very little time to try to understand Christianity on its own terms.
- How do new Jewish-Christian alliances affect views of other groups? For example, are Jews and Christians working for or against improved relations with Muslims?
- The State of Israel is often the elephant in the room, the topic off-limits in interfaith dialogue. Still, Jewish-Christian relations are sometimes judged by Jews on how much support is expressed for Israel. Some Christians who have moved the furthest from anti-Semitism and replacement theology are the ones who are critical of Israel, and others who are devoted supporters of Israel maintain traditional replacement theology.

Dabru Emet called for Jews to respond to changes in Christianity. It remains for religious leaders and scholars to think about assumptions, traditions, and actions, challenging us to live deeply within our own communities while considering God's plan not only for ourselves, but also for the rest of humanity.

---

13 "Between Jerusalem and Rome: Reflections on 50 Years of Nostra Aetate," Statement of the Conference of European Rabbis, The Rabbinical Council of America, and the Chief Rabbinate of Israel (August 31, 2017).

15. Jonathan D. Sarna, *American Judaism: A History*

Jonathan D. Sarna, *American Judaism: A History*, New Haven: Yale University Press, 2004

Dr. Jonathan D. Sarna (1955–) is University Professor and Joseph H. & Belle R. Braun Professor of American Jewish History at Brandeis University, where he directs the Schusterman Center for Israel Studies. He is also Chief Historian of the National Museum of American Jewish history.

With so many questions and issues and tensions confronting them, it comes as no surprise that as they approach their 350th anniversary on American soil, Jews feel bewildered and uncertain. Should they focus on quality to enhance Judaism or focus on quantity to increase the number of Jews? Embrace intermarriage as an opportunity for outreach or condemn it as a disaster for offspring? Build religious bridges or fortify religious boundaries? Strengthen religious authority or promote religious autonomy? Harmonize Judaism with contemporary culture or uphold Jewish tradition against contemporary culture? Compromise for the sake of Jewish unity or stand firm for cherished Jewish principles?

Simultaneously, indeed, Jews witness two contradictory trends operating in their community, assimilation and revitalization. Which will predominate and what the future holds nobody knows. That will be determined day by day, community by community, Jew by Jew.

Regularly, American Jews hear, as I did at the start of my career from a scholar at a distinguished rabbinical seminary—and as other Jews did in colonial times, and in the era of the American Revolution, and in the nineteenth century, and in the twentieth century—that Judaism in America is doomed, that assimilation and intermarriage are inevitable. Should high rates of intermarriage continue and the community grow complacent, that may yet prove true.

But history, as we have seen, also suggests another possibility: that today, as so often before, American Jews will find creative ways to maintain and revitalize American Judaism. With the help of visionary leaders, committed followers, and generous philanthropists, it may still be possible for the current "vanishing" generation of American Jews to be succeeded by another "vanishing" generation, and then still another.

"A nation dying for thousands of years," the great Jewish philosopher Simon Rawidowicz once observed, "means a living nation. Our incessant dying means uninterrupted living, rising, standing up, beginning anew." His message, delivered to Jews agonizing over the loss of 6 million of their compatriots, applies equally well today in the face of contemporary challenges to Jewish continuity. "If we are the last—let us be the last as our fathers and forefathers were. Let us prepare the ground for the last Jews who will come after us, and for the last Jews who will rise after them, and so on until the end of days." (373–374)

COMMENTARY BY MARC DOLLINGER

What's the difference between a rabbi and a Jewish Studies professor? That question, which could be the opening of a very bad joke, confronts Jewish scholars of the American Jewish experience who must navigate between the academic rules of critical analysis and their own personal love of Judaism and Jewish life. Rabbis know their jobs: building and strengthening Jewish life. Jewish Studies professors know their jobs: subjecting Judaism to the highest levels of impartial critique. What happens when a Jewish Studies scholar who is also a participant in Jewish life offers critical analysis that contradicts accepted communal beliefs or the attempts of the local Jewish rabbi to build and strengthen community? This dynamic puts some Jewish Studies professors in a no-win situation. Books that celebrate Jewish life fail the scholar's test of analytic objectivity. Treatments that criticize Jewish life can place professors at odds with their own religious communities. Jonathan D. Sarna's *American Judaism: A History* is one example of a work that bridges the chasm between the two. His already canonical work, a winner of the 2004 National Jewish Book Award, engages the most important historiographic questions for scholars. At the same time, Sarna also integrates the communal goals of rabbinic leadership with the professorial mandate of critical writing. With this navigation, his work rises to become the classic volume of Jewish Studies scholarship intended for his colleagues and for lay readers as well, especially as he makes no apologies for celebrating the American Jewish experience.

Published on the occasion of American Jewry's 350th anniversary, Sarna's 490-page *American Judaism: A History*, earned commendations from the Koret

Jewish Book Awards, Publishers Weekly, the American Jewish Historical Society, and the *Los Angeles Times*, where it enjoyed bestseller status, in addition to its National Jewish Book Award. Undergraduates read Sarna's book as the standard text in both American Jewish history and American Judaism courses while graduate students in Jewish Studies mine its pages both for large thematic frames as well as new interpretations of often-told episodes in the American Jewish experience.

The book traces the religious development of American Jews from their origins in mid-seventeenth-century colonial New Amsterdam to the early twenty-first century. It chronicles an American Jewish community mediating between the opportunities offered by Constitutionally-protected religious freedom and the threats to Jewish life posed by this voluntaristic approach to Judaism. Sarna searches for a better understanding of what it meant and what it might mean to practice Judaism in a pluralist, democratic nation.

Sarna presents a religious view of American Jews modeled on the path-breaking work of Sydney E. Ahlstrom, whose epic volume *A Religious History of the American People* provided much of the argumentative framing for *American Judaism*. An author of numerous books, articles, and even other synthetic treatments of American Jewish history, Sarna crafted his project as "the culmination of over thirty years of sustained interest in the history of American Judaism" (ix). With an integration of religion and history, he redefines multiple fields of academic inquiry just as he proffers a volume that interested lay readers will find important and valuable.

American Judaism dives into several of the most important questions in the historiography of American Jewish life, offering new and controversial perspectives on critical debates facing scholars and Jewish community leaders alike. In both its methodological approach and expansive content, Sarna's tome pushes all of us to reconsider some basic assumptions about the nature of Judaism, and even religion itself, on American shores.

First, Sarna's work asks us to consider the very purpose of university-level Jewish Studies scholarship. Asked another way, what *is* the difference between a rabbi and a Jewish Studies professor? While a rabbi seeks to develop stronger, better Jews as building blocks to Jewish communal strength, a Jewish Studies professor generally insulates herself from larger identity-based imperatives. She wants to judge Jewish sources by the same standards established throughout the academy: critical, third-person analysis unbounded to larger questions of one's personal belief system or the sources' impact on Jewish continuity. According to this classic view of the university, Jewish Studies professors must write from a dispassionate place, signaling a profound difference from the role of the congregational rabbi. Even as most Jewish Studies academics claim Jewish heritage, their decision to pursue professional lives within the university signals a willingness, if not a desire, to place their own religious identities on the margins. They will tell the truth, regardless of communal impact.

Elsewhere in the university, over the last few decades scholars from historically marginalized communities have often taken a different approach, seeking to leverage the university and higher education as a catalyst to bring needed social change. They regard their ethno/racial group's communal health as central to their academic mission. Even as many criticize a willingness to engage contemporary political issues in their classes, ethnic studies scholars tend to embrace what academics call "the identity project." Professors from disenfranchised groups understand categories such as race, gender, and class as central to their professional lives and to their role as classroom teachers. They strive to bring a deeper sense of consciousness to their students. To divorce themselves from the social truths their communities face day-to-day, to pretend to embrace the classic model of the university as a dispassionate place, would prove an abdication of the very privileges they enjoy as highly educated, and often tenured, members of university faculties.

Even as most Jewish Studies scholars distance themselves from this sort of identity-based approach to teaching and writing, Sarna dives right in, offering *American Judaism* as a volume dedicated to telling the story of American Jews to a readership interested in strengthening the Jewish community. He does not feign disinterest nor does he wish to offer a detached view of his subjects. Instead, Sarna lauds American Jews who, "over and over again for 350 years ... rose to meet the challenges both internal and external that threatened Jewish continuity" (xiv). In an American experience that some observers feared would fate Judaism "sooner or later to disappear" (xiii), Sarna pushes back, telling the story of a complicated engagement with the opportunities created by church/ state separation and the threats those very protections posed to a population of Jews who could enjoy their American experience without a strong sense of religious conviction. As Sarna writes, the history of American Judaism witnessed generation after generation of Jews purging older ways of Jewish expression and "reinventing American Judaism in an attempt to make it more appealing, more meaningful, more sensitive to the concerns of the day" (xiv). While he does chronicle moments of communal weakness, Sarna celebrates a population of Jews that, over time, returned to their faith, resisted the forces of assimilation, and ultimately told "a story of revitalization" (xiv).

American Judaism earned its place in the Jewish Studies canon with three important contributions to the historiography. First, the volume offers a lengthy analysis of religious developments during the colonial and early national periods. With the notable exception of Jacob Rader Marcus's epic three-volume, 1,713-page history of colonial American Jews, most American Jewish historians have paid short shrift to the early period, focusing instead on the twentieth-century experience of eastern European immigrants and their descendants. Earlier generations of scholars could not see the significance of the country's first practitioners of Judaism beyond what Marcus had chronicled. Not so with Sarna. He sees in colonial America the development of the synagogue-community model of religious expression. "Already in the late colonial period," Sarna argues, "American Judaism had begun to diverge from religious patterns that existed in Europe and the Caribbean" (xvii). Placing the Jews' house of worship at the center, Sarna describes how Jewish communities flourished. By the 1820s, though, a critical transformation occurred, lost on scholars who moved too quickly through the period. In what he considers "the first dramatic turning point in the history of American Judaism," the "synagogue-community" model that offered a more unified vision of Jewish religious expression gave way to a "community of synagogues" open to a plurality of different approaches to Judaism (xviii).

Second, Sarna abandons the generational approach to American Jewish history so common to many of us who learned about the "German" immigration of the nineteenth century followed by the eastern European wave of new arrivals in the twentieth. While most scholars deploy generational status to periodize their work, *American Judaism* argues that American Jews forged identities born more from the cultures surrounding them than from a static definition of American Judaism rooted only in their nation of origin or era of immigration. Sarna rejects "the false and tunnel-visioned assumptions that Jews are more influenced by their 'generation in America' than by their sur-roundings and the events of their day" (xix). To read this book is to abandon whatever you may have assumed about how or why American Jews engaged their Judaism as they did.

Finally, Sarna offers a new understanding of causality, the scholar's word identifying why history unfolded as it did, for the rapid social mobility of American Jews. Rooted in his religious interpretation of American Jewish history, Sarna credits the Jews' status as the nation's "largest and most visible non-Christian faith" (xv) for encouraging Judaism on American shores. While other non-Christian religious groups, and especially those from non-Western traditions, faced persecution, Jewish immigrants and their descendants enjoyed privilege as Christianity's religious forerunner. As Will Herberg argued in his path-breaking 1955 volume *Protestant-Catholic-Jew*, American Jews enjoyed one-third of the nation's religious heritage at a time when Jews constituted but a tiny fraction of the larger population. Thanks to this status, American Jews claimed significance beyond the narrow limits of their own religious communities. As Sarna argues, American Jews extended "the boundaries of American pluralism, serving as a model for other religious minorities and, in time, expanding the definition of American religious liberty so that they (and other minorities) might be included as equals" (xv). Ultimately, Sarna concludes that the positive impact of Jews on American religious life helped the nation expand its understanding of religious difference, especially among those who do not profess Christian beliefs.

When selecting the most important works in the field of Jewish Studies, *American Judaism* emerges as the essential volume on American Jewish religious life. It packs a narrative forged from important primary sources as it reads those documents in creative new ways. It spans the entirety of the American Jewish experience, detailing the nexus between Judaism and Americanism from a century before independence through the dawn of the twenty-first century. Ultimately, it offers its Jewish readers a scholarly treatment of their own religious history while it provides a compelling frame for academics in other religious spheres to investigate.

16. David Weiss Halivni, *Breaking the Tablets: Jewish Theology After the Shoah*

David Weiss Halivni, *Breaking the Tablets: Jewish Theology After the Shoah*, Lanham, MD: Rowman & Littlefield Publishers, 2007

Rabbi Dr. David Weiss Halivni (1927–) is a Holocaust survivor and Professor of Religion Emeritus at Columbia University, where he held the Lucius N. Littauer Chair in Classical Jewish Civilization.

To understand the full meaning of this prayer, we must first reflect deeply on the question that grounds all Holocaust theology: *Do we attribute the Shoah to sin?* Lest there be any doubt about my own response to this question, I will state my conclusions at the outset. *It is written in the Torah, a second time in the Prophets, a third time in the Writings, and a fourth time in the words of our sages, that the Shoah was not the consequence of sin.* (17)

I sympathize with those who claim that in order for a person to achieve responsibility for his actions, he must first be fully free, without any obstacles and external influences. To be sure, the knowledge of good and evil itself influences a person to choose the good; but, when he chooses evil, he must, in order to merit the punishment, have committed evil fully out of free choice, without any external intervention. Any kinds of intervention, even from God, reduces a person's responsibility for his actions. It is possible, therefore, that God will remain aloof. In order not to diminish a person's freedom to act—and thereby diminish his responsibility—God may stand apart, facing utter evil without intervening and without responding. Something like this happened in the time of the Shoah. God did not intervene and did not respond but stood apart. (31–32)

Intentionally, I have not made any use of the concept of "the hiding of God's face" (*hester panim*) that is so prevalent in the literature of Holocaust theology. According to this concept, God hid His face during the time of the Shoah and allowed whatever happened to happen. I reject this notion, because, as indicated in Deuteronomy, the "hiding of God's face" arises as a consequence of sin (31:17–18). This meaning appears explicitly in Isaiah: "Your sins have made Him turn His face away and refuse to hear you" (59:2). If we believed that, "the hiding of God's face" prevailed during the Shoah, then it would be as if we attributed the Shoah to sin, which is the very notion that we have rejected. God, as it were, restrained Himself from taking part in history and gave humanity an opportunity to display its capacities, for good or for evil. It is our misfortune that, in the time of the Shoah, humanity displayed its capacities for unprecedented evil. (32)

COMMENTARY BY DANIEL H. WEISS

A notable feature of David Weiss-Halivni's *Breaking the Tablets: Jewish Theology After the Shoah* is the parallel between his orientation towards the Shoah and his orientation towards engagement with Jewish texts. In other thinkers, these topics might be treated as highly disparate, but for Halivni, the struggles and challenges Jews face with regard to the former are inseparable from the challenges that they face with regard to the latter. In both cases, Halivni puts forth the counterintuitive stance that embracing a certain type of pessimism can in fact lead not to despair but rather to hope and to life.

With regard to the Shoah, Halivni uncompromisingly insists that the Nazi Holocaust should not and must not be explained as punishment for sins committed by members of the community of Israel. In order to support this position, he works through texts drawn from the Torah, from the Prophets, from the Writings, and from rabbinic literature, arguing that while God can indeed *punish* Israel for its sins, God has promised that God will never *destroy* Israel for its sins. Because the Shoah constituted such a major destruction and annihilation not only of individual Jewish lives, but of entire Jewish communities, cultures, and institutions, particularly in Eastern Europe, it cannot be thought of as a punishment for Israel's sins. This is a bold move on Halivni's part: other major events from Israel's past (including the destruction of the First and Second Temples) may be attributed to Israel's sins, but a destruction so great as the Shoah cannot be attributed to sin.

While Halivni's approach does avoid the problem of "blaming the victims" of the Shoah, which is no small achievement for a theological argument based on traditional Jewish texts, it does leave open the question of: if we don't make use of "punishment for sins," then how, theologically speaking, are we to account for the Shoah? While attributing the Shoah to Israel's sin may be highly problematic to moral conscientiousness, one must acknowledge that it does have the advantage of providing an answer in response the despairing cry of "Why?" By contrast, Halivni insists that the best and the right thing to do is to remain with our uncomfortable lack of good explanations, rather than try falsely to resolve our anxiety by explanations that are ultimately insufficient and harmful. Halivni appeals to the kabbalistic concept of *tzimtzum*, in which God deliberately contracts or withdraws God's direct presence from the created world in order to enable and affirm created beings' independence and free will. Yet, Halivni presents this theological idea not primarily in order to provide a reassuring explanation, but in order to say that while in principle all earthly events may be linked to a hidden divine cause or reason, the most appropriate response for us as mere humans to an event such as the Shoah is deliberately to treat it as an "unsolved enigma" (26).

In an important sense, Halivni's "pessimism" regarding the present impossibility of explanation enables us to preserve a robust sense of moral conscience, even in the face of an event that has ruptured Jewish spiritual life and cannot be healed by false balms. At the same time, this lack does not mean that all hope is lost: there remains a hope for the future even without having an explanation for the past. We can recognize that there are events that cannot and should not be conceived of as deserved or as just—yet we can still pray for a messianic future in God's sovereignty that will manifest on earth and in which justice and righteousness do reign (36–37).

When, later in the book, Halivni turns to the status and importance of Jewish textual study and engagement, we find a similar dynamic at play. While he affirms the revealed status of the Written Torah, he also holds that its text has been subject to corruption and "maculation" in its continued process of transmission, particularly as a result of Israel's sins and neglect in different generations, beginning with the sin of the Golden Calf that led to the shattering of the first set of tablets at Sinai (Exodus 32–34). This process, he holds, has resulted in a series of inconsistencies and irregularities in the text as we now have it. Notably, he also sees various early rabbinic texts as similarly acknowledging the non-immaculate status of the humanly transmitted texts and traditions of Scripture. In response to these ruptures, he asserts that the religiously faithful stance is to face up to the unfortunate situation bravely and honestly, rather than trying to "cover over, or rationalize" the text's problems through forced interpretation, *dochok* (59). While one can and should, with effort and prayer, try to repair the problematic texts to the extent possible in an attempt at *tikkun*, one must simultaneously be willing to live with a tradition that is not 'perfectly consistent' and with the limitations of even our best human reparative attempts. As Halivni puts it, "It is better to leave a difficult issue unresolved than to force the words to say something they do not mean" (62). Halivni thus rejects the "easier" path of forced interpretation of revealed but maculated texts, just as he rejects the path of forced explanations of history in the case of the Shoah.

Similarly, while Halivni upholds the basic authoritative status of the tradition of Oral Law, he maintains that it should not be treated as having been directly revealed at Sinai. Instead, he insists on the fallible human agency of the classical rabbinic sages who engaged in the interpretive production of the Oral Law. For Halivni, the production of the Oral Law arose from a need to interpret and apply the Written Torah in different practical contexts and in different situations, via the process of *midrash* (89). While he views the classical rabbis as retaining some degree (though diminished) of the divine presence, such that their halakhic-midrashic interpretations can be seen as a form of "partnership with God" (111), their ideas were still humanly fallible and remain so. Thus, against those who would insist on the revealed and thus absolute status of all classical rabbinic pronouncements, Halivni upholds the right to engage earlier texts critically and to posit that some Talmudic statements—such as Babylonian Talmud Shabbat 33b's "women are light minded"—"need not be viewed as essential to the Law" (100). While Halivni recognizes that this critical stance towards oral tradition marks a departure from much medieval and postmedieval Jewish theology, he argues that many streams of earlier classical rabbinic thought in fact held a theological view similar to the one he puts forth. Thus, while he presents the dogmatic notion of the Sinaitic revelation of the Oral Torah as "deeply dissatisfying to anyone sensitive to the reality of history" (97), he also maintains that his view is not simply a modern innovation, but marks a return to a prominent tradition within early rabbinic Judaism itself.

Moreover, while acknowledging the humanly fallible and maculated character of earlier texts may seem again like a type of pessimism that lacks the absolute certainty of some other theologies, Halivni maintains that being open to the human character of tradition can in fact foster "deeper discernment of the many expressions of Torah, past and present" and that such approaches "can serve as antidotes to intolerance" (98). If we no longer feel compelled to fit all of past tradition into a single authoritative unity, we can be more attentive to the richness of multiple differing voices from the past, and engagement with these different dimensions can generate new possibilities for reconstituting Jewish life in the present. Likewise, if we recognize human multiplicity in past tradition, we can find new ways of grappling with plurality in our own contexts. By contrast, if we refuse to recognize the fallibility of earlier rabbinic sages—and all the more so of contemporary rabbis and scholars—we are led again into the error of 'forcing' interpretations onto texts in a desire to quell our anxieties, generating social rigidity and authoritarianism. For Halivni, conversely, rather than leading us to abandon our texts and traditions in despair, a "pessimistic" acknowledgment that their divine status is always intermixed with human fallibility can in fact draw us closer to the texts, to engage them anew and discern hitherto undiscovered potentialities within them.

Thus, as in the case of his approach to the Shoah, we can view Halivni here as championing a "pessimism" of generativity and new life. Indeed, we can even view Halivni's approach to the concrete activity of text-engagement as a performative practice of enacting messianic hope and patience, akin to the classical sages who warned against those who would wrongly "force the end" (*lidchok et ha-ketz*) in pursuit of redemption. Instead, they affirmed that one should persist in Torah, *mitzvot*, and *teshuvah* in a broken world, while trusting in God to eventually bring about that which is not to be achieved by human force of will. Likewise, Halivni leaves us with the profound lesson that the present Jewish textual, social, and cultural task requires an ability to continue to strive for repair while acknowledging our human limitations, to refrain from "forcing" solutions in a misguided quest for certainty and security, and to retain hope that the future will give rise to new possibilities that are presently unseen.

17. Ruth Wisse, "How Not to Remember and How Not to Forget"

Ruth Wisse, "How Not to Remember and How Not to Forget," *Commentary*, January 2008

Dr. Ruth Wisse (1936–) is Martin Peretz Professor of Yiddish Literature and Professor of Comparative Literature at Harvard University.

Two approaches to memorializing the Holocaust might have yielded a worthier universal lesson. Were the "story" told from a Jewish perspective, it could function like the Passover text I described above. Jews, it might say, lived in Europe for over two millennia in such and such places, conducting themselves in such and such ways and achieving such and such things. In the late nineteenth century, a period of emerging nation-states, they too began their recovery of their national homeland, then under the rule of the Ottoman empire and later of Great Britain. But before they could secure their place of refuge, catastrophe overtook them in such and such a fashion and subjected them to such and such horrors; at the lowest point in European civilization, Jews were almost wiped off the continent. During the war, they responded in such and such ways. After it, they emerged with even greater national resolve.

This is the way I myself experienced my life as a Jew, and the way I would have preferred it to be known by others.

A second approach might be subsumed under the motto "Never Again." Here the emphasis would fall on the political process through which the Holocaust came about. Thus: anti-Semitism, an anti-liberal, anti-Jewish ideology and political movement, began in Germany in the 1870's, tapping sources in Christian and other anti-Jewish notions from the European past. In the 1920's, under such and such conditions, Hitler grabbed hold of this ideology and, in the name of protecting the institutions of society from the Jews, imposed his total control over those same institutions. The spread of anti-Semitism in many other countries of Europe created a common political bond among nations otherwise opposed to Hitler's aggressive aims. The war against the Jews escalated, blended into, and was subsumed by the war of the Third Reich.

One key element in such an exhibit would be the wartime alliance struck between Adolf Hitler and the Grand Mufti of Jerusalem, marking the point at which modern European anti-Semitism effected its entry into the Middle East. The last part of the exhibit would then move forward to today, illustrating how anti-liberal and anti-Jewish ideologies and movements continued to function, with variations, throughout the contemporary Arab and Muslim world. So documented, "Never Again" would be grasped not as some quasi-religious invocation but rather as simple political necessity, founded on the careful weighing of historical precedent and performance.

The United States Holocaust Memorial Museum, the largest and most important of such structures outside Israel, follows neither of these approaches. Its representation of the Jewish catastrophe is like a Passover Haggadah stuck in the section on slavery, recounting in great detail how many infant Jewish boys were drowned in the Nile, how many slaves were killed while building the cities of Pithom and Rameses, what cruelties were practiced against Jewish women, and so forth. In this dark telling, Jews are rescued in the end—by Americans, mostly—but there is no Jewish national resurgence, no emphasis on Jewish sovereignty, resilience, or self-defense. The theme song is not *Hatikvah*—the Jewish hope—but, if anything, "Over There," George M. Cohan's immortal American song from World War I, with its thrilling promise that "the Yanks are coming." Indeed, they came. Along the way, unfortunately, the effect of the museum's historical reconstruction of the Jewish side of the story is to make American visitors more comfortable with the idea of Jewish corpses than with the idea either of great rabbis or of Israeli soldiers.

Several years ago I watched an interview on public television with one of the museum's curators. When the phone lines were opened to viewers, one of the first to call was a self-identified Arab who asked why the museum did not document the "Israeli holocaust of the Palestinians." Looking out at the camera, the curator replied: "The museum only covers the years 1933–1945." She not only allowed the slander of Israel to go unchallenged but, like the museum itself, abrogated the responsibility to demonstrate the replicable features of anti-Semitism that had inspired not only her Arab caller but millions upon millions like him. That the museum "only covers the years 1933–1945" is precisely its moral and educational undoing.

When I was growing up I was certain that the worst was behind us, not because political evil had disappeared from the earth but because, through dreadful experience, Jews, Americans, and even Europeans had necessarily learned to guard against it. I believed that memorializing meant learning from history, and that the lessons of history were self-evident. I never imagined that, in the manner of Mahmoud Ahmadinejad, one could re-present history in such a way as to resurrect its most vicious patterns, bringing about yet another generation of perpetrators, collaborators, bystanders, and potential victims. I never imagined the possibility that political forces in the world could threaten a catastrophe as great as the one the museum now records.

COMMENTARY BY DARA HORN

In the twenty-first century, as we approach the inevitable moment when the last Holocaust survivor dies, I sometimes wonder if our ancestors felt any dread as similar moments approached. Did the death of the last survivor of the Crusader massacres prompt any soul-searching among Rhineland Jews? Ninety years after the Almohades invaded Spain and forced Jews to convert or die, was anyone collecting the last survivor's testimony? Did anyone acknowledge the death of the last survivor of the first Jewish revolt against Rome, the last Jew alive to see the Temple before it went down in flames?

If any of this seems absurd, it is because those generations of Jews, whose traumas were duly lamented and commemorated in their time—there is no shortage of legends, poems, testimonies, and lyrical remembrances for these and many other destroyed Jewish communities, in a Jewish literary tradition going back to the Book of Lamentations—were already knee-deep in the next existential challenge before the survivors of the previous destruction were in their graves. Our generation of Jews is confronting new challenges too, of course, nearly everywhere: redefining Jewish life under ongoing threats in Israel, and making difficult decisions amid resurgent hostility in Europe and elsewhere. It is only in North America that Jews have the luxury of wondering, as the last survivors die, what it all meant. Everyone else already knows.

Ruth Wisse's guidance through the moral perversity of so much official Holocaust remembrance is as bracing as all of her work, and it employs the same strategy that she has used in everything from her analyses of Yiddish literature to her opinion pieces on contemporary Israeli politics: recognizing within her personal experience the wider communal meaning. It is a rhetorical strategy that has served her well over the course of a life and career that spans Europe and America, the rise and fall of various political fashions both at home and abroad, and the twentieth-century rebirth of Jewish independence. It is also a style in keeping with the golden chain of Jewish literature going back to the Hebrew Bible's prophecies, in which every prophet's vision is inseparable from his personal awakenings, and every prophet's fate is bound up with the nation's. It is not too much to suggest that in this essay Wisse plays the role of the prophet, proclaiming to her community exactly what it needs to know but doesn't want to hear.

A European refugee herself, though at too young an age to remember her family's flight from Romania, Wisse has lived through two versions of North American Holocaust remembrance. What is most striking in this essay is how she documents the difference between the later institutionalized memorials, arranged by an organized Jewish community for a wider public, and the earlier communal memorial events, arranged by and for survivors and the relatives of those murdered. Her memories of these earlier events, with their openly weeping participants crying out for vengeance and rising to sing *Ha-Tikvah*, are startling in how vividly they reveal their participants' humanity—as adults who are rightfully grieving and enraged, and also rightfully proud of their people's resurgence in Israel and around the world—and in how vividly those events contrast with the dehumanizing effects of Holocaust museums and official communal memorials today.

Yes, dehumanizing. For what else can one call it when the most popular Jewish museum exhibitions are about the European Jewish community's destruction, when the largest public monuments erected by North American Jews commemorate that destruction, when the most widely read books about Jewish characters are about Holocaust victims, and when the most popular university courses in Jewish Studies are those that teach the Holocaust? Wisse would not deny the value of studying the destruction of European Jewish civilization for those already well aware of exactly what was destroyed. But studying or marveling at that destruction *instead* of studying or marveling at Jewish civilization itself—the more popular choice, as enrollment numbers show—is dehumanizing in the extreme. Lamenting the moment when she, too, found herself compelled to teach such a university course, Wisse captures exactly the compounded insult of this newer version of Holocaust remembrance: "Historically, Jews had provided an alternative civilization to the civilization that produced Hitler—yet there we were, analyzing the exploits and the culture of our destroyers. Why should *we* have felt obliged to teach German pathology?" She jokes about these courses, invariably better enrolled than any others: "Go argue with success." But the truth beneath this joke is the sickening lie that the creators of such public "lessons" invariably believe: "Everyone seemed confident that the representation of evil would have the appropriately redemptive effect."

Wisse is devastatingly right in calling out this lie, even more than she admits. I would suggest that this hallowing of victimhood extends well beyond museum culture to the novels, films, TV programs, and other imaginative works "inspired" by the Holocaust—the vast majority of which are based on an unspoken and fundamentally Christian premise pervasive in American culture, even if their creators don't realize it. I am referring to the idea that catastrophic events must somehow be redemptive, that suffering is somehow ennobling, that the end of any story, whether historical narrative or historical fiction, must involve some form of grace and salvation. This explains the popularity of stories about rescuers like *Schindler's List*, despite the historical fact that instances of Holocaust rescue were statistically insignificant—as were, incidentally, instances of Holocaust survival. But it also explains the pervasive assumption that we must "learn" something from the Holocaust, that rehearsing the nauseating dehumanization of the Jews is inherently a redemptive exercise, one that somehow brings honor to the memory of the murdered or spiritually enriches us.

This premise is perverse, first of all, because it is cruel to recall people only at the moment of their lives when they had the least agency; it is disrespectful, to say the least, to care about how people died without caring at all about how they lived. Wisse's report of pornographic comments made in front of images of naked women at a Holocaust exhibit is simply the most obvious evidence of the ultimately prurient result of this approach. For the most basic calculation of how Holocaust memorials erase lives at the expense of deaths, simply consider how many educated American Jews could name three concentration camps—and compare that with how many could name three Yiddish authors. (My choice of this particular indicator is no quirk: 80% of the Jews murdered in the Holocaust were Yiddish speakers, a famously literary culture.) This is disturbing enough. But this sanctification of victimhood is even more perverse for a second reason: its political potential, which we have unfortunately already seen. By adhering to this deeply Christian premise of hallowing the powerless sufferers, such memorials spread one of Western civilization's most pernicious ideas: that Jews are at their best and noblest when they have no power at all, that Jews who opt to build up their own civilization and to defend themselves against aspiring murderers are violating an unspoken rule about what the best and noblest Jews are supposed to do—which is to suffer and die. One only need to walk by any anti-Israel demonstration in any city in the world on any day of any year (they aren't hard to find) to see just how many people have taken the hint. In this brilliant essay, Wisse connects the dots, and as our new century progresses, there are only more dots to connect.

So if that's the wrong way to remember, what is the right way?

That question has an easy answer, although it takes a lifetime of devotion to render it into reality: continuing the civilization that the murderers sought to destroy. Wisse's most moving words in this essay are reserved not for her parents' murdered families, but for her teachers in her Jewish day school in Montreal, Holocaust survivors whose courage included their "willingness to be among children after having sometimes lost their own; [and] their respect for the Jewish subjects they taught despite the price they paid for being born Jews. That these survivors of the war against the Jews were prepared to instruct us in that civilization helped to convince me of its worth." As a life-changing teacher of multiple generations of students, Wisse speaks with absolute authority when she offers, almost as an aside, this essay's most important prophetic proclamation: "I have always thought it wrong to teach young children about the destruction of the Jews of Europe, unless and until they are first thoroughly informed about the staying power of Jewish civilization."

The achievements of that civilization, the "alternative civilization to the one that produced Hitler," is the greatest legacy of the Jewish people. One must praise all those parents and teachers who take on the daunting and holy and difficult and exhilarating task of transmitting the content of that civilization to the next generation, and do everything one can to support that sacred work. But I will quibble with Wisse on one minor point: The staying power of Jewish civilization need not be taught. It only needs to be lived.

As the last Holocaust survivor joins the last survivors of so many other destructions, the Holocaust will lose not only the intimacy of those communal gatherings Wisse remembers, but also the burdensome sanctification of powerlessness that she laments it has taken on in American Jewish life. Instead it will become, in collective Jewish memory, exactly what it was: one more moment in history when murderers attempted to extinguish the Jewish people—only to discover, like everyone before them, that Israel survives forever.

18. Yossi Klein Halevi, *Like Dreamers*

Yossi Klein Halevi, *Like Dreamers*, New York: Harper Collins, 2013

Yossi Klein Halevi (1953–) is a Senior Fellow at the Shalom Hartman Institute where he is also Co-Director of the Muslim Leadership Intiative (MLI). He is the author of the *New York Times* bestseller, *Letters to My Palestinian Neighbor*, and *Like Dreamers*, winner of the Jewish Book Council's Everett Book of the Year Award for 2013.

Yoel Bin-Nun approached the Lion's Gate. Spread before him was the landscape of messianic dream. Terraced into the Mount of Olives were thousands of flat tombstones, of Jews who had chosen to be buried directly across from the Temple Mount, to be resurrected when the Messiah came. In the Valley of Kidron rose the conical stone monument called the Pillar of Absalom, after the rebellious son of King David, founder of the messianic line. Nearby, embedded in the Old City wall, was the Gate of Mercy, through which, according to tradition, the Messiah would enter, and which had been sealed by Muslims to thwart the redeemer of Israel.

Yoel ran up the steep road leading to the Lion's Gate, past the still smoking bus, and through the crowded gate.

When he reached the steps leading to the Dome of the Rock, he abruptly stopped: beyond lay the region of the Holy of Holies.

He felt lightheaded, as if on a mountain peak. *To move from battle to this—*

He couldn't pray: prayer seemed inadequate. What was left to ask for? He felt himself to be an answered prayer to all those who had believed this day would come, that Jewish history would vindicate Jewish faith. (93)

The predawn streets of West Jerusalem filled with pilgrims. It was the holiday of Shavuot, Pentecost, celebrating revelation. The war had ended five days earlier, and all of Jewish Jerusalem seemed to be moving east. Many too had come from around the country, to be part of the first holiday at the Wall since its liberation—and the first mass pilgrimage of Jews to the area of the Temple Mount since Titus burned the Temple 1,900 years earlier. There were women wheeling baby carriages and grandmothers in kerchiefs and kibbutzniks in floppy hats and Orthodox men in prayer shawls and Chasidic fur hats and black fedoras and berets and knitted *kippot*. It was impossible, but here they were, sovereign again in Jerusalem, just as Jews had always prayed for and believed would happen. Strangers smiled at each other: We are the ones who made it to the end of the story.

Ada, on vigil in Avital's hospital room, heard the movement from the street. Through the arched window she saw the vast crowds heading toward the Old City. "There are thousands of people outside," she told Avital.

"Go join them," he urged.

Everyone seemed to be moving in slow motion. Ada felt as if she were floating. An Israeli crowd could be as edgy as a food line in a refugee camp, yet here there was no pushing, no concern that someone was cutting ahead or not moving quickly enough. They are all my family, she thought; I love them just for being Jews. (113)

COMMENTARY BY HANNAH KOBER

Like Dreamers brings the nerve-racking reality of the 1967 Six Day War and its aftermath to life through the stories of its best-known heroes: the 55th Paratroopers Reserve Brigade. A photograph of these soldiers at the moment they seized the Old City of Jerusalem (pictured on the cover of *Like Dreamers*) has become iconic, a symbol of Israel's triumphant and shocking victory in the Six Day War. Throughout the book, Klein Halevi portrays these protagonists as the embodiment of the struggle to make sense of concepts and realities new to their generation of Israelis: demonstrable sovereignty, a compelling sense of divine providence, and unprecedented access to Jewish historical sites. Over the course of their lives, the protagonists present a myriad of complex reactions to the trauma and excitement of the war—each of which is crucial for understanding both the beautiful and messy dimensions of ideology, identity, and memory in Israeli society. Klein Halevi adds multidimensionality to our understanding of Jewish and Israeli reactions to 1967 and seeks to elevate the collective memory of that time beyond an essentialized and flattened narrative of Israel as either victor/liberator or an oppressor/occupier. By tracing the varied lives of the paratroopers after the liberation of Jerusalem, Klein Halevi tells a richly textured and deeply human story of Israel's journey from past to present.

Klein Halevi employs the paratroopers' experiences to translate the political register into the language of human experience in two ways. The first is in his depiction of the liberation of Jerusalem and the subsequent theological and emotional shocks that came to define the experience, even across religious and political fault lines. The excerpts here capture a moment of spiritual speechlessness, a portrayal that amplifies the humanity and helplessness of the liberators themselves despite the power they held at that moment.

Klein Halevi continues to parse the reactions of Israelis to this pivotal moment throughout the book. Immediately after the war, as the discharged soldiers learn about the fallen, one soldier breaks out into uncontrollable, painful sobbing. The triumph of the victory was matched with or perhaps overwhelmed by a deep countervailing sense of grief. Later, interviewers from *Shdemot*, the kibbutz literary magazine, attempt to capture the feelings of the soldiers in the war's aftermath; their questions were met with a variety of emotional responses, ranging from tropes of messianic optimism to doubt and despair. Here, Klein Halevi emphasizes that the religious and political differences between the soldiers were not meaningfully divisive. He writes that "regardless of what they wore or didn't wear on their heads now, they had all worn the same helmets a few weeks earlier" (125). The trauma of the war led these individuals onto distinct paths, yet their individuality and difference cannot subvert their shared humanity.

The second means that Klein Halevi uses to convey the human dimension of the story is in the way he portrays the ideological complexities, ethical dilemmas, and emotional depths of each of the paratroopers and their respective communities. The paratroopers' stories reveal the evolution and maturation of these individuals and Israeli society more broadly. They also demonstrate that immediate aftermath of Israel's victory in the Six Day War was not defined by true consensus. Over the years since 1967, the protagonists come to include the forebears of the settler movement, a cynical singer-songwriter, a Peace Now activist and socialist, a far-left defector who collaborates with a Palestinian terror cell, and the devoted yet conflicted Chief Intelligence Officer of the brigade. Klein Halevi's portrayals show that the outcomes of the Six Day War have been and can be read as anything on the spectrum from messianic revival and national homecoming to a symbol of death, moral crisis, and occupation. Notably, he explores the integrity of each narrative regardless of the social acceptability of the protagonist's political and religious commitments in contemporary Israeli and North American Jewish discourse.

The narrative of Udi Adiv, the collaborator, is the most-groundbreaking element of this book. Adiv's story brings the emergence of a post-1967 Israeli anti-Zionist fringe to the fore. At the end of the war, a team of Israeli contractors demolished homes in the Mughrabi Quarter to create the Western Wall Plaza and enable public access to the site. The Quarter's residents were relocated to a refugee camp. Adiv reacts viscerally at the sight of the rubble, and thinks "whatever the Zionists touch, they destroy" (105). His disenchantment leads him down a path of activism against the Zionist enterprise, apathy in military settings and subsequent dismissal from the 55th Paratrooper's Reserve Brigade. Through Klein Halevi's portrayal of Adiv and the other protagonists, the reader swings on a pendulum between pride in Israeli political and military history, and shame or disgust for the morally challenging elements of those same political moments and trends.

Like Dreamers joins My Promised Land by Ari Shavit, The Accidental Empire by Gershom Gorenberg, and other recent books inviting both Israeli and Diaspora Jews into a process of national soul-searching without imposing conclusive value judgments on historical events. Writing with an eye toward English-speaking audiences, these authors attempt to fill out the Israeli historical narrative in order to curate a more honest discourse on internal schisms within Israeli society and the realities of discrimination and military occupation faced by Israel's Arab and Palestinian populations.

As it happened, Like Dreamers was released in 2013 following a second flare in tensions and violence in Gaza. The US Administration was engaged in attempts to bring the peace process back to the fore, and reports of settlement building freezes and partial thaws disproportionately dominated the news cycle. At the same time, protests over the costs of housing and dairy staples had revealed the extent to which the Israeli government had left domestic issues on the backburner while trying to stay afloat in a hostile region. Published nearly fifty years after 1967, with no end to the Israeli-Palestinian conflict in sight, this book brings readers into the intractable and heart-wrenching conflicts facing Israeli society.

Klein Halevi's transparent presentation of ideological diversity struck a chord in the North American Jewish discourse on Israel. The early 2010s saw a movement away from simple, unquestioning pro-Israelism in North America that had defined the years immediately following 1967 and became deeply amplified through the Second Intifada. North American Jews began reckoning on a larger scale with Israeli policies on religious pluralism, sovereignty, and nationalism that did not accord with their liberal sensibilities. North American readers of Klein Halevi become better acquainted with the network of diverse and complex Israelis who bore witness to and actualized the reality of a Jewish Jerusalem. The deeply personal nature of Klein Halevi's narrative compels the reader to bring an open mind and heart even to the protagonists whose values and political conclusions may be diametrically opposed to their own.

Klein Halevi has been criticized for leaving the story "unfinished" by not proposing a tenable policy position or definitive course forward. The book also does not bring all marginalized groups to the fore, as contemporary readers may expect from an expansive retelling of a historical narrative. Although the criticism may be resonant, it risks ignoring the book's mission and achievements.

Like Dreamers urges twenty-first-century Jews to make room for narratives that articulate their own convictions as well as those which deeply challenge their assumptions. Through the story of the paratroopers, Klein Halevi introduces a model of radical empathy that is largely unprecedented in literature on Israel, especially literature geared towards an English-speaking, North American audience. The Six Day War and its outcomes should not be seen as monolithic. Klein Halevi boldly elevates and coalesces the diverse stories of the paratroopers to achieve a more honest, holistic, and visionary discourse on Israeli history. The tension that emanates from the ideological schisms of the protagonists creates a forum for a productive and, ironically, non-polemical understanding of history. *Like Dreamers* presents Israeli pluralism, the Israeli-Palestinian Conflict, and the legacy of 1967 as both impossible to resolve and impossible to resist.

III
Religion and Religiosity

1. Joseph B. Soloveitchik, *Halakhic Man*

Joseph B. Soloveitchik, *Halakhic Man*, Philadelphia: Jewish Publication Society of America, 1983

Rabbi Dr. Joseph B. Soloveitchik (1903–1993) served as *Rosh Yeshiva* at the Rabbi Isaac Elchanan Theological Seminary of Yeshiva University, chaired the Halakhah Commission of the Rabbinical Council of America, and served as Honorary President of the Religious Zionists of America. He founded the Maimonides School in Brookline, Massachusetts.

When halakhic man approaches reality, he comes with his Torah, given to him from Sinai, in hand. He orients himself to the world by means of fixed statutes and firm principles. An entire corpus of precepts and laws guides him along the path leading to existence. Halakhic man, well furnished with rules, judgements, and fundamental principles, draws near the world with an a priori relation. His approach begins with an ideal creation and concludes with a real one. To whom may he be compared? To a mathematician who fashions an ideal world and then uses it for the purpose of establishing a relationship between it and the real world. ... The essence of the Halakhah, which was received from God, consists in creating an ideal world and cognizing the relationship between that ideal world and our concrete environment in all its visible manifestations and underlying structures. There is no phenomenon, entity, or object in this concrete world which the a priori Halakhah does not approach with its ideal standard. When halakhic man comes across a spring bubbling quietly, he already possesses a fixed, a priori relationship with this real phenomenon: the complex of laws regarding the halakhic construct of a spring. The spring is fit for the immersion of a *zav* (a man with a discharge); it purifies with flowing water; it does not require a fixed quantity of forty *se'ahs*; etc. ... When halakhic man approaches a real spring, he gazes at it and carefully examines its nature. He possesses, a priori, ideal principles and precepts which establish the character of the spring as a halakhic construct, and he uses the statutes for the purpose of determining normative law: does the real spring correspond to the requirements of the ideal Halakhah or not?

Halakhic man is not overly curious, and he is not particularly concerned with cognizing the spring as it is in itself. Rather, he desires to coordinate the a priori concept with the a posteriori phenomenon.

When halakhic man looks to the western horizon and sees the fading rays of the setting sun or to the eastern horizon and sees the first light of dawn and the glowing rays of the rising sun, he knows that this sunset or sunrise imposes upon him anew obligations and commandments. Dawn and sunrise obligate him to fulfill those commandments that are performed during the day: the recitation of the morning *Shema*, *tzitzit*, *tefillin*, the morning prayer, *etrog*, *shofar*, *Hallel*, and the like. They make the time fit for the carrying out of certain halakhic practices: Temple service, acceptance of testimony, conversion, *ḥalitzah*, etc. Sunset imposes upon him those obligations and commandments that are performed during the night: the recitation of the evening *Shema*, *matzah*, the counting of the *omer*, etc. The sunset on Sabbath and holiday eves sanctifies the day: the profane and the holy are dependent upon a natural cosmic phenomenon—the sun sinking below the horizon. It is not anything transcendent that creates holiness but rather the visible reality—the regular cycle of the natural order. (19–21)

COMMENTARY BY SHLOMO ZUCKIER

Rabbi Joseph Soloveitchik's *Halakhic Man* powerfully and passionately affirms the centrality of Halakhah to a Jew's religious experience. The work portrays the character of the halakhic man as a harmonious fusion of two personalities, *homo religiosus* and cognitive man. On the one hand, a person should not aspire to be a pure *homo religiosus*, a typological figure one might associate with a Chasidic and/or Christian temperament, seeking ecstatic religious experience at every turn and thereby fleeing this world. Nor, on the other hand, should one pursue the *gestalt* of a pure cognitive man, exemplified by the scientist who does not search beyond the surface level of reality. Rather, the halakhic man should seek to encounter God, as does *homo religiosus*, but should do so through his rigorous study of Halakhah, an intellectual endeavor analogous to cognitive man's pursuit of science. Through this study, halakhic man embodies a Hegelian dialectic between two contrasting personality types.

The selected passage represents several key and unique aspects of Soloveitchik's philosophy. It projects his halakho-centric worldview; view of Halakhah as science; this-worldly religiosity; hyper-intellectualist focus on Torah study; and existentialism-inspired quest for religious experience. In this passage, and in the essay overall, Rabbi Soloveitchik draws simultaneously upon his Lithuanian Talmudic roots and his neo-Kantian Idealist predecessors as he navigates the novel religious philosophy of halakhic man (which might or might not be identical with Soloveitchik's own perspective).

To a certain degree, Soloveitchik's approach to Halakhah draws upon the Lithuanian model of yeshiva life, largely originating with the opening of the Volozhin Yeshiva in 1806. In the Lithuanian yeshiva worldview, students should pore over volumes of Talmud at all hours of the day, sustaining the cosmos with their Torah study. Soloveitchik succeeded in taking this ethos and translating the theological significance of the study from a Kabbalistic (see *Nefesh ha-Chayyim*, Gate 4) idea of constructing ethereal worlds into a neo-Kantian, Idealist view of constructing one's own world, in this case by imposing halakhic structure onto one's sense perceptions. Kant had raised the challenge that human experience, or phenomena, might be mere creations of the human mind and have no connection to the world as it truly is, the noumena. One response to this utilized Idealism, the conception that human experience is in fact the ultimate foundation of reality, is to justify the construction of one's world out of sensory perceptions and mental categories. Faced with the Kantian challenge of bridging the gap between human experience and the world as it truly is, halakhic man "attempts to find within this concrete and physical world the traces of higher worlds, all of which are wholly good and eternal" (13).

This Idealist perspective is notable for the way it views the physical matter that correlates with halakhic categories. In addition to the vivid passage above, Soloveitchik touches on this point in his essay "*Mah Dodekh mi-Dod*," ostensibly a eulogy for his uncle, Rabbi Yitzhak Ze'ev Soloveichik, but also a companion essay to *Halakhic Man* (which has inexcusably gone untranslated into English).

In "*Mah Dodekh mi-Dod*," Soloveitchik praises the great revolution of Rabbi Hayyim Soloveitchik, his grandfather and founder of the Brisker school, as having "purified Halakhah from all forms of external influence." This includes his refutation of "psychologization and historicization," recognizing that Halakhah does not fall under these categories but is rather "ideal-normative." His ability—like that of a great scientist!—to organize legal content into one conceptual framework is celebrated by Soloveitchik the younger, both in "*Mah Dodekh mi-Dod*" and, at greater length, in *Halakhic Man*.

Soloveitchik further describes that the greatness of his grandfather was to abstract Jewish law from the level of physical objects to the level of concepts:

> Suddenly the pots and the pans, the eggs and the onions disappeared from the laws of meat and milk; the salt, the blood, and the spit disappeared from the laws of salting. The laws of kashrut were taken out of the kitchen and removed to an ideal halakhic world ... constructed out of complexes of abstract concepts.

This approach radically remakes the traditional view of Jewish law as a practical guide for living Jewishly. The practical aspects of halakhic decision-making become almost an epiphenomenon, as the imposing of the divine plan of Halakhah on the world becomes primary. Reinterpreting the Kabbalistic idea of *tzimtzum* along the way, Soloveitchik describes a world that God inhabits through the Halakhah, relying on the individual Jew to apply the rubric of Halakhah to the world. While this can also be accomplished to some degree through halakhic practice, its highest fulfillment relies on the great Talmudist alone.

In the passage from *Halakhic Man* above, the focus on halakhic concepts as the grounding of Jewish experience serves to render living in this world transcendent and simultaneously to define transcendence itself on the basis of this-worldly categories: "Halakhic man apprehends transcendence. However, instead of rising up to it, he tries to bring it down to him" (41). This theme of valuing this world, both material life and the human creative capacity therein, is emphasized throughout *Halakhic Man*. In fact, the World to Come itself merely consists of the righteous studying Torah (38–39). Humans, the apex of creation, are bidden to follow God in creating, most of all in self-creation through repentance (110–17).

Related to Soloveitchik's focus on this-worldly experience, his conception of holiness is also fundamentally grounded in human and physical reality. Sanctity is not dictated from above; rather, halakhic categories are presented through which human beings have the capacity to create holiness and live holy lives. "Holiness is created by man, by flesh and blood" (47). Rabbi Soloveitchik explains that this theme, present throughout several of his writings, renders religious life more democratic (43) and human-centered than alternative approaches to Judaism, which may have held a certain appeal to his twentieth-century American readership. Just below the surface is the implicit response to modern accusations that yeshiva study is elitist, cut off from the world, and stifling of human autonomy.

The anthropocentrism the Rav sees in Halakhah is represented well by the human experience of the bubbling spring and the charge to cognize it within a halakhic realm. Such a perspective focuses not only on Halakhah and the mind, but also reflects a certain focus on existentialism and phenomenology present in Soloveitchik's approach. While the centrality of human experience in no way diminishes the divine basis of the system, its significance is channeled through the experience of the religious practitioner, as the lived religious experience serves as the starting point for the creation of religious meaning. Halakhic man looks to the sunset and experiences God—not due to its beauty, but on account of its betokening a fundamental change in the (halakhic) world.

In a sense, *Halakhic Man*, and especially this passage, represents a broader move within the realm of Torah study, starting with Soloveitchik's grandfather Hayyim, wherein the goal of study shifts from clarifying halakhic details to building from those details a structure of Halakhah as a conceptual system. This shift has also occurred, to a large degree, not in Modern Orthodox circles but among the *Charedim*, inheritors of the Lithuanian yeshiva worldview who would never study philosophy, and for whom Torah study has come to be identified with the Brisker method of the Soloveitchik family.

This shift belongs in a German philosophical context as well. Soloveitchik draws upon a neo-Kantian conception (closely tied to Paul Natorp's philosophy of science) that sees knowledge as constructed of human sensory data. In a rigorous, mathematical process, halakhic data are subsumed under a broader, conceptual system in the same way that a physicist forges experimental data into theoretical laws of physics. Soloveitchik's association of Halakhah and science is manifest throughout his writing (see, for example, the 1986 essay *Halakhic Mind* and the recently published *Halakhic Morality*), as is his associated rejection of any psychologization or historicization of the law, in a manner very much in keeping with Natorp's work. Just as science is a hermetically sealed, internally defined realm that is unaffected by history, Halakhah must be seen the same way.

While *Halakhic Man* was originally published in Hebrew in 1944, the essay has enjoyed its broadest impact on the American Jewish and broader philosophical communities following its publication in English in 1983. This monograph has inspired many of the Rav's students and followers, who appreciate the volume's honoring the Brisker method. It has also been studied and valued for its role in the intertwined intellectual history of the Lithuanian and German strands, and as a bold and groundbreaking work of Jewish philosophy in its own right. And it has been critiqued by some as promoting a version of Judaism that is too elite or "ivory tower" to command the interest of the masses. Whatever one's perspective, *Halakhic Man* qualifies as one of the great theological works of the twentieth century.

2. Rabbi Yehoshua Yeshaya Neuwirth, *Shemirath Shabbath Kehilchathah*

Rabbi Yehoshua Yeshaya Neuwirth, *Shemirath Shabbath Kehilchathah*, English edition, New York: Feldheim Publishers, 1984

Rabbi Yehoshua Yeshaya Neuwirth (1927–2013) was a rabbi in Jerusalem.

In his mind's eye, Moses saw the people of Israel being swallowed up among the nations and totally disappearing, and this even while they were in their own land, let alone when they were scattered in exile. What did he do? "Moses assembled the whole congregation of the Children of Israel" (Exodus 35:1) and emphasized to them the importance of observing Shabbath. The Midrash (Yalkut Shim'oni at the beginning of *parsath vayakhel*) notes that the only time the Pentateuch expressly tells us that Moses assembled the people to give them a mitzvah is in connection with Shabbath. God told him to gather the people together and lecture to them in public on the laws of Shabbath, so that future generations of leaders would learn from this to gather their congregations together every Shabbath to teach them the Torah, to instruct them in the "do's and don't's" of life as a Jew. Shabbath was, thus, the instrument chosen by the Almighty to lift His children up spiritually to the level where they would sing praises to the glory of His Name.

The Mishna (Chagiga: Chapter 1, mishna 8) likens the laws of Shabbath to "mountains hanging by a hair," in that a multitude of precepts and rules, entailing the most severe penalties for their breach, depend on the slightest of indications given by a biblical verse. This is probably one of the reasons why the detailed observance of the Shabbath tends to be neglected by the populace at large more than other mitzvoth. The complications involved in the principles underlying the concept of Shabbath and in their practical application can be daunting not only for the man in the street. The Jerusalem Talmud (Tractate Shabbath: Chapter 7, halacha 2) tells us that Rabbi Yochanan and Rabbi Shimon ben Lakish spent three-and-a-half years on one chapter of Tractate Shabbath (Chapter 7, which deals with the thirty-nine major activities forbidden by the Torah on Shabbath). The Sifra (at the beginning of *parsath bechukothai*) points out that we are commanded not only to observe the Shabbath and remember it in our hearts, but also to refresh our memory by keeping it constantly on our lips. Unless one has been through the laws relating to the observance of Shabbath several times and continues to study them regularly, one has no hope of avoiding even the most elementary of pitfalls week after week. (xxx–xxxi)

COMMENTARY BY DAVID BASHEVKIN

In nearly any Judaica store where rabbinic books are sold, there is a section of works on Halakhah, Jewish law. On these shelves you will find a veritable treasure trove of compendiums on almost every aspect of Jewish life ranging from the laws of prayer to the laws related to sneezing. This proliferation and range of books suggest no halakhic topic is beyond the parameters of a book-length treatment. The renaissance of halakhic publishing in the late twentieth century owes much of its existence to the work *Shemirath Shabbath Kehilchathah*, by Rabbi Yehoshua Neuwirth, first published in 1965 by Feldheim Publishers. The work is a three-volume (as of the newest 2002 edition) digest of all the laws of Shabbat observance, with particular emphasis on the halakhic implications of modern technology. Now a staple of modern halakhic literature, this work ushered in a new age of halakhic digests as it reimagined Shabbat observance in the modern world.

In the introduction to the first printing, Neuwirth emphasizes that he does not intend to begin any sort of revolution. "This book," he writes, "did not arrive in order to innovate halakhic novelties." Rather, he explains, he is gathering all the relevant laws for Shabbat and Yom Tov (holidays) for those who are unable to study the relevant laws of Shabbat adequately on their own. His concern is that they do not forget *Torat ha-Shabbat*, the Torah of Shabbat. His phraseology is striking. It is not just the laws of Shabbat, which would have warranted the term *Hilkhot Shabbat*, that this work is coming to preserve; rather, his goal is far more overarching. The term *Torat ha-Shabbat* implies a grander set of values and traditions that the author hopes will emerge when the laws of Shabbat are properly observed in exacting details.

Following the publication of *Shemirath Shabbath Kehilchathah*, Rabbi Yaakov Yisroel Kanievsky (1899–1985), popularly known as the Steipler, penned a searing critique of this halakhic compendium in his work *Chaye 'Olam* (vol. 2, ch. 8). While acknowledging that some halakhic digests were already widely accepted, Kanievsky argues that *Shemirath Shabbath Kehilchathah* was treading into halakhic discussions that it was not equipped to handle. Kanievsky presents a startling analogy to those who would use such a work to resolve their Shabbat-related queries:

> Imagine for a moment if you were completely certain that one who desecrates Shabbat, whether biblically or rabbinically, would immediately develop cancer—how scared would such a person be?! They would never rely on just any person who comes along to tell you that something is permissible.

While perhaps jarring, this statement is a moving testimony of the determined sincerity with which the *charedi* community viewed Shabbat observance. Kanievsky, while the most notable, was not alone in his criticism. Rabbi Dov Landau (1930–), *Rosh Yeshiva* of Slobodka Yeshiva in Bnei Brak, wrote a ten-page pamphlet detailing issues and concerns he had with Neuwirth's halakhic methodology and conclusions. The pamphlet, entitled *Birur Devarim (Clarification of Matters)*, concludes by wondering: If Landau had so many concerns after only a cursory reading, how anyone could ever rely on this work?

Neuwirth never explicitly responded to his critics. In 1979, he published a second edition with a new introduction, in which he acknowledges that "beloved seekers of truth and pursuers of justice" had pointed out several issues with his first edition. Some of his language is also modified and some leniencies tempered. The book has been reprinted numerous times, and a third edition was released in 2010, suggesting that despite some the concerns, the work has been embraced by the *charedi* community for which he intended it. In America as well, the book has received widespread acceptance. First translated in 1984 by W. Grangewood and published by Feldheim, the work has become the first authority on many issues related to modern day Shabbat observance. It is not uncommon to hear an Orthodox Jew, considering whether to take advantage of some modern-day technological Shabbat convenience, say "does the *Shemirath Shabbath* discuss this?"

Indeed, in his first introduction to his work, Neuwirth notes the communal impact a work on modern Shabbat observance like his might have toward creating a set of uniform communal norms. He writes that Shabbat observance is the only commandment in the Pentateuch that is prefaced with the Hebrew word *va-yakel* [ויקהל], translated as "and he [Moses] gathered" (Exodus 35:1). This term was specifically used, he explains in his introduction, because of the power of Shabbat observance to build and sustain cohesive Jewish communities.

Others have been less critical of the work's contents and more critical of the effect that it has had on Orthodox communities. In his famed essay "Rupture and Reconstruction,"[1] Hayyim Soloveitchik laments changes in halakhic observance following the Holocaust. He argues that prior to World War II, halakhic observance was taught and preserved through a mimetic tradition and that since the Holocaust, halakhic observance had increasingly become a text-based tradition displacing much of the intuitive familial practice cultivated for centuries. In a footnote, Soloveitchik highlights the proliferation of topical halakhic compendia as evidence of this phenomenon. Referencing another popular English work on the laws of Shabbat, he writes:

> The first large-scale, serious halakhic presentation in English was, to the best of my knowledge, that of Shimon D. Eider, *The Halachos of Shabbos*, 2 vols. (Lakewood, New Jersey: S. D. Eider, 1970) which went through five printings in as many years. This, however, might yet be understood as an attempt to grapple with halakhic status and permissibility on Sabbath of the hundreds of new products of the modem consumer market, parallel to the groundbreaking work of Y. Y. Neuwirth, *Shemirat Shabbat ke-Hilkhatah* which had appeared in Jerusalem some five years earlier. Whatever its nature at the time of publication, in retrospect it was clearly a harbinger.

And a harbinger it was. As Soloveitchik persuasively claims, the shift from a mimetic tradition to a text-based tradition has repercussions far outside of the world of halakhic observance. As the immediacy of God's presence becomes obscured in the modern world, we are forced to turn to text-based halakhic analysis to rediscover the majesty we once knew in our quotidian lives. As Soloveitchik wonders about our New World:

> To what extent is there an ongoing experience of His natural involvement in the mundane and of everyday affairs? Put differently, the issue is not the accuracy of my youthful assessment, but whether the cosmology of Bnei Brak and Borough Park differs from that of the *shtetl*, and if so, whether such a shift has engendered a change in the sensed intimacy with God and the felt immediacy of His presence?

---

1   Hayyim Soloveitchik, "Rupture and Reconstruction," *Tradition* 28, no. 4 (Summer 1994): 64–130.

Absent a visceral mimetic tradition for God's intimacy, we are left with the details of halakhic observance with which we hope to find Godliness in the crevices of our lives.

The transition from the Old World to the New are at the center of *Shemirath Shabbath Kehilchathah*. At the end of his introduction for the third edition, Neuwirth recalls the travails his family faced while fleeing Nazi-occupied Berlin on their way toward Israel. Recounting the entire ordeal, he concludes with a story of being forced, contrary to normative Halakhah, to board a boat on Shabbat. "I accepted upon myself then," he writes, "that God should grant me the merit to do something on behalf of Shabbat." This book is the fulfillment of that promise he made in the aftermath of Shabbat desecration while fleeing to a new world. For his contemporary readers, that initial motivation remains the same. On any given shelf that houses Rabbi Neuwirth's work, the work continues to fulfill a promise of preservation of a certain kind, ensuring worlds Old and New continue to endure together.

3. *The Complete Artscroll Siddur*

The Complete Artscroll Siddur, New York: Mesorah, 1984

COMMENTARY BY DAVID ZVI KALMAN

Unlike the Hebrew Bible, whose text was essentially fixed by the Masoretes by the tenth century, the siddur has no "perfect" form. While the Masoretic text has remained constant for centuries, the latter has existed in a state of almost constant variation, and these variations appear to be growing by the year. This is understandable. Existing in tension with the spoken prayers whose texts it ostensibly documents, the power of the written word has meant that the siddur has frequently oscillated between between being a policy summary and a policy proposal, an extension of rabbinic authority and a supersession of that authority. At the same time, the siddur has always needed to respond to a wide range of literacy levels among the Jews who use them; some prayerbooks imagine themselves to be little more than handy reminders for the already well-initiated, while others aspire to be introductions to the practice of Judaism itself. These tensions, together with the constantly shifting goal of "relevancy," mean that the siddur, despite its canonicity, has always been in flux.

For most of its history, the siddur developed through slow accretions, absorbing favored liturgical poems (*piyyutim*) and other prayers without eliminating what had been inserted by generations past. This long and unmanaged evolution meant that, by the beginning of the nineteenth century, the siddur had become a kludge, the result of centuries of local needs and customs rather than a direct response to the needs of synagogues or individuals. It was the early Reform movement that first decided to reconstruct the siddur in its own image by translating select prayers into the vernacular, cutting substantial portions of both *piyyut* and prayer, removing or modifying ideologically problematic phrases, and even reversing the standard right-to-left pagination.

In reimagining the siddur as an ideological document, the nascent movement gained a responsibility for the upkeep and proliferation of the new book which had not previously existed. From 1815 onwards, ideological changes also meant siddur changes; the decision to leave text alone suddenly became ideological, too. While the changes did not necessarily correspond to changes in the lived liturgy, the use of the siddur as a proxy for ideological battles wreaked irreparable harm to the siddur's basic fungibility, excepting only minor regional variations. The choice of which siddur was "official" devolved upon

﴾ שמונה עשרה — עמידה ﴿

Moses advanced through three levels of holiness when he went up to Sinai. Therefore we take three steps forward as we "approach" God in the *Shemoneh Esrei* prayer.

Remain standing with feet together while reciting *Shemoneh Esrei*. Recite it with quiet devotion and without any interruption. Although it should not be audible to others, one must be able to hear his own prayers. See *Laws* §61-90 for a brief summary of its laws, including how to rectify the omission of phrases that are added at particular times of the year.

אֲדֹנָי שְׂפָתַי תִּפְתָּח,* וּפִי יַגִּיד תְּהִלָּתֶךָ.¹

אבות

Bend the knees at בָּרוּךְ; bow at אַתָּה; straighten up at ה'.

בָּרוּךְ אַתָּה* יהוה אֱלֹהֵינוּ וֵאלֹהֵי אֲבוֹתֵינוּ,* אֱלֹהֵי אַבְרָהָם, אֱלֹהֵי יִצְחָק, וֵאלֹהֵי יַעֲקֹב, הָאֵל הַגָּדוֹל הַגִּבּוֹר וְהַנּוֹרָא, אֵל עֶלְיוֹן,* גּוֹמֵל חֲסָדִים טוֹבִים וְקוֹנֵה הַכֹּל,* וְזוֹכֵר חַסְדֵי אָבוֹת, וּמֵבִיא גוֹאֵל* לִבְנֵי בְנֵיהֶם, לְמַעַן שְׁמוֹ בְּאַהֲבָה.

From Rosh Hashanah to Yom Kippur add:

זָכְרֵנוּ לְחַיִּים,* מֶלֶךְ חָפֵץ בַּחַיִּים, וְכָתְבֵנוּ בְּסֵפֶר הַחַיִּים, לְמַעַנְךָ אֱלֹהִים חַיִּים.

[If forgotten, do not repeat *Shemoneh Esrei*. See *Laws* §61.]

Bend the knees at בָּרוּךְ; bow at אַתָּה; straighten up at ה'.

מֶלֶךְ עוֹזֵר וּמוֹשִׁיעַ וּמָגֵן.* בָּרוּךְ אַתָּה יהוה, מָגֵן אַבְרָהָם.*

גבורות

אַתָּה גִּבּוֹר לְעוֹלָם אֲדֹנָי, מְחַיֵּה מֵתִים* אַתָּה, רַב לְהוֹשִׁיעַ.

﴾ שְׁמוֹנֶה עֶשְׂרֵה / SHEMONEH ESREI ﴿

The Talmud refers to *Shemoneh Esrei* simply as תְּפִלָּה, *The Prayer*, for in *Shemoneh Esrei* we formulate our needs and ask God to fulfill them. It was instituted three times daily by the Patriarchs. They are also in place of the daily Temple offerings (*Berachos* 26b). The *Zohar* refers to the *Shemoneh Esrei* as *Amidah* ["standing prayer"] and the two names are used interchangeably.

The term *Shemoneh Esrei* means eighteen, and, indeed, it originally consisted of eighteen blessings. The requirement of eighteen is based on various Scriptural supports (*Megillah* 17b). The text of the blessings was composed by the Men of the Great Assembly at the beginning of the Second Temple period and was put into its current form under Rabban Gamliel II after the Destruction, over four centuries later (ibid.). A nineteenth blessing was added later (see commentary to וְלַמַּלְשִׁינִים, p. 106), but the name *Shemoneh Esrei* was left.

Shemoneh Esrei has three sections: (a) In the first three blessings, the supplicant pays homage to God, like a servant praising his master before he presumes to make a request; (b) the middle section of thirteen blessings contains the suppli-

cant's requests; (c) in the last three blessings, he takes leave, expressing gratitude and confidence in his Master's graciousness (*Berachos* 34a).

The middle section is not merely a catalogue of requests. Each blessing acknowledges God's mastery and then makes the request. Thus, each is an affirmation of God's power (*Vilna Gaon*).

◆§ אֲדֹנָי שְׂפָתַי תִּפְתָּח — *My Lord, open my lips* .... Man may be ready for prayer, but he needs God's help to express himself properly (*Abudraham*). Alternatively, שְׂפָתַי, *my lips*, can mean *my boundaries*. We ask God to free us from our limitations so that we can praise Him properly (*Ramban*).

◆§ אָבוֹת / **Patriarchs**

The first blessing of *Shemoneh Esrei* is known as אָבוֹת, *Patriarchs*, because it recalls the greatness of our forefathers in whose merit God pledged to help Israel throughout history, even if we are unworthy.

בָּרוּךְ אַתָּה — *Blessed are You.* [Since God is perfect by definition, what benefit can man's blessing confer upon Him?]

— God is the Source of inexhaustible blessing, and has created the world in order to do good to His creatures. Since this is His will, we pray for

⊰{ SHEMONEH ESREI — AMIDAH }⊱

Moses advanced through three levels of holiness when he went up to Sinai. Therefore we take three steps forward as we "approach" God in the Shemoneh Esrei *prayer.*

Remain standing with feet together while reciting Shemoneh Esrei. *Recite it with quiet devotion and without any interruption. Although it should not be audible to others, one must be able to hear his own prayers. See* Laws *§61-90 for a brief summary of its laws, including how to rectify the omission of phrases that are added at particular times of the year.*

My Lord, open my lips,* that my mouth may declare Your praise.[1]

PATRIARCHS

Bend the knees at *"Blessed"*; bow at *"You"*; straighten up at *"HASHEM."*

בָּרוּךְ **Blessed are You,* HASHEM, our God and the God of our forefathers,* God of Abraham, God of Isaac, and God of Jacob; the great, mighty, and awesome God, the supreme God,* Who bestows beneficial kindnesses and creates everything,* Who recalls the kindnesses of the Patriarchs and brings a Redeemer* to their children's children, for His Name's sake, with love.**

From Rosh Hashanah to Yom Kippur add:
Remember us for life,* O King Who desires life, and inscribe us in the Book of Life — for Your sake, O Living God.
[If forgotten, do not repeat Shemoneh Esrei. See Laws §61.]

Bend the knees at *"Blessed"*; bow at *"You"*; straighten up at *"HASHEM."*

O King, Helper, Savior, and Shield.* Blessed are You, HASHEM, Shield of Abraham.*

GOD'S MIGHT

אַתָּה **You are eternally mighty, my Lord, the Revivifier of the dead* are You, with abundant power to save.**

(1) *Psalms* 51:17.

the Redemption, when man will be worthy of His utmost blessing (*Rashba; R' Bachya*).

— This is a declaration of fact: God *is* blessed in the sense that He is perfect and complete (*Sefer HaChinuch* 430).

אֱלֹהֵינוּ וֵאלֹהֵי אֲבוֹתֵינוּ — *Our God and the God of our forefathers.* We call Him *our* God because we must serve Him and know Him to the limit of *our* capacity. But there is much about His ways that we cannot understand. Therefore we proclaim that He is *the God of our forefathers*, and we trust the tradition they transmitted (*Dover Shalom*).

אֵל עֶלְיוֹן — *The Supreme God.* The word עֶלְיוֹן, *most high*, means that God is so exalted that He is far beyond the comprehension of even the holiest angels. We can understand Him only superficially, by studying His deeds — that He *bestows beneficial kindnesses* (*Siach Yitzchak*).

וְקוֹנֶה הַכֹּל — *And creates everything.* The translation is based on the consensus of commentators, both here and to *Genesis* 14:19. Some translate *the Owner of everything*. Either way, the sense of the phrase is that God is Master of all creation.

וּמֵבִיא גוֹאֵל — *And brings a Redeemer.* The phrase is in present tense. Every event, no matter how dreadful it may seem, is a step toward the ultimate redemption by the Messiah (*Siach Yitzchak*).

זָכְרֵנוּ לְחַיִּים — *Remember us for life.* During the Ten Days of Repentance, our prayers stress our pleas for life. But we request the sort of life that God considers meaningful — לְמַעַנְךָ, *for Your sake* (*Sefer HaChaim*).

עוֹזֵר וּמוֹשִׁיעַ וּמָגֵן — *Helper, Savior, and Shield.* God "helps" (עוֹזֵר) those who try to help themselves; He "saves" (מוֹשִׁיעַ) even without the victim's participation; and "shields" (מָגֵן) to prevent danger from approaching (*Iyun Tefillah*). Alternately, *Bnei Yissaschar* comments that עוֹזֵר refers to the help that God provides without any prayer on the part of the victim, while מוֹשִׁיעַ refers to God's response to a prayer.

מָגֵן אַבְרָהָם — *Shield of Abraham.* God preserves the spark of Abraham within every Jew, no matter how far he may have strayed (*Chiddushei HaRim*).

⊰§ גְבוּרוֹת / **God's Might**

מְחַיֵּה מֵתִים — *The Revivifier of the dead.* The concept that God restores life is found three times the congregations, allowing communities the opportunity—or the danger—of appearing to adopt a prayerbook's ideology as their own.

Ironically, this transfer of power from movements to individual synagogues ultimately had a moderating influence on the development of the siddur, since it was now necessary to create a book which satisfied a wide range of ideologies. Wanting to achieve commercial viability and/or denominational unity, many siddurim in the middle of the twentieth century began developing "options," obviating a synagogue's need to choose, for example, whether the Amidah should now also contain the names of the foremothers or only the names of the forefathers. At the same time, the drumbeat of continued relevance led to repeated revisions in the translations and accompanying readings.

By the middle of the twentieth century, with American synagogue and denominational affiliation still quite strong, these ideological and moderating forces had reached something of an equilibrium. The result was a small set of sanctioned siddurim produced by a handful of internal committees achieving wide acceptance. Aside from modern English translations—understood to be of paramount importance for increasingly unlettered congregations—most of these siddurim offered little beyond the text of the prayers themselves with some light commentary. Designed around the needs of the congregation, they provided everything necessary for the congregation to follow along and little else.

Beginning in the 1970s, the decline of centralized Jewish institutions, coupled with Jewish institutional desire to make Judaism relevant in non-traditional settings led to the "individualization" of the siddur. This had three major consequences. For denominationally affiliated publishers, it meant that the siddur now needed to appeal to people and not just institutions. For progressive Jewish thinkers, the siddur became a mold upon which to impress new ideologies and a laboratory for new designs. Finally, it meant that the rise of information technology, which Jews have embraced with a particular ferocity, had been translated into the idea of the dynamically reconfigurable siddur.

Ironically, the most important siddur of this era of individualization is also the most widely adopted by more traditional institutions. The current phase of siddur production was ushered in by the 1984 publication of *The Complete Artscroll Siddur*, an Orthodox volume whose innovative features and mass appeal transcended denominational boundaries and has, in various ways, influenced every other major siddur of the last thirty years. (The 1985 *Sim Shalom* and the 1989 *Kol ha-Neshama*, mainstays of the Conservative and Reconstructionist movements respectively, should be understood as the last manifestations of the pre-Artscroll denominational siddur.)

Whereas previous American siddurim had existed largely in relation to and for the sake of synagogue worship, the Artscroll siddur was designed as a largely self-contained volume, suitable for synagogues but accessible even to those with little prior knowledge of the liturgy studying its pages in isolation. This accessibility was achieved through a clever combination of text and design. Each page of the Artscroll siddur features not just prayer, translation, and commentary, but prescriptions about appropriate gestures and sequences at a level of granularity that had never before appeared in a liturgical text.

The massive success of the Artscroll siddur, even in Conservative and liberal Orthodox communities, put all other major siddur publishers on notice that placing good design on par with accessible language was necessary for viability. The Conservative movement's *Siddur Lev Shalem* and the Reform movement's *Mishkan T'filah* have both adopted and adapted Artscroll's accoutrements; Koren, an Israel-based Orthodox publisher with a strong reputation for design, entered the Anglophone market in 2009 with a Zionist, centrist-Orthodox, and typographically-sophisticated siddur featuring a commentary by Jonathan Sacks, then Chief Rabbi of the United Hebrew Congregations of the Commonwealth. These same principles have carried over into denominational machzorim, where the intricacy and length of Rosh Hashanah and Yom Kippur services has made a helpful and engaging book even more important.

The individualization of the siddur has developed the genre in other directions, as well. Siddurim have always existed in various physical formats to suit the needs of the owner, or to separate the weekday liturgy from the Shabbat and holiday liturgy, but recently it has also become common to redesign the text and commentary for specific sorts of Jews within a larger community. In 1998, Artscroll debuted a siddur with interlinear transliteration; it has also released variants for Zionists, those with a desire for more of the older *piyyutim*, and— in 2005—a siddur specifically for women. Koren, for its part, has released several children's siddurim, each designed for a different age cohort from preschool through high school; other siddur publishers have done similarly.

The individualization of the siddur, along with drops in the price of book publication, have led to a second key phenomenon: the proliferation of boutique siddurim meant to fulfill the needs of small communities of interest. Some of these siddurim are dedicated to the liturgical idiosyncrasies of specific regions of the Old World and others reflect the interests and customs of just a single congregation, but the most interesting publications are those driven by ideology. While officially sanctioned siddurim have continued to serve as ideological platforms—witness the inclusion or exclusion of the Prayer for the

State of Israel and the associated commentary in the various siddurim—these disputes are a pale shadow of the previous century's revisions, especially as the Reform movement's re-adoption of Hebrew and a more traditional liturgy have led to a greater convergence in the establishment liturgical space.

By contrast, these smaller-scale publications have been far more daring, especially in the realm of feminist and queer-positive publications. *Siddur Nashim*, published in 1976 by undergraduates at Brown University, includes both female God-language and new rituals around menstruation, as does Jill Hammer's *Siddur haKohanot*, which describes itself as "earth based." An atheist siddur appeared in 2008; Marcia Falk's 1999 *Book of Blessings* reimagines traditional prayers and invents new ones with entirely new language. Some of these siddurim eschew Hebrew, as with Zalman Schachter-Shalomi's *Sh'ma*; others contain only the Friday night liturgy, reflecting that service's popularity against the longer, less melodic Shabbat morning services. The rise of extradenominational minyanim has also led to the creation of bespoke siddurim, created by and for a single intentional community. Notable examples are the National Havurah Committee's *Chaverim Kol Yisrael*; the LGBT-inclusive *B'chol L'vav'kha*, produced by Congregation Beit Simchat Torah in New York; and the eponymously titled *Kitchen Siddur*, produced by a San Francisco community and infused with a Silicon Valley aesthetic. These labors of love are rarely commercially successful, though some have ultimately influenced more mainstream siddurim; nonetheless, their presence points to a continued desire for a relatable tradition, even outside the walls of long-standing American Jewish institutions.

In the last two decades, the trend towards boutique prayers and prayerbooks has been massively aided by the rise of the internet, which has served as both a repository for new prayers and an archive of old ones; platforms like the Open Siddur Project and Ritualwell have sprouted up to support these efforts. Importantly, the internet's ability to store music has dramatically increased access to *nusach*, the way in which prayers are chanted; to date, this is perhaps the internet's most important contribution to the accessibility of prayer. Even more recently, the growing sophistication of siddur apps has dramatically reduced the cost of creating accessible design. At present, however, neither of these new technologies has led to a fundamental reconsideration of the siddur; the internet largely serves as an enabler of siddur content, while the smartphone has only recapitulated the revolutions initiated by Artscroll more than thirty years ago. It remains to be seen whether these technologies will take the siddur in a radically new direction, or whether the siddur's longstanding relationship with paper will continue to show the way forward.

4. David Hartman, *A Living Covenant: The Innovative Spirit in Traditional Judaism*

David Hartman, *A Living Covenant: The Innovative Spirit in Traditional Judaism*, Woodstock: Jewish Lights Publishing, 1985

Rabbi Dr. David Hartman (1931–2013) was the Founding President of the Shalom Hartman Institute in Jerusalem and also served as Professor of Jewish Thought at Hebrew University.

This book attempts to characterize Judaism in terms of a covenantal anthropology that encourages human initiative and freedom and that is predicated on belief in human adequacy. I argue that a covenantal vision of life, with *mitzvah* (divine commandment) as the central organizing principle in the relationship between Jews and God, liberates both the intellect and the moral will. I seek to show that a tradition mediated by the Sinai covenant can encourage the development of a human being who is not afraid to assume responsibility for the ongoing drama of Jewish history. Passive resignation is seen not to be an essential trait of one whose relationship to God is mediated by the hearing of *mitzvot*. (3)

I argue strongly for the significance of Jewish particularity, not for its uniqueness. The covenantal election of Israel at Sinai, which is a central theme in this work, should not be understood as implying a metaphysical claim regarding the ontological uniqueness of the Jewish people. I do not subscribe to the view that a serious commitment to the God of Israel and Torah requires one to believe that the Jewish people mediate the only authentic way for the worship of God. I make no claims regarding all the non-Judaic ways of giving meaning and significance to human life. The range of my philosophizing about Judaism does not go beyond the range of my limited, particular experience as a Jew. Judaism does not provide me with an anchor point beyond a particular community and its history. The Jewish tradition and the Jewish people mediate for me the dignity and humility that comes from the full acceptance of particularity and human limitation. I only explicate a way in which the tradition can encourage a spiritual direction through its emphasis on the covenantal relationship of Israel with God. (3–4)

The breakdown of halakhic authority, the loss of a shared value framework for translating our historical consciousness into present day experiences, is one of the most significant challenges to which Jewish philosophical thought must address itself in the modern world. Can Jewish monotheism admit the legitimacy of religious pluralism? Can covenantal Judaism accommodate the various options through which Jews have chosen to give meaning to their existence?

My book does not attempt to work out the way in which ethics can control halakhic development, nor does it try to establish the limits of tolerance and pluralism. Nevertheless, it provides a framework and a religious sensibility from which to begin to chart a new direction for Judaism so that it might become a living possibility for a Jew who takes the modern world with radical seriousness.

Pluralism requires an epistemological framework that limits the claims of revelation. It requires a political philosophy in which the unity of God does not imply one universal way for all humankind. However, before epistemological and political theory can chart new directions for Judaism, we need a conceptual framework in which covenantal consciousness is permeated by a religious sensibility that celebrates finitude and creatureliness as permanent features of a covenantal life. A human sensibility that is open to and appreciative of the possibilities of pluralism is the foundation from which one can build a new epistemological understanding of revelation and *halakhah*. (17–18)

The Zionist quest for normalcy should free the Jewish people of any myth about the unique moral and spiritual powers of the Jewish soul. In taking upon ourselves responsibility for a total society, we must allow ourselves to be judged by the same standards as we have judged others. The Torah challenges us to becomes a holy people. It does not tell us that we are immune from the moral weaknesses and failures that affect every human being. The Jewish nation is not free from the same potential corruptions that affect any human community that has taken upon itself the bold challenge of living with power. Our newly gained sense of belonging and power enables us to look critically and honestly both at ourselves and at the halakhic tradition without the apologetic stance so characteristic of a community that saw itself as a persecuted and vulnerable minority. A community that feels dignified and secure in its identity and place in the world can allow itself the mature activity of honest critical self-appraisal.

To the degree that we can look at ourselves in a non-apologetic light, to that degree will we demonstrate our liberation from an exilic consciousness that is fundamentally timid, frightened, and outer-directed. We are free now to ask what we think of ourselves without being overly concerned with the way others will listen and respond to our agonizing self-appraisal. Because of our "role" as the suffering stranger in history, many have perceived the Jew as the moral conscience and critic of social and political injustice. In building the third Jewish commonwealth, our role must shift from the moral criticism of others to self-judgement. In coming home, the task before us is to clean up our own house. (296–297)

COMMENTARY BY DAVID ELLENSON

In *A Living Covenant*, David Hartman offered a picture of a living covenantal Judaism embedded in both the Jewish textual tradition and the reality of the land and people of Israel. In presenting this portrait of Judaism, Hartman rejected a notion of religion that distinguishes between law and spirit. Instead, he contended that an authentic Judaism incorporated both these elements.

To fully grasp the character of his thought, it is crucial to note that Hartman, like Martin Buber before him, insisted in *A Living Covenant* as well as his later writings that "genuine religiosity" requires "doing." However, in strong opposition to Buber, he completely rejected the notion that a commitment to Jewish law "damns" the Jews' "demand for freedom" and "degenerates into hairsplitting casuistry" that "enslaves religiosity."[1] Rather, he maintained that the values and beliefs that undergird Judaism are manifest in a "living covenant" that is concretized through a vibrant interpretive legal tradition. Hartman argued that Jewish law was capable of engagement with the modern world in a manner that is both faithful to the past and germane to the present, and he drew upon social, political, and religious categories of Western thought to present a spiritual-ethical vision of Judaism that called upon the Jewish people located in the State of Israel as well as in the Diaspora to manifest that vision and the values that flow from it in real life. His was a corporeal Judaism devoted to a commitment to all elements of traditional Jewish faith—God, Torah, and Israel.

Hartman strove mightily in *A Living Covenant* to articulate how the Jewish law might be approached so that an application of its resources could provide Jews appropriate and authentic guidance for the novel holistic venue created by the establishment of the third Jewish commonwealth. In order to do this, Hartman turned to the sobriety that marks the processes of the rabbinic tradition,

---

1   Martin Buber, *On Judaism* (New York: Schocken Books, 1967), 91–93.

particularly as that tradition finds expression in the writings of the great medieval philosopher Maimonides and other rabbinic teachers. From this rabbinic tradition, Hartman learned that God is not primarily discovered—as the Bible alone would have it—in the immediacy of personal encounter and experience. Instead, asserted Hartman, "From my many years of Talmud study, I learned that one can sense the living God of revelation … in the writings of any committed and learned covenantal teacher" (9).

Hartman called upon modern Jewish teachers to master the texts written by these past savants. He also challenged contemporary students of the Law to have the courage to assert their own authority by displaying the confidence past generations of rabbis did when they applied such textual mastery in new ways to meet the challenges of ever-changing situations. Hartman emphasized the authenticity and creativity he believed inherent in this process when he wrote:

> The Talmud contradicts the idea that "later" means "spiritually inferior" when it insists that the rabbinic sage is superior to the prophet. To accord the Talmud equal status with the Bible is to augment revelation not merely with a particular body of literature or school of teachers but with a method of interpretation that emphasizes the open-ended possibilities of learning from the received word. The covenant as reflected in the creative talmudic style of interpretation enables Jews to feel free to apply their own human reason to the understanding and application of the Torah. (9)

Maimonides, Hartman contended, properly understood all this, and Hartman asserted "that the covenant with the Jewish tradition was made for the sake of the oral tradition." The epistemological posture subsumed in this stance granted Hartman the license to maintain confidently that Judaism accords a rabbinic tradition of interpretation "the central place" in Judaism, and that such tradition is mediated through human understandings and discussions. On this basis, Hartman was able to state, "I philosophize within a tradition in which human teachers mediate my covenantal relationship with the God of Israel" (10).

By making this declaration, Hartman revealed his preference for what he long argued is a Maimonidean naturalistic approach to Jewish tradition that focuses upon the role that human agents play in establishing the parameters and demands of the covenant through the processes of rational legal interpretation. Some Orthodox colleagues were sharply critical of what they regarded as the anthropocentrism of this stance.[2] However, Hartman himself defended this position as true to the tradition and even contended that his own posture on this question was true to the legacy of his teacher Rabbi Joseph Soloveitchik.[3]

Nevertheless, Hartman recognized that this attitude stands in sharp contrast to another trajectory in Jewish tradition, one that Hartman identified with the Bible and the teachings of Judah Halevi. Both the Bible and Halevi, as Hartman viewed them, eschew a focus on the legal tradition. Instead, they focused upon an unmediated sense of God's immediacy which they believed resides at the heart of Judaism. In reflecting his preference in *A Living Covenant* for the mediation of the present in rabbinic tradition, Hartman not only built upon his previous work as expressed in books such as *Maimonides and the Philosophic Quest* (1977). He also foreshadowed a linchpin in the larger argument he would ultimately advance in his *A Heart of Many Rooms* (1999) and *Israelis and the Jewish Tradition* (2000) as well as other works.

The identification of these two poles of Jewish tradition as represented by Maimonides and Halevi also facilitated and supported Hartman's contention that Judaism is not monolithic but pluralistic. The polyvocality of Maimonides and Halevi provided him with an intellectual foundation to maintain that an examination of Jewish religious history legitimates pluralism. Consequently, Hartman was completely comfortable in candidly admitting that his own approach to Jewish tradition was selective. Indeed, he stated that his rendering of the tradition was totally "related to my philosophical concern to locate specific tendencies or possibilities within the rabbinic tradition that could be supportive of a covenantal religious anthropology capable of participating in the challenge of modernity" (13). Hartman made a persuasive case that Jewish tradition itself extends its blessing to this type of self-conscious and self-selective approach to Jewish law.

In arriving at this conclusion, Hartman underscored one of the major themes that long characterized his work. Throughout his lifetime, Hartman attempted to interpret and renew the Jewish legal tradition so as to demonstrate its vitality even in a modern setting where most Jews were so distant from this tradition that they neither resonated to its language nor found its holdings compelling. He argued that this was because so many teachers of rabbinic Judaism

---

2   For example, see Daniel Landes, "A Vision of Finitude: David Hartman's 'A Living Covenant,'" *Tikkun* 1, no. 2 (1986): 106–111, for a representative Orthodox critique of this type.

3   See Hartman's response to Landes in David Hartman and Daniel Landes, "Current Debate: Human Autonomy and Divine Providence," *Tikkun* 2, no. 1 (1986): 121–126, as well as *A Living Covenant, passim.*

neglected to emphasize its interpretive tropes that place the human decisor at the center.

As a result, it is hardly surprising to find this theme of rational human response to the words of the living God as found in Jewish legal texts articulated so intensely in the pages of *A Living Covenant*. Indeed, Hartman eloquently and passionately summarized his position when he wrote, "The living word of God can be mediated through the application of human reason ... to the revealed norms of Torah. This is the essence of the dialectical vitality of talmudic Judaism" (40). From narratives contained in the Talmud itself, Hartman found support for this posture. He maintained that the tradition itself teaches that the rabbi "is competent to introduce new legislation defining how the community is to behave. ... The intellectual mastery of the word of God ... is all the scholar requires to understand and define how ... the community of Israel ... [is] to behave" (51).

For Hartman, halakhic interpretation is an act of creative decision, not simply an uncovering of what is already there, for the text is always open to a number of meanings. Hartman would develop this point at greater length in *A Heart of Many Rooms*. However, it is enough to note that this argument already stood at the center of his concerns in *A Living Covenant*. He did not apologize for maintaining that rabbinic Judaism countenances the notion that an autonomous human moral sense can play a legitimately seminal role in covenantal Judaism.

However, it was by wedding this concern to an emphasis upon the State of Israel as the major (though not exclusive) venue for the expression of this ethos that Hartman marked himself as unique among modern Jewish thinkers. By lavishing his attention upon the State of Israel in *A Living Covenant*, Hartman developed a theme that while present, was more muted in his earlier writings.[4] In linking his emphasis upon Jewish law to the theological significance of the Jewish state in his 1985 book, Hartman heralded a new emphasis in his thought. He contended that the State of Israel now constituted the necessary precondition for the full realization of the Covenant inasmuch as only Israeli Jews were fully responsible for the homes they would build and the institutions they would construct.

This focus on the connection between a covenantal life grounded in Halakhah and the primary import accorded the Jewish state as the major

---

4   Moshe Sokol, "David Hartman," in *Interpreters of Judaism in the Late Twentieth Century*, ed. Steven T. Katz (Washington, D.C.: B'nai B'rith Books, 1993), 91–112, has pointed this out in his fine essay.

though not sole locus for its expression surely distinguished Hartman even at this juncture in his career from other Jewish thinkers with whom he was then identified.[5] While elements of his thought surely overlapped with ideals put forth by prominent Jewish thinkers such as Eugene B. Borowitz and Irving Greenberg, the differences between Hartman and these men were and are surely pronounced as well. His was not a covenantal theology that looked to the Holocaust as Greenberg did for direction, nor did he fail to accord preeminence to the richness of a living Jewish legal tradition or the centrality of an ever responsive and evolving Jewish state, themes that distinguished him from Borowitz. Indeed, his dual emphasis upon both a vital Jewish law and a vibrant Jewish state grant Hartman a unique position among the pantheon of contemporary Jewish thinkers. This singular posture characterized Hartman in *A Living Covenant,* and foreshadowed positions he would develop even further in his later thought. These insights from the pen of an Orthodox rabbi constituted a signal contribution to a modern philosophy of Jewish law as well as a significant gift to modern Jewish thought.

---

5   For such connections between Hartman and other prominent Jewish thinkers, see David Singer, "The New Orthodox Theology," *Modern Judaism* 9, no. 1 (1989): 35–54.

5. Neil Gillman, *Sacred Fragments: Recovering Theology for the Modern Jew*

Eugene Borowitz, *Renewing the Covenant: A Theology for the Postmodern Jew*

Neil Gillman, *Sacred Fragments: Recovering Theology for the Modern Jew*, Philadelphia: Jewish Publication Society, 1990

Rabbi Dr. Neil Gillman (1933–2017) was Aaron Rabinowitz and Simon H. Rifkind Professor of Jewish Philosophy at the Jewish Theological Seminary.

In an age that places a premium on individualism and autonomy, obedience to arbitrary divine decrees does not come easily. For those of us who were not raised in observant homes, ritual observances demand a choreography that is unfamiliar and threatening. It is not easy for adults to begin observing the dietary laws, turn their kitchens inside out, and accept the social limitations that this discipline demands. It is not easy to begin putting on *tefillin* in a public forum such as the synagogue chapel, or to adopt the practice of ritual immersion after menstruation—just to cite a few more examples. How can we justify these dramatic changes in lifestyle, first to ourselves and then to our families and friends?

Is it any wonder that many of us prefer to view religion as a matter of faith and belief alone, as inwardness or emotion ("I'm a Jew at heart!"), or as affecting primarily our interpersonal, ethical behavior? We may accept the fact that religion can dictate giving charity, dealing honestly with our fellows, remaining faithful to our spouses, and avoiding gossip or slander. What more can it legitimately require of us? Isn't it enough to be a good person? (215–216)

There is no question that Judaism wants us to be "good people." In fact, according to Isaiah 1, Hosea 6:6, and most of prophetic literature, God wants us, *above all*, to be good people. He abhors the Sabbath and Festivals and Israel's sacrifices when they are accompanied by flagrant violations of His moral law. Above all, He wants us to be concerned with the oppressed and the disadvantaged, with justice and compassion. His destruction of the Temple as punishment for the moral failings of the biblical community is powerful testimony to the hierarchy of values in prophetic religion.

But it is also clear that Isaiah is not denouncing the Sabbath, the Festivals, and the sacrificial cult themselves. After all, a later prophet, Ezekiel, prophesied at length about the rebuilding of the Temple, and the returning exiles did rebuild it with the explicit approval of that generation's prophets (Haggai 1:2ff). What Isaiah could not tolerate was the place that ritual has assumed in the life of the community. Jeremiah 7:8–15 is even more precise. The Temple had come to be viewed as a magical guarantor of security. The Israelites seem to have assumed that as long as there was a Temple, as long as the proper sacrifices were offered, they could do anything else they wished and still be safe, for God would never dare destroy His Temple. But He did—and in so doing, He said loudly and clearly that the Temple was created not for His sake but, rather, for the sake of a community of human beings. This seems to be the Bible's way of affirming what modern scholars have recently rediscovered: that ritual serves a powerful human—and not a divine—need.

The choice, then, is never between being a good person and a ritually observant Jew, but rather between competing ritual systems. Our problem is that we belong to multiple communities with multiple ritual systems. Sometimes our different communities cohere; we can have a kosher wedding dinner at the Plaza Hotel. But sometimes they don't; we can't serve shrimp cocktail at a kosher wedding. And then we have to choose. Who are we? Where do we belong? What is our identity? With that choice comes the choice of a ritual system. (242–243)

If we live in an age of communal fragmentation, anomie, and isolation, or rootlessness and emotional aridity, then more than ever we need ritual, even more theatrically performed than ever before—even if some of us no longer believe, as our ancestors did, that God explicitly commanded us to act in these seemingly arbitrary ways. If God did not command, then maybe we can discern a commanding voice in our very human nature and in our communal needs, and we may be prepared to hearken as obediently to this voice as our ancestors did to God's. (244)

Eugene Borowitz, *Renewing the Covenant: A Theology for the Postmodern Jew*, Philadelphia: Jewish Publication Society, 1991

Rabbi Dr. Eugene Borowitz (1928–2016) was Sigmund L. Falk Distinguished Professor of Education and Jewish Religious Thought at the Hebrew Union College-Jewish Institute of Religion.

In my view, Jewish autonomy becomes the use of our freedom in terms of our personal participation in the people of Israel's Covenant with God as the latest expression of its historic tradition.

Two intensifications of general human sociality arise from this conception of the Jewish self. As in all religions, living in Covenant involves a human being's most utterly fundamental relationship, namely, that with God. Hence our religious communities and duties cannot be peripheral to our lives but must be at their center; anything less than profound devotion and commitment profanes our professions of Jewish faith. Moreover, because the Covenant was made primarily with the Jewish *ethnos* and only secondarily with the Jewish *autos*, the Jewish people, its local communities, families, and progeny, remain the immediate channels through which we Jews sacralize existence. Since modern life immerses us in an individualistic ethos, all contemporary Judaisms must stress the sociality of Jewish spirituality so that we may live in proper Covenantal duality. (224)

Jewish critics of personalistic revelation charge it with invalidating a critical characteristic of Judaism, *halakhah*. As a logical observation, the indictment has merit: one cannot derive a legal structure from a theory that ultimately reserves authority for the self—even the self in relationship. But I reject the normative principle that authentic Jewish continuity requires the halakhic process. Our people did not lack Covenant-faithfulness in the millennium before the rabbinic period, when its primary religious structure appears to have been priestly and cultic. This precedent allows for the possibility that the rabbinic structuring of Jewish life that proved so effective until the Emancipation may now need to be drastically altered. Positively put, do the radically changed Jewish social status and cultural ethos that resulted from modernization prompt us to devise a more appropriate way of framing Jewish existence?

Two interrelated considerations, one practical and one theoretical, lead me to say "Yes." To begin with reality, almost all Jews who have modernized now consider Jewish law to be instructive rather than obligatory. Only the Orthodox and the few non-Orthodox ideologically committed to the necessity of *halakhah* discipline their lives by it. The remaining members of the caring community simply take for granted their right to determine what provisions of the *halakhah* they will and will not observe.

These Jews have negative and positive grounds for their insistence on autonomy. They do not believe God gave the Written and Oral Law and they remain unpersuaded that the Jewish desirability of the halakhic process should lead them to constrain their freedom by its rulings. Were there a non-Orthodox theory of revelation that indicated how God authorizes the corporate determination of individual Jewish duty, many might bend conscience to a newly flexible *halakhah*. But no one has yet provided one and the task seems presently undoable. The stumbling block remains the authority we have vested in selfhood. We have no compelling theories of corporate authority that still allow for something like the normativity we commonly grant to self-determination; mostly, we prefer to reason from self to society. (281)

COMMENTARY BY MICHAEL MARMUR

Neil Gillman's *Sacred Fragments* and Eugene Borowitz's *Renewing the Covenant* merit comparison for many reasons. Published within a year of each other by the Jewish Publication Society, these works brought European liberal streams of modern Jewish thought into the American Jewish mainstream. They both appeal to and epitomize a certain kind of reader: a postwar Western Jew rooted in modernity, compelled by Jewish affiliation, seeking a rationale for Jewish commitment.

Each of these works has had a palpable impact since their initial publication. JPS reports that sales for each of them have been impressive, Borowitz's work having sold some 5,500 copies, and Gillman's almost 15,000. Gillman's sales in particular are remarkable for a book of this kind. It is one of the most widely read books of Jewish thought of its era. Taken together, they represent the premier theological statements of the established non-Orthodox streams in the late twentieth century.

The true impact that these books and their authors have exercised on Jewish life in North America cannot be measured simply in terms of royalties. The primary reason for this is the role played by each of the authors in the formation of generations of non-Orthodox rabbis in America. Neil Gillman was associated with the Jewish Theological Seminary for over five decades, and in the course of that time he helped mold the theological orientation of the Conservative movement. Eugene B. Borowitz played a similar role at the New York campus of the Hebrew Union College—Jewish Institute of Religion. As well as his decades of service as a teacher at the College and his standing as the leading Reform theologian of his generation, Borowitz's role as the founder of *Sh'ma: A Journal of Jewish Responsibility* allowed to him to play a significant convening role for ethical discourse within the Jewish community across denominational lines.

These two men, then, lived in the same era and played comparable roles in their respective denominations. It is reasonable to predict that when the story of American Jewish thought in their era is told, Gillman and Borowitz will each command significant attention. Students who studied with them in a seminary setting went on to discuss and propagate their ideas with their congregants and in this way the key concepts of these books gained currency in non-Orthodox Jewish discourse in North America.

From amongst the canon of modern Jewish thinkers, both Gillman and Borowitz afford pride of place to two *zugot*, two pairs of contemporaries, who between them have helped define the agenda for contemporary non-Orthodox Judaism in America: Franz Rosenzweig and Martin Buber from the German context, and Mordecai Kaplan and Abraham Joshua Heschel from the American.

The influence of some others is common to both works. Both Gillman and Borowitz discuss Paul Tillich and Richard Rubenstein, and they both mention Arthur Cohen, Emil Fackenheim, and Louis Jacobs. It is in the discrepancies between the sources upon which they draw that something can be learned about their contrasting approaches. Maimonides is mentioned only in passing by Borowitz, but he figures prominently in Gillman's work, as does Judah Halevi, who plays no part in *Renewing the Covenant*. Gillman's palette includes Norman Lamm and Gershom Scholem, Harold Kushner and Will Herberg. Borowitz says nothing of these men in this book, but instead engages with the thought of Hermann Cohen, Leo Baeck, Ahad Ha'am, Michael Wyschogrod, and Arthur Green. To some degree these differences reflect denominational divergence and to some degree different intellectual appetites.

The authors also intend their books to serve different purposes. Gillman indicates at the very end of the work, in an afterword on "Doing Your Own Theology," his ambitions concerning the book itself. Suggesting that it may help individuals and groups as they struggle to formulate their own theologies, he notes that his work

... provides an outline of what our classical (i.e., biblical and rabbinic) sources have to say on a specific issue, traces some of the later formulations in medieval Jewish philosophy and mysticism, and outlines in more detail how contemporary thinkers have dealt with it. I suggest a set of criteria for evaluating each of these contemporary positions, and I conclude each chapter with my own position, indicating why it seems most adequate to me. (277)

Here in a nutshell is a description of the book's purpose and method. Gillman selects ten areas of theological speculation and with each of them he follows this approach. As he writes in the book's introduction, he hopes to engage his readers in a struggle for answers, and to provide them with tools to facilitate the struggle.

Gillman's choice of topics is remarkable, both for what it includes and for what is left off the list. He opens with revelation, arguing that "it is revelation that creates Judaism as a religion" (1). Taken together, these first chapters offer a discussion of the authorship, authenticity, and authority of Torah. The following five chapters all concern the central theme of classical theology—knowing, talking about, sensing, proving, and encountering God. The first of these chapters offers a broad grounding for the discussion, the second relates to the issue of symbolic language, and then empiricism, rationalism, and existentialism are discussed in turn.

The book's eighth chapter is an exercise in theodicy, asking why God allows suffering in the world. Theological responses to the Holocaust are discussed here, although unlike Borowitz's *Renewing the Covenant*, Gillman's work does not dwell on the impact of the Holocaust for the very possibility of doing theology. While chapter nine returns to the theme of ritual touched upon earlier in the work, the tenth and final chapter grapples with the end of days, a theme to which Gillman was to return in his 1997 work *The Death of Death*.

The issues represented here do not constitute a broad-ranging systematic theology. There is no place here for the people Israel, let alone for the modern State. Feminism is mentioned only in passing. There is next to no discussion of the encounter between Judaism and other religious traditions, and questions of political and social engagement are similarly de-emphasized. Instead of these and other possible components of an agenda of modern Jewish thought, Gillman offers his readers a way into a sophisticated modern discussion of God's essence, God's presence, God's expression, and God's promise.

No wonder, then, that the subtitle of Gillman's book is *Recovering Theology for the Modern Jew*. In contrast, Borowitz appended to the title of his book a different descriptor: *A Theology for the Postmodern Jew*. In order to understand what Borowitz means by the term "postmodern Jew," it is helpful to review the structure of his work. Twenty chapters are organized into four parts, the first of which, "Jewish Religious Experience in Our Time," serves as a preface. This opening section sets out Borowitz's critique of modernity, described in the title of chapter two as "The Betrayer." Borowitz's postmodernism, then, is not a matter of abstruse formulations favored by literary theorists of the French school. Rather, it is born of a post-Holocaust wariness about the promises of progress.

The next section of the work, "A Postliberal Theology of Jewish Duty," spans approximately two-thirds of the book. It is further divided into two parts, the first offering a discussion of "God, the Ground of Our Values," and the second "Israel, the People That Creates the Way." The closing two chapters relate explicitly to the theme of covenant, which—as Borowitz points out in his Preface to the entire work—had been a theological preoccupation of his since 1961. The final four chapters of the work are gathered under the heading "The Torah Born of Covenant." In this way Borowitz includes what he describes as the holistic context of the God-Israel-Torah triad of classical Jewish theology, and manages to present these perennial themes in the light of his analysis of modernity and its discontents, and through the prism of his particular approach, covenant theology. In the words of Borowitz himself, *Renewing the Covenant* is "a comprehensive theology pivoting on my understanding of "Covenant," although he then hastens to add that the book "deals with but one aspect of my theology," as if to say the naive belief of a previous generation in the possibility of a truly systematic theology is one victim of our postmodern condition (ix).

Gillman makes no secret of his own theological views in the course of his book. He states, for example, that "[t]here is simply no religious authority outside of a halakhic system" (59). Nevertheless, the core purpose of his work is not to promote his beliefs, but to encourage theological discourse among the clergy and lay readers to whom the book is directed. The afterword, a guide to "Doing Your Own Theology," makes this explicit. His method, summarizing millennia of thought and focusing on prevalent positions among contemporary thinkers, offers a way in to serious wrestling with Big Questions.

Borowitz, in contrast is not trying to summarize, but rather to offer an exploration of his own reading of some key modern thinkers, and an explication of his own position. The difference in sales may be a reflection of this difference in purpose. *Fragments* can be used as a kind of roadmap for personal theological search. *Covenant* may contribute to such a search, but as a thick and somewhat complex exploration of a leading theologian's point of view. The writing style of these two works also reflects this distinction—Gillman's prose is more accessible.

Gillman and Borowitz offer their readers examples of serious engagement with some of the great Jewish questions of the day. While Gillman's project is in essence to curate and convene an exploration of Big Jewish Ideas, Borowitz's primary goal is to express his vision of the postmodern Jewish self, living in covenant and striving to build a Jewish future. For most of the work, he speaks in general and theoretical terms, such as this formulation:

> Only when we end the distinction between our personhood and our Jewishness and understand ourselves as indivisibly Jewish selves, persons whose selfhood is inextricable from their participation in the Jewish people and its historic relationship with God, will we make possible a vigorous postmodern life of Torah. (181)

At the very end of the book, however, Borowitz offers some examples of how his covenantal approach to Jewish duty informs his stances on particular questions. He then outlines the reasons for his refusal to officiate at intermarriages. Here, then, is a Reform voice at the conservative end of the spectrum, a postliberal Jew in search of a grounding for the utterance of that least popular word in the liberal lexicon: no.

These two books appeared within a year of each other, and some twenty-five years later their authors died within a year of each other. In the intervening years both Gillman and Borowitz continued and deepened their endeavors as beloved teachers and respected writers, but more than any other of their works it is these two books which have come to epitomize their contributions to American Jewish discourse. With their passing, the mantle of serious, intellectual, pious, engaged, honest, and cogent non-Orthodox Jewish thought must pass to others committed to recovering theology and to renewing the covenant.

6. Rachel Adler, "In Your Blood, Live: Re-visions of a Theological Purity"

Rachel Adler "In Your Blood, Live: Re-visions of a Theological Purity," *Tikkun* 8, No. 1 (January/February 1993)

Rabbi Dr. Rachel Adler (1943–) is Rabbi David Ellenson Professor of Jewish Religious Thought and Professor of Modern Jewish Thought and Feminist Studies at Hebrew Union College-Jewish Institute of Religion.

When I was Orthodox, I thought that God's Torah was as complete as God: inerrant, invulnerable, invariable truth. I thought that I, the erring, bleeding, mutable creature, had to bend myself to this truth. Whatever I was or saw that did not fit had to be cut off, had to be blocked out. The eye—or the I—was alone at fault. I tried to make a theology to uphold this truth, and as hard as I tried to make it truthful, it unfolded itself to me as a theology of lies.

I do not believe the laws of purity will ever be reinstated, nor should they be. The worlds reflected in such rules are not worlds we inhabit. Neither should we seek to replicate such worlds. They are unjust.

In the mind of God, according to a midrash, is a Torah of black fire written on white fire. In the hands of Jews is a Torah written in gall on the skins of dead animals. And the miracle is that the fire of God's Torah flickers through our scroll. I continue to learn the purity texts, hoping for some yet unglimpsed spark, but that is not enough. I must learn what purity can mean in my own world and in the most human world I can envision. For if ours is a Torah of and for human beings, it may be perfected only in the way that we perfect ourselves. We do not become more God-like by becoming less human, but by becoming more deeply, more broadly, more comprehensively human.

We must keep asking the Torah to speak to us in human, this crude jargon studded with constraints and distortions, silences and brutalities, that is our only vessel for holiness and truth and peace. We must keep teaching each other, we and our study partner the Torah, all that it means to be human. Human is not whole. Human is full of holes. Human bleeds. Human births its worlds in agonies of blood and bellyaches. Human owns no perfect, timeless texts because human inhabits no perfect, timeless contexts. Human knows that what it weds need not be perfect to be infinitely dear.

COMMENTARY BY GAIL LABOVITZ

It is a rare thing to be a theologian who, in a single short article ("*Tumah* and *Taharah*: Ends and Beginnings," first published in *The Jewish Catalog* in 1973), makes an ancient practice—one long associated with deeply negative ideas about women's bodies and bodily processes—meaningful for a new generation of Jewish women (and men). Rarer still is for that theologian to decide two decades later that she was wrong, that moreover she needed to publicly retract her original work. Yet that is precisely what Rachel Adler is determined to do in this article, first published in *Tikkun* (and then included in the anthology *Lifecycles: Jewish Women on Biblical Themes in Contemporary Life*).[1]

The practice in question is actually a complex of laws, customs, and rituals around menstruation and sexual relations within heterosexual marriage. A menstruating woman is deemed in the Torah (Leviticus 15:19–21) to be *tameh*, a word typically translated as "(ritually) impure." A man is forbidden to have sexual contact with a woman while she is menstruating (see also Leviticus 18:19 and 20:18), and she conveys *tum'ah* (impurity) to items she touches, wears, or sits on. Even after the destruction of the Second Temple in 70 CE (the site at which concerns about ritual purity and impurity might be considered to be most relevant, and moreover a site necessary to the removal of some forms of impurity through sacrifice), the early rabbis of the Mishnah and Talmud further developed these laws and practices, indeed devoting an entire tractate to the topic, Tractate Niddah. To this day, many halakhically observant Jews continue to preserve these laws, including refraining from sexual intercourse and a variety of other forms of physical contact and other interactions that might be considered sexually provocative during the woman's menses, examination of blood stains to determine if they are menstrual, and the woman's immersion in a *mikveh* (a ritual pool of water) after the cessation of her blood flow and the counting of an additional seven "clean days."

The gendered nature of these laws (since typically only female bodies menstruate) has made them a topic of great concern for all. The historically male power structure of rabbinic Judaism and ordinary men in their role as husbands, were faced with a set of practice that must rely on women to report on and respond to their bodily functions if men are to have sexual access to them. Women were tasked with monitoring their cycles, maintaining restrictions

---

1 Debra Orenstein (ed.), *Lifecycles: Jewish Women on Biblical Themes in Contemporary Life* (Woodstock: Jewish Lights Publishing, 1997).

when warranted under the law, and seeing to their return to permissibility by proper immersion in the *mikveh*, and they lived with all the meanings and imagery, frequently quite derogatory, that were imposed in the course of Jewish history on this fundamental bodily function.

In her original article, Adler intended to break into the gendered, and more particularly androcentric or even misogynistic, discourse of regulating women's behavior and sexual availability during menstruation. She sought at one and the same time to find an explanation of these practices that could affirm women, their bodies, and female experiences of embodiment (on the one hand), and to situate these practices in a larger discourse of (ritual) purity and impurity that encompassed all Jews rather than being focused specifically on women (on the other). The two aims were linked in her earlier thinking.

She pursued these aims through a turn to "fields of secular learning: anthropology, literary criticism, comparative religion" ("In Your Blood," 39)—most notably the anthropological approach of Mary Douglas to concepts of purity and pollution, and the phenomenological approach of Mircea Eliade on the symbolism(s) of water and cycles of time. Thus, she observed that within the Torah, menstrual impurity laws are situated in a network of laws about multiple types of *tum'ah*, which is imparted from a variety of sources and in a variety of circumstances, including contact with a corpse of a human or animal, the skin disease known as *tzara'at*, semen, and childbirth. Adler argued that the components of the system as a whole share a common feature: "our confrontation with the fact of our own mortality" ("*Tumah* and *Taharah*," 64). That is, *tum'ah* arises at nexus points between life and death, and thus "is simply part of the human cycle. To be *tameh* is not wrong or bad. Often it is necessary and sometimes it is mandatory" ("*Tumah* and *Taharah*," 64). Menstrual blood, no more or less than any other source of *tum'ah*, marks the cycle of death and rebirth; that "which inside the womb was a potential nutriment, is a token of dying when shed," a potential pregnancy that did not come to fruition. If *tum'ah* and *taharah* represent universal themes of (contact with) death and (the return to) life, then women, too, should be understood (and experience themselves) as representatives of the most fundamental ontological distinctions of the human condition. In light of this understanding, women (and men) would not have reason to find themselves particularly stigmatized by these laws on the basis of their sex.

In "In Your Blood, Live" Adler enumerates and examines many of the textual and legal elements of this practice, which now suggest to her that her earlier thesis was incomplete, even inaccurate.

First, even if *tum'ah* and *taharah* indeed functioned in the biblical sys-tem as Adler initially suggested, so that all members of the society could cycle through the conditions of purity and impurity in basically equivalent ways, this is no longer helpful for understanding *tum'ah* in the post-biblical and particu-larly rabbinic Judaisms that followed. Post-rabbinic *tum'ah* is gendered particu-larly female, such that all females are (treated as) suspect of being in the process of menstruating and hence impure, while men, who certainly must have come into contact with sources of impurity such as seminal emissions and proximity to a corpse, nonetheless experience themselves as pure at all times. In addition, Adler demonstrates, even the biblical texts are filled with gendered assumptions about purity and a particular revulsion for female impurity that becomes a met-aphor for moral and ethical impurity (corrupt Jerusalem imagined as a woman whose skirts are stained by her menstrual blood, for example, a trope found in Lamentations and several prophetic books). While Adler does not directly mention this point in either essay, this highly negative view of menstruation and the menstruating woman was perpetuated and adapted in rabbinic texts (see, for example, Babylonian Talmud Pesachim 111a) and in later works such as the early medieval Baraita de-Niddah.

The rabbinic and post-rabbinic approach to menstruation, moreover, never addressed the relevant practices in terms of women's experiences or spiritual-ity. Rather, women in this body of law (as in many others as well) function as instruments and as a possible threat. At issue is men's sexual access to women, and women's potentially polluting effect on men. Within this framework, how is a woman to understand herself as a "God-created creature" ("In Your Blood," 38)? Adler's initial impulse had been to find a way into that difference between "how women were to comport themselves in their impurity" and "how a body that menstruates, a body that pollutes, could be a holy body ... what it might mean to be pure" (39). Her earlier stance, she argues, fell into (or itself cre-ated) a gap between the theoretical and the actual; that is, it failed to account for women's lives in a way that encompass not only their own bodies and expe-riences thereof, but also the societal context that (androcentrically and nega-tively) interprets and regulates their bodily experiences.

Along these lines, one of the most cogent analyses of the import of Adler's retraction is that of Jonah Steinberg.[2] Steinberg suggests that what is significant about the change of theorization for the laws of menstrual purity originally

---

2   Jonah Steinberg, "From a 'Pot of Filth' to a 'Hedge of Roses' (and Back)," *Journal of Feminist Studies in Religion* 13, no. 2 (1997): 5–26.

posed by Adler (as well as similar reinterpretations that have become popular especially among "Modern" Orthodox communities) is that it did not entail a change in actual practice. Adler's theorization could, as she herself acknowledged in her later essay, thus become for some rabbis "merely an effective apologia for getting educated women to use the mikveh" ("In Your Blood," 39) even as they ignored or overlooked some of the disturbing implications her methodology could have for understanding Judaism and Jewish theology. This, in turn, according to Steinberg, "allows multiple frameworks of theorization to exist superimposed," so that "the practices themselves are still amenable to a former, harmful justification that abides conspicuously in canonical sources" (24–25). For Adler, it was in fact seeing women create new rituals involving the *mikveh* (often as part of a healing process for uniquely female experiences of trauma around sex and sexuality, such as cancers of the reproductive system, miscarriages, sexual assaults) that brought her to an insight of this very sort in "In Your Blood, Live": "When Jewish women who were not Orthodox appropriated my reframing of immersion … to mark occurrences for which no ritual expression had existed, they taught me an important lesson about the possibility of salvage … for the feminist Jew, impurity seems to mean the violation of physical or sexual integrity, death by invasion" (41). She now holds that a truly new theological understanding must go hand in hand in hand with an actual feminist and female positive ritual expression.

Finally, Adler's essay also addresses another fundamental question in a very personal manner: what is a scholar's responsibility—that is, how should Adler engage with her own responsibility—for and towards a work which has been highly influential in other people's lives and practices, but which "I now cannot in good conscience endorse" (38)? As she herself notes, there is little precedent for what she felt she must do: "I had never heard a theologian say that he or she had been wrong" (41). In retrospect, Adler writes, "What I had succeeded in creating was a theology for the despised." The word "succeeded" is quite intriguing here, and I suspect carefully and deliberately chosen. Part of the challenge Adler faced was not just the sense that she could no longer stand by her earlier writing, but that the earlier piece had been so influential. Indeed, even long *after* Adler's 1993 retraction, one can see her thoughts in the first piece continuing to surface among Jews (including rabbis) trying to grapple with or provide justification for the presence of these concepts in Judaism's most sacred texts; for example, a simple online search yielded multiple homiletic pieces (particularly for the *parashah* of Tazria) from rabbis across the denominational spectrum using Adler's original approach to help make the laws of *tum'ah* that accompany childbirth comprehensible for modern Jews. A corollary question raised by Adler's retraction, then, is the extent to which an author can "own" something they have written once it is published and put out into the public domain. Adler's choice was to "tell a richly detailed story about a particular process of rupture and transformation in a particular time and place" (38); our response stands as our own choice before us.

7. Rodger Kamenetz, *The Jew in the Lotus: A Poet's Rediscovery of Jewish Identity in Buddhist India*

Rodger Kamenetz, *The Jew in the Lotus: A Poet's Rediscovery of Jewish Identity in Buddhist India*, San Francisco: Harper San Francisco, 1994

Rodger Kamenetz (1950–) is a poet and writer. He was LSU Distinguished Professor and Sternberg Honors Chair Professor in the Departments of English and Religious Studies at Louisiana State University.

In 1989, the same year he was awarded the Nobel Peace Prize for his nonviolent efforts, the Dalai Lama turned for the first time to the Jewish people for help. "Tell me your secret," he said, "the secret of Jewish spiritual survival in exile." (2)

Jews have survived twenty centuries of exile and dispersion, persecution and vilification, economic hardship, expulsion, forced conversion, Crusades, Inquisition, blood libel, pogrom—you name it, Jews survived it. But up until now few outsiders have ever looked upon this as much of an accomplishment.

In the Dalai Lama's eyes, and to many of the Tibetans, Jews are survival experts. The idea that Jewish history, with all its traumas, is relevant to another exiled people was inspiring.

But another attraction to Dharamsala was equally important. This dialogue would be an unprecedented meeting of two ancient religious traditions, an opportunity for leading religious Jews to immerse themselves in a living Buddhist community—that had never happened, as far as we knew, in thousands of years of Jewish and Buddhist history. (3)

Now he [the Dalai Lama] turned to address Yitz Greenberg. "Previously we referred to more traditional, more conservative ways. And you said modernity creates new problems. Due to that, if we try to isolate ourselves from modernity, this is self-destruction. You have to face reality. If you have reason, sufficient reason to practice a religion, sufficient value in that religion, there is no need to fear. If you have no sufficient reason, no value—then there's no need to hold on to it. Really. I feel that." He added that if a faith cannot provide satisfaction for someone, to insist on that person holding on to it is foolish.

"So you see, the time is changing. Nobody can stop it. Whether God created it—or nature is behind it, nobody knows. It is fact, it is reality. So we have to follow the time, and live according to reality. What we need, ourselves, as religious leaders, is to do more research, find more practices to make tradition something more beneficial in today's life" and more open to people. "Then they will choose which is more valuable, more useful." Either the modernity of the secular world or else traditional teachings. (231)

COMMENTARY BY OR ROSE

When Rodger Kamenetz first pitched *The Jew in the Lotus* to publishers, no one involved in the project expected it to be a bestseller. Since its original publication in 1994, however, the spiritual travelogue has sold tens of thousands of copies, has been translated into several languages, and led to the creation of a PBS documentary film by the same name (1999). While the subtitle of the *The Jew in the Lotus* focuses on the author's "rediscovery of Judaism in Buddhist India," it is a compelling read in large part because it contains several intersecting plot lines that together raise significant questions about identity, community, and spirituality.

The narrative framework of the book is an intercontinental journey to Dharamsala, India, undertaken by a delegation of eight rabbis and intellectuals in the fall of 1990 to meet with His Holiness, the fourteenth Dalai Lama. This remote town in the Western Himalayas has served as the center of Tibetan life in exile since 1959. Intrigued by the story of Jewish wandering over millennia, the Dalai Lama wants to know the "secret" of their survival. What could he learn from these esteemed Jewish leaders that might help his community thirty years after escaping an oppressive Chinese regime, now still taking refuge in this picturesque village? While the invitation was a noble gesture by a wise and aging leader, the challenge for this small, but fairly diverse group of Jewish delegates was that "they did not agree on which secrets to bring ... which of the secrets was relevant, or even if there was a secret" (24). With respect and humor, Kamenetz introduces the reader to several colorful and creative Jewish figures, sharing their process of navigating various theological and praxis-based matters, including tensions and compromises. The fault lines within the group serve as a window into discussions and debates in the wider Jewish community.

Among the individuals Kamenetz features are rabbis Zalman Schachter-Shalomi (Reb Zalman) and Irving (Yitz) Greenberg, who serve as the spiritual elders of the group, with Schachter-Shalomi playing the role of the heterodox, free-spirited mystic—"half beatnik and half Hasid" (113), and Greenberg the (modern) Orthodox, more circumspect, rationalist. Kamenetz—a poet and storyteller—is clearly more drawn to Schachter-Shalomi as a teacher, seeing in him an oral master, "best appreciated in person," who can inspire others through his "flow of ideas, images, and illuminating tales" (73). But by no means is Greenberg presented as a strawman or foil, but rather Kamenetz portrays him as a courageous traditionalist who worked diligently for decades at both intra-Jewish and interreligious engagement. In fact, one of the more touching moments in the book is when Reb Zalman says of Yitz, "He is bridging more tensions than any Jew I know at this point" (50). Learning about these two towering figures—including both their similarities and differences—is one of the gifts of the book.

Of course, part of the allure of *The Jew in the Lotus* is the opportunity to travel with the Jewish group to an exotic location and to encounter a world-famous, yet enigmatic, spiritual master and several of his associates, including an oracle and several learned monks and nuns. The actor and humanitarian Richard Gere even makes a cameo appearance early in the book. But Kamenetz is aware of the dangers of shallowness and condescension, reporting with both a critical and compassionate eye on the people he meets and the highs and lows of the dialogue. At the heart of the exchange between the Jewish and Buddhist participants is the complex subject of tradition and change. As the author notes, "The Buddhist leader had brought with him into exile a Noah's ark of practitioners" (45), but like the Jewish people themselves he and his advisors had to painstakingly sort out what to keep, what to adapt, and what to let go of. The reader also learns that for all of the ways in which the Dalai Lama is venerated, even deified, one attribute that makes him special is his finely developed ability to be present with other people. Reflecting on this point, Reb Zalman says, "There were times I was close to tears just from the intensity of his listening" (106).

In addition to the Dalai Lama's graciousness, part of what allowed for a rich and searching dialogue was that Jews and Buddhists do not have a long history of animosity. This allowed for a more appreciative interreligious exchange, without some of the usual defensive or polemical elements that can emerge in dialogue between communities with more complicated and entangled pasts. Participants were able to explore both the exoteric and the esoteric dimensions of the religious life, including matters of cosmology and consciousness. While some of the Jewish delegates were squeamish at times as Reb Zalman and Rabbi Jonathan Omer-Man discussed various Jewish mystical ideas—God's tenfold nature, angelology, and the transmigration of souls—Rabbi Moshe Waldoks quipped, "the esoteric is like gefilte fish to the Dalai Lama" (82). Presentations by Rabbi Joy Levitt (Reconstructionist) and Blu Greenberg (a pioneering Orthodox feminist leader) on the "secrets" of synagogue and family life were crucial to understanding the concrete ways in which Jewish men *and* women live out their spiritual and social commitments publicly and privately, and the evolution of these rites (including gender roles) throughout Jewish history. As Kamenetz notes, Blu's discussion also led to a fascinating discussion of inter-generational hopes and responsibilities, particularly since the Buddhist partici-pants were celibates who believed in reincarnation (215–217).

One thorny issue that arose in the dialogue and related conversations was the question of why there are a disproportionate number of Western Buddhist teachers and practitioners from Jewish backgrounds—including those who identify as JuBu, culturally Jewish but spiritually Buddhist, or simply as Buddhist. The members of the delegation grappled with issues of "religious switching" and "hybridity" (both terms that were not yet a part of the popu-lar discourse on religion), particularly in a post-Holocaust age in which issues of continuity are especially charged. Importantly, in exploring these issues, the delegates were brave enough to ask whether or not they and other Jewish lead-ers were offering their constituents compelling reasons to live engaged Jewish lives. Given the excitement about Kabbalah on the trip (which also dovetailed with its growing popularity in the United States) there were lively conversations about making Jewish mystical teachings and practices (including meditation and visualization) more accessible (148–149). There was also frank discussion about people's mis/perceptions about what is "real" or "mainstream" Judaism, and the universal truth that in "every religious tradition, what you invest is what return you get," as the famed American Hindu teacher, Ram Dass (formerly Richard Alpert), stated at a post-trip public event (268). Finally, the dialogue participants also grappled with the fact that some people—including some Jews—simply find greater fulfillment in a religious tradition other than the one into which they were born, and that others feel comfortable belonging to more than one tradition.

All of this brings us to the final plotline: the spiritual journey of the author himself. Reflecting on his Jewish identity early in the book, Kamenetz candidly states that for much of his adult life it was like a "strongbox," well protected by eth-nic pride, but lacking interior meaning—"much like the Hebrew letters I could pronounce but not truly read" (57). While the trip itself was brief, it helped open him to new possibilities for spiritual growth as a Jew. One of the strengths of the book is Kamenetz's openness about his questions and biases, as well as his insights. As he wrote in a new afterword in 2007, "I simply tried to tell the story as I experienced it, very personally, with feelings intact" (308). In so doing, he invites others to explore their inner lives through renewed engagement with their own traditions and in dialogue with people from other communities of practice. Interestingly, in Kamenetz's next book, *Stalking Elijah: Adventures with Today's Jewish Mystical Masters* (winner of the 1997 National Jewish Book Award in Jewish Thought), he returns "home" for extended conversations with Reb Zalman, Rabbi Arthur Green, and other American Jewish figures.

The *Jew in the Lotus* communicated several important insights for contemporary Jewish life that remain relevant today. Through his presentation of Reb Zalman and his students, Kamenetz helped share some of the intellectual and devotional riches of the Jewish mystical tradition (as distilled through a progressive, neo-Chasidic lens). By extension, the reader is asked to think expansively about making creative use of Jewish resources, ancient and modern, whether "normative" or not. In highlighting the lifelong work of Schachter-Shalomi and Yitz and Blu Greenberg, the author also provides examples of iconoclastic Jewish leaders who have labored on the edges of their communities to renew Jewish tradition in different ways. *The Jew in the Lotus* also helps us to gain a greater appreciation for the beauty and pain of the Tibetan Buddhist community in exile, and the dignity and humanity of His Holiness, the fourteenth Dalai Lama. The thoughtfulness with which the participants interact also serves as a model for anyone interested in genuine dialogue. Finally, in his conversations with various American Buddhist practitioners with Jewish roots or connections, Kamenetz helped further an important discussion of the possibilities and challenges of religious adaptation, permeability, and of dual belonging. Many years after the original publication of this popular memoir, *The Jew in the Lotus* serves at once as a tale of personal awakening, and as a call to spiritual and ethical renewal within and beyond our community.

8. Avivah Gottlieb Zornberg, *Genesis: The Beginning of Desire*

Avivah Gottlieb Zornberg, *Genesis: The Beginning of Desire*, New York: Random House, 1995

Dr. Avivah Gottlieb Zornberg (1944–) teaches Torah at a variety of institutions in Jerusalem. She holds a Visiting Lectureship at the London School of Jewish Studies.

The sense of not being able to understand their own story also constitutes the radical anxiety that Joseph inflicts on his brothers. His technique is a series of enigmatic questions whose drift is opaque to his victims. To be interrogated in such a way that one cannot construe the significance of the interrogator's "plot" is to experience the authentic terror of one caught in an *alilah*. Even the benign questions of, for example, a doctor may induce this special terror; for the doctor has a "narrative" in mind, a possible diagnosis, in the light of which he examines for symptoms. This narrative is "about" the patient, but he cannot decipher its meaning.

In Kafka's *The Trial*, for instance, K. suffers from this anxiety, as he tries unsuccessfully to decipher the plot, the case that he has to answer. There are multiple possibilities, which constantly interpose between K. and any single solution. As in any interpretation of a text, "The scriptures are unalterable and the comments often enough merely express the commentator's bewilderment." When K. and the priest debate interpretation of the story of the bookkeeper before the Law, K. finally experiences fatigue, a sense that he is not qualified for the task of interpretation. ... Joseph's brothers suffer a similar vertigo, as they lose control of their own "simple story," under Joseph's questioning. Finally, Judah, as their spokesman, expresses their radical outrage: "My lord asked his servants, 'Have you a father or another brother?'" (45:19). Judah begins his own narrative of the enigmatic relations between the ruler and his brothers: "You asked ... we said ... you said ... we said ... you said ..." On the surface, Judah is simply focusing the narrative on the issue of Benjamin, whose loss will send his father "in evil to the grave," and on his own responsibility for his brother. But Rashi quotes the midrash to pivot Judah's speech on the issue of Joseph's interrogation, which Judah presents as a kind of terror-tactics: "My lord asked ...: from the beginning, you came upon us with a plot [*alilah*]. Why did you have to ask all those questions? Were we seeking your daughter in marriage, or were you seeking our sister in marriage? But nevertheless, 'we said to my master ...'—we hid nothing from you."

In this midrashic account, Judah protests against the libel, the malicious narrative in which the ruler has tried to involve them. But even when it is not malicious, the experience of being in an *alilah* is painful and humiliating, for it undermines the central importance of intention in human life. The midrash calls on the intentionality of matchmaking as a sardonic example of personal purposes that justify submitting to interrogation. Judah protests not against the questioning as such but against the unnerving sense of being mere figures in the cryptic narrative ends of a "plotter." His words may sound conciliatory, but, in Rashi's reading, they breathe angry reproach.

For Rashi, this aspect of Joseph's treatment of his brothers seems to be radically significant. He evokes the problem of the *alilah* on another occasion, earlier in the story; but on this occasion, it is God whom the brothers sense as "plotting" their narrative. They find the money they have paid for corn returned inside their sacks—"Their hearts sank; and, trembling, they turned to one another, saying, 'What is this that God has done to us?'"(45:28). Rashi comments: "'*What is this that God has done to us?*'—to bring us the *alilah*, for the money was returned only in order to torment us."

The word *alilah* is used twice here, the second time in the verbal form (here translated "to torment"). It implies the humiliation, the sporting with the victim, by reducing his subject status—in effect, by removing his capacity to narrate his own experience. Clearly, the brothers fear that false charges will be brought against them: they will be victims of a libel. But Maharal describes their basic *harada*—"trembling"—the anxiety with which they respond to the returned money, as the unnerving effect of *any* sudden change in one's perception of reality. The integrity of one's world, one's capacity of describe one's own story, is undermined by unclassifiable, cryptic events.

Suddenly, the brothers feel that—like the prisoner in Kafka's story, *In the Penal Colony*—they are being written on, rather than writing their own narrative. And, like the wretched prisoner, who will be "written to death," they squirm with the effort to read what is written. Unlike Kafka's victim, however, the brothers have no mirror-mechanism in which to read their sentence. The strive to recategorize their perceptions, to find new meanings that will accommodate the invasion of the uncanny into their lives. But the main verb of the sentence describing their response is *va-yeherdu*—which the Targum translates *u-tevahu*—"they were perplexed, disoriented." The word indicates a shudder, almost of disgust, at a reality suddenly become unreadable.

This is the authentic *alilah* experience, as Isaac, for example, knew it, when Esau stood in front of him, crying betrayal: "Isaac was seized with very violent trembling [*va-yeherad ... harada gedola*]" (27:33). Rashi quotes the Targum, which again translates *u-tevahu*: "an expression of wonder and horror. The midrash reads, 'He saw Gehinnom—the inferno—open beneath him.'" (263–265)

COMMENTARY BY SHIRA HECHT-KOLLER

Avivah Zornberg's *Genesis: The Beginning of Desire* has taught many people that the biblical text can be approached as a meditation on humanity. Her unique approach to text-study—as an experiential mode of learning and one in which tensions, complexities, and ambiguities are a core part of the learning process—demonstrates that the text is just as interesting, fraught, and mysterious as life itself.

Zornberg has often been likened to Nechama Leibowitz (1905–1997): They are both Orthodox women, immensely learned in Torah and well-educated in broader ways as well, and both operated as commentators and teachers within the men's world of Torah study. But actually, Leibowitz can serve more as a foil than as a comparison for understanding Zornberg's method.

Leibowitz taught her students to read the sources carefully and meticulously, asking the same basic questions over and over, most famously, "What is troubling Rashi?" In contrast, Zornberg focuses on the experiential and the psychological, weaving together literary associations and, as Zornberg herself says, "personal meditations" (xii). For Zornberg, the personal aspect is central: the text, when read properly, should illuminate life, and life, in turn, illuminates the text.[1] Her approach is highly reflective, creative, and associative. A single page of her book might reference the medieval mystical Zohar alongside the work of modern philosophers Lev Shestov and Walter Benjamin within a discussion of Isaac and Esau or use the ancient Greek Euripides and the modern Kafka to probe the character of Joseph.

---

1   Tamar Ross, review of *Genesis: The Beginning of Desire*, by Avivah Zornberg, *Bekhol Derakhek-ha Da'ehu* 3 (1996): 51.

The resulting effect is a layered one, in which one text is added to another and juxtaposed with a third. There is often no argument to follow, but a journey to travel. The language is poetic, and the insights, especially the psychological ones, sometimes provoke moments of clarity and wonder. Ultimately, though, the style is one that interrupts and disrupts, leaving the reader with much to ponder, without a clear conclusion.

This meditative style is often lacking in structure and discernible order. Disorder has become, as Daniel Boyarin wrote, "a great source of comfort to us, as if it somehow validated and made bearable the disorder in the world around us."[2] Zornberg not only revels in the ambiguities of the text, but reveals others previously unappreciated, by "making the familiar strange."[3] Through a web that she weaves by crafting together a vast array of classical Jewish sources alongside the best of Western literature, she "fosters a dreamlike, fantastic comprehension of the text."[4]

Zornberg's essay on *Parashat Va-Yeshev* exemplifies the style and insights of the entire book. This section tells the story of the sale of Joseph and ensuing events. Her theme in this essay is the question of whether we are each truly the authors of our own story or if we are actually actors in someone else's play. She develops this in two ways relevant to this section of text. First, the all-too-real human emotions seen in the doting Jacob, the preening Joseph, and the jealous brothers are said later to have been part of a divine plan. But does this not ultimately trivialize the emotions felt by the biblical characters? Are our emotions trivialized when they are said to be in service of something beyond our control? Are the brothers not culpable for their actions if they are just doing, at the end of the day, what God wanted (or needed) them to do? The sense that although we experience life as if we are the protagonists, we may in fact just be playing predetermined roles is deeply unsettling for Zornberg. Second, Zornberg sees the same issue return as the brothers later stand before Joseph, now viceroy of Egypt. The brothers want to tell the story of their lives, but because of Joseph's interrogation of them, accomplished through questions Zornberg describes as "enigmatic," they are plagued by anxiety and the realization that they have lost the freedom to tell their own tale (263).

---

2   Daniel Boyarin, "Reading Genesis," *Tikkun* 11, no. 2 (March 1996): 72.
3   Shalom Carmy, review of *Genesis: The Beginning of Desire*, by Avivah Zornberg, *Jewish Action* 58, no. 3 (1998): 82–87.
4   Boyarin, "Reading Genesis."

The brothers are caught in the plot of Joseph's story. Their world, and the freedom and ability to describe it, is overridden. They experience "the vertigo of the ground cut away" from beneath them, and ultimately what Joseph prompts them to feel is the same "fragmentation of reality" that he himself felt at their hands (265). He needs them to feel this way before reconciliation can take place.

The question of what it means to construct one's own narrative and to craft one's story is a timeless one. In the more than twenty years since *Genesis: The Beginning of Desire* has been published, this question feels even more pervasive and looms large in the ethos of the early twenty-first century. In a time and age where it is so easy to craft one's own story, to tell it to the world, to share, to manipulate details to conform to the "perfect story" but equally as simple to craft the story of another through disruption and disorder, what does a personal narrative even really mean anymore? Are we all, as Zornberg writes, "mere figure(s) in the cryptic narrative ends of a plotter" (262)? Do we have the capacity to tell our own stories? The stories of others? What does it mean for our present selves and for our future if we don't?

More than twenty years since the book's publication, there are ways in which it speaks to our current ethos and other ways in which it stands starkly at odds with it. We live in an age of information overload and distraction, bombarded by articles, texts, tweets, and soundbytes. There is an aspect of Zornberg's work which accords well with this mode of reading. Because of the associative and layered nature of the writing, the reader can dip into each essay, sampling pieces, mulling them over, being enriched by a single sentence or a poignant connection, without trying to work through the whole thing.

On the other hand, Zornberg's material is hard, and each point and paragraph demands depth of thought, attention, and focus. In an age of shortened attention spans and the ongoing quest to digest as much as possible in as little time (and with as little effort) as possible, this book rejects that goal, insisting on attention and meditation as values in learning.

The focus on the self is also one that feels particularly resonant to a contemporary reader, but again, also sits in contrast with current trends and norms. We live in an age with an emphasis on the self, on crafting a personal brand that can be polished and shared with others. Zornberg demands that her readers bring themselves into the text, and in turn the text will inform and penetrate one's sense of self. But working through and internalizing her teachings is the serious and challenging work of self-exploration and identity formation. In recognizing motifs and patterns in the lives of biblical characters as *they* struggle, we too are meant to struggle, as they and we "learn the meaning of all existence."[5]

The danger of Zornberg's approach is the flipside of its beauty; creatively and idiosyncratically weaving together different ideas and texts can serve as a substitute for deep textual study, proficiency, and analysis. This is not the case for Zornberg herself: she is highly literate and engaged and is able to build upon her arsenal of Jewish literature in magical ways. But for the average student, a replication of her method and style is likely to result in deep personal connection to, but lower rates of proficiency with, the texts themselves.

Finally, as many have pointed out, Zornberg's work is work to be studied, learned, and meditated upon. It is a text that is best engaged with *be-chavruta*, in rigorous partnered study. The art of mulling over a text in tandem with another, pushing back, pressing forward, finding oneself in relation to the other in the text itself, is at the very heart of the work of *chavruta*. This is the mode that best suits study and reflection of Zornberg's works. This may be one of the best reasons to study Zornberg today: in contemporary society, with challenges being mounted upon an engaged and civil discourse, the art of *chavruta* feels more pressing now than ever.

---

5   Ross, review of *Genesis*, 50.

9. Abraham Joshua Heschel, Susannah Heschel (ed.), *Moral Grandeur and Spiritual Audacity*

Abraham Joshua Heschel, Susannah Heschel (ed.), *Moral Grandeur and Spiritual Audacity*, New York: Farrar, Straus and Giroux, 1996

Rabbi Dr. Abraham Joshua Heschel (1907–1972) was a Holocaust survivor and Professor of Jewish Ethics and Mysticism at the Jewish Theological Seminary.

Susannah Heschel: My father was a unique combination of a Hasidic voice of compassion and mercy, always seeing the goodness in other people, and a prophetic voice of justice, denouncing hypocrisy, self-centeredness, and indifference. My father wasn't interested in assigning blame or claiming victimhood, but as the Bible does, he showed us a vision of who we might become. His was a voice of inspiration, not argumentation, rooted in Jewish religious thought. What he once wrote of East European Jews applies to him as well: "Jewishness was not in the fruit but in the sap that stirred through the tissues of the tree. Bred in the silence of the soil, it ascended to the leaves to become eloquent in the fruit." So, too, Jewishness infused my father like the sap of a tree, and his eloquence was the fruit of his deep Jewish piety and learning.

Particularly extraordinary is the diversity of those who regarded him as their teacher: Catholics, Jews, Protestants, whites and blacks, liberals and conservatives, pious and secular, Americans, Europeans, Israelis. His life challenges our conventional expectations. Here is a rabbi whose books were praised by Pope Paul VI as helping to sustain the piety of Catholics; an Orthodox Jew with a white beard and yarmulke marching for civil rights and demonstrating against the war in Vietnam; an immigrant from Poland whose work is included in anthologies of exceptional English prose.

My father described himself as a "brand plucked from the fire of Europe," rescued from Poland by an American visa just six weeks before the Nazi invasion. His survival was a gift, because he became a unique religious voice in an era in which religion was in grave danger, according to his own analysis. The Hasidic Jewish world of Eastern Europe in which he was raised was far from the environment in which he wrote and taught in the United States. He came from a rebbe's family in Poland, from a Jewish civilization that was suddenly eradicated in the middle of his lifetime by the Germans, in whose universities he had studied and in whose language he had written about Jewish religious thought. Despite the horrors he experienced—the murder of his mother, sisters, friends, and relatives, the destruction of the world which had nourished him—his life continued to reflect the holy dimension he was able to evoke in his own original and unique words. (viii)

Abraham Joshua Heschel: There is immense silent agony in the world, and the task of man is to be a voice for the plundered poor, to prevent the desecration of the soul and the violation of our dream of honesty.

The more deeply immersed I became in the thinking of the prophets, the more powerfully it became clear to me what the lives of the prophets sought to convey: that morally speaking there is no limit to the concern one must feel for the suffering of human beings. It also became clear to me that in regard to the cruelties committed in the name of a free society, some are guilty, while all are responsible. I did not feel guilty as an individual American for the bloodshed in Vietnam, but I felt deeply responsible. "Thou shalt not stand idly by the blood of thy neighbor" (Leviticus 19:15). This not a recommendation but an imperative, a supreme commandment. And so I decided to change my mode of living and to become active in the cause of peace in Vietnam. (224–225)

What is needed at this very moment is to mobilize all human beings for one great task, to achieve world peace. As long as we do not make the problem of world peace a matter of absolute priority, I cannot be optimistic. Here is a parable: If my pockets are full of money, and I pass by a store which sells useless things, I will somehow be driven by all the money in my pockets to buy something, however useless. In the same way, we have so many atomic bombs now, do you think that we will not be tempted to use them?

I cannot say that I feel complacent about our chances for peace. Our terrible sin is in not giving peace absolute priority and in failing to realize that to attain peace, we have to make sacrifices. We are ready to make sacrifices for the sake of war, but not, apparently, for the sake of peace.

Let us assume that the religions represent moral powers in the world. They could do something, but they are scarcely on speaking terms. The ecumenical movement has made some progress in human relations, but on the top level I don't see much progress. It is conceivable for states to get together and have a United Nations, but it is still inconceivable to have a United Religions. The question is, Why do we not see the writing on the wall? The situation is very grave, and though many individuals feel it, most of us say, "Business as usual." What we must do is to alarm the world. People become more complacent and more involved in daily affairs, and their sensitivity, as I said before, is decreasing all the time. We continue to be ignorant of one another, of our fellow human beings, we really don't know what is happening in Vietnam, for example. ...

But what about life itself? What about humanity itself? We are doing too little, next to nothing, about peace. We leave it to a few individuals in Washington. Do they have the wisdom? Can I turn over my soul and conscience to them? Peace is our most important challenge and task, from every point of view and for all religions. But we leave it to others. We have delegated our conscience to a few diplomats and generals, and this is a very, very grave sin. (255–256)

COMMENTARY BY WILLIAM PLEVAN

On Martin Luther King Jr. Day in 1999, members and clergy of the Abyssinian Baptist Church and Congregation B'nai Jeshurun of New York City gathered to celebrate the life of Dr. King and his legacy. According to the *New York Times*, the event featured several significant references to Rabbi Abraham Joshua Heschel, whose *yahrtzeit* fell in the week prior.[1] Rabbi Rolando Matalon of B'nai Jeshurun read a passage from a speech Heschel had given to the Rabbinical Assembly, the organization of Conservative rabbis, in March 1968, abjuring those rabbis to follow King's lead in fighting against racism, poverty, and the Vietnam War. Rev. Calvin Butts of Abyssinian spoke extensively about Heschel in remarks entitled, "Moral Grandeur and Spiritual Audacity." The phrase is also the title of a collection of Dr. Heschel's writings that was edited with a biographical introduction by his daughter, Dr. Susannah Heschel, a professor of Jewish Studies who now teaches at Dartmouth, and published less than two years prior.

Moral Grandeur and Spiritual Audacity collects forty-two of Heschel's articles, speeches, and interviews. The title of the book (and of Rev. Butts's sermon) comes from a telegram that Heschel wrote to President John F. Kennedy in

---

1   Nadine Brozan, "For Blacks and Jews, Hopes for Renewed Link," *New York Times*, January 18, 1999.

June 1963 urging him to assert moral leadership on racial injustice. The telegram's terse words read in part: "Please demand of religious leaders personal involvement not just solemn declarations. We forfeit the right to worship God as long as we continue to humiliate negroes. Churches synagogues have failed. They must repent. ... I propose that you Mr. President declare a state of moral emergency. ... The hour calls for high moral grandeur and spiritual audacity" (*Moral Grandeur and Spiritual Audacity*, vii). Butts's use of Heschel's words at the Abyssinian-B'nai Jeshurun event is emblematic of both the influence of this particular volume and the powerful impact Heschel's teachings and personal example have had on Jews and non-Jews alike seeking a religious voice that speaks at once to both their spiritual longings and their social and political values.

Heschel is perhaps best known and recognized for marching with Martin Luther King Jr. at Selma in 1965 in addition to his other substantive efforts on behalf of civil rights and world peace. The iconic picture of Heschel with a long white beard appropriate to a Chasidic rabbi alongside King is one of the most influential images in postwar American Jewish consciousness. This collection's importance arises from the way it provides a deeper understanding of the underlying concerns that motivated both Heschel's social justice activism and his religious traditionalism. While all of the essays may also be found elsewhere, collecting them together in this single volume makes it expressly clear that for Heschel, genuine Jewish piety *must* find expression in political action. As he put it in a short essay, "The Reasons for My Involvement in the Peace Movement," "I did not feel guilty as an individual American for the bloodshed in Vietnam, but I felt deeply responsible. 'Thou shalt not stand idly by the blood of thy neighbor' (Leviticus 19:15). This is not a recommendation but an imperative, a supreme commandment. And so I decided to change my mode of living and to become active in the cause for peace in Vietnam" (225).

As the book shows, the predominant theme of Heschel's writings is the nature and meaning of piety as a virtue. Heschel devoted much of his work to explaining and vindicating a distinctively Jewish approach to piety, which he argued had been distorted or misunderstood by Western philosophy and scholarship in religion since the Enlightenment. Many of the essays in this volume are devoted either to his explications of Jewish religious concepts and practices or to a critique of modern theories of religion and how to recover piety as "the realization and verification of the transcendent in human life" (310). The essay "Jewish Theology" provides a helpful introduction to Heschel's theological language and touches on some of these key themes. Originally delivered as a speech to principals of Jewish day schools, Heschel's essay opens with reflections on the way his childhood home was suffused with traditional Jewish theological vocabulary. He describes preparing for Yom Kippur in his home as a child as "my great day of training in Jewish theology," because he experienced a relationship with God through concrete performance and deeply felt emotion, as opposed to philosophical concepts or didactic statements of faith (154).

Heschel's theology is not about the being of God but about what it means to be a religious person. In the Hebrew Bible, Heschel writes, God is in search of man, meaning that God calls out to humanity and the task of humanity is to hearken to the call for a divine-human partnership to make the world as God intended (158). Heschel tells a story in which he was invited to speak at the Pontifical Institute in Toronto about "The God of Israel and Christian Renewal," but prior to the event the organizers changed the title of his talk to "The Jewish Notion of God." For Heschel, the title change encapsulated what goes wrong with thinking about religion when Greek philosophy is given greater cultural authority than the Hebrew prophets (161).

Heschel's personal confrontation with the Holocaust is also a recurring motif in his theological reflections. In an essay on revelation, he writes: "It is, indeed, hard for the mind to believe that any member of a species which can organize or even witness the murder of millions and feel no regret should ever be endowed with the ability to receive a word of God" (188). As the reader grasps Heschel's understanding that revelation is a mark of God's disappointment with humanity as much as God's need for humanity, they might also remember his daughter's accounts of his harrowing escape from Germany and then Poland, the murder of his mother and sisters at the hands of the Nazis, and his avowal never to return to those countries (xix). In writing about racial injustice or the war in Vietnam, Heschel represents a form of Holocaust memory that eschews ethnic or religious inwardness and demands robust Jewish opposition to all modern forms of oppression, racism, and state-orchestrated mass death.

Because many of the selections in the book were delivered as public lectures, they offer some sense of Heschel as a rabbi who was concerned for the spiritual condition of Judaism as it adjusted to American society in the postwar era. Heschel saw that the Jews who had achieved economic, political, and cultural success and comfort in America were losing their connection to God and genuine Jewish piety. In "The Spirit of Jewish Prayer," Heschel issues a withering critique of prayer services in contemporary synagogues before a convention of American Conservative rabbis: "An air of tranquility, complacency prevails in our synagogues. What can come out of such an atmosphere? The services are prim, the voice is dry, the synagogue is neat and tidy, and the soul lies in agony. You know no one will scream, no one will cry, the words will be still-born" (101). Here, the poetic language and spiritual intensity of his books such as *Quest for God*, on the meaning of prayer, comes into direct confrontation with the reality of American synagogue life.

For Heschel, Jewish piety also required a theological humility that could allow one not only to be in dialogue with but to also learn from those of other faiths. He went to the Vatican to participate in discussions that led to the Church's statement *Nostra Aetate* in 1965, which represented an historic shift in the Catholic Church's approach to non-Catholic faiths, with a significant emphasis on Jews and Judaism. In the lecture he delivered upon beginning a vis-iting professorship at Union Theological Seminary, "No Religion is an Island," Heschel develops a nuanced Jewish theology of interfaith dialogue that reflects modern sensibilities and classical Jewish teachings: "Human faith is never final, never an arrival, but rather an endless pilgrimage, a being on the way" (245). Judaism does not claim exclusive possession of truth, and so despite a painful history of persecution, cooperation with other religious traditions is a deeply Jewish religious act and not just an act of political expediency.

Moral Grandeur and Spiritual Audacity serves as a compendium of Hes-chel's legacy as a model for authentic Jewish piety rooted in traditional Jewish texts and practices and committed to fighting for social justice and peace. As Jewish communal concerns have become increasingly divided along political lines, Jewish critics on the right have called into question the Jewish authentic-ity of progressive activism. At the same time, many Jews view interfaith social justice work and celebrations such as the Abyssinian-B'nai Jeshurun event as an essential part of their Jewish spiritual lives. Even if they don't fully embrace Hes-chel's religious traditionalism, these Jews want rabbis, teachers, and leaders who will also fight racism and oppose unjust wars. Heschel's vision of a theologically demanding and politically engaged Judaism that animates this book continues to inspire the next generation of such Jews.

10. Noam Zion and David Dishon, *A Different Night: The Family Participation Haggadah*

Noam Zion and David Dishon, *A Different Night: The Family Participation Haggadah*, Jerusalem, Israel: Shalom Hartman Institute; Englewood, NJ: American Friends of the Shalom Hartman Institute, 1997

Noam Zion (1948–) is a Senior Research Fellow at the Shalom Hartman Institute.

David Dishon (1949–) is Co-Founder of the Shalom Hartman Institute's Charles E. Smith High School for Boys where he currently directs and teaches Judaic Studies.[1]

COMMENTARY BY EMILY FILLER

According to the 2013 Pew Research survey of Jewish Americans, more American Jews attended at least one Passover seder in the previous year than observed any other holiday or participated in any traditional Jewish ritual.[2] Which is to say that even before the candles are lit, the *matzah* broken, or the green vegetable dipped in saltwater, Passover is already a "different night" for most American Jews. Passover marks the rare occasion when more Jews than not may look across a table and know that most other American Jews are doing the same. Noam Zion and David Dishon's "family participation haggadah," *A Different Night*, seeks to transform the seder ritual—often recalled as overly long and punctuated throughout with grumbling from hungry seder-goers— from a chore to a lively, conversational, and notably individualized experience.

Statistically speaking, the haggadah that American Jews know best is the "classic" Maxwell House Haggadah, a no-frills production first published in 1932 as a marketing tool to accompany Passover coffee sales and nearly continually since; it contains little beyond the haggadah text in side-by-side English and Hebrew and a few songs. Carole Balin traces the popularity of the Maxwell

---

1   See "Haggadahs-R-Us. A Different Night CLASSIC edition," https://www.haggadahsrus. com/ADN-classic.html.

2   Michael Lipka, "Attending a Seder Is Common Practice for American Jews," *Pew Research Center*, April 14, 2014, accessed August 07, 2018, http://www.pewresearch.org/fact-tank/2014/04/14/attending-a-seder-is-common-practice-for-american-jews/. Jenna Weissman Joselit notes that similar statistics are observable as far back as the 1920s, calling American Jews' valuation of Passover "both a statistical and emotional truth." See her *The Wonders of America* (New York: Hill and Wang, 1994), 227.

The Four Children

כְּנֶגֶד אַרְבָּעָה בָנִים

1. **The Haggadah** offers us educational advice about intergenerational storytelling. The midrash of the Four Children invites us to distinguish different character types and to suggest different approaches to our offspring. **Consider** the artistic interpretations of the Four Children, comparing and contrasting them.

2. **The Rabbis** turn the commandment of "ve-heegadta" (you shall **tell**) into a mitzvah of **dialogue** — with give and take on both sides. Successful dialogue means that each side, and especially the side anxious to "pass on the message," be keenly attentive to what the other is saying and feeling — to the particular personality and his or her needs.

❖

BLESSED be God,
Blessed be that One.
Blessed be the Giver of the Torah to the people Israel,
Blessed be that One.

THE TORAH alludes to Four Children:
One Wise or Thoughtful,
One Wicked or Rebellious,
One Simple or Innocent,
One Who Does Not Know How to Ask.

בָּרוּךְ הַמָּקוֹם,
בָּרוּךְ הוּא.
בָּרוּךְ שֶׁנָּתַן תּוֹרָה לְעַמּוֹ יִשְׂרָאֵל:
בָּרוּךְ הוּא.

כְּנֶגֶד אַרְבָּעָה בָנִים דִּבְּרָה תוֹרָה:
אֶחָד חָכָם,
וְאֶחָד רָשָׁע,
וְאֶחָד תָּם,
וְאֶחָד שֶׁאֵינוֹ יוֹדֵעַ לִשְׁאוֹל.

Kadesh
Urchatz
Karpas
Yachatz
Maggid

Four Children

56

Istavan Zador, Four Children (Budapest, 1924)

"Haggadahs-R-Us. A Different Night Classic edition," https://www.haggadahsrus.com/ADNclassic.html

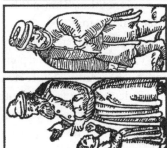

Prague, 1526

Education Through Dialogue

A Reminder for Parents!

Thus far the Haggadah has given guidelines to the parent who is full of earnest enthusiasm to pass on an historical and cultural "message" to the younger generation. If ever there was an event which appeals to the parent's desire to bring their youth-culture-centered children to appreciate the old values of cultural and ethnic pride and identification, the Pesach seder is it! Here lies a dangerous pitfall for the parent-educator. The leader of the seder is likely to concentrate on the text of the Haggadah without sufficiently taking into consideration the audience — the younger generation — and their level of interest. Absorbed with the sales-pitch, the salesperson often forgets the customer!

"The Four Parents:" Children Label Their Parents

IN THE DAYS of the patriarchal regime, we allowed ourselves to categorize our children harshly — accepting one as positive — the wise one.

The simple, the wicked and the one who knows not how to ask questions had to swallow hard and hide their sense of being insulted . . .

Now in our days no child is identified as "the offspring of the parent" and often the parent is identified as "the parent of that child." We have arrived at an era not of patriarchy or matriarchy but the rule of children. In our age it is then miraculous that our dear, delightful children don't divide us up and categorize us. At the best, we would be rated "naive or simple minded parents" or "parents who don't know how to respond to a question."

(Israel Eldad, "The Victory of the Wise Son")

The Pitfalls of Labeling

I INSTINCTIVELY recoil from static stereotypes that label persons simplistically. Therefore, I choose to interpret the midrash of the four children as a diverse set of strategies for addressing four different facets of each and every child. Each personality combines these facets in different ways. For example, the wise and the rebellious facets can be combined for evil. Then the cunning mind is used to inflict pain on one's parents. Alternatively, the combination can produce a revolutionary chalutz (pioneer) seeking not just to undermine the traditional order but to create new frameworks of meaning. This requires an intelligence which is not conservative like the traditional "wise child" but which looks beyond the horizon, beyond the existing laws and their pat rationale.

(Yariv Ben Aharon, Kibbutz author)

"Haggadahs-R-Us. A Different Night Classic edition," https://www.haggadahsrus.com/ADNclassic.html

House version to its accessibility, both literal—it could be easily found in the grocery store—and figurative; for rapidly assimilating American Jews, the Maxwell House Haggadah provided a clear, translated, and navigable script for the seder, regardless of a family's observance or level of traditional literacy.[3]

By contrast, Zion and Dishon's *A Different Night*, first published in 1997, seeks to make the seder more meaningful, not simply possible, for its participants. In their Foreword, Zion and Dishon assert that while still holding fast to the traditional haggadah text, "we have discovered that much can be done to make the seder more responsive to contemporary needs and simultaneously truer to the spirit of the Rabbis as educators" (3). The authors' commitment to ritual innovation authorized by rabbinic custom is on display even in the "user's guide" page preceding the official beginning of the seder; in what may be, from the point of view of many participants, the most important innovation of the haggadah, Zion and Dishon encourage seder-goers to embrace the custom of "extensive hors d'oeuvres" during the seder so as not to be distracted by hunger. Lest this practice be seen as an unacceptable, if appealing, departure from tradition, Zion and Rishon reassure the reader that "this was the original Rabbinic custom" (6).

The chief goal of this haggadah, then, is not difficult to discern. Zion and Dishon's stated intention is for this haggadah to "liberate" seder participants from the strict boundaries of the printed text, in hopes of generating a more creative, participatory, and free-wheeling conversation, particularly for families with impatient and hungry children. The haggadah's emphasis on drawing children into the discussion is evident in their introduction to the "storytelling" portion of the haggadah, wherein a version of the Exodus narrative of the Hebrews' liberation from Egypt is recounted. *A Different Night* suggests three questions for discussion with children, beginning with the query: "What was it like to be a slave?" The page of instructions is accompanied by a reflection by David Hartman on how he described slavery to his child with a story of a father unable to come home owing to work obligations; the prominent presence of this reflection indicates that parents and children at the seder table may try to generate their own accounts of slavery, based in the quotidian details of their own lives.

Perhaps the most notable of the three discussion questions suggested in *A Different Night* is the second prompt, which asks, "What do you know about Moshe as a baby and as a young man?" (48). In the context of a haggadah, such a question is quite striking—for, of course, Moses is conspicuously missing in the traditional haggadic account of the Hebrews' liberation. The traditional hag-

---

3   Carole Balin. "'Good to the Last Drop': The Proliferation of the Maxwell House Haggadah," in *My People's Passover Haggadah*, vol. 1: *Traditional Texts, Modern Commentaries*, ed. David Arnow et al. (Woodstock: Jewish Lights Publishing, 2008), 87.

gadah excises Moses from the story, ostensibly to emphasize God's singular role in bringing the people out of Egypt; as the English text says, "And the Eternal brought us forth from Egypt: not by means of an angel, nor by means of a Seraph, not by means of a messenger (*ve-lo al yadei shaliach*); but the most Holy, blessed by He, in His own glory."[4] Moses, informed by God that "I will send you to Pharaoh" (Ex. 3:10; *shlachakha el paro*), is nowhere to be found.[5]

Zion and Dishon unapologetically re-inscribe Moses in the haggadah, thus restoring his centrality to the narrative. In the pages that follow, *A Different Night* provides a script of sorts for parents with retellings—simplified and midrash-inflected—of Moses's birth and adoption into Pharaoh's palace, and his murder of the Egyptian slave driver, which compels his flight into the wilderness, where he will encounter God at the burning bush.[6] Both the explicit re-inscription of Moses in the haggadah and the suggested context—the question "what do you know about Moshe as a baby and as a young man?"—illuminate the assumptions and concerns that animate *A Different Night*. As one of the few biblical figures whom we know from his dramatic birth story to the very end of his life, Moses's presence in *A Different Night* provides readers, adults and children alike, with a more accessible personage with whom to identify. The haggadah's suggested questions about young Moses render him, if not precisely accessible, then at least literarily compelling, and a locus for further speculation and discussion.

It is well known that the traditional "four questions" that initiate the storytelling are to be asked by the youngest at table, and they are traditionally understood as a means of involving children in the ritual. Here, though, the suggested discussion questions are asked *of* children, not *by* them, and the responses are generated not by the haggadah text but by the children and their parents themselves. This turn effectively reveals not only the family-centered priorities of the haggadah, but a means of measuring the seder's familial success: by the degree to which children are verbally participatory.[7]

---

4   *Passover Haggadah* (Tarrytown, NY: Maxwell House Coffee, 1995), 17.

5   This translation is from the Jewish Publication Society's *Tanakh* (Philadelphia, PA: Jewish Publication Society, 1985).

6   The restoration of Moses's primacy in the Exodus narrative is acknowledged only briefly several pages later, where Zion and Dishon write that rabbinic seders of the distant past likely included Moses as parents sought to bring the story to life for their children, and that no less than Moses Maimonides recommended that Moses be part of the story.

7   In their qualitative and quantitative study of American Jewish families, Arnold Eisen and Steven M. Cohen observe that "The family context itself has become an arena for the expression of Jewishness that is second to none in its importance." *A Different Night*'s turn to child participation thus serves to assure parents that they are, in fact, legitimately acting as Jews; without the meaningful participation of their kids, an individual or couple might worry that their own Judaism was in doubt. See Eisen and Cohen, *The Jew Within*, 46.

The reintroduction of Moses, the person, thus represents Zion and Dishon's desire for people of all ages to re-inscribe themselves in the ritual, offering to the conversation not only Moses' experiences but their own. Hartman's account of slavery, after all, is based in a much more everyday experience of professional obligations; no doubt nearly everyone at the seder could generate an account of a time when they, as Hartman says, had little control over some aspect of their lives. More broadly, this personal and personality-based approach to the Passover story literally brings the story down to earth. In the reintroduction of the person Moses, the story is no longer a strange and distant account of an ancient people liberated by a vengeful deity, but a rather more manageable story about one flawed individual and his extended family.

What is less certain is whether the traditional object of regard—the epic account of an enslaved people fleeing Egypt on God's command—remains central to the family seder experience envisioned by A Different Night. For better or worse, the more distant and alien language of the traditional haggadah "script" does convey the expansiveness of the narrative. Consider, for instance, the opening description of Israelite oppression—"And they afflicted us: as it is said, and they set taskmasters over them, to afflict them with their burdens, and they built stone cities for Pharaoh, Pithom and Raamses"—and the Israelites' response: "And we cried unto the Eternal, the God of our fathers: as it is said, and it came to pass, after some time that the king of Egypt died, and the children of Israel sighed in consequence of the bondage, and they cried, and their complaint went up to God in consequence of the bondage."

Here, in a few terse phrases, we are given the fears and anguish of two peoples, and the scene is set for God's dramatic and violent intervention on behalf of the Hebrew people. But it is less clear that most contemporary American Jews would be able to truly "regard themselves" as enslaved Israelites with the collective consciousness of this people; the distance between the circumstances described and the circumstances of most American Jews is simply too great.

Zion and Dishon's insistence on the centrality of the person Moses and their haggadah's encouragement to participants to bring their everyday experiences to the fore marks an attempt to bridge this vast gap between the epic scope of the Exodus and the infinitely less dramatic and/or persecuted lives of most American Jews. And it is likely far easier to, as A Different Night effectively does, invite Jews—particularly children—to contribute in their own ways to a more accessible story, than it is to somehow draw those Jews into the strange and distant world of the Exodus. If all goes well, the resulting conversation may reassure American Jewish families that their Passover observance is substantive and meaningful—and that this substance and meaning was made possible not only by an improbable ancient narrative but their own American Jewish experiences.

11. Mendel Shapiro, "Qeri'at Ha-Torah by Women: A Halakhic Analysis"

Mendel Shapiro, "Qeri'at Ha-Torah by Women: A Halakhic Analysis," *The Edah Journal* 1, No. 2 (2001)

Rabbi Mendel Shapiro (1949–) is a lawyer and rabbi in Jerusalem.

This paper is not a manifesto to alter existing Orthodox Jewish synagogue practice. Although I believe that women's *aliyyot* and Torah reading may be halakhically sanctioned, it is clear that there is no live tradition of such a practice, or indeed any evidence that it was ever more than a sporadic phenomenon that took place in unusual circumstances. It would be wrong to create dissension in communities and synagogues by challenging hallowed practices that are seen as the hallmark of Orthodox Judaism, and I would not want this paper to be used for that purpose. By the same token, if my analysis of the sources is tenable, by what moral justification may women be denied a halakhic privilege if they exercise it in self-selected groups without directly impinging on others' sensibilities? I believe that the course for which I am arguing is at the very least a legitimate halakhic option that, by restoring to Orthodox women their halakhic capacity to participate in the *qeri'at ha-Torah* portion of the synagogue service, will invigorate and bring fresh energy to public religious life.

If the essential *halakhah* (*iqqar ha-din*) can countenance *qeri'at ha-Torah* by women in one form or another, how do we account for the Orthodox community's refusal seriously to face this possibility? It seems to me that the explanation lies not in *halakhah* per se, but in an ingrained conservatism, naturally suspicious of change, which is heightened by the perception of being under siege from a dynamic, attractive and sometimes unsavory general culture. Also not to be underestimated is the fear that flexibility on this issue would play into the hands of the Reform and Conservative movements. The terms of reference of this reflexive, intuitive opposition are not the open, precise, give and take of classical halakhic argumentation, but the evocative language of *minhag* (custom), *porets geder* (breaker of norms), and *lo titgodedu* (do not splinter the community). Women may not receive *aliyyot* or read the Torah because it goes against ingrained *minhag*; it upsets the received religious order. The implied operative halakhic principle, even if not explicitly enunciated, is simple and direct: "essential *halakhah* (*iqqar ha-din*) must submit to *minhag*."

COMMENTARY BY TOVA HARTMAN

In spring of 2001, *The Edah Journal* published Mendel Shapiro's "*Qeri'at ha-Torah* by Women: A Halakhic Analysis." Shapiro reviews key halakhic issues concerning *qeri'at ha-Torah* (chanting from the Torah) by women: *birkhot ha-Torah* (blessing the Torah before and after a portion is chanted), *kevod ha-tzibbur* (the dignity of the congregation), *qol ishah* (lit., "women's voices," a reference to the rabbinic notion that women's voices are inherently lascivious), *mechitzah* (separation of men and women for prayer), *minhag* (custom), *poretz geder* (not breaking the boundaries by violating customs of prayer), and *lo titgodedu* (not creating factions). He cites relevant biblical and rabbinic texts, and he examines the work of both medieval and modern *poskim* (halakhic decisors) like rabbis Ovadiah Yosef, Yehuda Herzl Henkin, and Dov Eliozrov. Indeed, Henkin judges Shapiro's work as "comprehensive and thoughtful." More specifically, he asserts that Shapiro has demonstrated "that *kevod ha-tzibbur* [the dignity of the congregation] can be waived, and does not apply today when everyone is literate" (1, 6).[1] This is a crucial observation, since the famous *baraita* [tannaitic rabbinic text not included in the Mishnah that nevertheless appears in the Gemara] in *Megillah* 23a specifically cites *kevod ha-tzibbur* as the reason why women may not read Torah in public.

After making a convincing halakhic case for *qeri'at ha-Torah* by women, Shapiro ends his article with a claim that women's reading of Torah "should not be introduced in a way that directly challenges existing practice or causes dissension within established synagogues, whose *minhagim* should be respected." Furthermore, we are told that that the practice ought to be limited to "self-selected groups." Shapiro thus puts halakhic argument aside and introduces one of the bugaboos that has long been used against women's rights: creating dissension in the community. Even though he has proven that *qeri'at ha-Torah* by women is halakhically permissible, Shapiro counsels against introducing such a change into one's synagogue so as to avoid dissension.

In considering the implications of Shapiro's article, Henkin too urges caution, adding a not very well veiled threat when he writes that despite the impressive

---

1   Yehuda Herzl Henkin, "Qeri'at Ha-Torah by Women: Where We Stand Today," *The Edah Journal* 1, no. 2 (*Sivan* 5761 [2001]): 1–6.

halakhic argument that Shapiro makes, "women's *aliyyot* [blessing of the Torah] remain outside the consensus, and a congregation that institutes them is not Orthodox in name and will not long remain Orthodox in practice" (6). Henkin uses a slippery-slope kind of argument ("will not long remain") as well as "go away and change" rhetoric.[2] As a result, people interested in change are subtly encouraged to presume that the problem lies with them, that the normative community does not have a stake in resolving their problem, and so rather than continue to cause dissension, they should go away and make changes on their own.

The reasoning behind Henkin's slippery-slope argument is skillfully turned on its head in Daniel Sperber's "Congregational Dignity and Human Dignity: Women and Public Torah Reading," published the following year.[3] Whereas Henkin is extremely critical of women's desire to take on more public roles in synagogue life, Sperber understands this desire to be borne of a legitimate religious quest. He writes: "We know that many women have a sincere desire, a yearning, to take an active and spiritual role in the life of the community and its pursuits, and excluding them from the synagogue or from involvement in worship ceremonies is a cause of great distress." Sperber argues that the halakhic value of *kevod ha-briyot* mandates that this distress be alleviated. This is a strong argument, for if *qeri'at ha-Torah* by women depends ultimately on *kevod ha-tzibbur* and the congregation in question is Orthodox, it actually relies on the beneficence of men, who have a monopoly on defining the *tzibbur* and what honors and dishonors it. Breaking this monopoly will undoubtedly lead to "dissension," as in any case where one group attempts to break a monopoly held by a privileged group, which is why Shapiro argues against it. Viewing *qeri'at ha-Torah* by women through the lens of *kevod ha-briyot*, Sperber gives weight to the subjective experience of "others" who are outside the *tzibbur*, namely, women.

That subjective experience has halakhic import can be seen from the Talmudic discussion of *ona'at devarim* (verbal wronging).[4] Tellingly, this halakhic concept is drawn from the relationship between husband and wife, and

---

2   I speak about this kind of rhetoric in my book, *Feminism Encounters Traditional Judaism: Resistance and Accommodation* (Lebanon, NH: University Press of New England, 2007). See Chapter 7, "Go Away and Change," 121–133.

3   Daniel Sperber's "Congregational Dignity and Human Dignity: Women and Public Torah Reading," *The Edah Journal* 3, no. 2 (*Elul* 5763 [2002]): 114. Sperber builds on this essay in his book: *On Changes in Jewish Liturgy: Options and Limitations* (Jerusalem: Urim Publications, 2010).

4   I look extensively at *ona'at devarim* in *Are You Not a Man of God: Devotion, Betrayal, and Social Criticism in Jewish Tradition* (New York: Oxford University Press, 2014). See especially Chapter 2, "'It is Not in Heaven!' and Other Hurtful Words," 46–81.

the Rabbis associated it particularly with women's subjective experience. This is epitomized by a text found in Bava Metsi'a 59a: "Rab said: One should always be heedful of wronging his wife, for since her tears are frequent she is quickly hurt." In a sense, women here become symbolic standard bearers for sensitivity to *ona'at devarim*. Their subjective experience is not only legitimated but is given a place of pride within Halakhah. The Rabbis stamp the "care voice" with the imprimatur of the "justice voice," making the two so interdependent that the line between them is substantially blurred.[5]

Like *ona'at devarim*, *kevod ha-briyot* is a subjective criterion, and also like *ona'at devarim*, it carries significant halakhic weight. Indeed, Sperber introduces several instances where *kevod ha-briyot* overrides traditional rabbinic law; this is seen in ancient halakhic practice where women were permitted to lay hands on sacrificial animals, as well as in more modern decisions, such as allowing deaf people to carry hearing devices on the Sabbath. Sperber thus demonstrates that women's subjective experience cannot be dismissed as easily as Henkin presumes. Saying in effect "you can't read Torah publicly because it's not Orthodox," does nothing to lessen the distress or humiliation women experience when they are not permitted to participate in this way. The halakhic principle of *kevod ha-briyot* mandates that we redress pain. The argument from *kevod ha-briyot*, then, powerfully undergirds the halakhic integrity of *qeri'at ha-Torah* by women.[6]

When Shapiro's essay first appeared, there was joy in the ranks of Orthodox feminists. Many felt that with the cogent halakhic reasoning presented in the first part of the article—by a rabbi, no less—halakhic change would proceed apace. Yet Henkin's position, which draws a strong distinction between learning Torah and the public ritual of chanting from the Torah, was also influential at the same time. Rabbis like Saul Berman and Aryeh Frimer maintained that while women should be encouraged to learn Torah at the very highest levels,

---

5 For the pioneering discussion of these "voices," see Carol Gilligan, *In a Different Voice: Psychological Theory and Women's Development* (Cambridge: Harvard University Press, 1982).

6 Henkin's basic criticism of Shapiro applies to Sperber's work. Indeed, Sperber himself puts the words into his hypothetical critic's mouth: "Yes, you selected a source here, a responsum there, and stitched them together to reach your desired result. Shouldn't you, instead, flow with the halakhic current, which says that *aliyyot* for women remain outside the consensus and that a community that provides for them is not Orthodox by definition and will not remain Orthodox in practice, as R. Henkin suggests?" (11). In answering this question Sperber calls upon the Orthodox community not to fear change because Halakha has always taken into account "changing situations, changing social conditions, and changing needs" (14).

Orthodoxy will not tolerate *qeri'at ha-Torah* by women. Their position then was also initially given a place of honor at Kolech and JOFA[7] conferences.

Today, however, within JOFA and Kolech there are no longer debates whether or not *qeri'at ha-Torah* by women is Orthodox—it is taken for granted that it is. Partnership minyans in which women regularly chant Torah are flourishing all over North America and Israel. What happened?

In 2002, as Shapiro's, Henkin's, and Sperber's work was first circulating, the first two partnership minyans were getting started, in Jerusalem and in New York. The divide between women's learning and women's participation in public ritual was no longer accepted by these communities. Torah scholarship and the accessibility of halakhic texts had reached a high enough level for some people to confidently speak—and listen to—their minds, their hearts, and their souls and not to rely solely on halakhic decisors or existing decisions. Without asking rabbinic authorities for confirmation, a grassroots movement came together to announce that times had changed. For many of us, *not* changing was causing dissension. With women getting doctorates from major universities around the world, with women performing life-saving operations on a daily basis, with women having positions of great power in business, law, politics, the judiciary, and the military, the idea that *qeri'at ha-Torah* by women was somehow still incompatible with *kevod ha-tzibbur* became patently absurd. It is true that for some people only an acknowledged rabbinical leader can acceptably say "times have changed."[8] We did not feel that way—we knew the world had changed, and we did not need anyone to tell us that it had. We knew what we knew, and we had finally lost patience with being told: "wait—soon."[9]

I call Shapiro's article the *teshuvah* to end *teshuvas* because we realized that in founding the partnership minyan Shira Hadasha we did not need a *posek* or a *teshuvah* to justify or explain what we were doing. We ourselves had direct access to relevant halakhic texts—and we knew how to read them. It felt disingenuous to rely upon the work of Shapiro for new practices taking place in our minyan. Rabbis were no longer the gatekeepers to Orthodoxy, and it was unnecessary to cite them as authorities. We founded Shira Hadasha not because

---

7   The Jewish Orthodox Feminists Alliance (JOFA) and Kolech, based in New York and Jerusalem, respectively, are the two major Orthodox feminist organizations.

8   The Chofetz Chayim, in issuing a *psak* at the beginning of the twentieth century permitting girls to learn Torah, famously said that "times have changed."

9   Martin Luther King, Jr., who fought a different battle but against similar rhetoric, teaches us that "'gradualism' … is so often an excuse for escapism and do-nothingism which ends up in stand-stillism."

an Orthodox rabbi had published a *teshuvah* permitting it; we knew there was halakhic integrity in what we were doing and that was enough for us.[10] We did not need consensus of the larger Orthodox world and we were not afraid that we appeared like other, more liberal religious movements. We did not view being called Conservative or Reform as an insult, and as a community, we wasted little time proving our commitment to Halakhah and traditional Judaism. We had too much work to do building and creating a religious community. It was patently apparent to us that we were within the bounds of Halakhah, and it was equally clear to us that many thought differently.

In the introduction to my book *Feminism Encounters Traditional Judaism*, I referred to Shapiro's article, noting that Shapiro seemed primarily interested in creating an "occasional refuge" where women could read Torah in a public setting, whereas I wanted "an ongoing, living *community* of prayer." Living communities are confronted with frequent challenges to which they must either respond or wither. In addressing these challenges, we ask our rabbis to be our teachers; we want to learn more. However, meta-halakhic assertions of dissension and warnings about slippery slopes do not hold a claim on us nor do they threaten us. Statements such as "well there is a way for you to do it but you can't"; "there is a way to do it but it will appear like you belong to another religious movement"; "well, there is a way for you to do it but your shul will not look like the shul my grandparents *davened* [prayed] in"; or "there is a way for you to do it but if you are really serious prove it by coming to morning minyan every day for a year" have lost credibility. This is a time of multiple religious truths, multiple subjective experiences, multiple religious experiments. Those who feared anarchy have been proven wrong: partnership minyans are not anarchic and the center holds within these communities of prayer. Those who said you can only change if you go away have also been proven wrong: we changed and we did not go away.

---

10 The concept of "halakhic integrity" can be seen from Shapiro's essay. Through his analysis of halakhic texts, Shapiro proves that the practice of *qeri'at ha-Torah* by women accords with the halakhic tradition. But implicit in Shapiro's ending—and explicit in Henkin's review—is that Orthodox Judaism does not permit *qeri'at ha-Torah* for women. It's clear then from Shapiro that something can be halakhic but not Orthodox.

12. Jonathan Sacks, *The Dignity of Difference: How to Avoid the Clash of Civilizations*

Jonathan Sacks, *The Dignity of Difference: How to Avoid the Clash of Civilizations*, London: Continuum, Second Edition, 2003

Rabbi Dr. Lord Jonathan Sacks (1948–) was Chief Rabbi of the United Hebrew Congregations of the Commonwealth. Since stepping down from this position, Rabbi Sacks has served as Professor of Law, Ethics, and the Bible at King's College in London, the Kressel and Ephrat Family University Professor of Jewish Thought at Yeshiva University, and the Ingeborg and Ira Rennert Global Distinguished Professor at New York University.

Religion can be a source of discord. It can also be a form of conflict resolution. We are familiar with the former; the second is far too little tried. Yet it is here, if anywhere, that hope must lie if we are to create a human solidarity strong enough to bear the strains that lie ahead. The great faiths must now become an active force for peace and for the justice and compassion on which peace ultimately depends. That will require great courage, and perhaps something more than courage: a candid admission that, more than at any time in the past, we need to search—each faith in its own way—for a way of living with, and acknowledging the integrity of, those who are not of our faith. Can we make space for difference? Can we hear the voice of God in a language, a sensibility, a culture not our own? Can we see the presence of God in the face of a stranger? Religion is no longer marginal to international politics. After a long period of eclipse, it has emerged with immense and sometimes destructive force. That is what lay behind an unusual assembly—and my first encounter with globalization—as the new millenium began. ... (4–5)

COMMENTARY BY MICHAL RAUCHER

In the wake of the September 11th terrorist attacks, Jonathan Sacks's *Dignity of Difference* argues that the predominant approach to differences of any kind (religious, ethnic, national, or economic, for example) is flawed. He notes that the United States in particular has approached differences through pluralism, a concept that acknowledges and accepts but does not celebrate distinctions between and among people. Instead, Sacks suggests looking at differences as dignified, indeed, even as originating with God. He writes, "God creates difference; therefore it is in one-who-is-different that we meet God" (59). In this way, Sacks provides an approach to diversity that is both celebratory and theological.

Therefore, instead of trying to find similarities between world religions, an approach that has left interfaith dialogue lacking in the wake of fundamentalist religious violence, Sacks argues that scholars and activists should be emphasizing the differences. Praising differences in this way will help us avoid a clash of civilizations. He explains that fundamentalism is the Tower of Babel of our times, attempting to build one language, one truth, and one faith. In contrast, focusing on differences will lead to a kind of universal morality, because when we notice differences in other people, we come to see them as individuals who are like us in important ways. Sacks explains,

> Because we know what it is to be a parent, loving our children, not children in general, we understand what it is for someone else, somewhere else, to be a parent, loving his or her children, not ours. There is no road to human solidarity that does not begin with moral particularity—by coming to know what it means to be a child, a parent, a neighbor, a friend. We learn to love humanity by loving specific human beings. (58)

These particularities and differences are lost not only due to the rise of fundamentalisms but also the spread of globalization. Despite our increased interconnectedness, we have a harder time, Sacks argues, seeing the value of the particular individual swimming in a sea of Others.

Religions tend toward tribalism because they emphasize the identity of the group, insisting that everyone within the group is the same and everyone outside the group is different and therefore excluded. The globalization of the twentieth and twenty-first centuries, however, stresses universalism. Its processes claim that we are all essentially the same, thus erasing any differences and leaving no place for religious tribalism. That being said, Sacks explains that these two approaches are mistaken because monotheistic religions actually embrace diversity on a global scale. Sacks suggests that monotheistic religions offer guidance in a variety of ethically challenging situations that arise from globalization, as we see in the passage excerpted.

The language of biblical monotheism shapes Sacks's philosophy here in a critical way. In contrast to the popular understanding of monotheism as promoting one faith, one truth, and one god, Sacks insists, "The glory of the created world is its astonishing multiplicity" (20).

Sacks tackles a few issues facing globalization and demonstrates how Judaism in particular offers remedies. First, Sacks considers the seeming amorality of the market economy. Through an analysis of biblical, Talmudic, medieval, and contemporary Jewish economic ethics, Sacks argues that Judaism appreciates wealth and commercial activity. From this perspective, the global markets provide opportunities to capitalize on the differences between us. Next, Sacks suggests that *tzedaka* and justice can correct global wealth inequality. Although the problem is caused by billions of transactions, many of them distant from us, citing Heschel's injunction that few are guilty but all are responsible, Sacks maintains, "The scope of our interconnectedness defines the radius of our responsibility and concern" (121).

Globalization also highlights gaps in education and access to knowledge across the world. Sacks states that education is the "basis of a free society. Because knowledge is power, equal access to knowledge is a precondition of equal access to power" (137). Judaism, from Ezra, the biblical scribe who was heroic as a teacher, to the importance of education in contemporary Jewish communities, shows us the imperative of equal access to education. Last, Sacks emphasizes the importance of cooperation over competition in our global economy. He suggests that the concept of cooperation is best understood through the language of covenant, which binds people together through their shared belonging and intertwined identities. Individuals do not stand alone but rather always within reciprocal relationships.

While Sacks's language of covenant and the theological significance of difference echo certain concepts raised by Martin Buber and Emmanuel Levinas, they differ in ways that connect back to the larger purpose of *The Dignity of Difference*. In Sacks's chapter on ethics, in discussing the relationship between Adam and Eve in the Garden of Eden, he references Buber's I-Thou philosophy: "Adam must pronounce the name of his wife before he can pronounce his own. He must say 'Thou' before he can say 'I'" (151). For Sacks, personal identity is found within the covenant of one to another. For Buber, this relationship is intimately also about God. In attempting to make this message more palatable to a wider audience, Sacks removes this theological language from the covenant between individuals. This secularization of Jewish religious concepts occurs throughout the later chapters of Sacks's work, as he uses Jewish concepts to correct the ills of globalization. It is notable that he doesn't stop with Jewish concepts. One will also find the words of Adam Smith and Amartya Sen, for instance, or examples from education schemes in Brazil to support the Jewish concepts that Sacks proposes.

The dialogue that Sacks creates between Jewish and non-Jewish ideas and language is one he has mastered in other work as well. This tactic creates rich conversation about concepts many people might think do not relate. It is difficult, though, to identify Sacks's main audience. Is *The Dignity of Difference* aimed at a traditional Jewish audience whose familiarity with the Jewish stories, history, and language will make his ideas seem authentic to Jewish tradition? In this way, is Sacks trying to appeal to members of his own community to take more responsibility in the globalized world in which they live? Or is he speaking to a non-Jewish audience and writing an apology for Judaism, attempting to explain that although religious fundamentalism is a problem in today's world, Judaism is not at fault?

Because Sacks has become such an important leader for the Orthodox Jewish community worldwide, I prefer to think that his work is meant to introduce the Orthodox community to concepts in philosophy and ethics that they otherwise might not encounter. To do this, he frames these ideas in language that they already use—the language of Jewish history, Jewish religion, and Jewish law.

In this, though, I want to suggest that perhaps Sacks's allusions to Levinas's concept of responsibility to the Other have missed the mark in an important way. Early on, Sacks beautifully captures Levinas's ideas of radical difference between individuals as something that is essential to human dignity. This is an important correction to the attempt to always try to find similarities with others. People demand our respect, Sacks says and Levinas would agree, because they are nothing like us. However, in his chapter on covenantal responsibility, Sacks talks at length about the reciprocal responsibilities between individuals in the covenant. It is here that his philosophy diverges greatly from Levinas. For Levinas, I am obligated to the Other not because of what he might do for me, but because the Other demanded something of me before I was even born. The Other demands our attention *because* she is Other and not ourselves. My obligation to the Other has nothing to do with what I might get in return. The relationship is not reciprocal but rather one of vulnerability and obligation.

This kind of responsibility, is, as I'm sure Sacks knows, difficult for most individuals to adopt. It is why, when Sacks demands a universal morality, he recognizes that although differences are what make us dignified, for us to feel morally obligated to one another, we have to find similarities. Those similarities mean that when I see another child suffering, I think of my own child and that drives me to moral action. But there is more that Sacks omitted. The implication, of course, is that I think of my own child and hope that if someone saw her suffering, they would take action as well. Reciprocity is how we imagine moral responsibility these days, and reciprocity involves similarities. Therefore, although differences are dignified, Sacks seems to be saying that we need to identify similarities to feel morally obligated.

Interestingly, Sacks stops short of explaining how his philosophy might affect our daily action. He insists on a reformulating of global challenges using the language of Jewish ethics, but it is not clear what the individual is supposed to take from his guidance. In the Prologue, Sacks suggests that religious leaders, business leaders, and politicians should be in conversation in the wake of the threat of religious fundamentalism and the dangers of globalization. He wants religions to take a stand, and it is in these conversations that he insists Judaism should be part of the solution. However, Sacks also maintains that a lot of this work resides within religious communities. Perhaps, in this way, Sacks's work is meant to spark important conversations within Jewish communities, and between Jewish and non-Jewish religious communities, in order to address the crises facing us all.

13. Rav Shagar, *Broken Vessels*

Rav Shagar, *Broken Vessels*, Efrat: Yeshivat Siach Yitzhak, 2004[1]

Rav Shagar (1949–2007) co-founded Yeshivat Siach Yitzhak in Efrat where he served as *Rosh Yeshiva*.

The paradoxical nature of postmodernism, as described above, is a feature of postmodern pluralism, which is stark and comprehensive in its acknowledgement that all stances are the product of historical and social circumstances, of conditionings that have no absolute metaphysical justifications. It is this acknowledgement that generates postmodernism's paradoxes, contradictions, and despair.

Yet I believe in pluralism, even if it differs from the pluralism of postmodernism: it is a positive pluralism, one of faith. The difference between the pluralism in which I believe and postmodern pluralism springs from the difference between uninspired relativism and a relativism open to inspiration; between a conception of postmodernism as an empty game and one that ascribes significance to it; between ascribing no weight or value to any opinion, including one's own, and seeing value in each and every opinion. Such a way of thinking deconstructs Rorty's dichotomy, mentioned above, between truth that is revealed and truth that is shaped or created. To me, the creative act reveals the divine through the human. All truths may be the product of human conditioning, but such conditioning constitutes the medium through which the divine manifests in the world. This is why the pluralist believer does not shy away from using the revelation metaphor; though he knows there are varying and conflicting revelations, the contradictions do not paralyze him. He is willing to concede that truth is a human construct, because he knows that human constructs are true creations, manifestations of God in a world that is "filled with his glory," not an empty, meaningless game. ...

I must take the ethical game as a given and play it, as I do the religious game: acting ethically and religiously out of a conviction that what I believe is true, but without going so far as to assert that faith in my own way renders

---

1   Translated from the Hebrew by Elie Leshem in Rav Shagar, Zohar Maor (ed.), *Faith Shattered and Restored: Judaism in the Postmodern Age* (New Milford: Maggid Books, 2017).

other ways worthless. To turn my faith into something absolute, objective, and contextless is to fashion it into an ideology, an idol. (116–117)

COMMENTARY BY TOMER PERSICO

Rav Shagar (Rabbi Shimon Gershon Rosenberg) had a complicated relationship with the truth. This should be understood in a positive way. His life of study and teaching had the quest for truth at its center, with Shagar coming to define and relate to it through different means and avenues. Indeed, it is his uncompromising passion for the truth that brought him to adopt the position of being both a postmodern thinker and an enthusiast for the mystical.

Born in 1949, Shagar participated as an IDF soldier in the 1973 Yom Kippur War. Fighting on the Golan Heights, his tank was hit and two of his crew members, young men with whom he had studied in yeshiva, were killed. Shagar himself suffered both physical and psychological trauma, and the war would be for him a catalyst for doubt and faith-related skepticism. It was because of his skepticism, in addition to a group of close students that formed around him, that he was expelled from his first teaching post at Yeshivat ha-Kotel and began his independent path. In 1984 he was invited (together with Rabbi Menachem Froman) by Rabbi Adin Steinsaltz to teach at Yeshivat Makor Chaim, where he exposed Religous Zionist students to Chasidic texts and ideas. Three years later, two of his students, Rabbi Benny Kalmanson and Rabbi Ami Olami, founded a rabbinical school at Otniel that in 1992 became a yeshiva that is now widely known for its emphasis on Chasidic studies and emotional worship. In 1996 Shagar (together with Rabbi Yair Dreifuss) founded Yeshivat Siach Yitzhak, which he headed until his death in 2007.

At its inception Shagar's thought was troubled by two major issues: the quest for truth in the Jewish tradition and the state of Talmud study in the yeshivot. Shagar was concerned by the crisis developing from the pointedly abstract and formal method of study inherited from the Lithuanian yeshivot of the nineteenth century. This sort of study was not fit for many, and the place that it occupied as the *summum bonum* of Jewish religious life meant that a large portion of young students would not find their place. Shagar countered Lithuanian formalism with the interest in the actual *Sitz im Leben* of the Talmudic text. In his teaching Shagar used some of the tools of modern academic research, a highly unorthodox step at the time, but one that has become more accepted, in part as a result of the work of the Beit Morasha house of study, founded in 1990, at which Shagar headed the Talmudic Beit Midrash.

The move away from formalistic study, while accommodating Shagar's distrust of dogma, accentuated the impossibility of combining the truth claims of the tradition with the conclusions of modern research. Holding fast to the quest for truth and simultaneously seeing intellectual honesty as a precondition to any real religiosity, Shagar did not shy away from this tension. He averted any direct collision between his different loyalties, however, by embarking on an effort to connect religious teaching to life through existential philosophy, which he learned independently at the beginning of the 1980s. Shagar turned towards the individual and the individual's inner struggles and experiences. At a time in which Israeli general society increasingly embraced an individualistic ethos, Religious Zionism was still very much absorbed with an intellectual and theological climate colored by the nationalistic interpretation of Rabbi Abraham Yitzhak Kook's writings. Shagar's emphasis on the individual—and even more so, on the inner life of the individual—was thus rare. Here also was the connection to Chasidic texts, which for Shagar echoed the existential thinkers he read and the existential issues he was struggling with. Alongside Froman, he was the first to offer young Religious Zionists inner-directed religious journeys that stressed the quest for authenticity and spiritual experience. Today these are can be found in almost every such community, as Shagar basically legitimized the subjective turn by teaching Chasidic texts that emphasize it and by creating a theological framework that presented it.

That theological framework was, from the mid-1990s, also deeply influenced by postmodern thinkers. Shagar studied postmodern thought on his own and found in it a solution that complemented both his yearnings for truth and his doubts about religious dogma. For Shagar postmodern deconstruction of social reality and truth claims opens up a clearing into which the divine light can shine. As he said in an interview with Yair Sheleg:

> Postmodernism liberates us from the mechanical structure of human reality, and mysticism also sees that structure as a limitation to be freed from. On the other hand, postmodern freedom turns in itself into a problem, what Sartre calls "the prison of freedom," when it causes nihilism. This is where mystical freedom comes in and gives meaning even in a postmodern world, when faith, in this situation, is liberated from the usual stress that impedes people, the stress of the lack of freedom identified with religion.[2]

---

2   Interview to Yair Sheleg, "Piskey ha-Seruv? Zo Teguva Galutit," *Haaretz*, November 1, 2005.

The collapse of modernistic narratives, as also of religious dogma, creates for Shagar an opportunity both for mystical intimacy and for the rejuvenation of religion. By breaking down collective truth claims, a personal mystical experience can be born, and with it a new, authentic, religious understanding. Postmodern thought also solves for Shagar the problem of validating religious truth in the world of modern research as now it seems that every truth is contested while at the same time religion itself can be validated through the avenue of personal spirituality.

Shagar did not express the usual anxiety seen in rabbinic circles about the possibility of a slide towards antinomian behavior. Though Shagar himself was thoroughly halakhic and insisted on the importance of observing the Jewish law, he viewed antinomian tendencies, especially amongst the younger Religious Zionist generation, as symptoms of a candid search for authenticity and meaningful faith.

It is in this context that Shagar saw the search for spirituality and religious authenticity as a revival of the classic Chasidic spirit. For Shagar we are now witnessing a spiritual revival equivalent to the one in eighteenth-century Podolia, which also rebelled against formalistic dogma and mechanical religion. This neo-Chasidic spirit (Shagar himself refers to this movement as "Neo-Hasidism") carries within it a promise of a religious revival that is on the one hand desperately needed, and on the other hand made possible by the postmodern breakdown of ideological frameworks. Indeed, neo-Chasidism for Shagar is itself a postmodern expression, characterized by the colorful mixture of different ideas and directions. It brings not only an authentic and timely Jewish answer to the woes of our era, but also gives birth to positive fruits such as creativity, a renewed awareness and intimacy with the body, and even social cohesion. "I have great faith that this [Neo-Hasidic revival] will have significance and weight no less than the former Hasidism," he wrote.[3]

Whether or not that will be the case, the neo-Chasidic religious renewal that Shagar helped initiate has expanded remarkably since his time at the Yeshivat ha-Kotel. In addition to Kalmanson and Olami's Yeshiva at Otniel, the 1990s also saw the founding of the Yeshivat Hesder Ramat Gan, headed by rabbis Yehoshua Shapira and Yaakov Ariel; Yeshivat Tekoa, headed by rabbis Haim Kafri, Ariel Holand, and Menachem Froman; Yeshivat Tsfat, headed by rabbis Shmuel Eliyahu and Eyal Yakobovitz; and, of course, Shagar's own Yeshiva,

---

3   Rav Shagar, Zohar Maor (ed.), *Lukhot Ve'Shivrei Lukhot* (Alon Shvut: Yedioth Seforim and Machon Ha'Rav Shagar, 2013), 169.

Siach Yitzhak at Efrat, headed by Rabbi Yair Dreyfuss. At all these yeshivot and more, emphasis is put on Chasidic ideas such as the demand for heartfelt, emotional prayer and Chasidic practices such as the festive *tish* dinner, playing Chasidic tunes, and talking time for solitary inner soul searching. Chasidic texts are unquestionably integrated into the curriculum, and indeed, parallel to the Chasidic shift in emphasis of the eighteenth century, these yeshivot place less emphasis on Talmudic study and more on the teaching of Kabbalistic and Chasidic material. Also similar to the dynamics at the inception of Chasidism, neo-Chasidism has also faced strong opposition, this time from Religious Zionist rabbis who feel the emphasis on personal connection to the Torah comes at the expense on strict adherence to the Halakhah and represents an excessive and distorted focus on the individual. The opposition to the growing enthusiasm for neo-Chasidism, though shared by rabbis both from the conservative end of Religious Zionism such as Rabbi Israel Zvi Tau and from its liberal end such as Rabbi Yehuda Amital, thoroughly failed, and has recently dwindled away.

Shagar can be said to have stood at the avant garde of the turn to personal, skeptical existential, Chasidic and experiential religiosity that since 1990s has become widespread among the Religious Zionist public. Moreover, the path he outlined provided tools for a growing culture of "self-care" that has characterized contemporary Western religiosity more generally. The increasing focus on the inner life of the individual is accompanied by Shagar with a turn away from the nationalistic sentiment coloring Religious Zionism and can be even seen as post-Zionist (such as in the works of Yishai Mevorach, Shagar's posthumous scribe). Shagar's work inspired not only rabbis, but poets, artists, free-spirits on the verge of leaving the life of observance and those who left, and above all many for whom the standard way of learning and living Halakhah was not religiously satisfying. Shagar is the emblematic postmodern figure of the Religious Zionist public in his embrace both of the postmodern crisis of truth and of the deconstruction of social narratives, but he is deeply existential in his quest for personal authenticity, and his emphasis on personal spirituality places him firmly as a neo-Chasidic theological thinker. His teaching, coming into distinction parallel to the rise of New Age spirituality in Israel and the breakdown of Kookist messianic nationalism for the Religious Zionist public, filled a vital need, and in doing so created a new religious language.

14. Arthur Green, *Radical Judaism: Rethinking God and Tradition*

Daniel Landes, "Hidden Master"

Arthur Green and Daniel Landes, "God, Torah, and Israel: An Exchange"

Arthur Green, *Radical Judaism: Rethinking God and Tradition*, New Haven: Yale University Press, 2010

Rabbi Dr. Arthur Green (1941–) is Director of the Rabbinical School and Irving Brudnick Professor of Jewish Philosophy and Religion at Hebrew College.

The need for ongoing human participation in the quest for redemption is the context of the volume you have before you. Radical Judaism means a reframing of our contemporary perspective on the great questions, a leap forward that shows we are not afraid to be challenged by contemporary reality, while we remain devoted to hearing the greater challenge of God's voice calling out "Where are you?" anew in our age. This means a Judaism that takes seriously its own claims of ongoing Creation and revelation, even as it recognizes all the challenges to them. To "take them seriously" in our day cannot mean simply holding fast to them without question, dismissing the challenges of science and scholarship or seeking to avoid dealing with them. It means rather to rethink our most foundational concepts—God, Torah, and Israel and Creation, Revelation, Redemption, to ask how they might work in the context of what we really believe in our age, and thus how they might speak to seekers in this century. Going back to the mountain and hearing the Word again, hearing it with clarity as the eternal voice speaks for our own day, will require a new sort of listening, one that has never yet existed, unique to this generation and to this moment. (163–164)

To be a Jew is still to think about the right way to live, to be challenged to respond. How do we live a holy life after the Holocaust, with a third of our people dead and so many wounded by cynicism and despair? How do we stand before Sinai as a people that fully includes the voices of women equally with those of men? How do we lift our heads in God's presence in a time when Jews are seen by many, and with some justification, as oppressors rather than victims? Our response needs to change shape and grow in each generation as it is confronted with the new and different challenges, but it still faces the same question. *Ayekah?* Where are you? How are you going to live? When we live badly, especially when we are selfish, mean, or uncaring, we are disgraced before our fellow Jews. "A Jew should know better" is something we all feel. What is "conduct unbefitting a member of the Jewish people?" We know it when we see it and we call it *hillul ha-Shem*, a defaming of God's name, that name we all bear as part of the word "Israel." The echo of covenant is commingled with the memory of Egypt and the long history of persecution in telling us when and how "a Jew should know better." (164–165)

I believe with complete faith that new forms of Judaism will emerge in the state of Israel, America, and elsewhere, distilled from the multiple experiments in Jewish living that are currently taking place in the lives of diverse individuals, households, and small communities. This is a process that will take several generations and cannot be rushed. Those who participate in this creative process are multiple and varied, including Jews by choice, refugees from ultra-Orthodoxy, and many whom they will meet in the middle. The new Judaism will not be created top-down by committees of rabbis or (God forbid) by presidents of major Jewish organizations. The *halakhah*, or pathway, of the future will be more flexible, more multistranded, than any we have known. It will only emerge from a new *aggadah*, a new articulation of Jewish faith that succeeds in capturing the hearts of generations of Jews. This narrative will take us back to the old tales, but with contemporary eyes and ears wide open. The voice calls forth each day. When we are ready, it will address us. My prayer is that this book constitutes a small step along that evolutionary path.

This is the moment for radical Judaism. We understand that all God can do is to call out to us, now as always. All we can do is respond—or not. The consequence of our failure will be monumental. God is indeed in need of humans; and we humans are in need of guidance, seeking out the hand of a divine Partner, one who "speaks" from deep within the heart, but also from deep within our tradition and its wisdom.

Such a time cries out for leadership, for covenant, and for *mitzvah*, all of them expanded and redefined for this hour. (165–166)

Daniel Landes, "Hidden Master," *Jewish Review of Books*, Fall 2010
Rabbi Daniel Landes (1950–) is Founder and Director of Yashrut and the former Director of the Pardes Institute of Jewish Studies.

There are dangers lurking in the kind of rhetoric that Green and like-minded thinkers employ. When Green urges, for instance, that we must "let others know that we and they are part of the same One when we treat them like brothers and sisters, or like parts of the same single universal body," he is perhaps contributing to the arousal of energies that may prove difficult to control. The dismissal of clear legal norms as nothing more than a transitory response to a wordless call, or the replacement of a firm prohibition of adultery with nothing more than self-selected boundaries ("make sure that all your giving is for the sake of those who seek to receive it"), is a failure to reckon with the power of temptation and the function of law, human or divine.

Compared with Green's God and his Torah, Green's Israel seems more familiar. It is still the people descended from Abraham. But it exists in some tension with what he calls "my Israel." The latter consists of the people he describes as "you for whom I write, you whom I teach, you with whom I feel a deep kinship of shared human values and love of this Jewish language." Green admits, "(partly in sadness!) that it no longer suffices for me to limit my sense of spiritual fellowship to those who fall within the ethnic boundaries that history has given us." He is, indeed, prepared to say:

> I have more in common with seekers and strugglers of other faiths than I
> do with either the narrowly and triumphally religious [or] the secular and
> materialistic elements within my own community.

Thus Green calls for a broader "Israel," imagining "an extended faith-community of Israel, a large outer courtyard of our spiritual Temple."

Although Green himself is a person who is clearly attached to the Jewish people, the logic of his position is disturbing. It leads him to privilege people possessing the proper spiritual consciousness, "my Israel," over the actual people of Israel. When Green lectured a decade ago at the Pardes Institute, where I am the current director, he spoke beautifully of Yehudah Aryeh Leib Alter's *ahavat Yisrael* (his love of Israel, or solidarity with fellow Jews), but I find no doctrine of *ahavat Yisrael* in Green's radical theology.

Arthur Green and Daniel Landes, "God, Torah, and Israel: An Exchange," *Jewish Review of Books*, Winter 2011

A rthur Green: The high point of my annoyance is Landes's claim that I offer "no doctrine of ahavat Yisrael." This book is written entirely in the spirit of love for both Judaism and Jews. Why else would I make the effort? Landes is unhappy that I admit openly my deep alienation from "the narrowly and triumphally religious" within our community. Honesty can sting. My claim to be "a religious Jew but a secular Zionist" is also intentionally distorted for polemical purposes. I meant simply that I remain committed to the vision of a Jewish and democratic state (There—I have signed my loyalty oath!) while according it no messianic significance. Has that gotten too hard to understand?

Landes lines up with the late Sam Dresner and others in expressing an overweening fear of anything that smacks of pantheism, celebrating God within nature, or an underlying sense of universal religiosity. But it is precisely this sort of religion that I believe humanity most urgently needs in this century, when our collective survival as a species is so threatened. I am here to teach a Jewish version of it, one relying deeply on our own sources and bearing our values, but without making an exclusive truth claim for Judaism. I rejoice that the deepest religious truths are known to men and women of many cultures, clothed in the garments of both east and west. See Malachai 1:11.

D aniel Landes: Green writes that the "high point of his annoyance" with me is in my contention that he presents a theology that has no doctrine of ahavat Yisrael, and then goes on to assert that he loves Jews and supports the State of Israel. I never asked for a loyalty oath or doubted Green's love of his fellow Jew. But neither of these adds up to a doctrine. In his book it would appear that he would replace simple Jews—if they have the wrong politics or a backward spirituality—with a member of Green's "extended faith community" ("my Israel") who is not Jewish but who shares his journey. My point was that ahavat Yisrael is about empirical (one might almost say carnal) Jews, an actual living community. But ahavat Yisrael also cuts both ways. Tradition leads me to maintain—as difficult as it might be to fathom from these exchanges—that Green and I are inextricably bound to (and stuck with) each other.

COMMENTARY BY SAMUEL HAYIM BRODY

The theological disagreement between Arthur Green and Daniel Landes is an important disagreement between two significant contemporary Jewish teachers. At the same time, it is a distant border skirmish, a report of which might be skimmed in the newspaper in the imperial capital before quickly turning the page. This is because of the relatively low rank of theology in the list of concerns bedeviling twenty-first-century Jewish communities. This is nothing new, of course; theology has often been the province of elites, while most people are content to muddle through without developing the kind of rigorous coherence between life and thought that professional thinkers demand.

Nonetheless, it would certainly be tempting to evaluate the debate between Green and Landes by scoring for points as in a boxing match. Each of them gets off a few good jabs: Landes is right that Green makes evolution meaningful only at the price of mischaracterizing the basic operation of natural selection! Green successfully calls out Landes's cheap shot about sex scandals in Renewal, forcing Landes to apologize! Landes defends the piety of the simple Jew, who just wants to talk to God! Green accuses Modern Orthodoxy of being theologically stagnant! But such an exercise would be beside the point. Rather than agree with one or the other, or even offer a critique of both, I would prefer to take a step back and to note the ways in which attention to the contours of the disagreement can tell us much about a particular set of contemporary religious Jewish worlds.

In one of these worlds, there is a hunger for a theology and an approach to Jewish traditions that can adequately confront an interlocking set of modern challenges: the challenge of modern scientific theories to traditional understandings of cosmological and human origins as well as of the possibility of miracles; the challenge of modern historical study to traditional understandings of the coherence, unity, and authorship of the Hebrew Bible and of rabbinic literature; and the challenge of modern liberalism, multiculturalism, and pluralism to traditional understandings of peoplehood and divine election. Since the nineteenth century, a number of such theologies have been tried and discarded, each one attempting to preserve particular aspects of Jewish tradition at the expense of others, trading off emphases and de-emphases in dynamic relation to contemporary philosophy and politics (and often with one eye on how Christians were dealing with the same issues).

Early on, the most pronounced tendency was to emphasize rationalism, selectively foregrounding elements of Jewish traditions that seemed to conform to the political, cultural, and religious parameters of the Enlightenment. Later generations, however, rebelled against what they perceived as the sterility and predictability of these rationalisms, and turned instead to those parts of Jewish tradition that emphasized mystery and ineffable experiences of the divine. Green stands squarely in this lineage. His neo-Chasidic mystical panentheism is not a rejection of modernity and its challenges, but rather a claim that religious rationalism fails to inspire and thus fails to offer Jews a way to meet those challenges. This is why it is somewhat strange for Landes to claim to find Green's "hidden master" in Mordecai Kaplan, founder of Reconstructionism and unabashed rationalist. But while this assertion may not reveal much about Green, it does reveal something about Landes and his world.

In the second world, the dominant mood is less hunger than anxiety. This world is confident that the traditional sources of Judaism (and it is always "Judaism," in the singular) can deal with all the challenges of modernity without losing itself. But it worries about mistakes being made in the process, about attempts to meet the challenges that tip too far in one direction or another, tumbling off the edge of the narrow ridge of Orthodoxy into an abyss. On one side, too much particularism (the *Charedim*); on the other side, too much universalism (liberal Jews). On one side, too much supernaturalism; on the other side, overweening and arrogant scientificity. On one side, blind allegiance to living *rebbes* as infallible channels of Torah; on the other side, unconstrained individualism and chaos. And on both sides (!), a failure to understand the political and theological significance and necessity of the State of Israel.

This latter point, while it is only one of many disagreements between Green and Landes, and at first pass not even close to the most important one, is worth dwelling upon because it provides a way of linking our "distant skirmish" back to the fault lines more fatally dividing Jewish communities today. Landes constructs his critique of Green according to the tripartite schema of God, Torah, Israel—themes represented as core to Judaism, such that any theology that fails to offer recognizable versions of them may be said not only to have fallen off the narrow ridge, but to be outside the bounds of Judaism completely. For Landes, Green's God, a classically panentheist substrate of Being, is insufficiently personal to count as a descendant of the speaking and commanding God of the Torah. Green's Torah offers no revelation that can serve to distinguish the nations of the world from the specific, elected covenant partner of God at Sinai, namely Israel. And Green's Israel is disturbingly defined as a community of elective affinity rather than of ancestry *and* affinity, together. Of course, there is precedent in Jewish traditions for all of these ideas, and much of the subsequent argument between the two men, played out in the virtual pages of *Jewschool* and of the *Jewish Review of Books*, involves dispute on the proper interpretation of these Maimonidean, Zoharic, and Chasidic sources.

But to read this debate as *primarily* about hermeneutics would, I think, put the cart before the horse. The debate is about boundaries. It is about what gets to count as Judaism in the twenty-first century. For Green and his world, the answer to that question is determined by hunger, whereas for Landes and his world, the answer is determined by anxiety. The State of Israel does not inspire liberal American Jews *Jewishly*, but it does assuage the anxiety of many Israeli and American Jews about the prospects of Jewish survival. What Landes does, in his critique of Green, is elide physical survival and spiritual survival by nearly imperceptibly eliding the people of Israel into the State.

This should not necessarily surprise us, since the most theologically exciting aspect of the State of Israel for non-messianically inclined Orthodox Jews has typically been the opportunity offered by renewed Jewish independence for the exploration of new vistas of Halakhah. Whole areas of halakhic creativity, constrained by the subservience of the Exile, are now free to develop, from the law of war to political economy to the treatment of non-Jewish minorities. Green's "radical Judaism," like much liberal Jewish thought, prefers to focus on religious experience and theological understanding rather than on Halakhah (something Landes alludes to as one of the many "dangers" of Green's thought), and so this particular aspect of Jewish statehood cannot be religiously inspiring for Green. What should not go unnoticed, however, is the revolutionary—or even "radical"—nature of *Landes's* view. In his anxious mood, he presents himself as the defender of that singular Judaism, with its personal God, its revealed written and oral Torah, and its elected and covenanted Israel. But then, all of a sudden, as if in mid-sentence—the State. This is new, and from a historical perspective it is just as "radical" as Green's own view.

After all, there is precedent for an impersonal, abstract God in Maimonides and the Zohar, but there is no precedent for identifying the people of Israel—God's elected covenant partner—with a secular state. To be sure, Religious Zionists, like any other stream of Jewish tradition attempting to answer modern challenges, has its preferred stable of precedents for citation: Yehuda Halevi on Jewish peoplehood; Nahmanides on the commandment to live in the Land; the *aliyah* of the students of the Vilna Gaon, etc. But the procedure of selecting and assembling these sources is not, from the outside, any more authentic or natural as an extension of "Judaism" than Green's own procedure. Green does not, himself, make this point; he reacts to Landes's claims about his lack of theological *ahavat Yisrael* by stressing his liberal Zionist credentials. But he correctly perceives the tone of Landes's critique as heresiological ("what's a Jew to do?"), and the justice of his reaction against this would be strengthened by the recognition of this authenticity sleight-of-hand.

None of this is to say, of course, that Green has hit upon the intellectual theological solution that will satisfy the hunger of his world. Perhaps many liberal Jews, regardless of denominational affiliation, implicitly conceive of God as "the infinitely varied self-garbing of an endless energy flow" (*RJ*, 25). But Landes had a point—even if I refrain from scoring the debate on points—that it is difficult to say, on Green's account, why we should not expect the progress of science to eventually eliminate the mystery upon which his theology relies.

15. Elie Kaunfer, *Empowered Judaism: What Independent Minyanim Can Teach Us About Building Vibrant Jewish Communities*

Elie Kaunfer, *Empowered Judaism: What Independent Minyanim Can Teach Us About Building Vibrant Jewish Communities*, Woodstock: Jewish Lights Publishing, 2010

Rabbi Dr. Elie Kaunfer (1973–) is President, Co-Founder, and CEO of the Hadar Institute and Co-Founder of the independent minyan Kehilat Hadar.

Independent minyanim have refocused the energies and resources of the larger Jewish world. This shift in focus, which could outlive any institutional presence of the minyanim, is perhaps their greatest opportunity for impact. Here are a few shifts in perspective brought about by the minyanim:

- **Vibrant, egalitarian, spirited prayer communities are now possible in the twenty-first century.** Those who had given up on the ability of American Jews to connect deeply with religion and modernity while forming community saw a workable alternative that inspired and engaged them.
- **In order to create spirited, vibrant religious communities, we do not need to reinvent Judaism.** The minyanim are not innovative in a groundbreaking, "new big idea" way. They took the power of traditional Judaism and made it compelling and energizing.
- **Empowered young Jews can make real change on the landscape, so we need to focus on how best to empower young Jews.** The minyanim were the outcome of a long educational and experiential process for their leaders. How can American Judaism invest its resources to make those opportunities for education and real, deep empowerment possible on a wide scale?

The Independent minyanim are one answer to the crisis of meaning in American Judaism. I see these minyanim as the most recent response to the perennial question: how can we connect to the age-old truths in Jewish tradition even as our world evolves rapidly? As an optimist, I look forward to the next contributions of Empowered Jews who struggle to answer that question. (83–84)

But the vast majority of Empowered Jews—for instance, the thousands of young Jews who attend independent minyanim—do not claim a particular denominational identity. When asked, they respond, "I don't want to label myself," or "Denominations don't represent who I am." Why is that and what does that mean? (145)

But an Empowered Judaism framework has an entirely different take on this phenomenon. That Jews are increasingly unwilling to settle for a broad definition is positive. Why? Because someone can no longer get away with telling you "I am Orthodox" and assume that you understand what kind of Jew she is. Instead, people are forced to explain *why* they practice in a particular way or *what*, specifically, they believe in. A world without convenient categories is a world that calls on people to take more ownership of the type of Judaism they want to practice in the world. This frame—with all its messy complexity—may frustrate those wishing to tell a simple story about American Jewish life. But it is a major step forward because it leads to a rich discussion about what being Jewish means in our richly textured, highly individualized, twenty-first-century lives. (147–148)

COMMENTARY BY JOSHUA AVEDON AND SHAWN LANDRES

Jewish history unfolds through periods of creative ferment and innovation interspersed between stretches of retrenchment and traditionalism. The unique beauty and strength of the Jewish tapestry relies on this warp and woof, and each new generation weaves together the strands of past eras. Rabbi Elie Kaunfer's *Empowered Judaism* is an essential source that describes a specific early twenty-first-century expression of ferment, namely, the phenomenon of the Independent Minyan (also known as the "indie minyan"). *Empowered Judaism* is both a revelatory recipe book written by and for the indie minyan enthusiast and a distillation of many of the defining characteristics of the broader ecosystem of Jewish innovation in the early 2000s. Its subtext is a call to ecclesiological revolution and organizational revitalization for all of Jewish life, seen through the lens of emergent prayer communities. The thesis is simple: "A Jewish world in which more people have the tools for the conversation means the conversation is more robust, more opinions are expressed, and a more dynamic society is created" (152).

Empowered Judaism describes the genesis of Kehilat Hadar (translated from Hebrew as "community of splendor"), arguably the most influential indie minyan, founded in 2001 by Kaunfer with his friends Mara Benjamin and Ethan Tucker. Their motivation to create a new place to pray—indeed, to *daven*—was born of frustration with their options for communal Jewish prayer. All three grew up in the heart of the Jewish community, Kaunfer and Tucker the sons of rabbis. Yet each had trouble finding the kind of meaningful prayer experiences they longed for as adults. The core of their idea was to combine the custom of fast-paced liturgically traditional prayer typical of Orthodox settings with the vibe of a radically inclusive atmosphere. Though passionately and comprehensively egalitarian (not only with respect to gender but also with respect to sexual orientation), thereby expanding the defining characteristics of who counts for the quorum traditionally required to perform major Jewish communal prayers, the format otherwise remained traditional and extremely focused. The community adopted a full Shabbat service, entirely in Hebrew, with little tolerance for textual innovation, lengthy sermons, or even the announcing of page numbers.

The indie minyan phenomenon spread across geographies and movements: Kehilat Hadar, Darkhei Noam, Kol Zimrah, and Altshul in New York; the Shtibl Minyan in Los Angeles; Mission Minyan in San Francisco; DC Minyan and Tikkun Leil Shabbat in Washington, D.C.; Washington Square Minyan in Boston; Na'aleh Denver; Shira Hadasha in Jerusalem; and dozens of others. They leveraged more than a decade of sustained communal and philanthropic investments in Jewish education and cultivated a new model for creating prayer-focused Jewish micro-communities. Indie minyans "stepped into a demographic vacuum in the Jewish institutional constellation and provided a meaningful and engaging option for Jews in their twenties and early thirties" (83). Easily replicable and sustainable, indie minyans blossomed in large and mid-sized Jewish population centers across North America. The founders of indie minyans built a self-organizing methodology that changed the Jewish landscape, and gave participants a do-it-themselves mode of communal expression for their religious identities and ritual practices.

Sometimes innovation is about a new idea or product. Other times it is about a novel process or delivery system. Indie minyans fall squarely in the latter category. There is nothing new about Jews praying together but in the nineteenth and twentieth centuries, especially in North America, the practice depended largely on the movement-affiliated synagogue. If, as Abraham Joshua Heschel suggested, synagogues gradually became "the graveyard where prayer is buried," then independent minyanim were created as spaces to bring prayer back to life.

Indie minyans live within a deliberately rigid framework of what Jewish prayer is. Kaunfer believes these constraints promote creativity: "When the basic expectations are clear, people feel freer to open up and experiment" (47). Setting aside any desire to innovate in content or basic procedure, Kaunfer and his peers instead focused on a delivery system that invited participation and sparked imitation to great and widespread effect. As he puts it, "Prayer is mystery, but improving prayer is not mysterious" (127). Their innovation wasn't about the "what" of Jewish prayer but the "how" of creating prayer spaces outside of the typical synagogue setting.

Empowered Judaism is an unabashed love letter to a kind of prayer-centric religious Judaism, and it sets itself apart from the collective communal neurosis of an establishment fretting about continuity and relevance. Instead, Empowered Judaism as a philosophy is obsessed with meaning and with creating a conduit to achieve the kind of ecstatic apotheosis only possible in communal prayer. In setting aside institutional obsessions, it also illuminates a potential path for addressing those concerns, not by gnawing at them, but by engineering transformative experiences and the platform to distribute them.

While the established Jewish communal infrastructure is often based on a top-down supply chain through which professionals and philanthropists provide programs and experiences to the Jews in the pews, modern Jewish innovation manifests itself most profoundly through compelling experiences devised by, for, and with the same group of people. Not only does that shift democratize the process, but it also reflects the proposition that a strong community is built by its members, not by a cadre of paid leaders providing a polished product for a passive third party to consume. Through the indie minyan, Kaunfer envisions "a Judaism in which people begin to take responsibility for creating Jewish community, without waiting on the sidelines" (3).

It is worth noting, however, that the indie minyan movement flourished mostly among Jews raised in the Conservative movement and what has come to be known as Modern Orthodoxy. As Kaunfer himself notes, "It is true that Empowered Jews may have connected to a range of Jewish communities throughout their lives, but they often feel most comfortable within a specific band of Jewish practice" (147). Indeed, there were few Reform- or Reconstructionist-inspired independent minyanim (though there were other types of spiritual communities led by Reform- and Reconstructionist-educated founders), and no ultra-Orthodox minyanim were identified with the movement.

Within that social context—and powered by dual commitments to lay empowerment and broad inclusion—the viral nature of the independent minyan concept is visible in its rapid proliferation into a vibrant national movement. Participants in Kehilat Hadar founded parallel minyans in other cities, and then those participants went on to create minyans further afield. Social networks spread the customs and melodies of indie minyans as dozens sprung up in the first decade of the twenty-first century. Kaunfer explains how this flowering of minyanim was unplanned and organic, "fueled by the mobility and transience of young Jews and relied on the power of each motivated individual who saw something in one city and said, 'I can do that in my town'" (66).

For Kaunfer, Empowered Judaism exists within a specific religious dimension—communal ritual expression—and has specific organizational consequences. In 2006, Kaunfer and Tucker, now ordained rabbis, along with Rabbi Shai Held, launched a new think tank and training academy to support the burgeoning movement called Mechon Hadar (now, Hadar Institute). Program begets pedagogy begets platform as Hadar translates the technology of independent minyanim from informally shared knowledge and practice into a formal network backbone organization. Hadar is an egalitarian yeshiva and institute whose goal is to create "a new type of lay leader—change agents who could go back to their home communities and engage their peers in experiencing Jewish heritage from a place of knowledge, substance, and confidence" (131). This leap from designing a new prayer product to building a system to reproduce and distribute it distinguishes the Hadar approach from that of many other Jewish innovations of the period.

Independent minyanim are one important stream within a broader emerging framework of communal practice and reinvention that has characterized early twenty-first-century Judaism. Like a handful of other individual organizations that evolved to build infrastructure for growth and scale such as Limmud, Hazon, and Moishe House, Hadar took the cottage of Kehilat Hadar and turned it into a cottage industry. What they all have in common is the combination of serious attention to Jewish content, the leveraging of existing social ties, and radically inclusive lay and volunteer empowerment. Kaunfer's *Empowered Judaism* demonstrates how creativity firmly rooted in historical soil can bring to flower something fertile, vibrant, and new.

IV
Identities and Communities

1. Menachem Mendel Schneerson, Letter to the Jewish Community of Teaneck

Menachem Mendel Schneerson (Lubavitcher Rebbe), Letter to the Jewish Community of Teaneck, December 1981[1]

Rabbi Menachem Mendel Schneerson (1902–1994) was the seventh and last Lubavitcher Rebbe.

Why is it so important for Jews to have a Chanukah Menorah displayed publicly? The answer is that experience has shown that the Chanukah Menorah displayed publicly during the eight days of Chanukah has been an inspiration to many, many Jews and evoked in them a spirit of identity with their Jewish people and the Jewish way of life. To many others, it has brought a sense of pride in their Yiddishkeit and the realization that there is no reason really in this free country to hide one's Jewishness, as if it were contrary or inimical to American life and culture. On the contrary, it is fully in keeping with the American national slogan "e pluribus unum" and the fact that American culture has been enriched by the thriving ethnic cultures which contributed very much, each in its own way, to American life both materially and spiritually.

Certainly, Jews are not in the proselytizing business. The Chanukah Menorah is not intended to, and can in no way, bring us converts to Judaism. But it can, and does, bring many Jews back to their Jewish roots. I personally know of scores of such Jewish returnees, and I have good reason to believe that in recent years, hundreds, even thousands, of Jews experience a kindling of their inner Jewish spark by the public kindling of the Chanukah Menorah in their particular city and in the Nation's capital, etc., as publicized by the media.

In summary, Jews, either individually or communally, should not create the impression that they are ashamed to show their Jewishness, or that they wish to gain their neighbors' respect by covering up their Jewishness. Nor will this attitude insure their rights to which they are entitled, including the

---

1   A complete reproduction of this text can be found in the endnotes of Chaim Miller, *Turning Judaism Outward: A Biography of Rabbi Menachem Mendel Schneerson the Seventh Lubavitcher Rebbe* (Brooklyn: Kol Menachem, 2014), 511–513.

privilege of publicly lighting a Chanukah Menorah, a practice which has been sanctioned by precedent and custom, as to become a tradition.

COMMENTARY BY JONATHAN D. SARNA

It began at the Liberty Bell in Philadelphia. In 1974, Rabbi Avraham Shemtov, a veteran emissary of the Chabad-Lubavitch movement, daringly organized the public lighting of a giant menorah overlooking that historic site to mark the festival of Chanukah. A year later, another Chabad emissary placed a twenty-two-foot menorah in Union Square in San Francisco. Four years after that, in 1979, the menorah came to Lafayette Park, just north of the White House. President Jimmy Carter ended one hundred days of self-imposed seclusion over the Iran hostage debacle to join in the lighting of that menorah, and delivered brief remarks.

These well-publicized menorah lightings anticipated two momentous changes in American Jewish life. One of them was the transformation of Chanukah from an essentially private Jewish festival, celebrated in homes and Jewish institutions, to a public one marked as well in outdoor squares and government institutions. The second was the emergence of Chabad on the national scene, led by "emissaries" (*shluchim*) of the Lubavitcher Rebbe, Rabbi Menachem M. Schneerson, and housed in Chabad houses and institutions that spread across North America, making Chabad the fastest growing Jewish religious movement of the postwar era. Those two developments, we shall see, were linked.

Chabad's menorah displays, as they proliferated, sparked a heated debate across the American Jewish community. Some, especially liberal Jews, insisted that the principle of church-state separation, championed by the American Jewish community since the nineteenth century, meant that the public square should be devoid of *any* religious symbols, Jewish or Christian. They viewed the Chabad menorahs as a violation of the "no establishment" clause of the US Constitution's First Amendment. Others, Chabad's proponents in particular, insisted that the Constitution guaranteed them the right "to practice their religion without fear," and that the public square should be open to religious symbols of *every* kind. They viewed public menorah displays, especially since they coincided with a season when Christmas displays were omnipresent, as an expression of the very neutrality with regard to religion that the First Amendment was supposed to guarantee.

A remarkable—indeed, unprecedented—1978 exchange between Rabbi Joseph B. Glaser, then the executive vice-president of the Reform Movement's

Central Conference of American Rabbis, and the Lubavitcher Rebbe articulated the two positions. Rabbi Glaser urged the Rebbe to "direct a cessation of ... lightings or other religious observances on public property," depicting these as being "as much a violation of the constitutional principle of separation of church and state as is the erection of Christmas trees and creches depicting the birth of Jesus. It weakens our hand when we protest this intrusion of Christian doctrine into the public life of American citizens." The Rebbe, in response, sought to "allay" Glaser's "apprehensions." After presenting his alternative understanding of the First Amendment, he emphasized that Chabad placed menorahs on public property to encourage Jewish religious identity and observance ("Torah and Mitzvoth") as well as Jewish religious pride. "Where Chanukah lamps were kindled publicly," he wrote, "the results have been most gratifying in terms of spreading the light of Torah and Mitzvoth, and reaching out to Jews who could not otherwise have been reached."[2]

The exchange between these two rabbinic titans from opposite ends of the Jewish religious spectrum highlights fundamental differences in outlook between them. Not only did they read the US Constitution differently, they also embraced different priorities and goals. Glaser believed that Jews flourished best in an America where religion and state remained totally separate. "The wall of separation between religion and state is like a dike," he argued. "The slightest breach is a dangerous portent of a torrent to follow." By contrast, for the Rebbe, as his biographer, Joseph Telushkin, observes, "what was paramount was reaching Jews who were not being exposed to Judaism, in this instance offering them as a point of entry the joyous 'festival of lights'. The Rebbe also wanted to show the non-Jewish world—and through them, nonobservant Jews as well—an image of Jews who were willing to be very public about their religious commitment."[3]

In a letter to the Jewish community of Teaneck (excerpted here), New Jersey, some three years after his exchange with Rabbi Glaser, the Rebbe put forth a portentous additional argument on behalf of the menorah displays. "Jews," he insisted, "either individually or communally should not create the impression that they are ashamed to show their Jewishness, or that they wish to gain their neighbors' respect by covering up their Jewishness." Having lived and studied in Paris prior to World War II, the Rebbe had first-hand knowledge

---

2   This exchange of letters is reprinted in Jonathan D. Sarna and David G. Dalin, *Religion and State in the American Jewish Experience* (Notre Dame: University of Notre Dame Press, 1997), 290–297.

3   Joseph Telushkin, *Rebbe: The Life and Teachings of Menachem M. Schneerson, the Most Influential Rabbi in Modern History* (New York: HarperCollins, 2014), 268.

of the French principle of *laïcité*, which *did* separate the French state from religion, distinguishing *private* life, where adherents believed religions belonged, from the *public* sphere, where all alike stood equal as citizens, devoid of religious or other particularities. Many enlightened European Jews had similarly embraced versions of this separationist principle. The nineteenth-century Hebrew poet Judah Leib Gordon, for example, in a poem entitled "Awake, my People," called upon the modern Jew to "be a human being (*adam*) in the streets and a Jew at home."

Precisely this dichotomy the Rebbe now flatly rejected in his letter to the Jews of Teaneck and elsewhere. He deemed it crucial for Jews to *publicly* adhere to their religion, even as he respected the right of other faith communities to also display their religions in the public square. The development of numerous ideologies promoting racial, ethnic, and religious pride, notably "Black is Beautiful" and "cultural pluralism," made it possible for him to defend his view in American terms that even his opponents had to respect. Menorah displays, he declared, were "fully in keeping with the American national slogan '*e pluribus unum*' and the fact that American culture has been enriched by the thriving ethnic cultures which contributed very much, each in its own way, to American life."

The arguments for and against public displays of the menorah on government property soon led to court challenges. One of them, in Pittsburgh, made its way all the way up to the United States Supreme Court which, in 1989, upheld the menorah display on the grounds that it formed part of a broader holiday display akin to the display of Christmas trees, which it likewise permitted. "Both Christmas and Chanukah," the court ruled, "are part of the same winter-holiday season, which has attained secular status in our society."[4]

Later that year, perhaps influenced by the Court's ruling, Chanukah made its way into the White House when President George H. W. Bush displayed a menorah there, given to him by the Synagogue Council of America. Twelve years later, his son, George W. Bush, became, in 2001, the first President to host an official White House celebration of Chanukah, and the first to actually light a menorah in the White House residence. In 2005, the Bush Chanukah party even became fully kosher—under the supervision of Chabad rabbis.

By then, just three decades after the first public Chanukah candle-lighting at the Liberty Bell, Chanukah menorahs had become ubiquitous in public and government venues across the United States. Chabad too had become ubiquitous, a familiar presence in communities and college campuses from coast to

---

4   County of Allegheny v. ACLU, 492 US 573 (1989).

coast. The widely publicized debates over menorah displays, followed by the US Supreme Court's vindication of Chabad's Constitutional claims (to the surprise and chagrin of Rabbi Glaser), helps to explain this development. So does Chabad's strategy of taking Judaism to the people—opening up its Chanukah and other celebrations to everyone at no cost—rather than confining Judaism to dues-paying congregants. So does Chabad's political savvy, displayed throughout the campaign to publicly display menorahs and then, annually, at crowded menorah lightings where politicians are honored. And so, finally, does the genius of the Rebbe himself, who initiated and steered the controversial menorah campaign; defended it in documents like his "Letter to the Jewish Community of Teaneck"; refused to compromise in the face of legal challenges; and encouraged his emissaries with messianic fervor to kindle more and bigger menorahs wherever they could, so as to "bring Jews back to their Jewish roots."

Following a lifetime of activism, and at an age when most Jewish leaders would have reposed in retirement, the Rebbe expanded his menorah campaign from a national into an international one, promoting public Chanukah displays and candle lightings on every continent. "We must," he insisted, "not only illuminate the inside of homes, but also the outside, and the world at large." "Go out into … the public domain," he entreated his followers, "and create light which illuminates the entire outside world."

2. Blu Greenberg, *On Women and Judaism: A View from Tradition*

Blu Greenberg, *On Women and Judaism: A View from Tradition*, Philadelphia: Jewish Publication Society of America, 1981

Blu Greenberg (1936–) is Co-Founder and first President of the Jewish Orthodox Feminist Alliance (JOFA).

Perhaps this is the only legitimate response one can make at this time: a series of tentative remarks. If feminism is a revolution, as I believe it is, and Judaism is and always has been the rock-bottom source of a Jew's values, thoughts, feelings, actions, mores, laws, and loves—how else can one respond to and be part of that turbulent encounter but with a stammer, one step forward and half a step backward. I envy those who can say, "This is Halakhah. That's it!" Or, "These are the absolute new truths, and nothing less will do!" I envy, but I also suspect, their unexamined complacency. I suspect that their fear is even greater than mine; therefore, they must keep the lid on even tighter and show no ambivalence, no caution, and no confusion.

So for me, despite the turbulence, or maybe because of it, it has not been all bad. I have had some very good feelings in the course of doing this work. The best of these has been a sense of being able to approach the sources without intimidation. The fact that I can think about the traditional sources without knowing them exhaustively, that I can bring to bear my own interpretive keys without diminishing the divinity and authority of the Halakhah and tradition—this has been a revelation for me. So, too, the experience, which all women alive today share, of stretching ourselves, our minds, our talents, our sights. Transition women, like myself, are taking everything less for granted and finding each step more exhilarating. (177–178)

COMMENTARY BY RACHEL GORDAN

It is impossible to examine the major changes in late twentieth-century American Judaism, without considering the influence of the writer and feminist Blu Greenberg. Her contributions to Modern Orthodoxy are quickly evident, but so too is her transformative effect on the entire landscape of American Judaism, by the twenty-first century, as a result of her feminist questions and commitment to Judaism.

In 1981, when Greenberg published *On Women and Judaism: A View from Tradition*, few Orthodox women were yet publicly grappling with feminism. It was three years before Geraldine Ferraro became the first woman nominated by a major political party, and six years before the US Congress designated a women's history month. Indeed, many Americans felt that they had already dealt with and then buried feminism, along with their bellbottoms and other trappings of hippie culture. Even within Judaism, by the mid-1980s, the debate over female rabbinical ordination seemed closed, with Reform, Conservative, and Reconstructionist Judaism having answered the question affirmatively. Few expected the issue of female ordination to be taken seriously within the most traditional of the movements of Judaism. Orthodox Jewish feminism was barely a blip on the radars of feminists or Jews. But through her writing and lectures, Greenberg brought Orthodox feminism into the foreground and became an agent of change, helping American Jews to think differently about a topic many had felt was destined to stay the same, forever: the role of women in Orthodox Judaism.

On Women and Judaism appeared fifteen years before Greenberg co-organized the first International Conference on Feminism and Orthodoxy, and less than a decade after she had, somewhat accidentally, accepted an invitation to give the opening address at the first National Jewish Women's Conference, in 1973, an event that proved eye-opening, as Greenberg experienced her first women's minyan, and received her first Torah honor ("I found it an exhilarating moment," she wrote of the experience. "It was the first time I had ever held a Torah scroll") (33). Coming as it did between these two important events in Greenberg's career as a Jewish feminist, *On Women and Judaism* provided readers with a template for confronting Orthodox Judaism with the questions of feminism, even as the book expressed Greenberg's personal struggles to bridge the two. As she engaged with Jewish texts, in preparation for her 1973 speech, now reading through the lens of women's equality, a thirty-something Greenberg discovered that she could "no longer accept the apologetic line so popular among those in the traditional Jewish community" (31). It was not just a matter of "different role assignments," as had been the customary Orthodox response to feminist challenges. By this point, Betty Friedan had given Greenberg important food for thought. "Once I had tasted of the fruit of the tree of knowledge," Greenberg wrote of her 1960s experience of reading *The Feminine*

Mystique that "there was no going back. The basic idea had found a resting spot somewhere inside me" (27). So, too, did *On Women and Judaism* plant seeds of change among Greenberg's late twentieth-century readers.

In *On Women and Judaism* and in later writings, Greenberg modeled a questioning posture toward Judaism and a process of transformation, as she explained how even a woman largely content with Orthodoxy ("I knew my place, and I liked it—the warmth, the rituals, the solid, tight parameters," Greenberg wrote of her experience growing up in an Orthodox home) had come to embrace feminism, despite her initial reservations. In the book Greenberg made clear where her loyalties lay: "My questioning never will lead me to abandon tradition. I am part of a chain of tradition. I am part of a chain that is too strong to break" (36). Readers of *On Women and Judaism* came to know a woman who had made a happy home within Orthodoxy. As Greenberg explained, far from resenting her second career as the wife of an Orthodox rabbi, who was expected to host and to visit along with her husband, she had deep appreciation for her role as rebbetzin. (As Sheryl Sandberg would do, a generation later, in her own feminist-inspired first book, *Leaning In*, Greenberg acknowledged that her spouse, and his feminist proclivities, had a large influence on her own ability to grow personally and professionally.) Her life was enriched, Greenberg explained, because of her ability, as the rabbi's wife, to be present for so many important moments in congregants' lives.[1] Her love of Jews and Judaism had grown as a result.

At the same time, Greenberg described her own mid-life interrogation of the tradition that had nourished her for decades. Newly sensitized to feminist issues, Greenberg discovered that she now took offense at certain precepts and gender norms emanating from Orthodoxy. *Kol ishah* was one example. The prohibition on a woman singing in the presence of men had not been popular in Greenberg's youth; its reemergence in the 1970s seemed, to Greenberg, like "a counterpoint to women's new freedom of expression. ... To me, kol ishah seemed nothing but an overt slur on the female sex, an arbitrary curb on women in the name of a one-sided modesty meter" (36).

Personal reactions like this were new to Greenberg. By noting them and the change in her that they evidenced, Greenberg allowed readers to witness her feminist awakening. She also demonstrated her acceptance that her feminist questioning of Orthodoxy would be a lifelong journey, now that the veil had

---

1   Shuly Rubin Schwartz, *The Rabbi's Wife: The Rebbetzin in American Jewish Life* (New York: NYU Press, 2006), 190–193.

been lifted: "I intend to keep my eyes wide open, watching to see what works and what doesn't, what is viable within the framework of Jewish tradition and what isn't" (36). Greenberg reminded her readers that Judaism, like all religions, has always been influenced by the surrounding culture. Recognizing that, "there is probably a great deal of tension in store for people like me," Greenberg wrote of those reconciling Judaism and feminism, that she nonetheless welcomed the challenge; she had faith that Judaism would emerge even stronger from its engagement with feminism.

Acknowledging the distance between Orthodox Judaism, on one hand, and feminism, on the other, Greenberg wrote a new kind of Orthodox rebbetzin's story: her narrative was honest and confessional, never preachy or moralizing. The path toward considering feminism was likely made easier for many readers because of Greenberg's own convincing attachment to Orthodoxy. In 1981, "feminist" was still a dirty word, often associated with man-hating, and an aversion for traditional family life. Not so in Greenberg's telling: "On those bitter cold Sabbath mornings I was absolutely delighted to linger an hour longer in a nice warm bed and play with the kids rather than to have to brave the elements," Greenberg confessed of her life as an Orthodox Jewish mother. "I could choose to go to the synagogue when I wanted or pray at home when I wanted; for my husband there was no choice" (25).

With its narrative of change in Greenberg's own attitude and in Judaism, *On Women and Judaism* was subtly inspirational. The engagement of Judaism and feminism offered a challenge that Greenberg portrayed as nearly irresistible to those who cared about religion: "new heights to scale, a deeper sense of maturity, and an enlarged scope of responsibility for oneself, society, and the continuity of tradition" (37). Indeed, the book became a guide for those hoping to navigate between Judaism and newer movements for freedom. Nowhere did that come through as strongly as in her dictum, "Where there's a rabbinic will, there's a *halakhic* way." Judaism included a tradition of change and the profound ability to assimilate new ideas. The key would be to draw on feminism in thoughtful ways, and with ultimate concern for welfare of Judaism. With *On Women and Judaism*, Blu Greenberg came to embody that goal for Jews at the turn of the twenty-first century.

3. Harold Kushner, *When Bad Things Happen to Good People*

Alan Lew, *This Is Real and You Are Completely Unprepared: The Days of Awe as a Journey of Transformation*

Harold Kushner, *When Bad Things Happen to Good People*, New York: Schocken Books, 1981

Rabbi Harold Kushner (1935–) is Rabbi Laureate of Temple Israel of Natick.

If a man who knew nothing about medicine were to walk into the operating room of a hospital and see doctors and nurses performing an operation, he might assume that they were a band of criminals torturing their unfortunate victim. He would see them tying the patient down, forcing a cone over his nose and mouth so that he could not breathe, and sticking knives and needles into him. Only someone who understood surgery would realize that they were doing all this to help the patient, not to torment him. So too, it is suggested, God does painful things to us as His way of helping us. (21)

Such answers are thought up by people who believe very strongly that God is a loving parent who controls what happens to us, and on the basis of that belief adjust and interpret the facts to fit their assumption. It may be true that surgeons stick knives into people to help them, but not everyone who sticks a knife into somebody else is a surgeon. It may be true that sometimes we have to do painful things to people we love for their benefits, but not every painful thing that happens to us is beneficial.

I would find it easier to believe that I experience tragedy and suffering in order to "repair" that which is faulty in my personality if there were some clear connection between the fault and the punishment. A parent who disciplines a child for doing something wrong, but never tells him what he is being punished for, is hardly a model of responsible parenthood. Yet, those who explain suffering as God's way of teaching us to change are at a loss to specify just what it is about us we are supposed to change. (23)

We have all read stories of little children who were left unwatched for just a moment and fell from a window or into a swimming pool and died. Why does God permit such a thing to happen to an innocent child? It can't be to teach a child a lesson about exploring new areas. By the time the lesson is over, the child is dead. Is it to teach parents and baby-sitters to be more careful? That is too trivial a lesson to be purchased at the price of a child's life. Is it to make the parents more sensitive, more compassionate people, more appreciative of life and health because of their experience? Is it to move them to work for better safety standards, and in that way save a hundred future lives? The price is still too high, and the reasoning shows too little regard for the value of an individual life. I am offended by those who suggest that God creates retarded children so that those around them will learn compassion and gratitude. Why should God distort someone else's life to such a degree in order to enhance my spiritual sensitivity? (24)

Alan Lew, *This Is Real and You Are Completely Unprepared: The Days of Awe as a Journey of Transformation*, Boston: Little, Brown and Company, 2003

Rabbi Alan Lew (1943–2009) served as the Rabbi at Congregation Beth Sholom in San Francisco. He was Co-Founder of Makor Or, a center for Jewish meditation.

Yom Kippur is the day we all get to read our own obituary. It's a dress rehearsal for our death. That's why we wear a kittel, a shroudlike garment, on this day; why we refrain from life-affirming activities such as eating, drinking, and procreating. We are rehearsing the day of our death, because death, like Yom Kippur, atones.

And what our tradition is affirming with these claims is the healing power of time. What our tradition is affirming is that when we reach the point of awareness, everything in time—everything in the year, everything in our life—conspires to help us. Everything becomes the instrument of our redemption.

The banks of the river roll by. We leave home to return home. Loss is inevitable. Entropy is a fact of life. What's done cannot be undone—but it can be healed; it can even become the instrument of our healing. The year rolls by with all its attendant loss and failure, death and disappointment, but at the end of the year there is a day that heals. Life rolls by, and the same is true of the end of life as well. (29)

And here is the bad news I have come to deliver. This is a true story, and it is not about me or my mother or a man desperate to blow the shofar. It is about you. It is really happening, and it is happening to you, and you are seriously unprepared.

And it is real whether you believe in God or not. Perhaps God made it real and perhaps God did not. Perhaps God created this pageant of judgement and choice, of transformation, of life and of death. Perhaps God created the Book of Life and the Book of Death, Teshuvah, and the blowing of the shofar. Or perhaps these are all just inventions of human culture. It makes no difference. It is equally real in any case. The weeks and the months and the years are also inventions of human culture. Time and biology are inventions of human culture. Language and stories, love and tragedy, are inventions of human culture. But they are all matters of life and death, all real and all inescapable. Even though we invented the idea of weeks, we die when our allotted number of weeks has gone by. So if this event is merely the product of human culture, it is the product of an exceedingly rich culture, one that has been accumulating focus and force for three thousand years.

Or perhaps God made the reality that all this human culture seeks to articulate. Perhaps God made a profoundly mixed world, a world in which every second confronts us with a choice between blessings and curses, life and death; a world in which our choices have incredible consequences; a world in which life and death, blessings and curses, choose us, seek us, find us every moment. And we live with the consequences of our choices. And perhaps we have chosen arbitrary spiritual language to express these things, or perhaps God made human culture so that we would express these things precisely as we have in every detail. It makes no difference. What makes a difference is that it's real and it is happening right now and it is happening to us, and it is utterly inescapable, and we are completely unprepared. This moment is before us with its choices, and the consequences of our past choices are before us, as is the possibility of our transformation. This year some of us will die, and some of us will live, and all of us will change. (105–106)

COMMENTARY BY JOSHUA LADON

There is likely no better selling book written by a rabbi than Harold Kushner's *Why Do Bad Things Happen to Good People?* The book, which tackles an eternal theological question in simple and clear prose, spoke to a generation of Americans reeling from a decade that saw Vietnam, Nixon, the OPEC embargo, and the Iranian hostage crisis. As America's stature in the world declined, on the heels of what Tom Wolfe called "the Me decade," Kushner's book found an audience much broader than the congregants of his suburban Conservative synagogue in Natick, Massachusetts. I first encountered it as a bar mitzvah gift in the 1990s.

As a work of Jewish thought, Kushner's account of suffering is a popular, updated version of Maimonidean free will. As an artifact of late twentieth-century American spiritual life, the book offers a snapshot of the American Jewish search for meaning. Together with Alan Lew's *This Is Real and You Are Completely Unprepared,* it tells the story of a spiritual Judaism that is increasingly inwardly focused, serving to answer questions of meaning but lacking commitment to any entrenched Jewish community. The power of these books is that they open doors. They meet the reader in their moment of need and bring them along to a fuller place. But they also predict a Jewish life that is increasingly niche and tailored for the individual to undertake alone.

It is difficult to understand how a book about God written by a rabbi would come to share the *New York Times* bestseller list with *Jane Fonda's Workout Book* and Dr. Joyce Brothers's *What Every Woman Should Know about Men.* Its reach was dramatic! In 1983, Philip Yancey, one of American Christianity's bestselling writers (fourteen million books sold) offered a serious treatment of Kushner's ideas in the Evangelical magazine *Christianity Today.* Noting the book's astonishing sales, he told of the way the book confounded church leaders, forcing a major Christian book distributor to issue a warning notice, "admitting that demand from readers virtually forced them to carry the book but acknowledging that Kushner's answers 'do not present an orthodox Christian theology of suffering.'"

Kushner's book emerges from the tragic loss of a child, his son Aaron, to progeria (rapid aging). It is written in a popular style, peppered with stories of the suffering he encountered as a young pulpit rabbi and his own efforts to comfort the bereaved. He strives for a universal tone and aims to set himself apart from popular notions of suffering. Reflecting on the funeral of a neighborhood boy who was hit by a car when he ran into the street, he references the boy's "clergyman" rather than specifying the officiant's religion by calling him a rabbi, pastor, or priest. Kushner is not interested in a religious polemic but wants to speak broadly to the needs of humanity.

Kushner quotes this clergyman as saying that, "This is not a time for sadness or tears. ... Michael has been taken out of this world of sin and pain with his innocent soul unstained by sin." While Kushner spends time later in the book offering theological arguments regarding suffering, his immediate desire is to comfort, leading him to reject this view. He writes, "I heard that, and I felt so bad for Michael's parents … they were being told by the representative of their religion that they should rejoice in the fact that he had died so young and so innocent." Kushner wants to remove God from a conversation about suffering. To Michael's parents and to others, he offers a vision of radical free will in which God steps back, providing humans the ability to be moral.

Beneath Kaplan's responses to individual vignettes of suffering lies the Holocaust. And when Kushner takes up the Holocaust directly, he does not try to explain it away, but he moves instead toward the cultivation of responsible moral action. The Holocaust does not teach us about God but about humanity, that our capacity for good comes with equal capacity for evil: "It happened because Hitler was able to persuade lawyers to forget their commitment to justice[,] … because democratic governments were unwilling to summon their people to stand up to Hitler as long as their own interests were not at stake." It is free will that enables moral action and it is free will that unleashes evil. And, what then, is religion for? God does not punish nor does God reward. Instead, God is transcendence, God is value, and God is comfort: "the goal of religion should be to help us feel good about ourselves when we have made honest and reasonable, but sometimes painful choices about our lives."

Kushner's book stands at the center of a popular inward turn from community to individuality, a towering example of the Jewish community's entrance in the popular self-help genre. Sociologist Micki McGee has identified the way the gospel of self-improvement employs a secularized version of Max Weber's Protestant ethic through a "therapeutic imperative to find self-fulfillment." It is telling then that Lew's *This Is Real and You Are Completely Unprepared: The Days of Awe as a Journey of Transformation*, published more than two decades later, has become *the* handbook for American Jewish High Holiday survival, aiming to wake up slumbering Jews from their everyday lives.

Lew, whose memoir *One God Clapping: The Spiritual Path of a Zen Rabbi* won the PEN Josephine Miles Award for Literary Excellence, was once on his way to becoming a Buddhist minister when he had an epiphany and decided to become a rabbi. Even after he was ordained as a Conservative rabbi, he never stopped meditating, building a center for Jewish meditation out of San Francisco Congregation Beth Sholom, the pulpit he served from 1991–2005.

Opening the book, we are immediately shaken awake: "You are walking through the world half asleep. It isn't just that you don't know who you are and that you don't know how or why you got here. It's worse than that; these questions never even arise. It is as if you are in a dream." The book's purpose is to sound an alarm as Lew maps out the "journey" of the Jewish High Holiday season from the ninth of Av in the middle of the summer through the end of Sukkot ten weeks later. This journey, Lew asserts, will be "one of self-discovery, spiritual discipline, self-forgiveness, and spiritual evolution."

If Kushner presents a God for humanity, unencumbered by religion, who has bestowed the gift of free will to all of God's children, Lew presents a Judaism designed for human self-fulfillment, with some God but much more conscious-ness. For Lew, the Jewish High Holiday cycle is a yearly exercise in attunement and an opportunity for self-transformation. Though Lew addresses the reader individually, there are moments when he draws attention to the need for com-munity and action. In preparation for Rosh Hashanah he exhorts the reader to consider the videotape of their lives, painting a portrait of his own synagogue in a San Francisco neighborhood where homes sell for millions of dollars but people are sleeping on the streets.

Over several pages, he points to the success and wealth of his community and his readers, while simultaneously bringing attention to the small hypocri-sies of their lives. From callous gossip to allowing poverty and drug addiction in the larger communities where they live, he weaves the good with the bad noting, "the tape didn't stop running in between the events we imagined were important. It caught all those small, in-between moments too, the moments when we thought no one was watching." But in the end, he does not implore his readers to join in fellowship with other Jews or service to the world around them. Rather, he ends on Sukkot, sitting under the stars, in a makeshift booth where the "illusion of protection falls away, and suddenly we are flush with our life, feeling our life, following our life." It is striking to me that he ends his book here and not with Simchat Torah, a day lived in community, focused on an ever unfolding heritage and tradition. It is not that I think he should have necessarily ended the book in synagogue, but why is he so alone?

These days, when the world's tragedies fly across the internet in moments, when videos of shootings and protests stream endlessly on individual handheld screens, when the boundaries of real and virtual blur into endless cycles of pings, beeps, notifications, and likes, messages of awareness and comfort are more rele-vant than ever. But in the networked individualism of the early twenty-first cen-tury, we cannot leave out the need for deep commitment to something beyond the self. In Abraham Joshua Heschel's *The Sabbath*, Shabbat observance serves as a protection against the far-reaching grasp of industrial society. To enter into the day, one "must first lay down the profanity of clattering commerce, of being yoked to toil." He calls it "a day for ourselves" and a "day for dominating the self."

He asks, "is there any institution that holds out a greater hope for [humanity]'s progress than the Sabbath?" Heschel's concern for the self is bounded with a concern for humanity and the world. For Heschel, the Sabbath enables recognition of God's dominion allowing us to "understand that the world has already been created and will survive without the help of [humans]."

The movement from Heschel to Kushner to Lew tells the story of an American Judaism hungry for meaning and ripe with ideas but simultaneously idiosyncratic and disconnected. These texts represent the possibility of American Judaism, full of vitality and transcending boundaries. But they also offer a warning. The next generation of American Judaism will have to further contend with the lonely Jew, not just sitting alone in their sukkah, but also alone behind the screen of their phone. How do we wake this person from their slumber into the life of service and purpose lived in community?

4. Evelyn Torton Beck (ed.), *Nice Jewish Girls: A Lesbian Anthology*

Susannah Heschel (ed.), *On Being a Jewish Feminist*

Evelyn Torton Beck (ed.), *Nice Jewish Girls: A Lesbian Anthology*, Boston: Beacon Press, 1982

Evelyn Torton Beck (1933–) is Professor Emerita of Women's Studies at the University of Maryland.

Pauline Bart, "How a Nice Jewish Girl Like Me Could"
I was never silent. Not then, not during the fifties, not now.

It is Erev Yom Kippur 1972. My lover, who has just returned from spending Rosh Hashanah with her family, and whom I have missed desperately (I got a kitten but it didn't work), tells me that she cannot sleep in the same bed with me. I promise that I won't "do anything" but she says that it doesn't matter. It is the Law. Since she has a degree in Talmud my case is hopeless. The next day she goes to the traditional, rather than the alternative services at a college campus and waits for the tenth man to arrive before they start. I tell her that she must confront the Jewish religious establishment and use her talmudic training to make Jewish feminism possible. She refuses. Confronting the Jewish establishment on religious issues is bad for the Jews. Later she temporarily refuses to join Jewish Women for Affirmative Action because that too was bad for the Jews. I tell her that she won't be able to go to Israel because I will denounce her to the Embassy as a lesbian and the Law of the Return does not apply to homosexuals. She cries. I am stunned because she never cries. I later write that she keeps her life in separate kitchen cabinets. In fact she is now a closet kosher since she can pass—indeed have high status—by being a vegetarian.

It is my sabbatical and I am in Paris, invited by a French sociologist to meet with French feminists. I put on my non-designer jeans and orange "A woman without a man is like a fish without a bicycle" T-shirt, and arrive at the prestigious address. The table is set for high tea and the women are wearing knit dresses, nylons and heels (This was before the "dress-for-success" epidemic hit). Some of the women teach at the Sorbonne; some have been active in International Women's Year, which I learned from *off our backs* was a fraud. I feel superior to them, for they are bourgeois feminists.

I see an interesting painting on the wall and ask about it. The hostess informs me that she had it painted with symbolic representations of parts of her life. She tells me what the various objects signify. When she gets to the lower left-hand corner, she says, "The barbed wire represents Auschwitz and that is my concentration camp number." I no longer feel superior.

My next stop is Amsterdam and I am speaking at the Women's Center about women and health issues, noting the dangers of the Pill. After the talk a woman concludes that the only logical solution is to become a lesbian. An obvious dyke, wearing a large Jewish star, she remarks that this kind of reasoning worries her. We talk and she takes me to the club where gay men and lesbians meet. She tells me that lesbians are about to separate, which makes her sad because she believes in pushing the boundaries back, not closing them. We arrange to meet the next day; she will take me to the museum and show me why Rembrandt was a greater artist than his contemporaries.

After the museum I assume the role of Pauline Bart, girl sociologist and intrepid interviewer. I ask her how she survived the war; she tells me that she was sent from Christian family to Christian family. I mention that she does not look Jewish. She says, "Of course not. If I looked Jewish I'd be dead." She gets a terrible headache and I feel guilty and stupid.

We return to her apartment where I learn of her role in the founding of Israel's gay liberation movement. She left after finding it impossible to live openly as a lesbian. In Israel she was in *galut* because she was a lesbian and in Amsterdam she is in *galut* because she is a Jew.

She tells me that on the Amsterdam tram people make nasty remarks when they pass the prosperous Jewish section which is prosperous only because the Jews received reparations for their losses during the Holocaust. She tells people, "You know how they got that money? Would you like to have gotten it that way?" She is clearly a woman who would have led strikes in junior high school. I have missed the last tram. We spend the night together. I feel as if I have come full circle. (59–61)

Susannah Heschel (ed.), *On Being a Jewish Feminist*, New York: Schocken Books, 1983

Susannah Heschel (1956–) is Eli Black Professor of Jewish Studies at Dartmouth College.

Sara Reguer, "Kaddish on the Wrong Side of the *Mehitzah*"

An unlucky *mitzvah* is Kaddish. Too bad. It was saying Kaddish for the past year that enabled me to keep my sanity. If I had not *had* to get out of bed at 6:30 A.M. in order to be on time for the beginning of services, I can guarantee that I simply would not have left my bed at all. Depression is a terrifying experience partly because one is virtually unable to fight it.

Did I mean what I was saying? Was I really reaffirming my belief in God's greatness (which is the meaning of the words of the Kaddish prayer)? Not for the first few months. Rather, I battled God every inch of the way. Catharsis came suddenly, violently, but it took almost the full eleven months before I again really meant the words I was pronouncing—meant them on the internal level.

Externally, there were some very interesting aspects to my Kaddish-saying career. I had my "home synagogue," the one that I attended most often, and after the initial shock of my appearance wore off and the old men agreed among themselves that I was right in saying Kaddish, I became one of the gang—or almost. For I sat behind a separation, in the corner. My anger at this particular *mehitzah* grew to the point that one rainy day, when a man came in and unthinkingly draped his wet coat over my "cage," I growled aloud. He jumped at the sound and looked at me questioningly. I said, "If you treat me like an animal, why the surprise if I growl like one?" He excused himself and removed his coat. I later found out from some of the men that this particular man did something unusual a few days after that incident. I was away for five days or so, and each morning during my absence the old gentleman I had growled at sat behind the *mehitzah* to see what it felt like. He agreed with my dissatisfaction and frustration, but neither of us could come up with a solution to the problem.

Most daily services are not held in the main synagogue but in a small room either downstairs or to the side of the main hall. Since women do not usually come to weekday services, most synagogues do not have facilities for them. When I appeared, the solution to the problem this posed was usually my standing to pray outside the room through the open door. Inevitably, there would be a scramble to get me a siddur, a chair, a Bible, and an embarrassed apology for the lack of a women's section. Inevitably, also, there would be a moment of stunned silence as I would rise to say Kaddish out loud. Some would come and ask if I had a brother, I would reply that it made no difference if I did or did not, for all children were obligated to say Kaddish for parents. Some would offer to say it for me. I repeated what I said about brothers. I also said that if it offended anyone for me to say it alone, they were welcome to say it with me, but not for me. A rush to the books, or to the rabbi, brought the usual—albeit sometimes reluctant—affirmation of my deed.

In one Hasidic synagogue, one man almost shouted at me to say Kaddish silently because my chanting aloud was against the injunction of *kol ishah*; the singing voice of a woman is considered by some to be sexually arousing to men and therefore is forbidden. I asked the man whether he spoke to women in public. He said yes. I said that I was merely speaking in public also, but to God. And if it still bothered him, he had no business sitting right near the *mehitzah* to start with.

Then there was the time I visited Boston and was praying in an Orthodox school attended by one of the most outstanding Jewish scholars and rabbis of our day [Rabbi J. B. Soloveitchik].[1] The sexton was nervous because I had already told him what I would be doing. He insisted on saying Kaddish with me. But I saw a flurry of activity in the corner where the rabbi sat, and when it came time to say it, I said the Kaddish alone and all answered, as they properly should have.

It has not been easy. This past year has been the worst of my life. It has been eased somewhat by my Kaddish-saying and by the positive reactions of most of the men I met at the services. On Sabbaths and holidays, women often came over to ask about what I was doing, usually adding that it was too bad they had not known about this during their own year of mourning, when they too had needed desperately some sort of ritual to lean on.

After much soul-searching, I decided at the end of this past semester to share my ideas and thoughts with my class at Brooklyn College, where I gave a course on "The Jewish Woman." At first I had hesitated; even though I felt strongly about the validity of my actions, I did not want to influence my students, who tend to be very much impressed by what I do. But if someone like myself is not going to teach this, who will? (179–181)

---

1   Eds.: Rabbi Soloveitchik is not named in the version of this essay that appears in Heschel's anthology. His name has been added here at the author's request.

COMMENTARY BY CLAIRE E. SUFRIN

In reflecting on the process of editing her 1983 anthology *On Being a Jewish Feminist*, Susannah Heschel notes that her book is not the first to address the subject of Jewish women.[2] For that, we would be well advised to look at least all the way back to the Mishnah, as one of its six major sections (orders) is titled Nashim, that is, women. What made Heschel's book different from so many that came before it is that she sought to flip the perspective: rather than discussing women as Judaism understands them, the essays in her book discuss Judaism as women understand it.

To privilege contemporary women over the inherited tradition as it was developed by generations of male rabbis was a daring move; Heschel pushed further by including essays on Jewish lesbians, on domestic abuse in Jewish homes, and other realities of Jewish life more typically ignored or denied. While each of the essays stands alone, to read this book cover-to-cover is to recognize the swelling force of Jewish women asserting their agency not only as women and not only as Jews, but as Jewish women.

That Jewish women would assert themselves as critics of and contributors to Judaism was a direct outgrowth of Second-Wave Feminism. In the essay excerpted from Heschel's collection that appears above, saying Kaddish becomes a consciousness-raising experience parallel to those that led many American women to the feminist movement as it gained steam in the 1970s. But within mainstream feminism, religion was often dismissed as unredeemably patriarchal. More specifically and more troubling for Jewish women, the association of monotheism with patriarchy sometimes took on an anti-Semitic tone. At its core, Jewish feminism was thus a critique of Judaism intended for other Jews and a defense of Judaism against those feminists who would deride it. Thus, for example, the one essay on women and Jewish law in the collection is titled "The Jew Who Wasn't There," and within it the author, Rachel Adler, describes in detail the mechanisms by which Halakhah excludes women from participation in the most important customs of the religion and thus distances them from God. But the essay ends not with a rejection of Halakhah or of Judaism more broadly but with a plea for a re-examination of Halakhah and the possibilities it might already contain for expanding women's access to the holy.

---

2   Susannah Heschel, "Twenty years ago, writing about Judaism from a feminist perspective, rather than discussing women from 'Judaism's' point of view, seemed audacious," Jewish Women's Archive, accessed July 11, 2019, https://jwa.org/feminism/heschel-susannah.

The link that Adler draws between being present in the synagogue and the study hall and having access to the Divine is one that runs throughout the anthology. Essays in the book's first part, titled "Old Myths and Images" address both positive and negative images of Jewish women inherited from the past with a focus on women as wives and as mothers. The book's second part focuses on the first half of Adler's equation, namely, women's presence and power within the Jewish community. It opens with Cynthia Ozick's "Notes toward Finding the Right Question," in which she laments:

> In the world at large I call myself, and am called, a Jew. But when, on the Sabbath, I sit among women in my traditional shul and the rabbi speaks the word "Jew, I can be sure that he is not referring to me. For him, "Jew" means "male Jew."
>
> When the rabbi speaks of women, he uses the expression (a translation from a tender Yiddish phrase) "Jewish daughter." He means it tenderly.
>
> "Jew" speaks for itself. "Jewish daughter" does not. A "Jewish daughter" is someone whose identity is linked to, and defined by, another's role. "Jew" defines a person seen in the light of a culture. "Daughter" defines a relationship that is above all biological. "Jew" signifies adult responsibility. "Daughter" evokes immaturity and a dependent and subordinate connection. (125)

Ozick ties the rise of Jewish women demanding respect primarily to the Holocaust. The desire of American Jewish women to be "counted" is, for her, a response to the decimation of European Jewry. In this formulation, Jewish feminism becomes a distinctly antinostalgic, constructive response to grief: rather than recreating what was lost, empowered Jewish women will build something new through which women and men will honor but also exceed the memories of what it is to be a Jew.

Essays in the remainder of this section show us how by addressing: women as leaders in Jewish Federations; the women learning to chant from the Torah; women becoming rabbis. Indeed, this last example offers us a quick way to measure the effect of Jewish feminism on Jewish religious life. The title of first woman rabbi belongs to the German Regina Jonas, who was ordained in 1935 and ultimately ministered to women in Theresienstadt before being killed in Auschwitz in 1944. But Jonas was very much an exception in her time and pursued ordination against significant opposition. In more recent history, the

Reform Movement's Hebrew Union College ordained Sally Priesand as a rabbi in 1972; the Reconstructionist Rabbinical College ordained Sandy Eisenberg Sasso in 1975; and the Conservative Movement's Jewish Theological Seminary ordained Amy Eilberg as a rabbi in 1986. The percentage of women rabbis in each entering cohort at these schools hovers now around 50%. Even more recently, Rabbi Avi Weiss made headlines when he ordained Sara Hurwitz as a Modern Orthodox "maharat" in 2009; Hurwitz, now using the title "rabbah," is the dean of Yeshivat Maharat, at which Orthodox women may study for ordination. At the same time, plenty of Modern Orthodox congregations—not to mention all other more traditional movements—continue to reject the very notion of a female clergyperson, and their synagogue services remain distinctly non-egalitarian.

The third section of Heschel's book focuses on theology. Here, it is Judith Plaskow who sets the tone, building on Adler's account of Halakhah and responding to Ozick. Ultimately, though, her focus is on the maleness of God-language. She writes:

> While the active presence of women in congregations should be bespeak our full membership in the Jewish community, the language of the service conveys a different message. It impugns the humanity of women and ignores our experience, rendering that experience invisible, even in the face of our presence. But since language is not a halakhic issue, we cannot change this situation through halakhic repair. It is not "simply" that *halakhah* presupposes the Otherness of women but that this Otherness reflects and is reflected in our speech about God. The equality of women in the Jewish community requires the radical transformation of our religious language in the form of recognition of the feminine aspects of God. (229)

This is a theme that Plaskow will develop at greater length in her 1990 book, *Standing Again at Sinai*. Within Heschel's anthology, the essay—and the entire third section of the book—serves as a counterpoint to the sociological emphasis of the other essays. Women might muscle their way into the synagogue and study hall and even into the leadership thereof, in a process that was already well underway by the time the anthology was published. But until the language for God found in the Jewish prayer book and sacred texts draw upon women's experience, women will always remain the Other to the male Jew and stand further from the Divine. Here, there is less progress to measure since the publication of *On Being a Jewish Feminist* than there is in the educational and sociological realms. Feminist agitation has succeeded in bringing mention of the biblical matriarchs into prayers citing the merits of the patriarchs in more liberal congregations. But most Jewish prayer communities have proven to be more resistant to changing the language they use to talk about or to God.

Evelyn Torton Beck's *Nice Jewish Girls: A Lesbian Anthology* was first published in 1982, predating *On Being a Jewish Feminist* by a year, with a second edition appearing in 1989. The center of the book is a photo essay entitled "That's Funny, You Don't Look Like a Jewish Lesbian," featuring portraits of Jewish lesbians of all ages in their everyday lives—hugging a friend or lover; holding a baby—and in their activism—marching in a Gay Pride parade; protesting the Ku Klux Klan. The photos and the autobiographical statements that accompany them echo the themes that run through the entire book: Jewish lesbians exist; their identities as lesbians and as Jews are intertwined to make them doubly outside the American mainstream; from this place of double outsiderness, they are ready to speak, and they want to be heard.

Beck writes in the introduction to the second edition that for her and many of her writers, "unexpectedly, the experience of coming out as lesbians was a crucial step toward our coming out as Jews. The experience of being outside the bounds of society as a lesbian makes a woman more willing to acknowledge other ways in which she stands outside. It becomes increasingly harder to ignore the signals of outsiderhood. And soon one doesn't want to" (xvii). The essay excerpted above illustrates but does not resolve the pain of negotiating one's way as a Jew, as a lesbian, and as a Jewish lesbian. Anti-Semitism looms during a 1940s childhood; a female lover chooses a traditional Judaism and rejects Jewish feminism; a friend who feels doubly exiled: from Amsterdam as a Jew and from Israel as a lesbian.

Here too we can quantify important changes in the Jewish community in response to books like Beck's and other activism. The larger rabbinical seminaries listed above now ordain openly gay and lesbian Jews. The most recent policy shift was at the Jewish Theological Seminary, in 2007. Debate about whether gay men can be ordained as rabbis is, as I write, a hot topic in more liberal branches of Orthodoxy. Most, if not all, liberal rabbis will marry same-sex couples with a ceremony adapted from the traditional Jewish wedding liturgy. *Keep Your Wives Away from Them* (2010), a more recent anthology edited by Miryam Kabokov, features the voices of trans Jews alongside those of lesbians.

And yet: just as there are pockets of the world in which anti-Semitism continues to rage, there are pockets of the Jewish community in which homophobia runs rampant. Feminism too remains a bad word among those who wish to protect The Jewish Tradition from "outside" influences. The experiences recounted in these anthologies bespeak pain and anger but the visions they foretell are hopeful. To live today is to see how far we have come and to know at the same time that there is work yet to be done.

5. Paul Cowan with Rachel Cowan, *Mixed Blessings: Overcoming the Stumbling Blocks in an Interfaith Marriage*

Paul Cowan with Rachel Cowan, *Mixed Blessings: Overcoming the Stumbling Blocks in an Interfaith Marriage*, New York: Penguin Books, 1987

Paul Cowan (1940–1988) was a staff writer at the *Village Voice*.

Rabbi Rachel Cowan (1941–2018) was Executive Director of the Institute for Jewish Spirituality and Co-Founder of the Jewish Healing Movement.

When Jews and Christians first fall in love, they usually regard themselves as individualists who will be able to transcend the specific cultural demands of the pasts that shaped their beliefs and laid claims on their loyalties. But that is a more difficult task than they imagine, for at some profound level of self and psyche, most will always be attached to the religious and ethnic tribes in which they were raised. They'll remain Americanized Eastern European Jews or German Methodists or Italian Catholics or Chinese Buddhists. They love the cultural assumptions that permeated their households when they were young: the background music of ordinary life, which a child takes for granted, which an adolescent or young adult tries to forget. If couples don't acknowledge such assumptions in the same way that people acknowledge music—as an interior melody that can't be articulated in words—they can damage the ecology of an intermarriage.

If a struggle over religion does begin, it often takes couples by surprise, thrusting them into confusing, seemingly endless discussions. For suddenly they discover that they are not interchangeable parts of an American whole, but two people whose different pasts have endowed them with a distinct set of feelings. How should they discuss their differences? How can each understand the ethnic and religious context in which the other's emotions exist? (128)

By the time children are old enough to ask about their identities, most patterns of a marriage are already established. Couples have negotiated their wedding ceremonies, the details of housekeeping, child care, wage earning, bill paying. They know what they'll do when one wants to make love and the other feels too tired. They have learned whether they can live with an annoying habit, like chronic lateness or bad table manners, or whether those habits may be the first step on the route to the divorce court.

But when the new person in their home asks questions which indicate uncertainty about his or her religious or ethnic identity, the interfaith couple may feel its marital ecology is imperiled. If the child asks a question indirectly, the couple may fail to acknowledge its importance or dismiss it as a cute remark. If the question suggests urgency, as our son Matt's question about Haman did, it may provide such doubt and disagreement that the parents ignore it altogether.

But they shouldn't. All youngsters need to feel secure. Often, when they ask questions about faith, they are seeking emotional reinforcement. But when children of intermarriage combine remarks about faith with questions about identity, they are trying to discover where they belong, as well. They are trying to ascertain *their* religion, *their* ethnicity, *their* place in a world that seems quite puzzling. They need to hear answers that show them their parents are comfortable with whatever spiritual choice they have made. (152)

Gentiles who feel pressure to convert to Judaism usually say that they haven't ruled out the prospect entirely. But, like Tim and Chris in our workshop, they want to feel as if they are making the decision for themselves, not for a spouse or for an in-law. They want to be treated as individuals, with their own histories, their own accomplishments, their own values. They bridle when a rabbi, an in-law, a spouse make them feel that the only important question about them is whether they'll become Jews.

In those situations, it is important that the spouse or in-law who hopes the gentile will choose Judaism find a program of Jewish study that is intellectually stimulating and doesn't demand immediate conversion. It is important that the gentile is exposed to a ritual life with meaning, and a community of Jews which welcomes newcomers. For people are far more willing to choose Judaism if they see it as an attractive way of life than if conversion is only portrayed as an homage to the 6 million. (236)

COMMENTARY BY SAMIRA K. MEHTA

When Paul and Rachel Cowan published *Mixed Blessings: Overcoming the Stumbling Blocks in an Interfaith Marriage* in 1987, they were drawing from over twenty years of marriage and from workshops they ran through several Jewish organizations including synagogues, the 92nd Street Y, American Jewish Committee, and Hillel. Their book, published by Penguin, was blurbed by Rabbi Harold S. Kushner (*When Bad Things Happen to Good People*) who wrote, "One of the most important books to come along in years. The right book on the right subject by the right people." The *New York Times Book Review* and the *Los Angeles Times* both agreed.

So, what allowed Kushner to give *Mixed Blessings* this endorsement? When *Mixed Blessings* was published, Jewish leaders and many active in Jewish communal life understood interfaith marriage (or intermarriage, as it was commonly called) to be the defining problem facing American Judaism. The National Jewish Population Survey, released three years after *Mixed Blessings*, offered statistical evidence for what many already knew to be true: 50% of American Jews were "marrying out." Their book was the "right subject" because it was of the moment.

While Jewish communities had rejected interfaith marriage for much of the twentieth century, the wildly increasing rates of interfaith marriage caused a shift in communal perspective. In 1971, the Central Conference of American Rabbis (CCAR), the Reform movement's rabbinic organization, had reluctantly rejected a policy that would have forbidden its clergy from performing interfaith marriages, a rejection rooted not so much in support for interfaith marriage as in autonomy for the rabbinic pulpit.[1] That said, some of the CCAR leadership saw a strategic reason for rabbis to perform interfaith weddings, namely, avoiding the alienation of interfaith couples. This faction advocated for performing the weddings if the couple agreed to certain conditions outlined by Rabbi David Max Eichhorn: they had to raise the children as Jews, with formal Jewish education; maintain a Jewish home according to the standards of the community providing the children's education; and lastly, keep their homes devoid of any non-Jewish religious symbols and celebrations. These conditions were intended to keep interfaith couples within Judaism, without weakening Jewish religion through assimilation.[2]

The Reform movement made other attempts to attract interfaith families. In 1983, they had decided to recognize patrilineal descent (counting people

---

1   Samira Mehta, "Chrismukkah: Millennial Multiculturalism," *Religion and American Culture* 25, no. 1 (2015): 22–24.
2   Mehta, "Chrismukkah," 25.

with one Jewish parent and a Jewish education as Jewish).[3] This decision was a notable break with Jewish law, which had, for centuries, seen Jewish identity as exclusively matrilineal. In addition, since the late 1970s, the Jewish Outreach Institute had worked, largely under Lydia Kukoff's direction, to make interfaith couples and their resultant families feel welcome in Jewish communities (even if those same communities had rejected them at the time of their weddings). They worked to meet the needs of interfaith families—offering training in practicing Judaism and in navigating interfaith life and working with congregations to help them welcome these families. The Cowans participated in this effort, giving talks and workshops on interfaith family life, and it was into this moment of crisis and shifting understandings of outreach that *Mixed Blessings* appeared.

The Cowans were the right people because they, through personal inclinations and explorations, had come to the conclusions that the Reform movement hoped interfaith couples would reach. When they married in 1965, Paul was from a secular and assimilated Jewish family that spent more time on Christmas and Easter than on Jewish holidays. He had gone to Choate, a prestigious Episcopal prep school that had provided a painful crash course in assimilation. Rachel was from a rational and skeptical family that had joined a Unitarian church for social acceptability (9–11). They had begun their marriage, and their early parenting, in the model of "doing both." Paul writes that they both saw the holidays fitting together in a secular calendar and were drawn to religious ceremony (though ironically, Paul was drawn to the pageantry of high church Episcopalianism and Rachel to the home-based celebrations of Judaism) (17). When their children were five and three years old, their son came running to his mother during a Purim celebration, seeking assurance that Haman would not get him as he was only "half-Jewish." Shortly thereafter, their daughter asked whether Rachel would be hurt if she chose to be Jewish. For the Cowan parents, these questions were "timebombs" that could hurt their children over the long run (24). They felt that the household needed one religion and, for reasons that *Mixed Blessings* traces, the religion they chose was Judaism.

They had independently come to the conclusion that the Reform movement hoped all interfaith couples would reach: a household must have one religion, and Judaism makes the most sense for a Christian-Jewish interfaith couple. They presented their decision as best for their family, not growing out

---

3   "Report of the Committee on Patrilineal Descent on the Status of Children of Mixed Marriages Adopted by the Central Conference of American Rabbis at Its 94th Annual Convention," March 15, 1983, 739 Box 8 Folder 13, American Jewish Archives.

of a sense of obligation to Jewish community. Rather than feeling deprived of her heritage, Rachel Cowan found such meaning in Judaism that she eventually converted to Judaism and entered rabbinical school. (*Mixed Blessings* is presented as "by Paul, with Rachel" because the demands of rabbinical school were such that Rachel took a less involved role in the book's creation than initially planned.) While the Cowans made it clear that Rachel's conversion did not remove all of the "stumbling blocks" in their interfaith marriage—they still had been socialized to different emotional needs, communication styles, and habits of grocery shopping—they also made it clear that choosing Judaism had been the best choice for all.

If the Cowans had created "the right book on the right subject by the right people," they were writing in accordance with the understood best practices at that moment; but those best practices were the product of a particular set of historically and culturally located understandings. *Mixed Blessings* was read for more than two decades by couples seeking insight into how to run their interfaith families. (It is now out of print, still read, though less frequently.) But in those decades, couples came up with many critiques.

The Cowans did not intend to outline a system in which the wife subsumed her culture to that of the husband, but rather one in which Jewish culture was preserved at the expense of Christian culture. Their story, however, modeled a trend in both prescriptive literature and popular culture. The model interfaith couple, in the American imagination, was a Jewish husband and a Christian wife. The solution, then, was for the Christian wife to give up her traditions and to do much of the work of raising Jewish children and maintaining a Jewish home. At the same time, they presented Judaism as a religion and a culture, seemingly undermining some of their own arguments about how Christian Protestant culture had shaped Rachel's world.

The next generation of interfaith couples would critique this model, not only for its failures in understanding Christianity, but also for feminist failings. These couples were looking for something more egalitarian, in which Jewish husbands participated more in raising Jewish children and the wives' traditions were not consistently the ones sacrificed. Many couple who chose to do both cited feminist values. Rachel Cowan certainly identified as a feminist, but that did not prevent critiques of the implicit gender dynamics of *Mixed Blessings* when seen in the broader context of literature for interfaith couples. Simultaneously, Jewish women married Christians at the same rate as their male coreligionists, and these homes presented different models for combining traditions. Some women married to non-Jewish men did maintain exclusively Jewish homes. Many, however, secure in their children's halakhic status and, perhaps, socialized to defer to their husbands, included more Christian traditions in their homes than their Christian counterparts were allowed.

The Cowans' sense that one could not be "half-Jewish," while in accordance with Jewish law, centered on understandings of identity that would be challenged by rising language of multiculturalism. Many people now present understandings of Jewish identity in combination with other identities using the language and logic of multiculturalism. Sometimes those responses have used the language of "halfness," such as we see in *The Half-Jewish Book* (2000) or *The Mozart Season* (2007).[4] Other times, they use the language of being entirely two things at once, for instance *Being Both: Embracing Two Religions in One Interfaith Family* (2006).[5] Other ways to discuss multiple identities have also been presented.[6] With *Mixed Blessings,* the Cowans ushered in a new era of Best Practices for Christian-Jewish interfaith family life, but it was not to be the last.

4   Daniel Klein and Freke Vuijst, *The Half-Jewish Book: A Celebration* (New York: Villard, 2000); Virginia Euwer Wolff, *The Mozart Season* (New York: Square Fish, 2007).

5   Susan Katz Miller, *Being Both: Embracing Two Religions in One Interfaith Family* (Boston: Beacon Press, 2013).

6   Laurel Snyder, *Half/Life: Jew-ish Tales from Interfaith Homes* (New York: Soft Skull Press, 2006).

6. Judith Plaskow, *Standing Again at Sinai: Judaism from a Feminist Perspective*

Judith Plaskow, *Standing Again at Sinai: Judaism from a Feminist Perspective*, San Francisco: Harper and Row, 1990

Dr. Judith Plaskow (1947–) is Professor Emerita of Religious Studies at Manhattan College.

Named by a male community that perceives itself as normative, women are part of the Jewish tradition without its sources and structures reflecting our experience. Women are Jews, but we do not define Jewishness. We live, work, and struggle, but our experiences are not recorded, and what is recorded formulates our experiences in male terms. The central Jewish categories of Torah, Israel, and God all are constructed from male perspectives. Torah is revelation as men perceived it, the story of Israel told from their standpoint, the law unfolded according to their needs. Israel is the male collectivity, the children of a Jacob who had a daughter, but whose sons became the twelve tribes. God is named in the male image, a father and warrior much like his male offspring, who confirms and sanctifies the silence of his daughters. Exploring these categories, we explore the parameters of women's silence.

In Torah, Jewish teaching, women are not absent, but they are cast in stories told by men. As characters in narrative, women may be vividly characterized, as objects of legislation, singled out for attention. But women's presence in Torah does not negate their silence, for women do not decide the questions with which Jewish sources deal. When the law treats of women, it is often because their "abnormality" demands it. If women are central to plot, the plots are not about them. Women's interests and intentions must be unearthed from texts with other purposes, for both law and narrative serve to obscure them. (3)

Clearly, the implications of Jewish feminism reach beyond the goal of equality to transform the bases of Jewish life. Feminism demands a new understanding of Torah, Israel, and God. It demands an understanding of Torah that begins by acknowledging the injustice of Torah and then goes on to create a Torah that is whole. The silence of women reverberates through the tradition, distorting the shape of narrative and skewing the content of the law. Only the deliberate recovery of women's hidden voices, the unearthing and invention of women's Torah, can give us Jewish teachings that are the product of the whole Jewish people and that reflect the more fully its experiences of God. (9)

Reform always begins in conviction and vision. Jewish feminism, like all reform movements, is rooted in deeply felt experiences and a powerful image of religious change. Wherever the individual feminist locates her active interests—in liturgy, theology, midrash, law—she acts out of commitment to an animating vision that has important repercussions for community life and practice. My central reason for writing a Jewish feminist theology, then, is to articulate one version of this vision and to foster its growth. If feminist theologies help to reanimate the connection between practice and belief in the Jewish world more generally, they will have made another important contribution to Jewish religious life. (23–24)

COMMENTARY BY JUDITH ROSENBAUM

It has been nearly thirty years since Judith Plaskow published *Standing Again at Sinai*, laying the foundation for an expansive Jewish feminist theology. Frankly, one might wish those thirty years had brought sufficient change to make it feel more dated. But to read it today is to recognize its enduring radicalism and relevance.

Though Plaskow begins with an explanation of the conflict she once felt between her feminism and her Jewishness, her argument is rooted in determined resolution. From the first page, she exhibits striking clarity about her unwavering commitment to the Jewish community as well as her right to challenge it. She asserts her entitlement to Jewish tradition and practice, even as she delineates the invisibility of women and their non-normative status within Jewish tradition. Both assertions reflect the many years of Jewish feminist work—her own and that of others, such as Rachel Adler, Paula Hyman, Arlene Agus, Martha Ackelsberg, Susannah Heschel, Aviva Cantor, and many more—upon which this book builds, converting the raw anger and pain of the early years of Jewish feminism into a constructive approach to change.

Plaskow lays out several bold claims: that the historic exclusion of women can't simply be dismissed as "tradition" or explained away sociologically, but rather must be recognized as a form of violence that continues to harm women and the Jewish community, and that the solution—the inclusion of women—is not just an additive process but a transformative one. Feminism, she argues, necessitates a radical reinterpretation of Judaism and its key categories: Torah, Israel (meaning the Jewish people), and God. This radical reinterpretation, however, should not be perceived as a threat to Judaism but rather as an opportunity for its renewal, and as an authentic expression of the Jewish practice of ongoing interpretation and adaptation.

One aspect of this radical reinterpretation is contained in her rejection of the compromise at the heart of emancipation—that, in return for citizenship, Jewish identity be compartmentalized as a private identity, "a Jew in the home and a man in the street." Instead, Plaskow demands her right to an integrated identity as Jew and feminist. "I am not a Jew in the synagogue and a feminist in the world," she declares. "I am a Jewish feminist and a feminist Jew at every moment of my life" (xi). Allowing the identity of "Jew" to be positioned in conflict with another identity, be it citizen or feminist, requires relinquishing the power of defining Judaism to others—a sacrifice Plaskow is unwilling to make.

At the same time, she describes several challenging paradoxes in the project of Jewish feminist renewal. One is the contradiction between the text's continual reinforcement of women's exclusion from the covenant and the inherent knowledge of many Jewish feminists that they are part of the covenant and, according to the tradition that all Jews were present at Sinai, can claim the Torah as their own. Plaskow's project is not to prove that women are covenanted—she assumes that this is true—but rather to address the dissonance that many feminists feel and to harness that dissonance to make change in the tradition. The otherness of women at the center of Jewish experience is not a closed door, Plaskow argues, but rather an invitation to engage in the powerful work of reinterpretation.

Another apparent challenge lies in Plaskow's insistence that women belong to the tradition and thus have the right to shape it, while also acknowledging that the existing structures—such as Halakhah—which exclude women's experiences and perspectives, can't be assumed to be the ones through which women will find meaning or shape the tradition. To paraphrase Audre Lorde, the master's tools may not be sufficient to dismantle the master's house.

Ultimately, however, Plaskow is less interested in dismantling than in renovating. True, this renovation requires some demolition—of the idea of Torah as perfect and complete, for example. Torah as we have received it is a distortion, she argues, for it is a male tradition, lacking the perspective of half of the Jewish experience. But Plaskow's optimism about the productive nature of Jewish feminist theology is palpable, and the theology she posits is a project of recovering and expanding Torah writ large, incorporating ongoing revelation in the form of women's history, midrash, liturgy, and ritual. Plaskow contributed an innovative approach to Jewish feminism by insisting that (as she titled her groundbreaking 1982 essay) "The Right Question is Theological," thus creating a field of Jewish feminist theology where none previously existed. Theology, however, in Plaskow's hands, is not limited narrowly to conceptions of God; rather, it addresses broader questions of authority, law, and reconsideration of concepts such as chosenness, called into question by the feminist claim that difference need not necessitate hierarchy.

Though certainly intellectually rich and rigorous, Plaskow's theology is not only an intellectual project but also one that is personal, critical to her identity and the meaning of her Jewishness. In framing this work as rooted in personal commitment (and asserting her right to do so, another contribution of feminism), she also reveals what's at stake in this project: real people and their ability to live fully as Jews.

Nearly two decades into the twenty-first century, aspects of Plaskow's work are eerily resonant. She wrote *Standing Again* in the 1980s, as a flare-up of anti-Semitism in the women's movement cast into sharp relief Jewish feminists' double outsiderness as Jews in the women's movement and feminists in the Jewish community. This conflict is, sadly, again asserting itself today, with exclusion of Jews sporting Jewish symbols from some progressive rallies and renewed debate about whether one can be both a feminist and a Zionist.

In *Standing Again*, Plaskow pointed out that giving women roles in Jewish practice did not magically turn Judaism into a feminist tradition but merely allowed women to participate in a male religion. So, too, did revelations of the #metoo movement force the Jewish community to acknowledge again that inclusion and access are not sufficient to create meaningful change. Women's increased participation in Jewish communal leadership hasn't meaningfully shifted unequal structures of power or standards of acceptable behavior.

Of course, some aspects of *Standing Again at Sinai*, such as the chapter on sexuality, in which the gender binary is firmly in place, reveal their age. But Plaskow's argument is nimble enough to transcend these limitations, as she argues for a vision of feminism that targets not only the oppression of women but all forms of oppression. Feminism, in her words, "aims at the liberation of all women and all people, and is thus not a movement for individual equality, but for the creation of a society that no longer construes difference in terms of superiority and subordination" (xvii). And Plaskow herself has continued to explore issues of sexuality in her subsequent work on Jewish theology and ethics.

While defining a very thorough approach to Jewish feminist theology, *Standing Again at Sinai* extends a framework and an invitation, rather than offering a comprehensive new theology. Plaskow makes a strong case for a new vision of Torah, Israel, and God, and suggests that this creativity will blossom through continuing innovations in history, Halakhah, midrash, ritual, and liturgy. Her feminist theology, then, is a collective and ongoing project—one that encourages and inspires more specific programs for change, such as those of Rachel Adler and Tamar Ross, in addition to those in her own later scholarship.

What does it mean, in Plaskow's formulation, to stand again at Sinai? It is an act of reparation—a statement of belonging—and it is also a claim to authority, for Sinai is where the Rabbis locate the right to be interpreters of the tradition—a right reserved, of course, to those who are its inheritors. These are lessons that the Jewish community is still learning, and Plaskow's masterful work remains one of the best texts to teach them.

7. Letty Cottin Pogrebin, *Deborah, Golda, and Me: Being Female and Jewish in America*

Letty Cottin Pogrebin, *Deborah, Golda, and Me: Being Female and Jewish in America*, New York: Crown Publishers, 1991

Letty Cottin Pogrebin (1939–) is Founding Editor of *Ms. Magazine*.

My mother's kashruth fraud is part of a category of family secrets that I think of as "cheating on Judaism." Among other such fakeries were our violations of the Sabbath.

Jews are not supposed to travel on the Sabbath, but my father, pillar of the Jewish community and model of pious propriety, drove to shul on Friday nights and Saturday mornings. He parked the car three or four blocks away, then we got out and walked, ostentatiously arriving by foot. (Only on the High Holy Days did we actually trek the mile or so to the Center.)

Second, Jews are not permitted to smoke on the Sabbath. But Daddy was a two-pack-a-day man. After three or four hours at services, he could hardly wait to light up, which he did about a block away from shul. If one of the congregants approached, he quickly stamped out the cigarette beneath his shoe.

Jews also are not allowed to carry money, cook, work, or shop on the Sabbath. But it was okay for Daddy to go into his office on Saturday because he had a heavy caseload. It was okay for us to carry money or buy some bagels or coffee cake on the way home from shul. It was okay for Mommy to cook on Saturday if she hadn't prepared enough food in advance of the Sabbath. It was okay for me to go to the movies on Saturday if I was bored stiff and getting on my parents' nerves. Exceptions were made but never exactly acknowledged. They were our secret.

Besides cheating on Judaism, there was the category of family secrets that related to life-cycle events, especially sex, marriage, and death. I was in my early teens when I learned that my mother's mother—my sweet, shy, strictly kosher, God-fearing Grandma—was a runaway bride. Back in 1898 or thereabouts, in her little shtetl in Hungary, she was the victim of an arranged marriage to a man she loathed. After vows were exchanged but before the union was consummated, she ran away to the man who was to become my Grandpa. I wasn't exactly shocked when I found out about it as much as I was struck by disbelief that my meek, dour grandparents could once have been such impulsive lovers.

Also, on my mother's side there was my aunt and uncle's secret marriage. At this writing, Aunt Tillie and Uncle Ralph are well past their sixty-fifth wedding anniversary. However, they were legally married for two years before their public religious ceremony. Custom required that a man not be wed until his two older sisters were married. Ralph and Tillie kept their earlier marriage date a secret until their daughter discovered the licence. She was ten years old.

My Uncle Herbie and Aunt Joan were the objects of family-wide pity because they were childless. "Such a shame, she's barren," everyone whispered. I was in my thirties before I discovered Herbie and Joan's secret: they didn't *want* children. In fact, Joan had had at least one abortion. But in our family, Joan had concluded, it was easier for her to pretend infertility than to assert her wish to remain childless. One of my cousins insists Joan later invented the abortion story to cover for her sterility, which was considered the worst failure of womanhood.

Oh, yes, the secret abortions. Between them, my mother, sister, aunts, and cousins must have had a half-dozen abortions, but of course I never knew about any of them. These secrets were revealed to me many years later, after I survived an illegal abortion which I too had kept secret from my female relatives.

There were secrets on my father's side as well. Two sisters unhappily married—don't ask *how* unhappy—and making the best of it. (10–11)

COMMENTARY BY ARIELLE LEVITES

Letty Cottin Pogrebin's *Deborah, Golda, and Me: Being Female and Jewish in America* is part memoir, part journalistic account, and part manifesto. It's also a how-to manual for building and expressing a Jewish feminist self. Pogrebin was one of several Jewish women who were leading figures in Second-Wave Feminism nationally and globally. As historian Joyce Antler writes, "the place of Jewish women in women's liberation is highly significant. … Jewish women in second-wave feminism helped to provide the theoretical underpinning and models for radical action that were seized on and imitated throughout the United States and abroad. Their articles and books became classics of the movement and led the way into new arena of cultural and political organizing."[1] As a

---

1   Joyce Antler, *Jewish Radical Feminism: Voices from the Women's Liberation Movement* (New York: NYU Press, 2018).

founder of *Ms. Magazine*, Pogrebin was part of this core circle of Jewish women agitating for the transformation of gender roles in American life.

Pogrebin was also one of many Jewish feminist activists whose feminism extended to Judaism, leading them to reimagine Jewish traditions through a feminist lens that centered women's experiences. For these women, few aspects of their lives were free from scrutiny and reappraisal. Theology, ritual, communal and domestic roles all needed to be re-examined and remade. In particular, Pogrebin was one of the "Seder Sisters," a group of women who participated for decades in an annual women's seder, later recounted in E. M. Broner's *The Telling*. Pogrebin understood herself as more of a traditionalist in these experiments in Jewish ritual innovation, wanting to retain the old seder melodies with the weight of memory and the sacred they carried for her. Tellingly, when Broner threw one of the group's only material artifacts into the fireplace as a declaration of maturity and coming of age, it was Pogrebin who rescued the "sacred *shmatte*" from the flames. Even a radical can feel the pull of tradition.

Putting Things on Paper

Pogrebin opens *Deborah, Golda, and Me* with a discussion of two items served on paper: first, bacon masquerading as lamb served on a paper plate, and second, the revelation of closely guarded family secrets on the printed pages of a memoir. "Lamb on paper" is what Pogrebin's kosher-keeping mother told her she was eating when she gave her bacon in the hopes of encouraging her to gain weight. Pogrebin calls this—and some of her mother's other choices—"cheating," but she also recognizes her mother's act as not only hypocrisy but also an expression of love. As such it exemplifies what feminist scholar Carol Gilligan has called an "ethics of care" to describe choices made by people operating within webs of relationships that require them to negotiate between competing needs and obligations.

Pogrebin's mother's choices remind us that shifts in what it means to be Jewish in America often take place beyond the purview of the public eye, outside of the denominational landscape and institutions. Sometimes Jewish life is shaped, not only by ideology and law, but by improvisation and simply doing the best we can.

Second-Wave Feminism sought to dissolve the dichotomy between public and private, which was seen as fundamental to loosening the bonds of the patriarchy. Adopting "the personal is political" as a rallying slogan, a central part of this feminist agenda was turning an eye to what happens behind closed doors, by bringing to light the lives women actually live and the choices they actually make, and why and how they make them. Pogrebin's book serves this agenda as she describes the secrets of her own mother's kitchen, the abortions and gender reassignment surgery planned there, saying out loud the things that couldn't be said before, putting them on paper and making them a matter of public record, even when the disclosure of intimate secrets might be seen as act of betrayal.

Rebellion as Love

Love, alienation, and rebellion are inextricably linked in Pogrebin's book. When Pogrebin was a teenager her mother died of cancer. At shiva one evening, only nine men were present instead of the ten traditionally required for a minyan, the quorum needed to recite the Mourner's Kaddish. Pogrebin begs her father to allow her to count as the tenth. Instead her father calls for the synagogue to send a tenth man—a stranger—to complete the minyan. As she recounts, many women of her generation, including E. M. Broner, Bella Abzug, Susannah Heschel, and Blu Greenberg, were first forced to reckon with the limits of women's participation in Judaism when a parent or other beloved relative died. Wanting to recite the Mourner's Kaddish, they found that their prayers were not recognized as having the same status as that of a man. This experience felt like a denial of their filial love and devotion. They saw themselves, not just as daughters, but fiercely loving daughters, and they wanted to stand as mourners and have their grief and love acknowledged. They wanted their words of prayer to be seen as acts of devotion to those they sought to remember and honor. This desire to have their love count often fueled their activism in the Jewish sphere.

Pogrebin's sense of fierce loving comes through in her descriptions of more overtly political settings as well. She is happy to tell us what's wrong with the United States, with Israel, and the women's movement because she loves them all. Throughout she seems dismayed to see how loving critiques motivated by a sense of commitment and devotion are sometimes rejected as destructive and undermining acts. Her activism for gender equity earns her the label of man-hater; her support for Israeli-Palestinian dialogue leads some to denounce her as a Zionist apologist or a self-hating Jew.

Showing Up

As a teenager mourning her mother, Pogrebin opts to leave the Judaism that refused to count her. Over time, though, she comes to see that to shape the world to her vision she must instead demand to be let in. Transformation requires a persistent engagement. To that end, much of the book focuses on Pogrebin's efforts to facilitate conversation across difference. When Pogrebin sees a moral issue—whether it's anti-Semitism in the women's movement, misogyny in Jewish communal life, or injustice and discrimination in the United States or in Israel—she wants to name it, call it out, and talk about it. This is her model for what feminist activism looks like. She identifies areas of conflict around fundamental ethical principles and rushes headlong into the discomfort. To advance justice, her instinct is: show up for your people and for other people, invite precisely those you disagree with, demand the space to tell your story, and fall back to listen to the painful truths of others.

Much has changed since Pogrebin wrote her book; in particular, the rising numbers of Jewish women who have reached great heights of erudition as Jewish scholars and the flowering of new Jewish rituals that center women's experiences and belonging. But many of the problems that seemed intractable more than twenty-five years ago still feel intractable, and that realization hangs heavily. Still Pogrebin is an excellent diagnostician, able to zero in unflinchingly on the sources of metastatic disease.

The passage of time sometimes makes her remarks feel too optimistic. At one point in the book, she comments that African-Americans will soon have their own museum on the mall, not far from the United States Holocaust Memorial Museum, which was then being constructed. Now we know that it would another be twenty-five years from when she wrote those words until the National Museum of African American History and Culture opened in 2016. In particular, her reckoning with racism and the relationship between Jewish women in the United States and whiteness seems undeveloped. But her overall assessment of the fundamental problems that must ultimately be addressed seems eerily prescient.

The chapters about anti-Semitism in progressive movements and the need for Jewish women's participation in interfaith dialogue remain particularly resonant. She devotes several pages to her attempts to understand black feminist leaders who will not disavow Louis Farrakhan, the anti-Semitic leader of the Nation of Islam. In 2019, associations between leaders of the Women's March and Farrahkhan led many Jewish feminists to disavow this contemporary feminist movement. How does a person committed to social justice movements and the advancement of women of color confront anti-Semitism? In the face of deep conflict, what do you do? Pogrebin says: You show up and you try to talk through difference in the hopes that it will lead to action. Whether her prescription for the cure—dialogue across difference—will create new paths forward remains to be seen.

In her introduction Pogrebin explains that she looked to the biblical judge Deborah and to Golda Meir, the fourth Prime Minister of Israel, as Jewish female archetypes. They offered her latent paradigms for the person she could become. An archetype is a form of cultural inheritance, not always manifest, but always possible. As new generations of Jewish feminists look for resources to move toward a more equitable society, Pogrebin, now an archetype in her own right, offers a set of possibilities from her own experiences charting the Second Wave. These include: say out loud what you know; insist that nothing is outside the bounds of reimagination; know that rage is sometimes the most caring response; cultivate empathy for those operating under different constraints and circumstances; listen carefully to discern that which produces dis-ease from that which is hateful; show up for yourself and others. Will these strategies for action ultimately prove successful? Pogrebin might advise, don't throw things out just because they are old, but never fear to reimagine what your ancestors gave you.

8. Barry Kosmin, *Highlights of the CJF 1990 National Jewish Population Survey*

"A Portrait of Jewish Americans," Pew Research Center

Barry Kosmin, *Highlights of the CJF 1990 National Jewish Population Survey*, New York: Council of Jewish Federations, 1991

Dr. Barry Kosmin (1949–) is Research Professor in Public Policy & Law and Founding Director of the Institute for the Study of Secularism in Society and Culture (ISSSC) at Trinity College, Hartford, Connecticut.

One way to assess intermarriage is to note the identification of the current marriage partner of anyone who was born Jewish and is now married, irrespective of their present Jewish identity. This population numbers 2.6 million. ...

68 percent of all currently married Born Jews (1.7 million) are married to someone who was also born Jewish. It should be remembered that this includes people from 18 to over 80 years of age. Four percent (105,000) are married to a Jew by Choice while 28 percent (739,000) are married to a Gentile. This last figure includes Born Jews (160,000) who converted to another religion (JCO). ...

The choice of marriage partners has changed dramatically over the past few decades. In recent years just over half of Born Jews who married, at any age, whether for the first time or not, chose a spouse who was born a Gentile and has remained so, while less than 5 percent of these marriages include a non-Jewish partner who became a Jew by Choice (JBC). As a result, since 1985 twice as many mixed couples (Born Jew with Gentile spouse) have been created as Jewish couples (Jewish, with Jewish spouse). This picture also tends to underestimate the total frequency because it does not include currently Born Jews divorced or separated from an intermarriage, nor Jew-Gentile unmarried couple relationships and living arrangements. (13–14)

Although the opposition to intermarriage is greatest amongst the [Jews by Religion], even a third of them would support such a marriage and another

46 percent would accept it. These results suggest that across all types a general acceptance of intermarriage has developed coinciding with the rapid rise in the incidence of intermarriage in recent years. (29)

"A Portrait of Jewish Americans," Washington, D.C., Pew Research Center, 2013

A key aim of the Pew Research Center survey is to explore Jewish identity: What does being Jewish mean in America today? Large majorities of U.S. Jews say that remembering the Holocaust (73%) and leading an ethical life (69%) are essential to their sense of Jewishness. More than half (56%) say that working for justice and equality is essential to what being Jewish means to them. And about four-in-ten say that caring about Israel (43%) and having a good sense of humor (42%) are essential to their Jewish identity.

But observing religious law is not as central to most American Jews. Just 19% of the Jewish adults surveyed say observing Jewish law (halakha) is essential to what being Jewish means to them. And in a separate but related question, most Jews say a person can be Jewish even if that person works on the Sabbath or does not believe in God. Believing in Jesus, however, is enough to place one beyond the pale: 60% of U.S. Jews say a person cannot be Jewish if he or she believes Jesus was the messiah. (14)

Where have the Jews by religion gone? Some have converted to other faiths, but many have become Jews of no religion—people who describe their religion as atheist, agnostic or "nothing in particular" but who were raised Jewish or had a Jewish parent and who still consider themselves Jewish aside from religion. A Pew Research reanalysis of the 2000–2001 National Jewish Population Survey suggests that at that time, 93% of Jews in that study were Jews by religion and 7% were Jews of no religion (after some adjustments to make the NJPS and Pew Research categories as similar as possible). In the new Pew Research survey, 78% of Jews are Jews by religion, and fully 22% are Jews of no religion (including 6% who are atheist, 4% who are agnostic and 12% whose religion is "nothing in particular"). ...

The increase in Jews of no religion appears to be part of a broader trend in American life, the movement away from affiliation with organized religious groups. Surveys by Pew Research and other polling organizations have shown a decline in the percentage of U.S. adults who identify with Protestant denominations and a rapid rise, beginning in the 1990s, in the number of Americans who do not identify with any religion. This group, sometimes called the "nones," now stands at about 20% of the U.S. public, including roughly a third of adults under 30. (32–33)

Overwhelming majorities of both Jews by religion and Jews of no religion say they are proud to be Jewish (97% and 83%, respectively). Most Jews by religion also say they have a strong sense of belonging to the Jewish people (85%) and that they feel a responsibility to care for Jews in need (71%). Far fewer Jews of no religion share these sentiments. (52)

More than half of Jews by religion (55%) say being Jewish is mainly a matter of ancestry or culture, while 17% say it is mainly a matter of religion, and 26% say it is a combination of religion and ancestry/culture. Roughly eight-in-ten Jews of no religion (83%) say being Jewish is mainly a matter of ancestry or culture, while just 6% say it is mainly a matter of religion. (54)

COMMENTARY BY MIJAL BITTON

At first glance, it seems like not very much changed between the release of the 1990 National Jewish Population Survey (NJPS) and the 2013 Pew Research Center's Survey of American Jews. Both of these surveys, quantitative studies conducted on a national scale, study Judaism as a "religion" and measure modes of traditional Jewish affiliation. These studies also tell a similar and—many argue—continuous American story: one in which non-Orthodox Jews exhibit a weakening of ethnic Jewish identity and, increasingly, the dissolution of previously normative communal boundaries.

One important factor differentiating these studies, however, is the way each was received in the American Jewish community. The publication of the 1990 NJPS—especially the statistic of a "52% intermarriage rate" reflecting marriages that included a non-Jewish partner between 1985 and 1990—deeply affected the policy of American Jewish institutions. In its aftermath, many organizations promoted initiatives to ensure "Jewish continuity" including Jewish day schools, Jewish life on college campuses, and the founding of Birthright Israel.[1]

---

1   To get a sense of how Federation professionals used this data to further a Jewish continuity agenda see: Hayim Herring, "How the 1990 National Jewish Population Survey Was Used by Federation Professionals for Jewish Continuity Purposes," *Journal of Jewish Communal Service* 76, no. 3 (2000): 216–227.

Though it is much more recent, it is already clear that the reaction to the 2013 Pew Survey marks a change from the discourse surrounding the earlier survey. In particular, while reactions to the 1990 NJPS coalesced more or less around a single "story" meant to advance Jewish continuity, the post-Pew discussion reveals the absence of communal consensus, as two opposite and often polarized schools of thought related to the study of American Jews have emerged.[2]

The first school of thought is that of respondents who react with alarm to the data of the 2013 Pew Study, concerned by the steady rise of intermarriage, decreasing fertility rates, and fewer forms of traditional affiliation for non-Orthodox American Jews. Some in this camp express concern over the future number of Jews in America, while others focus on the declining number of non-Orthodox yet highly engaged Jews. At its core, this orientation maintains that there are certain standards of Judaism against which the behavior of American Jews should be measured—and that American Jews are largely falling short of what is deemed to be a healthy Jewish demographic.[3]

The second school of thought is made up of academics, activists, and educators who reject this pessimistic assessment of the 2013 report. While some explain why the data should be read in a way that does not show the breakdown of certain traditional measures of Jewish life, many simply argue that Jewish life in America has indeed become different than it was in the past, and that the shift is not a cause for communal anxiety. Thought leaders in this camp argue that Judaism must be defined by what Jews do, and, as such, we must interpret the weakening of traditional modes of affiliation as a result of the new ways Jews are enacting Judaism.[4]

---

2 I understand the first school of thought I describe to generally correspond to social scientific research invested in studying behavior and boundaries and the second school of thought to correspond with research focused on sentiment and subjectivity. See Riv-Ellen Prell, "Boundaries, Margins, and Norms: The Intellectual Stakes in the Study of American Jewish Culture(s)," *Contemporary Jewry* 32, no. 2 (2012): 189–204. For a defense of a behaviors and boundaries based approach see Charles S. Liebman, "The Marshall Sklare Memorial Lecture: Some Research Proposals for the Study of American Jews," *Contemporary Jewry* (2001): 99–114. For an argument on behalf of a more subjective approach to studying Jewish identity see Bethamie Horowitz, *Connections and Journeys: Assessing Critical Opportunities for Enhancing Jewish Identity* (New York: UJA-Federation of Jewish Philanthropies of New York, 2000).

3 See, for example, "Strategic Directions for Jewish Life: A Call to Action," EJewishPhilanthropy, October 1, 2015, accessed July 11, 2019, https://ejewishphilanthropy.com/strategic-directions-for-jewish-life-a-call-to-action/.

4 See, for example, Bethamie Horowitz, "Assimilation Anxieties and the Case of American Jews," *American Jewish Yearbook* (2014): 51–55.

What, then, should we make of the emergence of a polarized discourse regarding the sociology of Jews?

One way to understand the debate about how to read the Pew study is through developments in the discipline of the social scientific study of Jews. More specifically, general trends in the social sciences have shifted away from relying upon hard categories for identity and belonging, instead privileging performance and the dynamics of human interaction. These trends have given rise to new understandings of the flux inherent in Jewish identity. For instance, the increased popularity of qualitative research has allowed for the examination of intermarriage in a more nuanced way than that captured in depersonalized statistics produced by quantitative surveys. This shift also highlights an important disciplinary and epistemological difference between those social scientists who see their role as advocating for policy recommendations based on their research, and those who seek to describe what is happening in the Jewish community without producing recommendations for policymakers or otherwise evaluating the populations they survey. It should be noted that the second group of scholars often have fewer public platforms by which to publicize their views, as communal organizations tend to seek the former.

This divide among researchers, however, is about more than different methodologies, interpretations of survey data, or disciplinary approaches. I would suggest that at their core, the emerging disagreements over how to interpret and analyze the data reflect conflicting moral approaches towards Judaism itself.

What we are witnessing in conflicting reactions to the 2013 Pew survey is a debate about two different conceptions of the values that guide or should guide American Jewish life: continuity, on the one hand, and inclusivity, on the other. By this, I do not claim that the social scientists arguing over assessments of the Pew Survey data are intentionally constructing moral arguments. Rather, their responses align with—and are often amplified by—competing sets of communal values.

Those who react to Pew with alarm at the increasing dissolution of traditional forms of Jewish life see contemporary American Jewry as abdicating the moral imperative of Jewish continuity. Those who engage in producing this morality speak of it unselfconsciously, as one that requires no explanation or justification. For them, "Jewish continuity" is a modern-day *mitzvah* (commandment). If Jewish continuity is the sacred goal, then whichever forms of social life help reproduce current communal structures are idealized and valorized. One of the consequences of this moral orientation is the prioritizing of working for some unknown future over the present. Sidney Goldstein, a principal investigator for the NJPS, has noted that a major concern about intermarriage is that the children and grandchildren of Jews who marry non-Jews are less likely to identify as Jews than those born to two Jewish parents.[5] This correlation has led communal leaders—who are often themselves Jewish parents and grandparents—to focus on these future generations as a justification for their present-day interest in Jewish continuity. Expressed in theological terms, then, this approach means that those focused on Jewish continuity are often less concerned for their own *olam ha-zeh* (this world) than they are for their own *olam ha-ba* (the world to come)—namely, the spiritual future of their grandchildren.

On the other side of the equation are those who seek to elevate Jewish inclusivity as the most sacred of American Jewish values, a moral orientation that often correlates to the responses that express optimism in reaction to the 2013 report, or who at least reject the pessimistic assessments of others. Upholders of this morality often not only disagree with the standards used to measure Jewish behaviors and identity, but find the very idea of standards to be morally problematic. Standards inherently produce boundaries, which essentially exclude and pass judgement over individuals. American Judaism—whether understood as a faith, tradition, ethnicity, religion, or heritage—must remain malleable to contain within it the multitudes of individual negotiations of Jewishness. On this basis, some of these interpreters object to using words like "assimilation" to describe American Jewish life. The morality of inclusivity sacralizes and reifies the status of Jews. If all that is needed for an activity or behavior to be authentically Jewish is for a self-identifying Jew to define it as such, then the actor's Jewishness (inherited or by choice) becomes the most significant determinant in the production of American Judaism.

The problem with much of the public communal discourse around the social scientific study of American Jews is that data are often used to advance specific values, without making explicit that the conversation has veered into moral discourse. Lila Corwin Berman compellingly describes the ascent of sociology as the primary discourse (one based on an intimate relationship between social scientists and the organized Jewish community) through which American Jews learned to compare themselves, both their similarities to and their differences from, broader American society.[6] Michal Kravel-Tovi characterizes statistics

---

5   Sidney Goldstein, "Profile of American Jewry: Insights from the 1990 National Jewish Population Survey," *American Jewish Yearbook* (1992): 77–173.

6   Lila Corwin Berman, *Speaking of Jews: Rabbis, Intellectuals, and the Creation of an American Public Identity* (Berkeley: University of California Press, 2009).

related to American Jews as "wet numbers" carrying with them the presumed "dryness" of statistics but invested with the "wet" emotional baggage of American Jewish dreams and nightmares.[7]

A way forward would be to elevate the discourse and debates over social scientific research of American Jews by having researchers and communal stakeholders insist upon openly distinguishing the differences between describing data and assigning it moral value or deriving policy recommendations from it. This approach would acknowledge both that moral lenses ultimately shape collective self-understanding and communal assessments, which means they belong in our conversations, and that there are dangers in masking moral discourse in the discipline and authority of social science.

---

7 Michal Kravel-Tovi, "Wet Numbers: The Language of Continuity Crisis and the Work of Care among the Organized American Jewish Community," in *Taking Stock: Cultures of Enumeration in Contemporary Jewish Life*, ed. Michal Kravel-Tovi and Debra Dash Moore (Bloomington: Indiana University Press, 2016), 141–64.

9. Joseph Telushkin, *Jewish Literacy*

Paula Hyman, "Who is an Educated Jew?"

Vanessa Ochs, "Ten Jewish Sensibilities"

Joseph Telushkin, *Jewish Literacy*, New York: William Morrow and Company, Inc., 1991

Rabbi Joseph Telushkin (1948–) is a rabbi, lecturer, and author.

Judaism believes that the goal of Jewish existence is nothing less than "to perfect the rule under God" (from the *Aleinu* prayer).

In Jewish teachings, both clauses—the world's ethical perfection and the rule of God—are equally important. Human beings are obligated to bring mankind to a knowledge of God, whose primary demand of human beings is moral behavior. All people who hold this belief are ethical monotheists, and thus natural allies of religiously committed Jews.

Unfortunately, although ethical monotheism is the goal of Judaism (*see Micah/To Do Justice, and to Love Goodness, and to Walk Modestly with Your God*) and the purpose of the Jewish mission in the world, more than a few Jews have lost sight of this goal. As the late Rabbi Abraham Joshua Heschel lamented: "The Jewish people are a messenger who have forgotten their message." Among religious Jews today, disproportionate emphasis often is placed on rituals, as if Judaism's ethical laws were offered merely as advice and are not as binding or important as the rituals. The Israeli Bible scholar Professor Uriel Simon has noted the paradox that Jews who most passionately believe that the Jew are God's Chosen People are the ones most likely to justify any acts of the Israeli government on the grounds that "we have a right to act like any other nation."

Strangely enough, however, secular Jews are as likely as religious Jews to believe that the Jews have a special mission. As Simon goes on to note: "And those Jews who don't believe in chosenness are the ones who are most likely to hold Israel to a higher standard than they hold any other nation."

The principle of ethical monotheism, the obligation to try to "perfect the world under the rule of God," is reiterated three times a day in the *Aleinu* prayer, which closes the morning, afternoon, and evening prayer services. The term "ethical monotheism" itself is generally credited to nineteenth-century Reform Judaism, and remains nineteenth-century Reform's most enduring contribution to Jewish thought. (549)

Paula Hyman, "Who is an Educated Jew?," *Sh'ma: A Journal of Jewish Ideas* (February 2002)

Dr. Paula Hyman (1946–2011) was Lucy Moses Professor of Modern Jewish History at Yale University.

Modernity fractured Jewish experience, destroying the hegemony of rabbinic Judaism and the authority of traditional Jewish elites. Contemporary currents of thought like postmodernism and multiculturalism have challenged virtually all certainties and shaken all canons. No canon is fixed, and all guardians of cultural transmission are required to make hard choices. We are fortunate that the Jewish canon has always been a relatively open one, for the traditional Jewish system of interpretation of classical texts has provided a mechanism for ongoing revision. The development of interpretive strategies, in midrash, for example, as literary scholars have argued, demonstrates a way to recover oppositional strands within traditional texts. Insofar as we focus on the spaces for debate and contestation within the traditional Jewish canon, we acknowledge the need for, and sustain the possibility of, multiple cultural expressions for the diverse people that we are. Although the term "open canon" sounds like an oxymoron, it simply reflects the recognition that every canon is constructed and merits a healthy combination of respect and skepticism and regular revision if it is to speak to its intended audience. A truly "open canon" affords opportunities for choice and for the inclusion of ongoing cultural creativity.

Once we acknowledge that unity is neither possible nor desirable, though, we must ask what models of educated Jews we seek to promote. What, if anything, will educated Jews of different paideias (educational visions and curricula in the broadest sense) share?

I can think of three prerequisites—necessary but not sufficient—for all educated Jews: the Hebrew language (in all its variants, from the Bible to the present—not just street Hebrew); an acceptance of biblical and rabbinic texts as one's own; and a general knowledge of Jewish history. Hebrew is an essential tool for reading much of what Jewish culture has produced. But it is more than a tool. Without Hebrew there is no visceral, as distinct from intellectual, connection to Jewish creativity across time and space. Accepting Tanakh and rabbinic texts as one's own does not necessitate ascribing to them sacredness or religious authority. But it does necessitate grappling with their meaning and their role in world culture as well as Jewish culture and in the choices that contemporary Jews make. The knowledge of the broad outlines of Jewish history enables us to understand the societal and intellectual contexts in which Jewish culture has developed.

Accepting this core curriculum is only the first step in becoming Jewishly educated. An open Jewish canon in the twenty-first century draws upon a variety of voices and genres. It must embrace all the Jewish cultural products of the past two centuries—that is, the different forms that Jews have chosen to make meaning of their existence as Jews. Secular forms in many languages—including literature, memoirs, folkore, film, and the visual arts—are too often dismissed as lacking in cultural significance.

What I am suggesting, then, is that educated Jews would share a core curriculum of Hebrew language, foundational texts, and knowledge of historical development. They would then follow a multiple-track model of curriculum development, choosing, according to their own interests, from a far broader range of cultural expression than is commonly considered "Jewish knowledge." Although biblical and rabbinic texts would define a core of Jewish knowledge, further learning would not privilege any single genre of cultural production or any single text.

Changes within the past generation necessitate a rethinking of Jewish learning as thorough as the Haskalah critique of two centuries ago. While the majority of Jews have acquired secular education, as maskilim advocated, they have not always applied their knowledge to Judaism or Jewish culture. I am not referring here to the willful ignorance of what modern scholarly inquiry has to say about classical Jewish texts. Rather, I am speaking about the failure of most Jews who consider themselves Jewishly educated to contend with recent trends in studies of culture. ...

The multicultural model, which disputes the very idea of canon (but may also accept the concept of an open canon) and pays heed to the voices that resist and subvert authority, appears quite suitable to the diversity of Jewish patterns of behavior and thought in a post-emancipation world. It mandates willingness to acknowledge the multiplicity of Jewish voices and accept their authenticity. The multicultural model is particularly appropriate to the ambiguous position of Jews in Diaspora, who create Jewish culture in the space between being a part of the larger society and apart from it (or, in the words of a recent book, insider/outsiders). The adoption of a multi-cultural stance, however, requires a recognition of the diversity of Jewish life as a value rather than an unfortunate fact; that is, it requires a conversion of diversity into pluralism.

Living in a multicultural society, we have the opportunity and the obli-gation to shape a fluid Jewish canon for our own time and for the future. Engaged with the richness of the culture we have inherited, which links us with Jews of other times and places, we must be sensitive as well to the incom-pleteness of our legacy, to the voices that have been suppressed (women's and others) and to the interpretations that have lacked authority. The legacy of our generation may well be a postmodern hermeneutics of suspicion and a recognition that a diverse people requires cultural diversity.

Vanessa Ochs, "Ten Jewish Sensibilities," *Sh'ma: A Journal of Jewish Ideas* (December 2003)

Rabbi Dr. Vanessa Ochs (1953–) is Professor of Religious Studies at the University of Virginia.

I've heard it said, "I'm not really religious but I like to think of myself as a good Jew." This line references an unarticulated code that many Jewish Americans try to follow—even judge themselves by—a code that overlaps but is not synonymous with the requirements of Jewish law or traditional practice. ...

My understanding of Jewish sensibilities is influenced by two major Jew-ish thinkers, Max Kadushin and [Irving] "Yitz" Greenberg. What differentiates my list of sensibilities from Kadushin's value concepts and Greenberg's contin-uum concepts is that I see the sensibilities as categories that emerge primarily from the real lives of a diverse population of Jews, characterizing how Jews self-describe and live out their ideals, rather than as prescriptions imposed by sacred texts.

The Sensibilities
1. Making Distinctions: Havdalah
   Making distinctions matters to us. They may be temporal — such as making a distinction between special times and everyday times.

We take calendars seriously: we honor vacation time, family time, and birthdays. While we celebrate the blessings of everyday life, we understand that special occasions have a holy dimension that we mark. Some distinctions are personal and create new situations, like marriage ceremonies or graduations.

2. Honor: Kavod

We are aware that we do not live in a social vacuum and that our actions have consequences. We want to be respected. Thus, we aspire to act in ways that will bring honor to ourselves, to our families, and to the communities we belong to. We want to be worthy of honor after we have passed on and our deeds and choices are remembered.

3. Turning: Teshuvah

We believe it is possible to reflect upon one's life, turn it around, and experience forgiveness from others while also feeling a sense of renewal for ourselves. We are works-in-progress, and self-improvement is always possible. We give ourselves and others opportunities to change.

4. Dignity; Being in the Image of God: Tzelem Elokim

We seek ways to conduct ourselves and to treat others with the greatest of respect in order to preserve our own dignity and the dignity of each individual and to prevent humiliation. We are aware that dignity is possible only when one is free and self-sustaining. We care about education because having knowledge enhances one's self-respect and ability to live in a dignified manner. We might care about appearances, knowing that dressing appropriately enhances one's self-respect and honors others. We are likely to engage in political, charitable, and volunteer activities (such as mentoring the underprivileged, working for civil rights, or building housing for the homeless) that increase the dignity of others.

5. Saving a Life: Pikuach Nefesh

We believe that as long as one is healthy there is reason to celebrate. We toast, "L'Chaim!" "To life!" We do not take health, the number one blessing, for granted, and we feel the miraculous nature of every recovery. We understand that life is fragile and go to extremes to save a life.

6. Being a Really Good Person: "Be a Mensch"

We aspire to be a mensch, someone who acts with compassion toward others. In ourselves and in others, we value the human qualities of being attentive, empathetic, and discrete, and of making sacrifices when necessary. We try to be good friends and neighbors. A mensch's broad reserve of compassion extends toward all Jews, wherever they live, and toward all people, particularly the vulnerable.

7. Keeping the Peace: Shalom Bayit

Certain decisions or gestures are made not only because they are appropriate but also because they serve to keep the peace, settle differences, keep a family together, and create harmony instead of divisiveness.

8. Repairing the World: Tikkun Olam

We hold that each person should find ways to make the world a better and more just place. This stance of compassionate engagement occurs in simple individual ways as well as on larger platforms. We use our money and talents to make a difference. Engaging in world repair, we may feel as if we are "doing a *mitzvah*," doing something that we are divinely ordained to do even though it is our choice. We feel that doing good works justifies our having been put on this earth. If we have been fortunate, we feel responsible to "give back."

9. Maintaining Hope: Yesh Tikvah

We try to hang on to hope and resist despair. In romance, we believe we will meet our beshert, our intended one. We dream expansively and even set off on uncertain journeys with feelings of promise on the horizon. At the same time, we accept that some things seem fated not to be. When a door closes, we face reality and move on to new possibilities.

10. Memory of One's Ancestors: Z'chut Avot

We feel connected to the people who came before us. We draw insight and wisdom from the experiences of our ancestors and seek to honor them with our actions. And we expect the same of our children. Thus, we honor our ancestors by transmitting the sensibilities that characterized their ideas and actions onto the next generation.

Regardless of orientation, these sensibilities can help Jews formulate decisions in keeping with one's Jewish "compass" in at least three particular areas: health care, ritual practice, and personal moral choice. ...

These sensibilities help us understand how our Jewishness defines or contributes to the way we live. For example, according to halakhah, sexual relations between an unmarried man and woman are forbidden. Yet Jews who do not heed halakhah concerning premarital sex still bring Jewish consciousness to sexuality. Two sensibilities in particular govern premarital relations. First,

"Saving a Life": the majority of Jews involved in romantic relationships feel duty-bound to take precautions for safe-sex both for themselves and their partners. Second, "Distinctions": many Jews tend to honor both themselves and their partners by maintaining monogamy in relationships.

Drawing upon the ten sensibilities and relating them to a situation at hand requires creative thinking and the ability to juggle. That is, a sensibility that mattered more at one time or to one generation might give way to a different sensibility that now takes precedence. Sometimes multiple sensibilities are at play, and they may compete for the strength of influence. At the core, however, is the weightiness of the sensibilities, what Kadushin calls the "primary factors in the experience of significance."

COMMENTARY BY HANNAH S. PRESSMAN

These texts by Joseph Telushkin, Paula E. Hyman, and Vanessa L. Ochs help us to consider the shape of a comprehensive Jewish education. Telushkin offers a core curriculum; Ochs, a list of essential Jewish values that one might explore and study; and Hyman, a plea to make the canon more inclusive. Further, each scholar proposes criteria that would qualify a Jew as having met the communal standard of knowledge. Yet, perhaps unsurprisingly, none of the formulas is the same.

At their heart, all three texts are about *tokhen*, the modern Hebrew word for content or substance. From this word, a cluster of questions emerges: What should be the actual substance of a Jewish education in the twenty-first century? How do we inculcate authentic Jewish values? What is the connection between Jewish literacy and Jewish identity? Can we draft a list or write a textbook that will satisfy most, if not all, of these (and other) visions for an informed Jewish perspective on the world?

It is not a coincidence that the meaning of the word *tokhen* in biblical Hebrew extends to include measuring, estimating, and weighing. In Exodus 5:18, Pharaoh declares that, despite lacking the necessary straw, his Israelite slaves still have to deliver "the *tokhen*, quota, of bricks." In 1 Samuel 2:3, having finally given birth to a son, the grateful Hannah hails the Lord as "an all-knowing God; by Him actions are *nitkenu*, measured." These aspects of *tokhen* serve as an apt metaphor for the intellectual notion of content: a substantial idea has measurable weight and impact. Our idioms follow suit. A student gradually piles up her knowledge "brick by brick"; a deep discussion can likewise be called "weighty."

What, then, is the measure of an educated Jew? This essay will consider points of overlap and divergence among the three texts, suggesting how they create and contribute to a communal conversation about how to equip Jews with knowledge of Judaism.

Telushkin's *Jewish Literacy* has become the industry standard for introducing Judaism, a go-to text for modern conversion classes and those seeking to broaden their Jewish knowledge base. An Orthodox rabbi and scholar, Telushkin applies E. D. Hirsch's notion of a content-based educational approach to Judaism. Providing a comprehensive collection of what he calls "basic Jewish terms," Telushkin hopes that this book will stage an intervention against the "Jewish ignorance" (that is, illiteracy) he sees as rampant in American Jewish life.

The scope of *Jewish Literacy* is remarkable, offering historical overviews from ancient to modern times, with appearances by Maimonides, Moses Mendelssohn, and Golda Meir. There are explanations of the Hebrew calendar, the Jewish life cycle, and how things work in a synagogue. The short essays are often accompanied by anecdotes or jokes taken from Telushkin's own life, giving the book the warm feel of a conversation with a chattily authoritative friend. Standout entries, like those on Ruth and the definition of *mensch*, convey the essence of Jewish peoplehood in pithy yet powerful prose.

Here's the rub, however: any collection subtitled "the most important things to know" inherently marks other things—whether voices, viewpoints, or cultural products—as less important, even outside. An early review politely noted that "the women's movement and its relation to Judaism" was a "missed" topic;[1] one of *Jewish Literacy*'s only nods to popular culture comes in a later edition, when Telushkin added Oskar Schindler to the entry on righteous gentiles after the 1993 film *Schindler's List*. Additionally, the risk of creating a curricular catalogue, as well-intentioned as it may be, is that it encourages a checklist-based approach to education and assessment—what's often called "teaching to the test." In his recent critique of *Jewish Literacy*, Jon Levisohn raises these concerns about Telushkin's adoption of Hirsch's method, concluding that students should instead be empowered to "use their knowledge for constructive purposes."[2] That is, we should aspire to cultivate readers who can also create their own meaning and not just recite what they've read. Nevertheless, Telushkin's *Jewish Literacy* is an incredible accomplishment, even if the lacunae are just as stimulating as the *tokhen* that made the cut.

---

1   Ilene Cooper, review of *Jewish Literacy: The Most Important Things to Know About the Jewish Religion, Its People, and Its History*, by Joseph Telushkin, *Booklist* 87, no. 18 (May 15, 1991): 1757.

2   Jon A. Levisohn, "Redeeming Jewish Literacy," *Hayidion* (Spring 2016): 12–13.

Ten years after *Jewish Literacy*'s first edition, Hyman's and Ochs's think-pieces appeared in close succession in *Sh'ma: A Journal of Jewish Ideas,* each offering an alternative to Telushkin's mode of organizing Jewish knowledge. For these scholars, *tokhen* is not an end in itself, but a means of *being* and *doing* Jewishly in the world. Their essays shift the conversation away from Telushkin's opposition of literacy versus illiteracy and away from any single book. Instead, Ochs and Hyman encourage us to consider the potential of flexible frameworks with open boundaries. The result, they assert, will be an approach to Judaism that is more accepting of secular and popular culture, as well as new ritual practices—all of which can effectively engage and retain lifelong Jewish learners.

In "Who Is an Educated Jew?," Hyman, a historian who often trained her lens on gender issues, argues for a more inclusive approach to composing a core curriculum while also upending the notion that mastery of any particular list is sufficient. Her forceful critique lays bare an internal (and eternal) tendency to create hierarchies within the cultural and intellectual life of the community. In a piquant genealogy of Jewish educational standards, Hyman identifies the spread of *Haskalah* (Enlightenment) ideas in the late eighteenth century as marking the end of a general consensus about a basic Jewish curriculum. She argues that the turn of the twenty-first century is a similarly critical time: Jewish life now is increasingly diverse, and a one-size-fits-all educational model will not work. Like Telushkin, Hyman sees a need for intervention, but devises a nearly-opposite strategy for meeting the moment.

Hyman's boldest move is to emphasize the canon's inherent flexibility. The Jewish textual tradition is always already being reworked, so it should not seem revolutionary to embrace more variety within the canon. In making space for silenced voices, texts, and swaths of Jewish experience that have not been viewed as mainstream, Hyman is consciously adopting some of the changes that cultural studies have brought to the Academy over the past few decades. The "multicultural model" offers a means of disrupting the top-down power dynamics whereby elites determine what is worth learning—which *tokhen* counts and has weight in our minds. In her view, popular culture is a prime example of something that is typically shunted aside but actually should figure into "the sum total of Judaism."

Importantly, though, Hyman does not throw out all of tradition. Instead, she identifies three essential pieces that must form the foundation of any Jewish education: Hebrew language, biblical and rabbinic texts, and "general knowledge of Jewish history." These are to serve as a stepping stone to accessing anything that is of further interest to the student. Hyman particularly endorses contemporary and secular cultural expressions such as film, literature, and visual art, "the different forms that Jews have chosen to make meaning of their existence as Jews." Jewish education becomes a "Choose Your Own Adventure" story, with roots in a timeless tradition but potential to grow, wildly and fruitfully, in any direction. In addition, Hyman's proposal raises questions of implementation on the ground. Teachers who are trained in teaching *Mishnah* aren't necessarily comfortable dissecting episodes of "Transparent" or probing a Liana Finck graphic novel, and vice versa. Yet if the goal is growing lifelong learners, then welcoming popular and secular culture into the fold feels like a win-win. Hyman's thesis supports empowering educators to provide engaging access points for American Jews with a variety of backgrounds and interests.

Hyman writes that the times demand a vision of a core curriculum—a center—that is "malleable … created by Jews through a combination of consciousness and behavior." Her emphasis on laypeople and the flexibility of her framework resonate strongly with Vanessa Ochs's approach in her "Ten Jewish Sensibilities."

An anthropologist who earned rabbinic ordination in 2012, Ochs defines the Jewish "sensibilities" she lists as "ethical precepts, values, principles, and ways of being." The framework is descriptive rather than prescriptive, "emerg[ing] primarily from the real lives of a diverse population of Jews." She initially generated these guidelines to help Jews and their caregivers navigate healthcare decisions, but felt they were potentially useful for the broader community as a tool of engagement for "the spiritually disenfranchised." Ochs points out an additional, intriguing benefit: the sensibilities offer ways to support emerging ritual practices, a crucial function as Jewish communities respond to new needs and demographic trends.

Reading through the sensibilities, I was struck by how many of the items inspired personal reflection. For example, the entry for "Teshuvah" focuses on forgiveness and renewal without referencing the High Holy Days as a context: "We give ourselves and others opportunities to change." Framed this way, renewal is a perpetual possibility, not a one-off confined to Rosh Hashanah and Yom Kippur. The entry for "Being a Really Good Person" does not dwell on the sociolinguistic origins of *mensch* and *menschlikhkeit*, but rather on the mandate to act compassionately to all people, Jews and non-Jews alike.

Few would argue against the notion of a Jewish "compass" to guide our actions. However, the matter of these sensibilities' *tokhen*, their core substance, has provoked some debate. In the *Sh'ma* discussion accompanying this piece's original publication, respondents questioned how Jewish the sensibilities actually are. While a Protestant chaplain declared the list "distinctively Jewish,"[3] a Reconstructionist Rabbinical College professor reacted by claiming that, "Not one of the sensibilities she highlights comes from the particularistic strand of Jewish sacred texts, communal customs, or liturgical ideals."[4]

Despite this critique, Ochs contends that these ways of acting and being are the weightiest in our tradition, the ones most likely to be absorbed from generation to generation. In a later version of the article, she describes specific instances where the sensibilities are expressed.[5] Notably, she ends the list with the principle of Z'chut Avot (Memory of One's Ancestors) and the importance of transmission for honoring those who came before us. This principle unites all three authors gathered here, who, despite their differing viewpoints, criteria, and presentation of tokhen, want the golden chain of Jewish knowledge to continue. That their strategies vary widely only underscores that the past three decades have been a fertile period for the evolving conversation about Jewish learning and living, in concert with the shifting dimensions of contemporary Jewish identity.

On some level, creating a list is an act of provocation: as soon as it is written, the document invites commentary on what has been left out. On another level, though, creating a list is an act of hope: hope that someone, somewhere, will find therein the recipe they have been seeking for a fulfilling Jewish life. These three authors recognize that in the modern world, we cannot live Jewishly by default; instead, we must craft this life consciously, with love and intention. Ultimately, the measure of an educated Jew might be to feel lightness in one's steps while carrying the weight of tradition.

---

3   Karen L. Wood, "Christian and Jewish Sensibilities," Sh'ma (December 2003): 6.
4   Nancy Fuchs-Kreimer, "Rooting Universal Sensibilities in Jewish Life," Sh'ma (December 2003): 8–9.
5   Vanessa Ochs, "The Jewish Sensibilities," Journal of Textual Reasoning 4, no. 3 (May 2006).

10. Yaakov Levado, "Gayness and God: Wrestlings of an Orthodox Rabbi"

Yaakov Levado, "Gayness and God: Wrestlings of an Orthodox Rabbi," *Tikkun* 8, No. 5 (September/October 1993)

Yaakov Levado is the pseudonym under which **Rabbi Steve Greenberg** (1956–) wrote his groundbreaking essay "Gayness and God" in 1993. Greenberg is Co-Founder and Director of Eshel, a support, education, and advocacy organization for Orthodox LGBT Jews, Senior Teaching Fellow and Director of the Diversity Project at the National Jewish Center for Learning and Leadership (CLAL), and a faculty member at the Shalom Hartman Institute of North America.

As a traditionalist, I hesitate to overturn cultural norms in a flurry of revolutionary zeal. I am committed to a slower and more cautious process of change, which must always begin internally. Halacha, as an activity, is not designed to effect social revolution. It is a society-building enterprise that maintains internal balance by reorganizing itself in response to changing social realities. When social conditions shift, we experience the halachic reapplication as the proper commitment to the Torah's original purposes. That shift in social consciousness in regard to homosexuality is a long way off.

If I have any argument, it is not to press for a resolution, but for a deeper understanding of homosexuality. Within the living Halacha are voices in tension, divergent strands in an imaginative legal tradition that are brought to bear on the real lives of Jews. In order to know how to shape a halachic response to any living question, what is most demanded of us is a deep understanding of the Torah and an attentive ear to the people who struggle with the living question. Confronting new questions can often tease out of the tradition a *hiddush*, a new balancing of the voices and values that have always been there. There is no conclusive *psak halacha* (halachic ruling) without the hearing of personal testimonies, and so far gay people have not been asked to testify to their experience. ...

Holding fast to the covenant demands that I seek a path toward sanctity in gay sexual life. The Torah has much to say about the way people create *kedushah* in their sexual relationships. The values of marriage, monogamy, modesty, and faithfulness that are central to the tradition's view of holiness need to be applied in ways that shape choices and lifestyles.

Holding fast to the covenant means that being gay does not free one from the fulfillment of *mitzvot*. The complexities generated by a verse in Leviticus need not unravel my commitment to the whole of the Torah. There are myriad Jewish concerns, moral, social, intellectual, and spiritual, that I cannot abandon. Being gay need not overwhelm the rest of Jewish life. Single-issue communities are political rather than religious; religious communities tend to be comprehensive of the human condition. The richness of Jewish living derives in part from its diversity of attention, its fullness.

For gay Orthodox Jews, this imagination of engagement between ourselves and the tradition is both terribly exciting and depressing. Regretfully, the communities that embrace us, both gay and Jewish, also reject us. The Jewish community wishes that we remain invisible. The gay community is largely unsympathetic and often hostile to Judaism. There are some in the gay community who portray Judaism as the original cultural source of homophobia. More often, the lack of sympathy toward Jewish observance derives from the single-mindedness of gay activism. Liberation communities rarely have room for competing loyalties.

COMMENTARY BY ZEV FARBER

It is difficult to step back in time and imagine ourselves in the place of Rabbi Steve Greenberg when he wrote this piece. Our world has changed drastically since 1993.

In the United States, gays were still barred from military service; "Don't Ask Don't Tell," which was progressive for its time, became law only in 1994. Sodomy laws were still on the books in many states; they were declared unconstitutional only in 2003, in the wake of *Lawrence vs. Texas*. Some of the seeds for openness to gays in American society, however, had already begun to take root. Most significantly, in 1973, the American Psychiatric Society had updated its *Diagnostic and Statistical Manual of Mental Disorders* (DSM), removing homosexuality from the list.

On the Jewish front, openness to homosexuals was gaining ground in the non-Orthodox movements. The Reconstructionist Rabbinical College (RRC) began ordaining openly homosexual clergy in 1984 and crafted a non-discrimination policy in 1990, making it out of bounds for synagogues not to hire rabbis on the basis of sexual orientation. In 1986, an ad hoc committee on homosexuality and the rabbinate made an official recommendation to the Reform Central Conference of American Rabbis (CCAR) to ordain homosexuals, which was eventually accepted by that body in 1990 and became the policy of the movement's rabbinical school, Hebrew Union College-Jewish Institute of Religion (HUC-JIR).

In the Conservative movement, however, a similar push to accept homosexuals for ordination was blocked in 1992, and only revisited ten years later (2002), with a split decision in the movement's Committee on Jewish Laws and Standards. Actual acceptance of homosexuals into the movement's rabbinical schools only began in 2006 at the Ziegler School of Rabbinic Studies (American Jewish University) and in 2007 at the Jewish Theological Seminary.

In the Orthodox world within which Greenberg functioned, this progressive trend had barely made a dent. Perhaps the most daring statement about homosexuality in Judaism made by an Orthodox rabbi was that of Rabbi Norman Lamm who, in the *Encyclopedia Judaica Yearbook* (1974), suggested that homosexuals should not be seen as liable for the sin of homosexual congress because they are compelled to be the way they are by their biological wiring. (It seems hardly coincidental that this was penned one year after the APA declared homosexuality to be a normal human orientation.)

Lamm's suggestion could have had real power, halakhically speaking, as it suggested way to incorporate traditional notions of sexuality while leaving room for homosexuals to live a full Jewish life. Nevertheless, it had virtually no impact on the Orthodox world, and was only seriously picked up decades later by Rabbi Nathan Lopez Cardozo in 2003 as part of an interview for the documentary, *Trembling Before God*, which also featured Greenberg (more on this later), and by Greenberg himself in 2004, in his book *Wrestling with God and Man*. Over the past few years, the claim has gained traction, and has been used by Rabbi Benny Lau, Rabbi Shlomo Riskin, and by this author, but in 1993, this idea had produced nary a blip on the screen.

A much more common conception among Orthodox rabbis and laypeople, and one that Greenberg painfully describes in his article, was that homosexuality is fake. This position was articulated in halakhic literature, most famously by the giant of American halakhists, Rabbi Moshe Feinstein, who, in 1976, wrote a responsum (*Iggerot Moshe, Orach Chayyim* 4:115), in which he addresses a young homosexual man asking for some words of advice to help him control his urges. Feinstein does so by informing him that there really is no such thing as homosexual desire. Nature dictates, Feinstein wrote, that people are attracted to members of the opposite sex and not to members of their own sex. Therefore, the only explanation for homosexual behavior was as an expression of rebellion against God. If the questioner could get his anger against God under control, he would be able to live a "normal" heterosexual life.

A related stance was taken by Rabbi Barry Freundel in 1986 and was meant to be a progressive position for the educated Modern Orthodox community. In answering the question of what Judaism's view of the Jewish homosexual is, Freundel writes, "there is no such individual." He expands on this point to say, "halacha rejects the notion of an individual called a homosexual, rejects the necessity of the homosexual act for any individual, rejects the idea of an irrevocable homosexual orientation." Why is Freundel so certain that a "wired" homosexual is impossible? Because such a person would mean that God is unfair. He writes, "it is difficult to imagine G-d creating a situation wherein those who feel themselves to possess a homosexual orientation cannot change and are consequently locked in a living prison with no exit and no key."

In short, since God must be fair, and God's Torah prohibits (male) homosexual congress in the strongest terms, then homosexuals as such, that is, men who can only feel attraction to other men and are repelled by the idea of heterosexual sex, must not exist. Into this world jumped Yaakov Levado, Greenberg writing under pseudonym literally meaning Jacob Alone.

Perhaps most importantly, Greenberg simply said, "here we are." He begins with a description of his journey with which a reader can identify. A *frum* boy who wants to get married and have children, who loves Torah study and becomes an Orthodox rabbi, who never considered the possibility that he was gay until it became undeniable. He didn't want it, he says, but there it is. Although in retrospect, this may not seem like such a novel point, in the Orthodox conceptual universe of the early-to-mid-90s, in which there are no homosexuals but only naughty and confused heterosexuals, the effect is poignant, as is the anguish he describes over how the reality of being a gay Orthodox Jew tears at his loyalty: "I still feel ripped apart by these feelings—wanting a woman at the Shabbat table and a man in my bed. If I am judged for some failure, perhaps it will be that I could not choose the Shabbat table over the bed."

As a product of the Orthodox world, Greenberg is well aware of the view he is up against, and he calls it out: "The unfairness of this argument begins with the recasting of homosexuals as heterosexuals with perverse desires. The Torah is employed to support the idea that there is only one sexuality, heterosexuality."

This is Yaakov Levado's first major contribution. To burst the absurdity bubble: *"Of course there are homosexuals,"* he is saying, *"and I am one of them. Here is my story."*

This leads to the next major contribution of the article. Greenberg realizes that the only thing that can change the status quo would be for people to really get to know actual homosexuals face to face. As long as the matter remains theoretical, homosexuals are easy to write off. He makes this point most starkly in his description of how *poskim*, legal decisors, should deal with the question.

> There is no conclusive *psak halacha* (halachic ruling) without the hearing of personal testimonies, and so far gay people have not been asked to testify to their experience. How can halachists possibly rule responsibly on a matter so complex and so deeply foreign, without a sustained effort at understanding? Whatever the halachic argument will be, we will need to know much more about homosexuality to ensure that people are treated not merely as alien objects of a system but as persons within it. Halachists will need to include in their deliberations the testimony of gay people who wish to remain faithful to the Torah. ... one wonders what the impact might be if Orthodox rabbis had to face the questions posed by traditional Jews, persons they respect and to whom they feel responsible, who are gay.

This insight, that Halakhah will only begin to change once rabbis and communities are confronted with actual gay members, was likely the push for Greenberg to eventually help produce the documentary, *Trembling Before God.* This documentary, which simply tells the stories of various gay and lesbian Orthodox Jews, had a tremendous effect on the discourse. Real people are harder to ignore than theoretical constructs. (This is also one of the reasons why Greenberg's eventually coming out and shedding of his pseudonym were so important.)

I will add three more small, but key, points. First, as can be seen in the above quote, Greenberg understands that a stable solution will only come with halakhic language, with creative solutions accompanied by the concern for real people. This creative engagement can be seen, for example, in Rabbi Chaim Rapoport's 2004 *Judaism and Homosexuality,* a book that would have been impossible in the climate of 1993.

Second, Yaakov Levado's description of his personal community of like minded *frum* gay people led to the tremendously important step of creating an organization, Eshel, which would provide a support network for religious gay Jews, in 2010. (There were already groups for gay Jews in general, such as Nehirim founded in 2004, but Eshel took this into the *frum* community.)

Finally, Greenberg describes his "fantasy" community towards the end of the article. He does not envision the final step as gay shuls, but regular Orthodox shuls that are gay friendly, in which gay singles and coupled (nowadays married) gays can join as regular members and feel part of the community. This is exactly what the Orthodox world—at least the progressive Orthodox world—is struggling with now. Other matters are hardly (yet) on the horizon in the Orthodox world, such as ordination of gay rabbis or performance of gay marriages or even commitment ceremonies, but they likely will be. Whatever comes next, the confession of Yaakov Levado, with his bold opening statement, "I am an Orthodox rabbi, and I am gay," was a crucial orienting and unprecedented step for the Orthodox community.

11. Leonard Fein, "Smashing Idols and Other Prescriptions for Jewish Continuity"

Leonard Fein, "Smashing Idols and Other Prescriptions for Jewish Continuity," The Nathan Cummings Foundation, 1994

Dr. Leonard Fein (1934–2014) was Professor of Politics and Social Policy and Klutznick Professor of Contemporary Jewish Studies at Brandeis University, Founder of the National Jewish Coalition for Literacy, Co-Founder and Editor of *Moment Magazine*, and Founder of MAZON: A Jewish Response to Hunger.

Here were come upon a fourth generation in search of a rationale, of an ideology, of a reason to be and to do Jewish, and to it we offer instead Judaism as an act of spite—that is, as one version or another of the notion that so long as there are antisemites in the world, it would be dishonorable to abandon the Jewish ship.

In one version, this argument is cast in historic terms. Who are the Jews? We are the people who in this, the twentieth century, were hunted and hounded and hanged and slaughtered, we are the people with tattoos burnt into our forearms. What is all this talk of purpose? We have been bound together in fire. Following Fackenheim, we insist that we will not grant Hitler a posthumous victory, which amounts to saying that so long as there are antisemites in the world, we must remain Jews. Why not intermarry? Because of Auschwitz. Why not assimilate? Because too much Jewish blood has been spilled. We may march behind the Star of David, but it is the swastika that urges us on. Our vision is not of the end of days, but of the camps; our slogan is not a blessing, but a curse: "Never again!"

But "never again," for all its moral force, is at best a way of telling Jews what to avoid; it says nothing about what we are to embrace. It induces a Judaism that comes as a reaction to antisemitism, but is wholly lacking in any substantive pro-semitism. We stay in the Jewish room, but we stay there neither to pray together nor to play together; we stay there to sulk and to resist together. We stay there out of Jewish honor rather than Jewish conviction.

Lacking conviction, we pay the Anti-Defamation League to protect Jews and the Lubavitch movement to practice Judaism, thereby satisfying the claims of honor—but ignoring the claims of Jewish continuity, which, in an era of choice, requires conviction. Like Zionists who assert Israel's centrality but themselves choose to live at the the periphery, we become Jews who assert Judaism's merits—but only for others, not for ourselves. For our underlying motive is that there be Jews, not that we ourselves be among them. And so the mere advocacy of Jewish rights becomes the sum and substance of our Jewish praxis. ...

How do we begin to reshape the culture of community? For let there be no mistake: A community that sees itself (or large segments of which see themselves) as a community of purpose, as a community of intention rather than merely of coincidence or of fate, is a very different community from the one we now have.

COMMENTARY BY ARYEH COHEN

The coda to Leonard (Leibl) Fein's essay is the key to the whole. He writes:

> It is time to imagine and then invent a strategy for Jewish continuity that hinges more on the "how" of Judaism than on the "why" of it, a Judaism in which the "why" is immediately implied by the "how." It is time to build a community whose ways are a complete response to the question of why we should be, in which the home of Israel is not merely the place where when you have to go there, they have to take you in, but a place so magical and so nurturing and so satisfying and so ambitious and so purposeful that when the modern world hands you, as it does and as it will, a change of address card, you'll say, "No, thanks, this is not only where I belong, this is where I choose to stay. There are still idols to be smashed, there is still justice to be pursued, there is still mending to be done." (56)

This coda reminds me of the last paragraph of what I consider to be the finest of Emmanuel Levinas's so-called "Jewish" essays, "Cities of Refuge," in the collection *Beyond the Verse*. Here, Levinas writes that

> What is promised in Jerusalem, on the other hand, is a humanity of the Torah. It will have been able to surmount the deep contradictions of the cities of refuge: a new humanity that is better than a Temple. Our text, which began with the cities of refuge, reminds us or teaches us that the longing for Zion, that Zionism, is not one more nationalism or particularism; nor

is it a simple search for a place of refuge. It is the hope of a science of society, and of a society, which are wholly human. And this hope is to be found in Jerusalem, in the earthly Jerusalem, and not outside all places, in pious thoughts. (51–52)

Fein, the secular apostle, who often said that the God he didn't believe in handed Torah down to Israel at Sinai, and Levinas, the philosopher of the Other, whose transcendent theology, and theology of transcendence was not about God, but rather about the other person, seem to have sat at the same table in the back of the *shtibl*. Zionism for Levinas, in this passage though not necessarily everywhere, is not focused on the geographical locus of Jerusalem. Jerusalem itself is not a specific city but, rather, any city, any actual city—a city of people going about their lives inattentively, a city on whose streets homeless people sleep, homeless people whose faces we must look at and respond to. Our waking up and our response is the Zionism that will get us to the Heavenly Jerusalem that Levinas reads into a *sugya* in Tractate Makkot.

Similarly, Israel for Fein is the place in which there is "a community whose ways are a complete response to the question of why we should be." It is the place here, not there, where there are still idols to smash and justice to be done. Writing at a moment in which there was a lull in the ongoing struggle in Israel-Palestine, he misdiagnoses it as "the beginning of a very different time, an ordinary time. Suddenly, peace between Israel and its neighbors has been transformed into something more than a prayerful yearning; not speedily, to be sure, but yes, quite possibly in our time." (Looking back we realize how beautifully naïve this hopefulness was.) At that moment in which it might seem that the siren call of Jerusalem, of Zionism was most seductive, Fein powerfully turned his back and declared that Zion (my term, not his) is here. The telos is the creation of peace in this place. The early twentieth-century Yiddishist socialists called it *doikayt*. Jeremiah exhorted the exiles to "seek the welfare of the city to which I have exiled you and pray to the Lord in its behalf; for in its prosperity you shall prosper" (29:7).

Fein's visionary insight was not that the work of justice was Jewish work or work that Jews should do. This insight came first with the Eastern European Jewish immigrants to these shores; yes, obviously, the members of the International Ladies Garment Workers Union, and the martyrs of the Triangle Shirtwaist Factory fire; but also the sage of the Lower East Side Rabbi Moshe Feinstein—whose study hall was mere blocks from Abe Cahan's Yiddish *Forverts*, which preached the gospel of assimilation and survival—who declared that organizing workers and creating unions was obviously permitted.

Fein's insight was twofold. First, he was not panic-stricken by the prophets of doom who read the future in the National Jewish Population Survey and then dispersed money hither and yon in the service of "continuity." Jews were attracted to Judaism when they resonated with its mission.

Second, doing justice is central to the mission of Judaism. "We were taught and now we teach that the question of God is not a question of whether He is jealous or of whether He is a he or even of whether He exists, but of food and of work and of shelter, of love and fidelity and the capacity for wonder. ... *Judaism is a vocation; it is not the services we attend but the services we perform that define us*" (italics in original). The question of God is a question of justice. The Transcendent is the Other who is beyond my conceptual grasp and therefore can only be responded to in her vulnerability.

However, and this is essential to this point: the reason to do justice is not to attract the youth, not as a continuity program, but because it is right, because this is the answer to the question: "What does the Lord your God demand of you?"

This field of play, as limned by Fein twenty plus years ago, is still the field today.

We are shorn of the belief that peace will break out in Israel-Palestine anytime soon. Some of us are shorn of the belief that the Israeli government is interested in peace, or in an end to a more than fifty years' occupation and its attendant sins against human rights, sins against God. However, the centrality of the demand for justice—economic justice, racial justice, criminal justice reform, human and civil rights—to Judaism, especially among those who were not yet around to hear Fein's call, is no longer questioned.

The diasporist reflexes of those who grew up in the fifth decade of the Occupation, post 9/11, in the first decade of America's seemingly endless war in the Middle East, in the time of the first African-American president, are strong. They resonate to Fein's cry that "There are still idols to be smashed, there is still justice to be pursued, there is still mending to be done." They solidly agree that this is where Jerusalem is and might be rebuilt so that we can get to the Heavenly Jerusalem.

Fein saw the way forward in institution building:

> The creation of a service agency, a community consulting service, brought into being by all the world-menders and community-menders we can gather. Think of that aggregation of people, for now, as distributed over a normal curve, with the one tail encompassing people who are principally

devoted to the internal life of the community, the other tail composed of people whose principal activities are in the larger world. The key group is the center group, people equally comfortable in both worlds, equally committed to the repair of both.

In the past two decades, a large part of Fein's vision has been fulfilled. (Interestingly, it is his very original and still germane suggestions for internal *tikkun*, such as a community wide effort to guide divorce toward more ameliorative paths, or establishing community rules about who might be honored, which have not been advanced.) There is no one agency, but there is a collection of organizations such that there is a movement. (There is the Jewish Social Justice Roundtable, established in 2009, in which many, though not all, of the organizations of the movement sit, though each organization is independent, and there is disagreement on positions and tactics among the organizations.) More importantly, perhaps, the intellectual foundations of the movement have been articulated and inscribed in a growing bookshelf.

The argument for doing justice Jewishly includes Maimonides's understanding that the path of the philosopher is the path of the one who performs *hessed, mishpat u-tzedakah*, acts of kindness, justice, and righteousness (*Guide for the Perplexed* III:54); Heschel's claim: "What is an idol? Any god who is mine but not yours, any god concerned with me but not with you, is an idol" ("Religion and Race"); the rabbinic tradition's mythologization of God as the one who supports the poor, visits the sick, buries the dead, or who wiles away eternity in the dense distinctions which comprise the materiality of Jewish ethical practice; the Alter of Kelm's audacious claim that the prerequisite to receiving Torah is becoming one who acts out of radical empathy (Rabbi Simcha Zissel Ziv Broida, *Sefer Hokhmah u-Mussar*). *Tikkun olam* is no longer a catch-all substitute for an understanding of Jewish ethical commitments and obligations. There is a depth and breadth to the current writing in the field of Jewish social justice: responsa, broadsides, blogs, books both popular and academic, scholarly articles.

The question of scholarly indebtedness is always tricky. However, it is clear that Leibl Fein was one of the first to proudly embrace the idea of social justice as the reason for Jewish continuity and not the other way around.

12. Steven M. Cohen and Arnold M. Eisen, *The Jew Within: Self, Family, and Community in America*

Steven M. Cohen and Arnold M. Eisen, *The Jew Within: Self, Family, and Community in America*, Bloomington: Indiana University Press, 2000

Dr. Steven M. Cohen (1950–) served as Research Professor of Jewish Social Policy at Hebrew Union College-Jewish Institute of Religion and Director of the Berman Jewish Policy Archive at Stanford University.

Dr. Arnold M. Eisen (1951–) is Chancellor of the Jewish Theological Seminary in New York.

We can state with confidence that the quest for Jewish meaning is extremely important to our subjects, just as the search for meaning is important to contemporary Americans more generally (Bellah et al. 1996; Withnow 1994; Roof and McKinney 1987). Middle-range American Jews seek an abiding significance in their lives that goes beyond the activities of daily life and the limits of their own mortality. They readily discussed their highly personal searches for transcendent meaning, and confessed (to a degree that surprised us) to belief in God. Our subjects reported a strong desire to find a sense of direction and ultimate purpose, and the wish to find it largely or entirely in the framework of Jewish practices and beliefs. The fact that decisions concerning Judaism are inextricably wrapped up in the search for personal meaning to life is perhaps the reason that our subjects most often expressed their Judaism in the private sphere, where transcendent purpose is most readily discovered and located by contemporary Americans of whatever tradition. Judaism "happens" at home, with family or good friends. It transpires in it the place within the self given over to reflection, longing, faith, and doubt.

This development marks in several crucial respects a veering away from the modern story: the "grand narratives" of emancipation and enlightenment in which the rejection of religion has figured prominently. Far from leaving faith behind in favor of secular national or communal loyalties, as many of their parents and grandparents did, the Jews we interviewed are dissatisfied with secular affiliations and are in search of personal spiritual meaning. Where previous generations abandoned ritual practice almost entirely, believing it outdated or superstitious, Jews today are returning to ritual observance and making it a major locus of personal meaning. Avowed discontent with the disruptive and alienating aspects of modern life has led many of them to seek out religious communities that hold the promise of personal meaning as well as of enriched and enduring family relations. Finally, where the parents and grandparents of those we inter-viewed had in many cases lost faith in God and lost interest in all but the ethical and historical aspects of the Jewish tradition, moderately affiliated Jews today are not abandoning tradition but refashioning it. They have no wish to sacrifice the particularity of ethnic and religious loyalty in the name of America or humanity. (8)

The sovereign Jewish self, in its search for personal fulfillment, may turn out to be the stimulus for personal growth and fulfillment in a Jewish context and may even prove the stimulus of Jewish communal renewal and creativity as yet unimagined in America. Or—more likely, in our view—it will contribute to the dissolution of communal institutions and intergenerational commit-ment, thereby weakening the very sources of its own Jewish fulfillment and making them far less available to succeeding generations. (12)

COMMENTARY BY ALAN BRILL

During the 1990s, contemporary sociologists of religion Wade Clarke Roof and Robert Wuthnow documented how American religion had changed from long term commitments and congregational membership to a voluntary religion of seeking for meaning in life. They showed that for baby boomers, American reli-gion is now individualistic, focusing on personal journeys, spiritual moments, self-help, and the inner self.[1]

Steven M. Cohen and Arnold M. Eisen, a demographer and a historian of modern Jewish religion respectively, wrote an important work called *The Jew Within: Self, Family, and Community in America*, which addressed the Jewish community in light of the shift shown by these studies.

Cohen and Eisen indisputably show that that the American Jewish com-munity does indeed follow the trends of general American religious life. Their

---

1   Wade Clarke Roof, *A Generation of Seekers: The Spiritual Journeys of the Baby Boom Generation* (New York, HarperCollins, 1993); Robert Wuthnow, *After Heaven: Spirituality in America since the 1950s* (Berkeley: University of California Press, 1998).

work suggests that current American Jewish life is personal and freely chosen, based on powerful individual memories and experiences performed one individual at a time. Moreover, most baby boomers "view personal meaning as the arbiter of their Jewish involvement."

The Jew Within alternates between personal stories of how baby boomers live their lives based on personal choice and discussions of the values and tensions of this Judaism of personal meaning. The work shows the important role of nostalgia and memory as the basis for religious life. Experiences from childhood or adolescence figured prominently in personal religious decisions. The memory and ambivalence of family gatherings, conversations with grandparents, rites of passage, and youthful practices inform current decisions.

Judaism, as practiced in the United States, is a series of one-time experiences, personally constructed. Jews selectively borrow from diverse Jewish sources and freely mix culture and religion. Contemporary Judaism is also highly syncretic, freely and routinely combining Jewish elements with a variety of cultural tropes and non-Jewish religious or spiritual traditions. Finally, treating one's religion as one-time experiences allows one to be a perpetual seeker of meaning as one keeps changing one's direction, time and again.

Based on these results, Cohen and Eisen argue that one cannot understand Jewish life by one's organizational affiliations or charitable donations or synagogue visits. Rather, "only by hearing personal stories can one comprehend the Judaism wrapped up in those stories." The baby boomers define themselves far less by denominational boundaries (Reform, Conservative, Orthodox) or institutional loyalties (Hadassah, Jewish community centers, synagogues) and do not "center on concern for the State of Israel, and do not arise out of anxiety about anti-Semitism."

The Jew Within notes that for American Jews, their Judaism is simultaneously given from birth and a choice one makes "even if one chooses not to choose it." One's Jewish identity is a given and one does not become more Jewish by becoming more involved and one does not become less Jewish by not choosing any Jewish practice.

The people interviewed took the compatibility of being both Jewish and American for granted; and they are even less interested in denominational differences than their parents' generation was, insisting on the right of individual autonomy when it comes to deciding the details of Jewish practice. Spirituality is a felt concern; ritual and texts resonate with religious meanings that they view positively.

Cohen and Eisen conclude that Jewish life is entering the era characterized by the breakdown of a grand narrative of Jewish peoplehood into local narratives of personal stories of family and self. Significantly, they explain this breakdown as a particularistic story, rather than as part of a broader American trend. They present premodern, modern, and now the postmodern era of Jewish life. They present traditional premodern Jewish community as possessing a collective sense of divine duty. Modernity ruptured this sense of community, hence observance of Jewish ritual fell and ritual was adapted not to conflict with Western life.

In the United States, for the children of immigrants who took advantage of political and economic opportunities that promised unparalleled acceptance by the surrounding non-Jewish society, integration and Americanization were prime goals. Jews built an impressive array of communal institutions including synagogues and secular organizations. There was a modern Jewish "civil religion" which triumphed among Jews in this period, consisting of commitment to peoplehood and collective identification.

Cohen and Eisen see the current era as a breakdown of the commitment to the civil religion of Jewish communal life. This individualism is a challenge to the standard Jewish narrative that Judaism should be a communal commitment to continue a heritage of a people. This book became a clarion call to figure out how to return to the golden age of post-World War II collective Jewish identity, advocating the need to get American Jews to give up their individualism in favor a return to community.

Subsequent studies have shown that younger Jews, who are either Generation X or Millennials, have even fewer ties to Jewish organizations and define Judaism as entirely personal meaning.

The Jew Within received over two dozen major reviews, all of them seeking to return the genie back into the bottle. Many reviewers thought that the study is nothing to be positive about since it speaks of the decline of traditional values, while others opined that optimism would be entirely misplaced after such a report and that pessimism would be the more appropriate response. Some reviewers advocated a return to a commitment to community, a binding sense of covenant and a non-individualistic approach to ritual. Other reviewers simply considered the data and personal narratives another example of the narcissism and shallowness in American religion that was presented fifteen years prior by Robert Bellah.[2]

2　Robert Bellah et al., *Habits of the Heart: Individualism and Commitment in American Life* (Berkeley: University of California Press, 1985).

One young Reform thinker commented that "a 21st century Reform Judaism can no longer afford to have 'personal choice' as its core principle because it eclipses other more central Jewish values that are needed now more than ever. Rather, personal choice must be seen as a given and the starting point for a variety of commitments."

Several important theological reviews called for a return to a Divine perspective in which the God of history commands the Jew to keep the Torah. They considered this new approach as fundamentally being one's own god, an idolatry of self-veneration.

A more global reaction was to blame postmoderns for digging a hole to bury themselves and the community because people cannot each have their own interpretations and still maintain community.

Some Jewish organizational descriptions picked up Roof's phrase "spiritual marketplace" and proceeded to compare the Jewish choices made by today's Jew to the banal choices of the market, implying a degree of pampering and meaningless luxuries. However, according to Roof and Wuthnow, these religious choices reflect a sincere attempt to create meaningful lives.

Not one of the reviews of *The Jew Within* contextualized this change as part of changes in American religious life to understand that the Jewish community is only following broader trends as it has always done. For example, historian of American religion Martin Marty documented that American religion alternates between periods of institutional affiliation and individualism; Jewish life fits this broader cyclical pattern.[3]

Seven years after this book was published, the philosopher Charles Taylor wrote his seminal work describing the theological underpinnings of the new condition. The mid-twentieth century approach, in which individuals expressed themselves in collectives and institutions, no longer holds true in its original meaning. Religion is functional as a source of individualized meanings and moral orders.[4]

Religion today, Taylor argues, can be found in "the continuing multiplication of new options, religious, spiritual, and anti-religious, which individuals seize on in order to make sense of their lives." Taylor stresses the complex ways in which religion is now even more a part of our daily lives, and the importance of a multiplicity of textual interpretations to deal with this variety.

---

3   Martin Marty, *Modern American Religion* (Chicago: University of Chicago Press, 1986–1996).
4   Charles Taylor, *A Secular Age* (Cambridge: Harvard University Press, 2007).

According to Taylor, we live in a postsecular age, in which religious functions are now found in our ordinary lives of work, family, education, and philanthropy. We are concerned with fullness of life and a healthy flourishing existence, based on a social image and intuition of a flourishing life. Taylor notes, that we especially use religion for our ethical motivation, our sense of *tikkun olam* (his term).

I used to teach *The Jew Within* as part of contemporary Jewish thought because it documents the movement away from the Jewish thinkers of the twentieth century and offers an opening to discuss the wider social changes.

However, I no longer assign the work. In the time since I first wrote this essay, women have come forward to reveal Cohen's long history of sexual harassment, sexual assault, and abuse of power spanning several decades. In addition, in Cohen's later work, when he has attempted to address these social changes, he has ignored examples of cultural renewal and creativity and instead obsessed over the age at which Jewish women marry and how many children they have as the key to communal survival.

Nevertheless, the negative reaction to the description of American Jewish life presented in *The Jew Within* is indicative of a much broader truth. The older models for conceptualizing Judaism fail to accurately describe our contemporary Jewish communities. In light of the reality described by *The Jew Within* and conceptualized by Taylor and others, we needed to reframe our understanding of Judaism in the current decades.

13. A. B. Yehoshua, "The Meaning of Homeland"

A. B. Yehoshua, "The Meaning of Homeland," in Steven Bayme, Leonard J. Fein, Samuel G. Freedman, Eric Yoffie, "The A.B. Yehoshua Controversy: An Israeli-Diaspora Dialogue on Jewishness, Israeliness, and Identity," American Jewish Committee (AJC), August 2006

A. B. Yehoshua (1936–) is a novelist, essayist, and playwright.

What I sought to explain to my American hosts, in overly blunt and harsh language perhaps, is that, for me, Jewish values are not located in a fancy spice box that is only opened to release its pleasing fragrance on Shabbat and holidays, but in the daily reality of dozens of problems through which Jewish values are shaped and defined, for better or worse. A religious Israeli Jew also deals with a depth and breadth of life issues that is incomparably larger and more substantial than those with which his religious counterpart in New York or Antwerp must contend.

Am I denouncing their incomplete identity? I am neither denouncing nor praising. It's just a fact that requires no legitimating from me, just as my identity requires no legitimating from them. But since we see ourselves as belonging to one people, and since the two identities are interconnected, and flow into one another, the relation between them must be well clarified.

As long as it is clear to all of us that Israeli Jewish identity deals, for better or worse, with the full spectrum of the reality and that Diaspora Jewry deals only with parts of it, then at least the difference between whole and part is acknowledged. But the moment that Jews insist that involvement in the study and interpretation of texts, or in the organized activity of Jewish institutions, are equal to the totality of the social and political and economic reality that we in Israel are contending with—not only does the moral significance of the historic Jewish grappling with a total reality lose its validity, there is also the easy and convenient option of a constant flow from the whole to the partial.

COMMENTARY BY JAMES LOEFFLER

My favorite description of diasporic Jewish identity dates from the first century. In the year 38, the Jews in the city of Alexandria suffered a terrible outbreak of anti-Jewish violence. In the aftermath, the Greek Jewish philosopher Philo responded with a spirited defense of Jewish life in the Diaspora: "For so populous are the Jews that no one country can hold them, and for that reason they settle in the most populous and most prosperous cities in Europe and Asia," he wrote, "and while they believe the sacred city [of Jerusalem], where the Holy Temple of the Most High God is established, to be their mother-city, yet they consider the various cities which they have inhabited from the time of their fathers and grandfathers and great-grandfathers and ancestors still farther back, where they were born and reared, to be their fatherlands." Even in the worst of times, Philo argued, life in the Diaspora should be understood as a permanent home, not temporary exile. Generations of Jewish life had left Jews rooted in cities and countries around the world without compromising the central place of the Land of Israel in their hearts and minds.

Philo might just as easily have been speaking for modern American Jews. Here too Jews proudly celebrate their dual birthright of diasporic fatherland and Jewish motherland. American Jews routinely insist that the two complement one another in harmonious fashion. And just like Philo, they react with alarm when someone, whether friend or foe, questions the legitimacy of their diaspora.

That is precisely what happened in the spring of 2006, when the distinguished Israeli writer A. B. Yehoshua launched a polemic that would have made Philo rush for his quill. The occasion was the 100th anniversary celebration of the founding of the American Jewish Committee. The venerable communal organization, founded in New York in 1906 to combat anti-Semitism and defend vulnerable Jewish communities around the world, hosted the Israeli author for a panel at the Library of Congress together with Cynthia Ozick, Rabbi Adin Steinsaltz, and Leon Wieseltier, with Ted Koppel moderating. The assigned topic was the suitably weighty question: "What Will Become of the Jewish People?" In a set of highly emotional extemporaneous remarks, Yehoshua angrily eviscerated American Jewish ignorance, passivity, self-indulgence, and self-delusion. Diaspora Jews were engaged in a mental game of merely "playing with Jewishness," like an ethnic costume dress, while Israeli Jews were the real Jews. "[Being] Israeli is my skin," he proclaimed, "it's not my jacket. You are changing jackets—from Argentina you take your jacket to Brazil, from Brazil ... to America, from there, there, and then you're moving. You are changing countries like the Jews have done all the time, changing countries like changing jackets."

Not content to dismiss American Jews as inauthentic imposters, he continued by blaming American Jews for anti-Semitism. As he explained, American

Jews "play all the time with the pathological interaction with the anti-Semite, what he thinks about you, what he speaks about you." Yet all that loud worrying about anti-Semitism came a little too late. He suggested that had American Jews seized the chance to immigrate in large numbers to British Mandatory Palestine after 1917, a Jewish state could have been established before World War II, saving at least some of the millions of Jews trapped in Europe. No amount of European or American Jewish Nobel prizes or contemporary vigilance about anti-Semitism should obscure what he called that "very big failure" to avert the catastrophic scale of the Holocaust.

Having thus savaged the American Jewish past and present, Yehoshua saved his harshest words for the subject of the American Jewish future. "If ... in 100 years Israel will exist and ... I will come to the Diaspora [and] there will not be [any] Jews, I would say it's normal. I will not cry for it," he declared. By contrast, if Israel should disappear, no Diaspora life could possibly replace it. "There is no alternative to be a post-Zionist Jew," content to live without Israel. By implication, such an outcome would spell the end of Jewish history.

An explosive controversy ensued. American Jews, who rarely agree on much, reached a quick consensus that the Israeli writer had deeply insulted both their American honor and their Jewish dignity. Many Israeli leaders and commentators joined the chorus of criticism. Contrarian voices from Israel and the United States praised Yehoshua's candor, if not his intemperate tone. He, in turn, responded with a half-apology published in *Haaretz*, in which he justified his critique as tough talk from a cranky but honest relative. Israeli Jews lived in "a binding and inescapable relationship with one another," thanks to their homeland and national language. By contrast, American Jews possessed an optional, "incomplete identity." The American Jewish fixation on religious meaning could hardly substitute for the existential character of Jewishness in a Jewish country: "What I sought to explain to my American hosts, in overly blunt and harsh language perhaps, is that, for me, Jewish values are not located in a fancy spice box that is only opened to release its pleasing fragrance on Shabbat and holidays, but in the daily reality of dozens of problems through which Jewish values are shaped and defined, for better or worse."

Yehoshua's fiery bromide stands as a contemporary reformulation of one strain of classic Zionist thought, associated with thinkers such as Yosef Haim Brenner and Micha Josef Berdyczewski, that sees the Negation of the Exile as a fundamental aspiration of the Jewish return to national sovereignty in the historic Land of Israel. Harsh as his words were, Yehoshua is not alone in believing that Jewish Diaspora is a relic destined to be transcended through immigration to the State of Israel. However hyperbolic, his challenge is also the extreme version of a longstanding trope of American Jewish self-critique. Commentators have long decried the complacency of American Jews, who subscribe to a myth of exceptionalism, whereby individual Jewish self-realization requires few hard choices about identity, language, education, or other forms of thick collective responsibility and commitment.

At the same time, I would suggest, Yehoshua's diatribe betrays his own profound insecurity about the Israeli Jewish future and the meaning of Zionism in Jewish history. That is, in arguing about American Jewish failings, Yehoshua reveals just how much he relies on the Diaspora to define the content of his Israeli Jewish identity.

The most obvious place where Yehoshua projects Israeli fears and doubts onto his American brethren is in his strangely counter-factual account of the Holocaust. The charge that mass *aliyah* by American Jews in the 1920s would have stopped the Holocaust and/or the Arab-Israeli conflict is based on a willful misreading of the basic facts of twentieth-century Jewish history. There is no reason to believe that large-scale Jewish immigration of the kind Yehoshua suggests would have been permitted by the British authorities even in the 1920s. The British were concerned about Arab-Jewish demographic relations from the outset. Nor, is it at all clear this would have led to a Jewish nation-state before the Holocaust. Furthermore, as Yehoshua reproaches American Jews for not migrating in this era, he ignores the fact that the largest Jewish community at the time was not in the United States but in Eastern Europe, particularly Poland. In truth, the mass migration of Jews to the United States around the turn of the twentieth century gave rise to a political mobilization that made possible both the Balfour Declaration in 1917 and the State of Israel in 1948. In short, Israel could not have come into existence as it did without American Jews.

What explains Yehoshua's historical fantasy? The answer lies in his critique of the American Jewish obsession with meaning. Yehoshua mocks American Jews for their obsession with religious identity and ethnic heritage, which he says cannot compete with the power of language and nationhood. But in discussing the Holocaust, he laments not the death of millions of Jews, but the fact that millions of Jews died *for no reason.* "If there was a state" before the Holocaust, Yehoshua remarks, "when the big wave of fascism and Nazism was entering Europe we could [have] defended ourselves totally differently. We would [have] die[d] for something. We would [have] die[d] for the territory." Elsewhere, he repeats this peculiar lament. The tragedy of the Holocaust was that the Jewish people lost "a third of its members for nothing—not for territory, not for religion, not for money, not for ideology." In fact, Jews died during the Holocaust for all of those reasons and for none. Some fought the Nazis as Zionists, others as Bundists, still others as rabbis. But all who died, died as Jews. Yehoshua craves more meaning, a larger meaning, from the Jewish past. Yet he seems uncertain about the content of that meaning.

Yehoshua returns to this theme of meaning in his *Haaretz* postscript, appropriately titled "The Meaning of Homeland." There, after dismissing the American Jewish impulse to find Jewish meaning in texts and rituals, religion and culture, he boasts of how Israeli Jewish life is "immeasurably fuller and broader and more meaningful than the Jewishness of an American Jew." Yet it turns out that what unnerves him most is the lessening place of "the meaning of Zionism" in the lives of American Jews. Throughout his remarks and afterword he expresses a palpable insecurity that Israel without American Jews will some-how lose its *own meaning*. In "The Meaning of Homeland," he admits that what originally piqued his anger was the fact that no one at the Washington event sufficiently acknowledged the coincidence that it was happening on the eve of Israel's Memorial Day. These together suggested that "that the deep and natu-ral identification that a large portion of American Jewry once felt with Israeli life has been steadily and seriously weakening in recent years." He worries that, "You are not coming anymore, or you are coming very few. There is not Aliyah ... you will find your Jewishness reading another book of history and going to synagogue."

Why is this bad? Because, Yehoshua writes, he sees a black-and-white choice between nurturing the "concrete and living value of 'the homeland,' rather than the dull and worn-out value of Jewish spirituality." It is as if the American Jewish choice of spiritual and cultural renewal somehow invalidates the narrower Israeli narrative of meaning through land. If American Jews do not visit and do not immigrate, he worries, Israeli Jews will suffer, too. That is why, at the end of the essay, he writes, "If we don't want this kind of Jewish mindset (with the help of our Palestinian rivals for the homeland) to pull the rug out from under our feet, we ought to reiterate the basic, old concepts to Israelis just as much as to American Jews." Though he denies it, Yehoshua's remarks sug-gest how he needs American Jews to validate his own Israeli Zionism—and to assuage his fears that Israel itself might disappear one day.

Dichotomies are helpful. They allow us to clarify what we are and what we are not. But they also represent artificial exercises in imposing a comfort-ing binary order on a messy world. Throughout history, Jewish communi-ties have always defined themselves through debates about their differences.

Those arguments over Diaspora and Zion do reflect real, profound differences. Yet they also betray an ongoing story of mutual interaction. For in truth, Jewish interdependence is a signal characteristic of Jewish life, then and now. Yehoshua concedes as much in a postlude. "The debate between us is a basic one that goes to the root of things," he writes, "but we are one people, and I have never ceased to stress this cardinal principle."

14. Elliot N. Dorff, Daniel S. Nevins, and Avram I. Reisner, "Homosexuality, Human Dignity and Halakhah: A Combined Responsum for the Committee on Jewish Law and Standards"

Elliot N. Dorff, Daniel S. Nevins, and Avram I. Reisner, "Homosexuality, Human Dignity and Halakhah: A Combined Responsum for the Committee on Jewish Law and Standards," December 2006[1]

Rabbi Elliot Dorff (1943–) is Professor of Jewish Theology at the American Jewish University in Los Angeles, California.

Rabbi Daniel Nevins (1966–) is Pearl Resnick Dean of The Rabbinical School and Dean of the Division of Religious Leadership for JTS.

Rabbi Dr. Avram Reisner (1952–) is Rabbi Emeritus of Chevrei Tzedek Congregation in Baltimore, Maryland.

The halakhic status quo is deeply degrading to gay and lesbian Jews. Quite apart from social and literary trends that have taught contempt for homosexuals, legal norms that either ignore them or cruelly demand the absolute suppression of their libido create an environment of humiliation. At this point it is impossible for responsible poskim to ignore this dynamic. (9)

We are concerned for the dignity of gay and lesbian Jews not only because we are sympathetic to their dilemma, but also because their humiliation is our humiliation. We wish to welcome them, but we do so in such a forbidding fashion that they are repeatedly humiliated. Looking at our own congregations, we too are embarrassed by our cold welcome. For example, a gay man told us of going to minyan to say kaddish during shloshim for his father. The rabbi prevented him from leading services because he was gay, and then showed him an entire list of "leadership activities" from which he was banned

---

1   Available for download at http://www.rabbinicalassembly.org/sites/default/files/public/halakhah/teshuvot/20052010/dorff_nevins_reisner_dignity.pdf.

based on that rabbi's interpretation of the CJLS's [Committee on Jewish Law and Standards] 1992 consensus statement. This humiliation was experienced not only by an individual, but by an entire congregation. When gay and lesbian Jews are finally welcomed to take their rightful places in our community, then we will have safeguarded their dignity as individuals, and our dignity as a community.

It is difficult to imagine a group of Jews whose dignity is more undermined than that of homosexuals, who have to date been told to hide and suppress their sexual orientation, and whose desire to establish a long-term relationship with a beloved friend have been lightly dismissed by Jewish and general society. They have, in effect, been told to walk alone, while the great majority of Jews are expected to walk in pairs and as families. In such a context, where is the dignity of homosexual Jews? How can we hide from their humiliation? What halakhic recourse is available to integrate gay and lesbian Jews into the observant community with full dignity? (16)

COMMENTARY BY JANE KANAREK

On December 6, 2006, the Committee on Jewish Law and Standards of the Rabbinical Assembly (CJLS) approved a responsum entitled "Homosexuality, Human Dignity, and Halakhah: A Combined Responsum for the Committee on Jewish Law and Standards." Jointly authored by rabbis Elliot N. Dorff, Daniel S. Nevins, and Avram I. Reisner, this responsum sought to effectively normalize the status of gay and lesbian Jews within the Conservative Movement. In evaluating rabbinic concepts of sexual norms and human dignity, the authors argued for the importance of stable, committed relationships for homosexual Jews as much as for heterosexual Jews. The authors argued that the halakhic principle of human dignity could supersede rabbinic level prohibitions on same-sex intimacy, leaving only an explicit ban on anal sex between men. Crucially, Dorff, Nevins and Reisner advocated for the admission of openly gay and lesbian Jews into the Movement's professional schools and associations. As a result of this responsum, on March 26, 2007, the Jewish Theological Seminary of America decided, for the first time, to open its doors to openly gay rabbinical and cantorial students.

The approval of "Homosexuality, Human Dignity, and Halakhah" was the culmination of a years-long process of study and discussion and was not without controversy. Indeed, while Dorff, Nevins, and Reisner's responsum was approved by a vote of thirteen in favor and twelve against, another responsum, "Homosexuality Revisited," by Rabbi Joel Roth was approved by the same number of votes, thirteen, with only eight opposing (four members of the CJLS abstained). In contrast to Dorff, Nevins, and Reisner, Roth argued for maintaining the status quo, welcoming openly gay and lesbian Jews into the Movement's congregations but prohibiting all same-sex sexual intimacy and continuing a ban on admission into the Movement's clergy schools. Additionally, the Committee published an important dissenting paper, "דרוש וקבל שכר: Halakhic and Metahalakhic Arguments Concerning Judaism and Homosexuality," by Rabbi Gordon Tucker. Tucker argued that Jews living sexual lives with same-sex partners, "should be considered subject to the same obligations and entitled to the same rights as those whose sexual lives are with members of the opposite sex." However, Tucker designated his paper not only as a responsum but also as an essay on legal theory and more specifically methodologies for deciding Halakhah. These three works on the status of gays and lesbians thus provide us with an important lens for understanding not only the issue at hand—the status of gay and lesbian Jews—but also the role of law and legal theory and the place of the CJLS within the Conservative Movement.

The CJLS sets halakhic (legal) policy for the Conservative Movement and the membership of the Rabbinical Assembly, the international association of Conservative/Masorti rabbis. Its procedures can best be understood as operating under a modified and non-authoritarian majoritarianism. It is a modified majoritarianism because a responsum becomes an official position when it receives a minimum of six favorable votes. It is non-authoritarian in that individual rabbis are not mandated to accept the rulings of the CJLS; rabbis are asked to consider the decisions of the CJLS, but they are not required to accept them. Further, this type of majoritarianism means that responsa with diametrically opposed positions can both become official positions of the Conservative Movement. Indeed, the two approved *teshuvot* on homosexuality came to opposite conclusions, with Roth maintaining the status quo of a second-class status for Jews in same-sex relationships and Dorff, Nevins, and Reisner arguing for the full integration of gays and lesbians into the Conservative Movement. On the one hand, this outcome is ethically problematic: how can one Movement simultaneously exclude and include? On the other hand, at its best, the ability of the CJLS to accept multiple answers speaks to an implicit theological recognition of the indeterminacy of human knowledge. While multiple legal answers may result in less ideological coherence, they also open up the possibility for more experimentation within the legal order and thus the development of a new legal consensus.

Indeed, not only does the CJLS accept multiple and conflicting positions on one halakhic question, but these positions often reflect different legal philosophies, that is, theories of how best to decide a legal question. This divergence in legal philosophy is strikingly reflected in these three CJLS papers on homosexuality. Dorff, Nevins, and Reisner operate in what I would term a values-based jurisprudence. That is, they argue that values can have normative consequences in rabbinic law and, where appropriate, should be utilized in the decision-making process. In the case of same-sex relationships, these three rabbis contend, "that the permanent social and sexual loneliness mandated by halakhic precedent for homosexuals undermines their human dignity." The authors acknowledge that established Halakhah comprehensively bans sexual intimacy between males. However, they argue that the core biblical prohibition is only against anal intercourse between males; other prohibitions are rabbinic decrees that create a preventative fence around this central prohibition. Because rabbinic law does not value celibacy and does value sexual intimacy in the context of a committed relationship, maintaining the rabbinic ban on homosexual intimacy would violate another rabbinic value: that of human dignity (*kavod ha-briyot*). Because homosexuality is innate, dignity demands that Jews be able to live a life of *mitzvot* (commandments) within the context of a same-sex relationship. Citing numerous cases where halakhic decisors translate *kavod ha-briyot* into normative practice, the authors argue that *kavod ha-briyot* supersedes rabbinic (but not biblical) decrees. In this case, that means that while anal intercourse remains prohibited, all other forms of sexual intimacy are permitted to same-sex couples. The authors thus argue that when values are viewed as holding normative force, a legal pathway does exist within established Halakhah for recognizing the dignity of same-sex relationships.

In contrast to the methodology of Dorff, Nevins, and Reisner, Roth takes a positivist approach to law, an approach that posits law as growing out of basic norms from which legal pathways are then derived. Positivism is also characterized by the separation of law and morality, arguing that a law, once legislated, is law regardless of whether or not it is a moral law. Roth's *teshuvah*, removed as it is from the actual experiences of gays and lesbians, and filled with detailed, explicit, and technical language is best understood in this context. Arguing that there is no derivational legal pathway towards the normalization of same-sex sexual intimacy, Roth maintains the ban. Reading Roth's *teshuvah* involves stepping into a closed discourse of a world of legal certainties.

Tucker's dissenting paper called for a more expansive model of halakhic decision making, one that included the particular issue of same-sex relationships but also reached beyond it. Tucker argued that legal positivism, with its systemic certainties and search for stability, is a useful legal philosophy in the large majority of cases, that is, those that are easy or ordinary. However, positivist modes of decision making fail in cases where systemic precedents are absent and do not accord with the personal experiences and narratives of both individuals and the larger community. Such, Tucker contended, is the situation with gay and lesbian Jews. Drawing on the work of the legal theorist Robert Cover, Tucker argued for a vision of halakhic methodology—Halakhah with a capital "H"—that gives legal standing to formative aggadic or narrative texts. These aggadic texts are represented by older textual traditions and also generated through the actions of committed communities. In the case of gay and lesbian Jews, Tucker advocated a merging of Halakhah and Aggadah that recognizes personal narratives of more than one human sexuality along with midrashic narratives of God's empathy.

As an indication of Conservative Judaism's commitment to multiple opinions, all three of these works are available on the website of the Rabbinical Assembly. Yet, indicative of the limits of that pluralism, the *teshuvot* of Roth and Dorff, Nevins, and Reisner are accepted positions of the Movement while that of Tucker is not. Perhaps more important for the Movement, though, is the effect of these papers. While Roth's *teshuvah* remains an official position of the CJLS, the *teshuvah* of Dorff, Nevins, and Reisner became determinative for the Movement's future. While not proposing an opening of the halakhic toolbox as expansive as that of Tucker, the work of Dorff, Nevins, and Reisner has had a transformative influence on the nature of the Conservative Judaism. In proposing that values have normative force and must be taken into account when deciding law, the *teshuvah* of Dorff, Nevins, and Reisner opened the door to the narratives of gay and lesbian Jews, bringing them into the center of a key conversation: how a Jew continues to observe Jewish law in a modern context.

Following this CJLS decision, the North American rabbinical schools of the Jewish Theological Seminary and Ziegler welcomed gay and lesbian students; the Schechter Rabbinical Seminary in Jerusalem followed in 2011. The Rabbinical and Cantorial Assemblies began welcoming openly gay members. Perhaps more significantly, liturgies for gay marriage and divorce were adopted in 2012, even prior to the United States Supreme Court's decision striking down the Defense of Marriage Act in 2013. Indeed, the Conservative Movement submitted amicus curiae briefs in support of this change, and the majority opinion of the Supreme Court used similar arguments based on human dignity to justify the rights of gay couples to marry. The CJLS decisions were thus not restricted to the internal context of Conservative Judaism but were embedded in a larger social and legal discourses about justice and human dignity.

15. Noah Feldman, "Orthodox Paradox"

Jay Lefkowitz, "The Rise of Social Orthodoxy: A Personal Account"

Noah Feldman "Orthodox Paradox," *New York Times*, July 22, 2007

Noah Feldman (1970–) is Felix Frankfurter Professor of Law at Harvard Law School and Senior Fellow of the Society of Fellows at Harvard.

My own personal lesson in nonrecognition is just one small symptom of the challenge of reconciling the vastly disparate values of tradition and modernity—of Slobodka and St. Paul's. In premodern Europe, where the state gave the Jewish community the power to enforce its own rules of membership through coercive force, excommunication literally divested its victim of his legal personality, of his rights and standing in the community. The modern liberal state, though, neither polices nor delegates the power to police religious membership; that is now a social matter, not a legal one. Today a religious community that seeks to preserve its traditional structure must maintain its boundaries using whatever independent means it can muster—right down to the selective editing of alumni newsletters.

Despite my intimate understanding of the mind-set that requires such careful attention to who is in and who is out, I am still somehow taken by surprise each time I am confronted with my old school's inability to treat me like any other graduate. I have tried in my own imperfect way to live up to values that the school taught me, expressing my respect and love for the wisdom of the tradition while trying to reconcile Jewish faith with scholarship and engagement in the public sphere. As a result, I have not felt myself to have rejected my upbringing, even when some others imagine me to have done so by virtue of my marriage.

Some part of me still expects—against the judgment of experience—that the individual human beings who make up the institution and community where I spent so many years of my life will put our long-standing friendships ahead of the imperative to define boundaries. The school did educate me and influence me deeply. What I learned there informs every part of my inner life. In the sense of shared history and formation, I remain of the community even while no longer fully in the community.

If this is dissonance, it is at least dissonance that the modern Orthodox should be able to understand: the desire to inhabit multiple worlds simultaneously and to defy contradiction with coexistence. After all, the school's attempt to bring the ideals of Orthodox Judaism into dialogue with a certain slice of late-twentieth-century American life was in many ways fantastically rich and productive. For those of us willing to accept a bit of both worlds, I would say, it almost worked.

Jay Lefkowitz, "The Rise of Social Orthodoxy: A Personal Account," *Commentary*, April 1, 2014

Jay Lefkowitz (1962–) is Senior Partner at Kirkland & Ellis LLP and Adjunct Professor at Columbia Law School.

Social Orthodox Jews fully embrace Jewish culture and Jewish community. And they are committed to the survival of the Jewish people. Indeed, that is their raison d'être. Furthermore, because religious practice is an essential component of Jewish continuity, Social Orthodox Jews are observant—and not because they are trembling before God.

As for me: I start my day each morning by donning my tefillin before heading to my office at a law firm. I eat out in restaurants several times a month only to pass up 90 percent of the menu in favor of vegetarian fare because I keep kosher. I occasionally find myself stuck in cities on a Friday far from home because I cannot travel back to New York City in time for the arrival of the Sabbath. I go to synagogue each week and celebrate all the Jewish holidays. My children attend a Modern Orthodox day school, and my college-age daughter served as a soldier in the Israeli army. And I am proud to be a Zionist. Unless one were to look very carefully, I would appear to be the very model of an Orthodox Jew, albeit a modern one. But I also pick and choose from the menu of Jewish rituals without fear of divine retribution. And I root my identity much more in Jewish culture, history, and nationality than in faith and commandments. I am a Social Orthodox Jew, and I am not alone.

COMMENTARY BY ELLI FISCHER

In his influential essay "Orthodox Paradox," Noah Feldman describes how he found confirmation that his alma mater had deliberately edited him and his non-Jewish then-girlfriend out of the class's tenth anniversary reunion photo that appeared in its alumni newsletter: "I bumped into the photographer, in synagogue, on Yom Kippur ... his pained expression told me what I already knew. 'It wasn't me,' he said."

In his essay, Feldman uses the tale of his exclusion from the school publication and other examples from his schooling at the Maimonides School in Brookline, Mass to make the case that Modern Orthodoxy's attempt to achieve "consilience of faith and modernity" ultimately falls short of its goal. When push comes to shove, he contends, Modern Orthodoxy, despite its engagement with the modern world, still fails to "normalize the observance of traditional Jewish law." Feldman primarily addresses two areas in which Modern Orthodoxy has not managed to reconcile tradition and modernity: sexuality and the treatment of non-Jews—two areas that converge in his exogamous relationship and eventual marriage. His school's non-recognition of his most important life decisions is a vestige of excommunication, a way to demarcate communal boundaries that leaves him and his non-Jewish spouse on the outside. He thus concludes that the synthesis of Orthodoxy and modernity remains aspirational, that is, that Modern Orthodoxy is not really modern.

The configuration known as "Modern Orthodoxy" seeks to integrate complete observance of Jewish law with full participation in American life and culture. A century ago, it was extraordinarily difficult to find employers willing to accommodate Sabbath observance; the "Modern Orthodox" ideal seemed far away indeed. By now, as Feldman notes, a major party has nominated a Sabbath-observant Jew for the Vice Presidency of the United States.

Nevertheless, throughout that century, the "modern" and the "Orthodox" seemed to be on a non-convergent path. To be Orthodox, one had to give up less and less "modernity," and vice versa. Feldman's point is that this convergence is not asymptotic; there are certain fundamental and irreducible differences between Orthodox Judaism and modern sensibilities.

Orthodox opposition to same-sex marriage seems to confirm Feldman's thesis. As Facebook profile pictures across the globe turned rainbow colors to celebrate Obergefell v. Hodges in 2015, the Orthodox Union issued a statement condemning homosexuality and calling upon principles of religious liberty as a justification for Orthodox rabbis to refuse to marry gay couples. Orthodoxy thus became part of America's conservative counterculture. The Supreme Court decision represented a major milestone in the normalization of homosexuality. Yet Orthodoxy privileges heterosexuality and considers homosexual relations sinful. Inclusiveness and tolerance of homosexuals within Orthodox communities are attainable, and indeed, great strides have been made toward those goals. As the statement from the OU indicates, however, normalization, however, is incompatible with Orthodox Judaism. Thus, even if Feldman overplays his hand in some respects—school newsletters are, after all, carefully curated documents that project how the school wants to be seen by parents and donors and not objective sources of news—he is correct in his diagnosis of the ultimate incompatibility of Orthodoxy and modern sensibilities.

But there is another side of the "Orthodox Paradox" that Feldman does not address. Let us return to his Yom Kippur meeting with the school photographer. Feldman does not identify the synagogue for his readers, but would they be surprised if it turned out to be Orthodox? The presence of Jews who are far from Orthodox doctrine and practice in Orthodox synagogues is increasing. Chabad, where the gap between the movement's doctrine and practice and the practices and beliefs of rank-and-file worshippers is perhaps greatest, has met with phenomenal success during the past decades. And Chabad is not alone. So how does one account for the increasing presence of those who are Orthodox in neither belief nor practice in the pews of Orthodox synagogues?

In truth, outside of Anglophone North America, and even within it until the post-World War II decades, non-practicing and often non-believing Orthodoxy is the prevalent mode of Jewish religion. (For several historical reasons, Jewish denominationalism only caught on in a handful of countries, and almost always those with strong Protestant traditions.) In this configuration, synagogue rabbis and perhaps other clergy members are expected to uphold Orthodoxy in creed and deed, while the membership reflects a broad spectrum of observance and belief. A façade of observance is maintained within the synagogue: the sexes remain separate, only kosher food is served, and the parking lot remains closed on the Sabbath. Non-observant members who drive can park nearby and walk the rest of the way. The liturgy continues to reflect theological beliefs that many congregants would find problematic, to say the least, should they stop to think about it.

At first glance, it would seem that the wide gap between synagogue lip-service and actual belief and behavior is likely to produce dissonance amongst congregants and clergy alike. And indeed, for Jews raised in nominally Orthodox homes who came of age in the United States during the decades after World War II, nonobservance by Orthodox standards often led to affiliation with the Reform or Conservative denominations as they raised their own families.

A small chart in the 2014 Pew Research Center Study of American Jews indicates that this trend is changing, that is, that Orthodox-raised Jews are increasingly likely to continue affiliating or identifying (Pew, unfortunately, makes no distinction between these two terms) with Orthodoxy, and are increasingly less likely to join non-Orthodox denominations.

Orthodox Retention, by Age

	Among those raised as Orthodox Jews by religion who are now age...			
	18–29	30–49	50–64	65+
% who are currently...	%	%	%	%
Orthodox Jews by religion	83	57	41	22
Conservative Jews by religion	1	9	17	29
Reform Jews by religion	0	7	7	23
Jews by religion – other denom.	0	1	3	6
Jews by religion – no denom.	3	22	11	9
Jews of no religion	6	4	4	6
Not Jewish	7	*	17	4
	100	100	100	100

Source: Pew Research Center 2013 Survey of U.S. Jews, Feb. 20–June 13, 2013. Figures may not sum to 100% due to rounding.
PEW RESEARCH CENTER

Much has been written about the top line of this graphic, which shows a linear and dramatic increase of Orthodox retention from the Silent Generation to the Millennials. As the survey notes, it is possible that this does not represent a generational shift, but a steady attrition rate from Orthodoxy across ages. Still, it is difficult to believe that one fifth of dropouts from Orthodoxy make the leap as senior citizens.

The more interesting—even astounding—data appears below the top line, which quantifies not how many Jews leave Orthodoxy, but where they go. Almost three-fifths of Jews from the Silent Generation raised in Orthodox homes stopped identifying as Orthodox Jews. By Generation X, that ratio had shrunk to about one-sixth. Among Millennials, it has all but disappeared. This trend passes the eye test as well: I was the Orthodox rabbi at a university popular among graduates of Orthodox day schools, and I know hundreds of people who dropped Orthodox observance and/or belief. Very few identify or affiliate with other denominations. The shrinking ranks of Conservative Judaism have been the subject of much analysis and discussion, yet a primary factor has been all but ignored: in previous generations, Conservative Judaism benefited significantly from Orthodox attrition. That is no longer the case.

Jay Lefkowitz explains the attraction of Orthodoxy for those who practice its tenets but do not accept its theological premises in his "The Rise of Social

Orthodoxy: A Personal Account." Feldman contends that Modern Orthodoxy, as a religious configuration, is not truly "modern"; Lefkowitz seeks to obviate this concern when he posits: that "if unwavering acceptance of the Torah as divine is the precondition for Orthodoxy, then the term 'Modern Orthodox' may well be a misnomer for many Jews who identify as Modern Orthodox." Lefkowitz's task is thus to explain those modern non-Orthodox (even if "Orthodox") Jews who continue affiliating with non-modern (even if "Modern") Orthodoxy.

Lefkowitz labels those who do not espouse Orthodox doctrine even while they are personally observant "Social Orthodox," and he counts himself among its adherents. In his telling, for the Social Orthodox like him, "the key to Jewish living is not our religious beliefs but our commitment to a set of practices and values that foster community and continuity." He contends that Modern Orthodoxy provides the most robust framework for a fully engaged Jewish life, and is therefore attractive to those who are not very concerned with dogma or doctrine but are strongly interested in the perpetuation of Jewish culture and civilization. For Lefkowitz, the primary way to effect this perpetuation is through the practice of Jewish ritual. It is behavior that binds Jews across generations and around the world, and which engenders a sense of belonging and community. As for belief, Lefkowitz seems to oscillate between considering it to be of secondary or tertiary importance, or in fact unimportant.

In the final analysis, both Feldman and Lefkowitz are correct. There is certainly a doctrinal barrier that prevents the full integration of Orthodoxy and modernity. It is equally certain that there are modern individuals who embrace Orthodox practice for reasons other than its doctrine.

Nevertheless, important questions remain. Lefkowitz's thesis can partially explain why a typically non-dogmatic Millennial who was raised Orthodox but no longer believes in or practices Orthodox Judaism might feel comfortable in the orbit of a less doctrinaire group, but it cannot explain the resurgence of non-practicing Orthodoxy in its entirety; once again, Chabad provides an instructive example. It may be that no explanation is necessary. Perhaps most Jews no longer feel compelled to harmonize their Judaism with their modernity and will adopt the trappings of non-modern tradition for the Jewish moments of their lives. Perhaps American Judaism will become more like Judaism in other countries, where Judaism is identified with Orthodoxy by default, even by those who do not practice it. Alternatively, perhaps attitudes toward accommodating non-practicing and non-believing Jews will precipitate schism within Orthodoxy itself. Time will tell.

16. Tamar Biala and Nechama Weingarten-Mintz (eds.), *Dirshuni: Midrashei Nashim*

Tamar Biala and Nechama Weingarten-Mintz (eds.), *Dirshuni: Midrashei Nashim*, Tel Aviv/Jerusalem: Yediot Acharonot/Jewish Agency, 2009

Tamar Biala (1970–) is a writer and lecturer.

Nehama Weingarten-Mintz (1972–) is a lecturer, educator, and activist.

Rivkah Lubitz, "Midrashim of the Daughters of Tzelophchad"[1]
"And the daughters of Tzelophchad drew near ... and these are his daughters' names: Machlah, Noa and Choglah and Milkah and Tirtzah" (Numbers 27:1).

Why were they referred to, first, as "the daughters of Tzelophchad" and only afterwards by their own names?

Because of the *tzel* and *pachad*, shadow and fear, that was in them at first. For at first they dwelled in their father's shadow, and feared to raise their heads. Once they drew near to one another, they were empowered, and known by their own names, as is written, "And the daughters of Tzelophchad drew near ... and these are his daughters' names."

"Rightly [*kein*] do Tzelophchad's daughters speak" (Numbers 27:7).

Tanot asked God: "If Tzelophchad's daughters spoke the truth, why didn't you write that in Your Torah in the first place, for after all, You are truth, and Your Torah is truth, and Your word endures forever?"

God answered, "Truth will grow from the ground" (Psalms 85:12).

Tanot asked: "But is it not written, 'God's Torah is whole' (Psalms 19:8)?"

God answered her: "I already wrote in My Torah, 'Be wholehearted with God your Lord' (Deuteronomy 18:14). And what's more, I wrote: 'Walk before me, and be wholehearted' (Genesis 17:1)."

There is truth that descends from on high, and there is truth that grows from below. Blessed is the generation in which truth from above meets truth from below. And this is what Scripture means when it says "Truth will grow from the ground, and justice look down from Heaven" (Psalms 85: 12).

The cynics of the time said: "Tzelophchad's daughters are hypocrites."

---

1   Translated from the Hebrew by Yehudah Mirsky.

They said: "They're doing this for their own power, their own prosperity, to make themselves men's equals when it comes to inheritance."

"They aren't doing this for the sake of Heaven."

That is why the Torah says *kein*, [which means] "rightly" as in "honest" (*keinut*), and "rightly" as in "correct" (*nakhon*). They act for their own power, they act for their prosperity, they act to make themselves men's equals when it comes to inheritance, they act for the sake of Heaven. (92–93)

COMMENTARY BY SARAH MULHERN

Dirshuni, like collections of feminist midrashim which preceded and followed it, sets out with the explicit goal of expanding and reframing the Jewish canon to include the wisdom of the whole community. In the eyes of the modern midrashists whose work is included, the Torah was written by men for primarily male audiences, leaving the Jewish tradition fundamentally incomplete. To be whole, it needed insights and inspiration which could only be drawn from Torah written by women, from their distinct perspectives and in their voices. In the words of *Dirshuni*'s co-editor, Tamar Biala, the goal of teaching and publishing midrashim written by women was to "tell whoever was ready to listen that the other half of Judaism is being written in our days."[2]

The turn specifically to midrash, the body of rabbinic literature which interprets and expands on the biblical text, as a technique for this work is perhaps unsurprising. As Barry Holtz writes in his discussion of classical midrash of the rabbinic period:

> The central issue behind the emergence of Midrash [is] the need to deal with the presence of cultural or religious tension and discontinuity. Where there are questions that demand answers, and where there are new cultural and intellectual pressures that must be addressed, Midrash comes into play as a way of resolving crisis and reaffirming continuity with the traditions of the past.[3]

Thus, for Jewish feminists, creating midrash is a way of working with the tensions between their feminist impulses and the patriarchal nature of Judaism,

---

2   Tamar Biala, "Filling the Missing Half of the Sacred Bookshelf," *My Jewish Learning*, January 22, 2015, accessed July 12, 2019, https://www.myjewishlearning.com/the-torch/filling-the-missing-half-of-the-sacred-bookshelf/.

3   Barry Holtz, *Back to the Sources* (New York: Summit, 1984).

between the absence of women's voices and perspectives from the canon and their profound love for Torah. Midrash gives these authors the tools they need to express their anger, love, puzzlement, hurt, and fidelity to Torah. It allows them to articulate their values Jewishly and to bring Torah in line with them. It gives them a traditionally legitimate language in which to critique and subvert canonical texts. Most of all, it allows them to grow Torah into a sacred conversation of which they feel a part and of which they can approve.

Midrashim written by women first began to appear in the United States in the 1970s, alongside the emergence of innovative women's rituals. The genre exploded in size and in scope through the 1980s and 1990s. It took many forms, but narrative expansions of the female characters of the Bible, beginning with Mary Gendler's 1973 "The Restoration of Vashti," and Midrashic poems, such as Merle Feld's influential early 1980s "We All Stood Together," were primary. In this period, these and other works were widely read by American Jewish feminists and were often incorporated into Jewish ritual life and text study in those North American Jewish circles where the challenges and opportunities of feminism loomed large.

In her groundbreaking 1990 feminist theological work *Standing Again at Sinai*, Judith Plaskow expressed the motivations and goals of feminist midrash: "We must render visible the presence, experience, and deeds of women erased in traditional sources. We must tell the stories of women's encounters with God and capture the texture of their religious experiences. ... To expand Torah, we must reconstruct Jewish history to include the history of women, and in doing so alter the shape of Jewish memory." This clarion call spurred even more prolific creativity in the genre, which came to include a diversity of additional forms such as biblical commentaries like Ellen Frankel's *The Five Books of Miriam: A Woman's Commentary on the Torah*, published in 1996, novels such as Anita Diamant's *The Red Tent*, published in 1997, and even visual and performance art, including the work of poet, songwriter, and violinist Alicia Jo Rabins.[4]

Published in 2009, *Dirshuni* is in many ways a continuation of the genre of feminist midrash as it already existed and in other ways highly innovative. The book, co-edited by Biala and Nehama Weingarten-Mintz, contains ninety

---

4   Thanks to Rivkah M. Walton (see her article "Lilith's Daughters, Miriam's Chorus: Two Decades of Feminist Midrash," *Religion & Literature* 43, no. 2 [Summer 2011]: 115–127) and Jody Myers (see her chapter "The Midrashic Enterprise of Contemporary Jewish Women," in *Jews and Gender*, ed. Jonathan Frankel [New York: Oxford University Press, 2001]). I have relied extensively on both of these works in my understanding of the development of feminist midrash.

midrashim written by thirty-seven women, as well as a brief introduction and conclusion framing the intent and goals of the editors. The midrashim vary in length between a few lines and a few pages and are grouped into fourteen topical sections. The midrashim deal with most of the narrative arc of the Hebrew Bible including sections on Creation and the Garden of Eden, the biblical foremothers and forefathers, slavery and redemption from Egypt, and Israel's wanderings in the wilderness, as well as with selected narrative sections of the Prophets. The collection also includes midrashim on some rabbinic and liturgical texts, organized around themes like the study of Torah, different types of human relationships, theology, fertility and infertility, justice, and others.

The works' continuities with previous feminist midrash are seen specifically in the editors' acknowledgment of Plaskow and Chana Thompson's midrash "Imagining Sarah" as important inspiration for their work, and more broadly in the shared goal of using the creative power of midrash to bring women's voices and experiences into the Torah. Together with those who came before them, they insist that access to classical texts—which girls and women now enjoy more than at any other point in Jewish history thanks to the influence of feminism on Jewish education—is insufficient. They assert that women must now step forward as the authors of new sacred texts, as an act of repair for the women who will read and write them, and as an act of repair for Judaism and the Torah itself.

At the same time, *Dirshuni* is quite innovative. It is the first collection of women's midrash to be both written and published in Israel. While Biala and Weingarten-Mintz both credit their "miraculous" discoveries in the early 2000s of informal collections of midrashim by Israeli women with showing them the "redemptive power" of this kind of work, and while a few individual Israeli women's midrashim had previously appeared in print, theirs was the first project to solicit midrashim from a politically, ethnically, and religiously diverse group of Israeli women and to make women's midrashim widely available to Israeli readers in Hebrew from a popular press. The specifically Israeli nature of the collection can be seen in several of the midrashim such as those dealing with agricultural issues and those that subtly critique the Rabbanut, the state rabbinic authority. For these reasons of language and culture, *Dirshuni* has had a deeper and broader impact on Israeli Jewish feminist ritual, study, and thinking than earlier English-language works published in North America.

The primary contribution of *Dirshuni*, however, is one of form. In selecting which midrashim to include, the editors chose to restrict the collection to midrashim that worked within the interpretive rules, techniques, and structures of classical rabbinic midrash. Very few such midrashim had previously appeared in print. This was done with the hope of bringing feminist midrash more directly into dialogue with midrashim from the previous millennium and as an expression of the editors' view that these works ought to be read not as literature but sacred text. In striving to write in the forms of the Rabbis' midrashim, the midrashim of *Dirshuni* audaciously claim to be their equal.

Like other midrashim in the collection, the midrash included here by Rivkah Lubitz shares many structural elements with classical rabbinic midrash. It is written in a tight form, with short comments responding to small pieces of text from the Hebrew Bible. The text assumes the omnisignificance of each word of the biblical text on which it comments, and yet feels free not only to elucidate but to subvert it. It relies on word play and the creative use of interbiblical references to make its claims, and it makes use of the familiar rabbinic motif of dialogue with God.

Unlike rabbinic midrash, Lubitz's midrash is distinctly feminist. She emphasizes sisterhood: women are fearful and can be overshadowed by men when they are separate, but united they are strong, able to voice their needs, and able to articulate their individuality. The voice that can challenge God does not belong to a familiar male rabbi or prophet, but to Tanot, a female character created by Lubitz based on her interpretation of a biblical verse about the daughter of Yiftach. Tanot appears several places throughout the collection, serving, according to the editors of *Dirshuni*, as a kind of female Eliyahu haNavi, Elijah the Prophet, a presence who occasionally jumps into the discourse of the Beit Midrash in rabbinic midrash. Here, her voice is strongly confident as it pushes God for both clarity and justice using God's own words, and God takes her questions seriously and as deserving of response.

Further, in this midrash, it is God who expresses the claim that a perfect Torah must be created through the work of humans in partnership with the Divine, clearly a claim for the authenticity of the work of feminist midrash. It goes on to celebrate the good fortune of a generation, presumably our own, wherein God's revealed truth can be in relationship with the truths generated from "below"—meaning the new expansions of human understanding brought by feminism and the truths generated by human, including women's, experience. The text challenges a traditional view of revelation by insisting that only such a meeting of Divine and human truths will produce justice. The midrash ends by responding directly to the experience of many women who learn and teach of Torah of cynics asserting that they do so not out of love but only in pursuit of power by contending that the very construction of the biblical verse comes to teach the sincerity of such women. In a powerful twist, the midrash affirms that the pursuit of power and equality for women is justified and is itself a sincere and holy task, done for the sake of heaven. This powerful combination of classical structures with feminist insights is what makes *Dirshuni* such a unique and transformative contribution.

Dirshuni is widely taught and has become influential in Israeli Jewish feminist circles and some North American ones. In 2018, a second collection of midrashim was published. An effort is also under way to translate the work into English, so that it might influence Jewish communities outside Israel more deeply. The central idea advanced by the work, that Torah will change for the better when women create material in its classical forms and demand they be included in the canon, has continued to inspire parallel work in other such forms, most notably the emergence of responsa written by women to answer queries about Jewish law.

The Jewish canon has always been a living thing. The texts which Jews relate to as holy, as fitting for Talmud Torah, grow and change, and as they interpret and assign fresh meaning to what came before, so too do our understandings of lessons and values of the earlier texts grow and change. Feminist Midrash works from the assumption that this process will be more dynamic and healthier if the doors of the Beit Midrash are opened wide to women and others with perspectives not represented by the historic rabbinic elite, from the belief that Torah will be better and more holy when such people are equal partners in cocreating it with God.

Dirshuni opens with the words of Isaiah 58:2—"Every day they seek Me … they desire that God should be near." The word for seek, *yidreshun*, shares a root with the word "midrash" as well as the book's title, *dirshuni*, which is best translated as an imperative: seek me! *Dirshuni* and its sister texts represent this longing and command to draw closer to the Divine through an active seeking in God's Torah. This has been, in many ways, the central work of Jewish spiritual life since the destruction of the Temple. The beautiful midrashim of *Dirshuni* show us a glimmer of the beauty and the closeness to God that will emerge as the Jewish people—in all its diversity and fullness—continue to step up to this sacred task.

17. Leon Wieseltier, "Language, Identity, and the Scandal of American Jewry"

Leon Wieseltier, "Language, Identity, and the Scandal of American Jewry," *Journal of Jewish Communal Service* (Winter/Spring 2011)

Leon Wieseltier (1952–) was Isaiah Berlin Senior Fellow in Culture and Policy at the Brookings Institution and Literary Editor of the *New Republic* as well as a critic and Contributing Editor at *The Atlantic*.

The Spoiled Brats of Jewish History

Surely the standard by which we must judge ourselves as Jews, and by which our children and our historians will judge us, is not an American standard, even if we are also Americans; and it is not even an American Jewish standard. It is a Jewish standard, the Jewish standard, the classical Jewish standard, the standard of our tradition. I take it to be a fundamental principle of Jewish life that it is by our tradition that we must measure ourselves. So the questions that we must ask ourselves are these: How does what we have created compare to what we inherited? Did we add to our tradition or did we subtract from it? Did we transmit it or did we let it fall away? Did we enrich it or deplete it? Among the great Jewries, what is our distinction? Measuring ourselves by the standard of our tradition, we should note immediately one distinction of the American Jewish community; and it is with this distinction that I have come here to trouble you. The distinction that I have in mind is the illiteracy of American Jewry. I mean, its Jewish illiteracy.

Jews without a Language

The American Jewish community is the first great community in the history of our people that believes that it can receive, develop, and perpetuate the Jewish tradition not in a Jewish language. By an overwhelming majority, American Jews cannot read or speak or write Hebrew, or Yiddish. This is genuinely shocking. American Jewry is quite literally unlettered. The assumption of American Jewry that it can do without a Jewish language is an arrogance without precedent in Jewish history. And this illiteracy, I suggest, will leave

American Judaism and American Jewishness forever crippled and scandal-ously thin. There are two ways in which we can educate our children, two instruments of identity with which we may equip them. One is conviction, the other is competence. I have no doubt that the future of Jewish culture in America will be determined more by Jewish competence than by Jewish conviction. We cannot teach our children what to believe; or rather, we can try to teach them what to believe, but we can never be certain of the success of our effort. They will believe what they wish to believe. We cannot control their belief. Indeed, we must be grateful for their freedom of mind. But it is not an illusion of control to think that we can permanently arrange matters so that our children will never be shut out of their own tradition, out of their own books. If we cannot make sure that we will be followed by believing Jews, we certainly can be sure that we will be followed by competent Jews. Indeed, competence leaves a Jew favorably disposed to conviction. A com-petent Jew is not destroyed by his questions, because he can look for the answers himself. He, or she, has the tools. Ignorance, I think, is much more damaging than heresy.

COMMENTARY BY JON A. LEVISOHN

In "Language, Identity and the Scandal of American Jewry," Leon Wieseltier offered what appeared to be a devastating critique of the cultural condition of the Jewish community in the United States.[1] That community is the most highly educated in the world—but it is embarrassingly uneducated in Jewish culture. That community has achieved astonishing material success—but astonishingly little spiritual success. American Jews, he said, are "the spoiled brats of Jewish history." He went on to lament the "thinness of Jewish culture in America," the "calamitous decline in Jewish competence," and especially the "noisy profes-sions of their identity." If these words wound, they must capture something true.

We need to look more closely, however. Wieseltier populated his essay with numerous examples of illiteracy from other periods in Jewish history, displaying the habits of mind of the academic historian he once was, happily shattering the myths of a glorious past. But the logic is problematic. The more we notice illiteracy elsewhere, the less we are inclined to believe that there is something

---

1 In October of 2017, Wieseltier was accused of a pattern of workplace sexual harassment stretching back for two decades or more, which he did not deny and for which he publicly apologized. This essay is intended as a critique of his ideas, rather than an adjudication of his behavior, his punishment, or his rehabilitation.

special about the illiteracy of American Judaism. Wieseltier then says, in effect, "Still, American Jewry is worse." Is it?

The evidence is thin. Wieseltier has told us a story about four thousand medieval manuscripts. He has told other stories about the spoken Hebrew, uncomprehended by an American Jewish audience, of Haitian politician Jean-Bertrand Aristide and Palestinian author Anton Shammas. He even shared a passage from a Philip Roth novel. Significantly, he showed—rather than told—what it looks like to be a scholar of Jewish history familiar with all its various time periods and some of its languages. He never actually said, "Why can't more people be like me?," but on my reading, a good deal of the energy of his argument came from this question.

But it is not only the case that Wieseltier provided so little evidence. More importantly, he was unclear about the capacity that he was criticizing. Was it the ability to read? To write? To understand spoken Hebrew? To understand classical texts? Or perhaps he was simply disturbed by ignorance of Jewish culture and tradition? This slipperiness ought to concern us.

In one location, Wieseltier made the strong claim that the "American Jewish community is the first great community in the history of our people that believes that it can receive, develop and perpetuate the Jewish tradition *not* in a Jewish language." Maybe this is the heart of the issue. Language is the basis for culture. Without a distinctive language, you cannot have a distinctive culture. It may well be true that Hebrew literacy (or even general literacy) has been limited in other times and places. Nevertheless, other Jewish communities have shared a spoken Jewish vernacular—Yiddish, or Aramaic, Ladino, Judeo-Italian, or dozens of others. American Jews do not.

But this is a simplistic argument. Indeed, in a classic 1966 essay, the great Jewish historian Gerson Cohen debunked it explicitly; he pointed to the Jews of ancient Alexandria whose culture survived because they translated it into Greek.[2] More recently, sociolinguist Sarah Bunin Benor wrote: "Wherever Jews have lived, their speech and writing have differed from those of their non-Jewish neighbors." Even in America? Yes, even in America, where Jews speak "Jewish English."[3]

In fact, Wieseltier and Benor (following Cohen) represent two general attitudes towards North American Jewish culture. Prominent sociologist Charles

---

2   Gerson Cohen, "The Blessing of Assimilation in Jewish History," reprinted in his *Jewish History and Jewish Destiny* (New York: Jewish Theological Seminary of America, 1997).

3   Sarah Benor, "Do American Jews Speak a 'Jewish Language'? A Model of Jewish Linguistic Distinctiveness," *The Jewish Quarterly Review* 99, no. 2 (2009): 230–269.

Liebman called them "traditionalists" and "transformationists." The former are the pessimists who lament the departures from tradition. The latter are the optimists who celebrate the new. When Wieseltier says that American Jews have no Jewish language, Benor responds that they do. If Wieseltier says that they have not produced any significant cultural contributions, Benor responds that they have. To the transformationists, the traditionalists are hopelessly nostalgic. To the traditionalists, the transformationists are hopelessly naïve. Regardless of the particulars of the argument about Jewish languages, this divide remains a deep one in our Jewish communal discourse.

But Wieseltier did not merely offer a negative assessment of American Jewish culture. He also explained how it came to be that way. American Jewish culture, Wieseltier wrote, has "lived off of the spiritual and historical resources of other Jews." Indeed, he wondered whether any immigrant community could act otherwise: "A transplanted culture will always have a powerful anxiety about authenticity." There seems to be some kind of psycho-socio-cultural law: Newly planted communities cannot help but see themselves as pale imitations of a romanticized past.

This, in a word, is nonsense. Surely there are historical examples of such derivative communities. But there are at least as many historical examples of transplanted cultures that have thrived. One does not need trendy postmodern theory to understand the importance of "hybridity," that is, the way in which it is precisely the dislocation and relocation of cultures (for example, through immigration) that generates unprecedented interactions, which lead to new cultural forms and often to new cultural vitality. And scholars have long argued that the ideology of "traditionalism," and the search for authenticity in (invented) traditions, is a hallmark of modernity itself, rather than a pathology particular to the American Jewish immigrant community.

But perhaps we are over-analyzing, expecting too much precision in what was, after all, a *cri de coeur*? If so, we might notice that such laments themselves have a history, famously documented by the great historian Simon Rawidowicz in his "Israel: The Ever-Dying People." "He who studies Jewish history," Rawidowicz wrote, "will readily discover that there was hardly a generation in the Diaspora period which did not consider itself the final link in Israel's chain."[4] He calls the Jewish people "a nation that has been disappearing constantly for the last two thousand years," and humorously claims that "there is no nation

---

4   Simon Rawidowicz, "Israel: The Ever-Dying People," in his *Studies in Jewish Thought* (Philadelphia: Jewish Publication Society, 1974).

more dying than Israel," before concluding that "incessant dying means uninterrupted living, rising, standing up, beginning anew." I have no doubt that Wieseltier knew Rawidowicz's classic essay. Perhaps he forgot the conclusion.

So how should we think about the cultural condition of American Jewry? Should we rejoice in its non-traditionalist cultural successes, applaud its robust institutions, and celebrate Jewish English as a distinctive language? If we are interested in data, should we cite the 98% of non-Orthodox Jewish singles who say they are proud to be Jewish,[5] or the 83% of the "nones"—those who supposedly reject Judaism as a religion— who express pride in being Jewish?[6] Or should we lament the vacuity of what Wieseltier called their "noisy professions of identity"?

There is a better way to think about these issues, to which Wieseltier himself gestured when he wrote that "the future of Jewish culture in America will be determined more by Jewish competence than by Jewish conviction." Competence in what? His answer, of course, was linguistic competence. Notably, he was not after the "cultural literacy" made famous by E. D. Hirsch's eponymous work, and imported into the Jewish publishing world by Joseph Telushkin and his *Jewish Literacy*, a concept with broad appeal but little coherence. Instead, he had in mind the older idea of literacy as a capacity, an ability to do something with what one knows.

"Jewish linguistic competence" is not simply a matter of fluency in Hebrew. Instead, we should look to the philosopher of Jewish education Michael Rosenak, who developed the twin concepts of language and literature. "Education," he wrote, "is the teaching of a language and helping learners to see it as their home."[7] But "language" here is used metaphorically, to mean a set of basic assumptions and frameworks, the linguistic and conceptual infrastructure of a culture. The cultural products themselves, whether written or oral, are "literature." And education, he continued, "is, at the same time, cultivating an appreciation of its literature and enabling the next generation to make literature in the language." This is what it means to teach a culture: helping students to understand the language in which the literature is written, to appreciate (and to critique) the literature, and especially, to produce new contributions to the culture of their own. What Rosenak did not say explicitly, but which is particularly important in the context

---

5   Steven M. Cohen and Ari Y. Kelman, *Uncoupled: How Our Singles are Reshaping Jewish Engagement* (New York: Andrea and Charles Bronfman Philanthropies, 2008).

6   Theodore Sasson, "Pew Data Shows Children of Intermarriage Still Identify as Jews," *Tablet*, November 11, 2013.

7   Michael Rosenak, *Roads to the Palace: Jewish Texts and Teaching* (Providence: Berghahn Books, 1995).

of Wieseltier's arguments, is that the metaphorical usage of language-and-literature takes us out of the realm of an elite textual culture and incorporates as well a popular, mimetic culture.

Rosenak, I believe, was almost exactly right about the purpose of education. What is missing is pluralization: languages, not language. Jewish education ought to teach Jewish languages, both metaphorical and literal, as many as possible, as deeply as possible. Jewish education ought to cultivate Jewish linguistic competence in this metaphorical sense, ought to produce speakers and writers in the languages of Hebrew, and Yiddish, and Ladino, and American Jewish English; the languages of the Hebrew Bible and of Talmud; the languages of Jewish philosophy, and law, and mysticism; the languages of modern Hebrew literature and contemporary Israeli hip-hop; and on and on. And it ought to cultivate Jewish linguistic competence, as well, in the mimetic languages of ritual practice and Kaplanian "folkways," of food and celebration, of Jewish dance and music, of Jewish charitable giving and *tikkun olam*, of communal innovation, and on and on.

Are American Jews scandalously illiterate? No, they are not, particularly when we expand our conception of language to include the metaphorical languages in which they are competent, as we ought to do, and when we are attuned to the multiplicity of metaphorical languages, as we ought to be. On the other hand, are American Jews as competent in Jewish languages as we would like them to be? Surely the answer to that question is negative as well. Where Wieseltier was right, I believe, was not so much in his cantankerous condemnation of the condition of American Jewish culture, but in his concern for competences. What, we should ask descriptively, are American Jews good at? What specific cultural competencies do they develop? What practices do they enact? And then, allowing ourselves to move to the prescriptive, we should ask: What practices and cultural competencies do we want to promote?

Wieseltier lamented that American Jews are outside of Jewish language and Jewish culture, and therefore suffer a kind of self-alienation. This is too strong. But even if we look suspiciously at claims about Jews being alienated from some essential Judaism, we may still find that the worry resonates. We do want Jews to be at home in ways that many currently are not. The path to that at-home-ness is not through "noisy professions of identity" but through Jewish languages—learning to speak and write in as many Jewish languages as possible, as richly and robustly as possible. There is no scandal of American Jewry, but for Jewish educators, there is much work to be done.

18. Ruth Calderon, "The Heritage of All Israel"

Ruth Calderon, Inaugural Knesset Speech, "The Heritage of All Israel," *New York Jewish Week*, February 14, 2013[1]

Dr. Ruth Calderon (1961–) is Co-Founder of Elul, the first Israeli secular and egalitarian Beit Midrash and Founder of Alma, a Tel Aviv institution which seeks to acquaint secular Israelis with Hebrew culture. She served as Knesset Member for the Yesh Atid Party from 2013 to 2015.

I am convinced that studying the great works of Hebrew and Jewish culture are crucial to construct a new Hebrew culture for Israel. It is impossible to stride toward the future without knowing where we came from and who we are, without knowing, intimately and in every particular, the sublime as well as the outrageous and the ridiculous. The Torah is not the property of one movement or another. It is a gift that every one of us received, and we have all been granted the opportunity to meditate upon it [as] we create the realities of our lives. Nobody took the Talmud and rabbinic literature from us. We gave it away, with our own hands, when it seemed that another task was more important and urgent: building a state, raising an army, developing agriculture and industry, etc. The time has come to reappropriate what is ours, to delight in the cultural riches that wait for us, for our eyes, our imaginations, our creativity. …

I long for the day when the state's resources are distributed fairly and equally to every Torah scholar, man or woman, based on the quality of their study, not their communal affiliation, when secular and pluralistic yeshivot, *batei midrash*, and organizations win fair and equal support in comparison to Orthodox and Haredi *batei midrash*. Through scholarly envy and healthy competition, the Torah will be magnified and glorified.

COMMENTARY BY YOSSI KLEIN HALEVI

It is February 2, 2013, the opening session of the 19th Knesset, and Ruth Calderon, newly elected parliamentarian on the centrist Yesh Atid (There

---

is a Future) list, ascends the podium to deliver her inaugural address. She is carrying a volume of Talmud. Better known as an educator than as a politician, she is a founder of a movement to empower secular Israelis in reclaiming traditional Jewish study without necessarily taking on religious observance. And she is here today not so much to declare that cultural revolution as to embody its maturation.

"This book that is in my hands changed my life, and it is to a great extent the reason why I am here today," she begins in a soft, slightly hoarse voice. She presents her life story as her first text. She is, she says, every Israeli: daughter of refugees—right-wing Sephardi father from Bulgaria, left-wing Ashkenazi mother from Germany. They created a home imbued with faith—not with religion but with the secular faith of Zionist rebirth. "I did not inherit a set of Talmud from my grandfather," she says. Her state education began with the heroic figures of the Bible, ignored the irrelevant and vaguely shameful centuries of exile, and leaped to the heroic figures of the Zionist revolution—"from the Tanach to the Palmach. ... I was not acquainted with the Mishnah, the Talmud, Kabbalah or Hasidism."

As a teenager, she began to sense the absence of two thousand years of Jewish civilization. "I missed depth. ... The new Hebrew, created by educators from the country's founding generation, realized their dream and became a courageous, practical, and suntanned soldier." Her irony is affectionate: Even in her disaffection, she is a loyal daughter of secular Zionism. "But for me, this contained—I contained—a void. I did not know how to fill that void. But when I first encountered the Talmud and became completely enamored with ... its language, its humor, its profound thinking, its modes of discussion, and the practicality, humanity and maturity that emerge from its lines, I sensed that I had found the love of my life, what I had been lacking."

There is a past, says the MK from Yesh Atid, and it belongs not only to the Orthodox but to me, too. "The Torah is not the property of one movement or another. It is a gift that every one of us received, and we have been granted the opportunity to meditate upon it as we create the realities of our lives. Nobody took the Talmud and rabbinic literature from us. We gave it away, with our own hands, when it seemed that another task was more important and urgent: building a state, raising an army, developing agriculture and industry and so on. ... The time has come to reappropriate what is ours, to delight in the cultural riches that await us."

Her first reckoning, then, is with the secular Zionist establishment that ignored the "Jewish bookshelf," as Israelis call the body of traditional literature.

But there is a second reckoning: with the Orthodox establishment that claims exclusive right to it. MK Calderon proceeds to challenge that hegemony by doing what no one has ever done before on this podium: open a volume of Talmud and teach. "I will read it once in Aramaic, for the music, and then in Hebrew."

She chooses a disturbing Talmudic story. She has, after all, come here to disturb the status quo, the second-class status of women in Israeli Judaism. The story tells of a rabbi named Rehumei who was so devoted to his own rabbi, the renowned Rava, that he would remain with him throughout the year, returning home only for Yom Kippur. One Yom Kippur he forgot to come home altogether. His wife "shed a tear. ... He was sitting on a roof. The roof collapsed under him and he died."

In this place and time, it is a loaded metaphor, implicitly aimed at *Charedi* men who study Torah full-time and have separated themselves from "home"— the national home. But Calderon hasn't come only to disturb and rebuke; she has come to study, to engage ideological rivals, rather than humiliate and defeat them.

"*Rehumei* in Aramaic means 'love,'" she explains. "*Rehumei* is derived from the word *rehem*, womb, someone who knows how to include, how to completely accept, just as a woman's womb contains the baby. This choice of word for 'love' is quite beautiful. We know that the Greek word for 'womb' gives us the word 'hysteria.' The Aramaic choice to take the womb and turn it into love is a feminist gesture by the Sages."

Presiding over the session is Yitzhak Vaknin of the ultra-Orthodox Shas party. Whatever skepticism he may have had about this woman with a Talmud has vanished. The word *rehem*, he tells Calderon, is the numerological equivalent of 248, the same number as positive *mitzvot*, commandments.

"*Yasher koach*!" says a delighted Calderon, "May you have strength."

"I think the idea she is saying is wonderful," the MK from Shas tells the Knesset.

Suddenly this place of divisiveness and cynicism and bombast has turned into a study hall. And the incongruously warm exchange between ideological rivals—Yesh Atid, after all, represents a backlash against ultra-Orthodox power and military exemptions—becomes part of the "oral tradition" of Calderon's speech.

"What can we learn from the story of Rabbi Rehumei?" asks Calderon. "First, I learn that one who forgets that he is sitting on another's shoulders"— whether those of a neglected wife or of IDF soldiers—"will fall. Righteousness is not adherence to the Torah at the expense of sensitivity to human beings."

But then, abruptly, she softens again. "I learn that often, in a dispute, both sides are right ... that both my disputant and I, both the woman and Rabbi Rehumei, feel that they are doing the right thing and are responsible for the home." The metaphor becomes explicit: "Sometimes we [non-*Charedim*] feel like the woman, waiting, serving in the army, doing all the work while others sit on the roof and study Torah; sometimes those others feel that they bear the entire weight of tradition, Torah, and our culture while we got to the beach and have a great time. Both I and my disputant feel solely responsible for the [Jewish people's] home. Until I understand this, I will not perceive the problem properly and will not be able to find a solution."

This is her challenge to the Knesset, to the people of Israel: Can we replace a zero-sum discourse with the dialectic of Talmud, in which argument sustains rather than threatens relationship?

Calderon's own dialectic is balancing outreach to rivals with asserting her truth. And she turns now to her agenda as an MK: "I aspire to bring about a situation in which Torah study is the heritage of all Israel, in which the Torah is accessible to all who wish to study it, in which all young citizens of Israel take part in Torah study as well as military and civil service." Torah study and military service aren't mutually exclusive but complementary expressions of citizenship in the people of Israel.

"I long for the day when the state's resources are distributed fairly and equally to every Torah scholar, man or woman, based on the quality of their study, not their communal affiliation, when secular and pluralistic yeshivot, houses of study and organizations win fair and equal support in comparison to Orthodox and haredi study halls. Through scholarly envy and healthy competition, the Torah will be magnified and glorified."

MK Calderon is declaring an end to the culture war of Israel's early years. That war was fought between the "Israelis"—those who saw their new country as a break with the Jewish past—and the "Jews," those who saw Israel as the natural continuity of an unruptured story. The war between the "Israelis" and the "Jews" is over, Calderon is saying, and the Jews won. Jewish identity and Jewish texts are no longer peripheral to Israeliness.

But even as she is laying to rest the old culture war, she is implicitly announcing a new one: a struggle *within* Israeli Judaism. What kind of Judaism will prevail here: a Judaism imported wholly from the ghetto, developed under the most extreme conditions of insecurity and insularity; or new, more open forms of Judaism reflecting a self-confident people's return to sovereignty? Who are the rightful conversation partners with the Sages: only the Orthodox or any

Jew, "secular" or "religious," male or female, drawn to the discourse? Who owns Judaism?

MK Calderon ends by reciting an improvised—and egalitarian—prayer to "the God of our fathers and mothers"—for success in her work as a public serv-ant, for keeping "my integrity and innocence intact." MK Vaknin loudly says, "Amen." It is a stunning affirmation to Calderon's dare: that religious pluralism in Israel will happen not through protests and recrimination but with generosity and self-confidence, holding a volume of Talmud and claiming ownership to a shared tradition.

19. Rick Jacobs, "The Genesis of Our Future"

Rick Jacobs, "The Genesis of Our Future," Union for Reform Judaism Biennial Address, December 12, 2013

Rabbi Rick Jacobs (1956–) is President of the Union for Reform Judaism (URJ).

In a Jewish world where many more Jews are outside than inside, how can we not practice audacious hospitality? When women finally became rabbis, cantors, and board presidents, they didn't just fill the previously conceived roles; they critiqued and reshaped Jewish life. We need to do the same now with the LGBTQ community, with multi-racial Jews, with intermarried families, and with Gen X and the millennials, all of whom have much to teach us.

Let's be frank. Even when they get inside our doors, many of these folks are convinced of not much more than the fact that we can smile. Are they equally certain that we want them? That's the question. The answer is an emphatic yes. Only by being inclusive can we be strong; only by being open can we be whole. ...

Incredibly enough, however, I still hear Jewish leaders talk about intermarriage as if it were a disease. It is not. It is a result of the open society that no one here wants to close. The sociology is clear enough; anti-Semitism is down; Jews feel welcome; we mix easily with others; Jewish North Americans (researchers say) are more admired overall than any other religious group. So of course you get high intermarriage rates—the norm, incidentally, in the third or fourth generation of other ethnic groups as well.

In North America today, being "against" intermarriage is like being "against" gravity; you can say it all you want, but it's a fact of life. And what would you prefer? More anti-Semitism? That people did not feel as comfortable with us?

In any event, we practice outreach because it is good for the Jewish people. Interfaith couples can raise phenomenally committed Jewish families, especially when they do it in the Jewish community that is offered uniquely by the Reform Movement.

The Talmud brags that no person ever greeted Yohanan ben Zakkai first, not even a non-Jew in the marketplace; it was always ben Zakkai who was first to extend his hand—to Jew and non-Jew alike. Yohanan ben Zakkai is known for completely reimagining Jewish life when the Second Temple was being destroyed. The architect of the biggest turnaround in Jewish history knew what it was to be audacious. And so must we.

It is not just sociology that demands that we be serious about welcoming interfaith families. It is theology as well. We have a sacred obligation to open our doors, to add to our ranks, and to make sure that progressive Judaism has a growing, not a shrinking, voice in proclaiming what Torah must mean for our time and for our world. It is a veritable gift of God to have the opportunity of a millennium: more non-Jews who want "in" than Jews who want "out." That has never happened before. We dare not squander this gift out of fear of what new voices may say and where new opinions may lead.

COMMENTARY BY DAN FRIEDMAN

In October 2013, the release of a massive chunk of demographic data gave the leaders of American Jewry pause for thought. After the National Jewish Population Survey had stopped its annual reports in 2001, the community had labored with a relative dearth of information about its constituents. Suddenly, and with more breadth and depth than ever, the Pew Research Center's survey of American Jews provided a new focus for surprise, delight, and, of course, concern.

Surprise was elicited by the substantial growth of the Orthodox community (to 10%), by the number of "nones" (22% of Jews identified as Jews of no religion) and by the fact that more than twice as many respondents (42%) thought that a sense of humor was more important to being Jewish than observing Halakhah (19%). Delight came from the overwhelming sense of pride that American Jews had in their Jewishness. Although, presumably, there were many different reasons for their assertions, a breathtaking 94% of the respondents said they were "proud to be Jewish."

But one of the major concerns raised by the report was the traditional worry about the rate of interfaith marriage. Pew found that 58% of American Jews who married between 2005 and 2013 had non-Jewish spouses—the percentage even reached 72% for non-Orthodox couples. For proponents of "in-marriage" this was an alarm bell that the community was in danger of complete assimilation, for proponents of inclusion it was a reminder of how important it was to count those interfaith couples as Jewish.

Into this debate strode Rabbi Rick Jacobs. Installed as the president of the Union for Reform Judaism only the year before, he was heading into the first biennial conference under his leadership. The convention took place in

December 2013, barely two months after the Pew Study, and was meeting in California where Jacobs had grown up and, as he would emphasize in his address to the group, learned to surf. He was determined to take this opportunity to stamp his signature on the meeting and onto the URJ. Promising to "Reimagine Jewish Life," the head of the largest Jewish denomination in North America (representing 35% of all American Jews, according to the Pew Study) gave an impassioned and upbeat keynote speech.

It was a clarion call. Though his address bore the official title of "The Genesis of Our Future," it became known as Jacobs's "Audacious Hospitality" speech. In it, he enumerated the ways in which Jews had found a welcoming home in America — and among Americans — and he called for an equally enthusiastic Jewish reciprocation. For Jacobs, this was not a time of obstacle, but of opportunity: "Surf's up!" The statistics about interfaith marriage showed a literal love and embrace of Jews by America that represented a deep validation of the American Jewish community. And the only proper response to such an embrace was a fearless welcome of interfaith couples into the open spaces, progressive traditions, and warm communities of Reform Judaism.

Jacobs described fighting interfaith marriage as akin to fighting gravity. For a significant number of engaged American Jews, that rhetoric was tantamount to admitting defeat in the face of assimilation. Both Gary Rosenblatt at the *New York Jewish Week* ("[interfaith marriage] becoming the norm poses a threat to the sustainability of American Jewish life") and Jane Eisner at the *Forward* ("encouraging Jews to marry other Jews is too essential to surrender to the uncertainties of American assimilation") editorialized against his exhortations. Indeed, the Pew Study and Jacobs's words sparked a January meeting of twenty-five Jewish leaders in New York to discuss how to stimulate inmarriage.

But Jacobs had not ceded ground in the marketplace of ideas. Advocating the practice of hospitality exemplified by the Jewish progenitors Abraham and Sarah, citing the example of twentieth-century Reform leader Rabbi Alexander Schindler and drawing on the boldness of the word "audacious" in the Obama era, Jacobs called on Reform Jews to embrace America as it had embraced them. He looked to the "radical hospitality" program of the Shir Tikvah Congregation in Minneapolis as a model to expand and deepen so that the URJ could reach out with openness and "courage" to interfaith families as well as to all the underserved and under-recognized sections of the community.

The reward of such an approach, Jacobs maintained, would exceed the satisfaction of having done the right thing. Congregations across the continent had already seen such acts succeed. He put the idea in general terms: "Only by being inclusive can we be strong; only by being open can we be whole." And he also spelled out the benefits that the URJ had already enjoyed from welcoming families new to Judaism. They are "bringing the creativity, leadership, and service of hundreds of thousands of interfaith families to enrich our congregational lives, while countless thousands of children are being raised with meaningful Jewish experiences and commitments."

Because of the anxieties over assimilation and the rate of interfaith marriage, some significant findings of the Pew Study and Jacobs's response were somewhat overlooked. When Jacobs spoke of his commitment to audacious hospitality he was not simply prescribing more outreach to interfaith families, he was looking to make Judaism in general and his congregations in particular, attractive to those who, whether by dint of affection (for Jewish spouses) or disaffection (for instances of Jewish practice) were adjacent to, but not members of, Reform congregations.

The demographic opportunities outlined by Pew were not just limited to interfaith families, but were available in a number of generational (Gen X, millennials) and other identity segments. In his speech Jacob specifically mentioned the need to include interfaith families, Jews with disabilities, and LGBTQ Jews, but he also refers implicitly to the group that Pew called the "Jews of no religion" or the "nones" by saying that Reform congregations should provide refuges for "spiritually homeless souls."

He also picks out the generally undercounted and under-acknowledged Jews of Color as a group in particular need of recognition. This is a group that the Pew Survey relegates to a paragraph on page 46 but which later demographers suggest was undercounted and, rather than being around 7% of the whole, is closer to 10% and growing, or, in other words, very similar to the number of Orthodox Jews in America. Jacobs quotes Congregation Or Ami in Calabasas, CA which identifies as "Mosaic" because their members, "connect back to Moses, a Hebrew child, raised by Egyptians, who married a non-Jewish woman of color and became the leader of his people."

Jacobs's rhetoric was not hollow. In his first years as head of the URJ he included significant focus on the audacious hospitality project. Having spent nearly thirty years as a congregational rabbi (nine years in Brooklyn and twenty years in Westchester), he understood that hospitality started locally and knew some of what was needed for local congregations to implement audacious hospitality. A budget line was opened up, a section of the website appeared and an Audacious Hospitality Toolkit gave congregations not just tone, but tools to make welcome all the aforementioned groups.

April Baskin was appointed to the role of Vice President of Audacious Hospitality in April 2015 to embody the organization's welcoming stance. A millennial with experience at Interfaith Family and at Jewish Multiracial Network she was a professional whose life had been spent opening doors and making people welcome.

With his biennial address, Jacobs further stirred the waters of anxiety, which had already been muddied by the Pew Survey. But his actions were designed to make his denomination more inclusive, not more exclusive. Although he took a clear position, his actions were in accord with the words of Rabbi Joy Levitt, then the executive director of the JCC in Manhattan. When the JTA asked her about the in-marriage furor, she said:

> I'm not particularly interested in a food fight between people who think intermarriage is here to stay and we should embrace it and people who think intermarriage is a problem and we need to fight it. … I'm interested in how we build a Jewish life that is attractive, engaging and deeply meaningful to the people who are in it.[1]

Jacobs's 2013 keynote itself ended with surfing words of encouragement. "There are tremendous waves cresting all around us, my friends, and I, for one, refuse to sit on the shore in fear and trembling. This is our moment. It's time to for us to ride the biggest waves with newfound skill and balance."

---

1   Julie Wiener, "After lull, intermarriage debate reignites," *Jewish Telegraphic Agency*, January 28, 2014.

Contributing Authors

Joshua Avedon's business strategy experience in the early days of online commerce has informed his writing on startups, social ecosystems, and change-making, including the first academic study of IKAR (a community he helped found). He and Shawn Landres created the original Jewish Emergent Initiative at Synagogue 3000 and co-founded Jumpstart Labs.

Rabbi David Bashevkin is Director of Education for NCSY, the youth movement of the Orthodox Union and Instructor at Yeshiva University. His book, *Sin-a-gogue: Sin and Failure in Jewish Thought*, was published by Cherry Orchard Books, an imprint of Academic Studies Press.

Dr. Hillel Ben-Sasson studies and teaches Jewish Thought and Political Philosophy. He is a Research Fellow at the Jewish Theological Seminary and Head of the Misholim honors program at Oranim Academic College in Israel.

Dr. Judah M. Bernstein received his PhD in History and Hebrew-Judaic Studies from New York University in 2017, with a thesis on American Zionism in the early twentieth century. He also served as a Shalom Hartman Institute Kogod Research Fellow from 2016–2018.

Dr. Mijal Bitton is a Fellow in Residence at the Shalom Hartman Institute of North America and the cofounder and *Rosh Kehilla* of the Downtown Minyan. She earned her doctorate at New York University conducting a groundbreaking sociological study of Sephardic Jews in America.

Rabbi Dr. Alan Brill is the Cooperman/Ross Endowed Chair for Jewish-Christian Studies at Seton Hall University. His most recent book is *Rabbi on The Ganges: A Jewish Hindu Encounter*.

Dr. Samuel Hayim Brody is Associate Professor in the Department of Religious Studies at the University of Kansas. His first monograph, *Martin Buber's Theopolitics*, was a finalist for the National Jewish Book Award in 2018.

Rabbi Dr. Aryeh Cohen is Professor of Rabbinic Literature at the Ziegler School of Rabbinic Literature of the American Jewish University. He is also Rabbi in Residence of Bend the Arc: A Jewish Partnership for Justice. His latest book is *Justice in the City: An Argument from the Sources of Rabbinic Literature*.

Dr. Julie E. Cooper is Senior Lecturer in the Department of Political Science at Tel Aviv University. She is the author of *Secular Powers: Humility in Modern Political Thought*.

Dr. Sarah Cushman is Director of the Holocaust Educational Foundation of Northwestern University. She is currently writing *Auschwitz: The Women's Camp*, based on her dissertation.

Dr. Marc Dollinger is the Richard and Rhoda Goldman Chair of Jewish Studies and Social Responsibility at San Francisco State University. He is author, most recently, of *Black Power, Jewish Politics: Reinventing the Alliance in The 1960s*.

Rabbi Dr. David Ellenson is Chancellor Emeritus and former President of Hebrew Union College-Jewish Institute of Religion. He is also past Director of the Schusterman Center for Israel Studies and Professor Emeritus of Near Eastern and Judaic Studies at Brandeis University. His most recent book is *Jewish Meaning in a World of Choice*.

Rabbi Dr. Zev Farber is Senior Editor of TheTorah.com for Project TABS and a Research Fellow at the Shalom Hartman Institute's Kogod Center. He is the editor of the two-volume *Halakhic Realities: Collected Essays on Brain Death/ Organ Donation*.

Rabbi Dr. Joshua Feigelson is Executive Director of the Institute for Jewish Spirituality. He is the author of "Halakhah As an Ethic of Power: Yitz Greenberg and the War in Vietnam," published in *A Torah Giant: The Intellectual Legacy of Rabbi Dr. Irving (Yitz) Greenberg*.

Dr. Emily Filler is Chair and Assistant Professor of Jewish Studies at Earlham College, and Co-Editor of the *Journal of Jewish Ethics*.

Rabbi Elli Fischer is a writer, translator, and editor pursuing a doctorate in Jewish history at Tel Aviv University. He was Founding Editor of the Lehrhaus and is Co-Creator of a Digital Jewish Studies project called HaMapah.

Dr. Rachel Fish is founding Executive Director of the Foundation to Combat Anti-Semitism. She is co-editor of the book *Essential Israel: Essays for the Twenty-First Century*.

Dr. Sylvia Barack Fishman, Foster Professor of Contemporary Jewish Life Emerita at Brandeis University, is Editor of the Hadassah Brandeis Institute Series on Gender and Jewish Women. She is the author of eight books and numerous articles on sociology, literature, and culture of American Jewry, including *Love, Marriage, and Jewish Families: Paradoxes of a Social Revolution*.

Dr. Dan Friedman is Director of Content and Communications at the Shalom Hartman Institute of North America. He was previously Executive Editor of the *Forward*.

Dr. William A. Galston is the Ezra K. Zilkha Chair and a Senior Fellow in the Brookings Institution's Governance Studies Program. His most recent book is *Anti-Pluralism: The Populist Threat to Liberal Democracy*.

Dr. Rachel Gordan is Shorstein Fellow in American Jewish Culture at the University of Florida where she teaches in the Religion Department and the Center for Jewish Studies. She is working on a book about post-World War II American Judaism.

Rabbi Dr. Donniel Hartman is President of the Shalom Hartman Institute and holds the Richard and Sylvia Kaufman Family Chair. He is author of *Putting God Second: How to Save Religion from Itself*.

Dr. Tova Hartman is Dean of Humanities at Ono Academic College. Her current research focuses on two areas: male trauma and multicultural Jewish education. Her most recent book is *Are You Not a Man of God? Devotion, Betrayal, and Social Criticism in Jewish Tradition*, co-authored with Charlie Buckholtz.

Dr. Christine Hayes is Weis Professor of Religious Studies at Yale University. Her book *What's Divine about Divine Law: Early Perspectives* won the 2015 National Jewish Book award in scholarship and additional awards from the American Publishers Association and the Association for Jewish Studies.

Shira Hecht-Koller, Esq., is Director of Education for 929 English, a platform for the global study of Tanakh, and Faculty Member at Drisha. She also serves as Educational Ambassador for Paideia: The European Institute for Jewish Studies in Sweden.

Dr. Sara Yael Hirschhorn is Visiting Assistant Professor of Israel Studies at the Crown Family Center for Jewish and Israel Studies at Northwestern University. She is the author of *City on a Hilltop: American Jews and the Israeli Settler Movement* (winner of the 2018 Sami Rohr Prize in Jewish Literature Choice Award and 2017 Finalist for the National Jewish Book Award).

Dr. Dara Horn is a scholar of Hebrew and Yiddish Literature and the author of five novels, most recently *Eternal Life.*

Dr. David Zvi Kalman is a Fellow in Residence at the Shalom Hartman Institute, Manager of Print-O-Craft Press, and Co-Founder of Jewish Public Media. His primary research is on the intersection of Jewish history and the history of technology. His work has appeared in *Haaretz, Tablet,* and the *Forward.*

Rabbi Dr. Jane Kanarek is Associate Professor of Rabbinics and Associate Dean of Academic Development and Advising at Hebrew College. She is the author of *Biblical Narrative and the Formation of Rabbinic Law.*

Dr. Alexander Kaye is the Karl, Harry, and Helen Stoll Chair of Israel Studies and Assistant Professor in Department of Near East and Judaic Studies at Brandeis University. His book, *The Invention of Jewish Theocracy,* deals with Religious Zionist attitudes to law in the State of Israel and the origins of the struggle for a halakhic state.

Yossi Klein Halevi is a Senior Fellow at the Shalom Hartman Institute where he is also Co-Director of the Muslim Leadership Intiative (MLI). He is the author of the *New York Times* bestseller, *Letters to My Palestinian Neighbor,* and *Like Dreamers,* winner of the Jewish Book Council's Everett Book of the Year Award for 2013.

Hannah Kober is a doctoral student at Stanford Graduate School of Education. She previously served as Program Associate at the Shalom Hartman Institute of North America.

Ambassador (Ret.) Daniel Kurtzer is the S. Daniel Abraham Professor of Middle East Policy Studies at Princeton University's Woodrow Wilson School of Public and International Affairs. During a twenty-nine-year career in the Foreign Service, he served as US Ambassador to Egypt and Israel, and he is the co-author of *The Peace Puzzle: America's Quest for Arab-Israeli Peace, 1989–2011*.

Dr. Yehuda Kurtzer is President of Shalom Hartman Institute of North America and author of *Shuva: The Future of the Jewish Past*.

Rabbi Dr. Gail Labovitz is Professor of Rabbinic Literature at the Ziegler School of Rabbinic Studies at the American Jewish University, and an ordained Conservative rabbi. She is the author of *Marriage and Metaphor: Constructions of Gender in Rabbinic Literature*, as well as numerous articles in the areas of rabbinics, gender, and Jewish law.

Rabbi Joshua Ladon is West Coast Director of Education for the Shalom Hartman Institute of North America and a doctoral candidate at the Jewish Theological Seminary. His writing has appeared in the *New Republic*, the *Forward*, and the *J Weekly*.

Dr. Shawn Landres, Co-Founder of the original Jewish Emergent Initiative at Synagogue 3000 and of Jumpstart Labs, has been cited in the *Forward 50* as "an essential thinker in explaining the new Jewish spirituality and culture." He is the co-editor of *Religion, Violence, Memory, and Place*.

Dr. Erin Leib Smokler is Director of Spiritual Development at Yeshivat Maharat Rabbinical School and a Research Fellow at the Shalom Hartman Institute of North America. She is the author of *God in the Years of Fury: Theodicy and Anti-Theodicy in the Holocaust Writings of Rabbi Kalonymus Kalman Shapira*.

Dr. Marcie Lenk has devoted her intellectual life and career to organizing educational programs and teaching Jews and Christians (and people of other faiths) to understand and appreciate the basic texts, ideas, history, and faith of the others. She received her PhD in Early Christianity at Harvard University, an MTS from Harvard Divinity School, as well as an MA in Bible from Yeshiva University.

Dr. Jon A. Levisohn is the Jack, Joseph, and Morton Mandel Associate Professor of Jewish Educational Thought at Brandeis University, where he directs the Jack, Joseph, and Morton Mandel Center for Studies in Jewish Education. He is the co-editor with Ari Y. Kelman of *Beyond Jewish Identity*.

Dr. Arielle Levites is Managing Director of CASJE (Consortium for Applied Studies in Jewish Education). She is writing a book about contemporary American Jewish spirituality.

Dr. James Loeffler is the Berkowitz Professor of Jewish History at the University of Virginia. He is the author of *Rooted Cosmopolitans: Jews and Human Rights in the Twentieth Century* and editor of *The Law of Strangers: Critical Perspectives on Jewish Lawyering and International Legal Thought*.

Dr. Shaul Magid is Distinguished Fellow in Jewish Studies at Dartmouth College and a Kogod Senior Research Fellow at the Shalom Hartman Institute of North America.

Dr. Yehuda Magid holds a PhD in Political Science from Indiana University. His current research projects explore the phenomenon of right-wing extremism in Israel-Palestine, Palestinian responses to Israeli military actions in the West Bank, and the global phenomenon of civilian targeting by pro-government militias.

Rabbi Dr. Michael Marmur is Associate Professor of Jewish Theology at HUC-JIR in Jerusalem. He is the author of *Abraham Joshua Heschel and the Sources of Wonder*.

Dr. Samira K. Mehta is Assistant Professor of Women and Gender Studies and Jewish Studies at the University of Colorado Boulder. She is the author of *Beyond Chrismukkah: Christian-Jewish Interfaith Families in the United States*.

Judge Dr. Yigal Mersel is currently Director of Courts in Israel, having previously been the Registrar of the Supreme Court of Israel, District Court Judge, and an assistant to Aharon Barak while the latter was President of the Supreme Court. He holds LLB, LLM, and LLD degrees from the Hebrew University and has published books and articles on various eras of law.

Dr. Sarah Anne Minkin is an educator, activist, and philanthropic advisor focusing on Israel/Palestine, human and civil rights, and feminist social change. She is a lecturer at the University of San Francisco and an affiliated faculty member at University of California, Berkeley's Center for Right-Wing Studies.

Rabbi Sarah Mulhern is a faculty member and Manager of the Created Equal Project at the Shalom Hartman Institute of North America.

Dr. Tomer Persico is Koret Visiting Assistant Professor at Berkeley Institute for Jewish Law and Israel Studies at the University of California, Berkeley and the Shalom Hartman Institute Bay Area Scholar in Residence. He is the author of *The Jewish Meditative Tradition* (Hebrew).

Dr. Noam Pianko is the Samuel N. Stroum Chair of Jewish Studies and Professor in the Jackson School of International Studies. His recent book, *Peoplehood: An American Innovation,* won the American Jewish Historical Society's Saul Viener Book prize.

Rabbi Dr. William Plevan holds rabbinic ordination from the Jewish Theological Seminary and a doctorate in Religion from Princeton University, where he wrote a dissertation on the philosophical anthropology of Martin Buber. His article "Holiness in Hermann Cohen, Franz Rosenzweig, and Martin Buber" was published in *Holiness in Jewish Thought,* edited by Alan Mittleman.

Dr. Benjamin Pollock is the Sol Rosenbloom Chair in Jewish Philosophy and Associate Professor of Jewish Thought at the Hebrew University of Jerusalem. He is author of *Franz Rosenzweig's Conversions: World Denial and World Redemption.*

Dr. Hannah S. Pressman, a scholar of Hebrew literature and Jewish culture, has published widely for general and academic audiences. Her essay "Curating Connections: Public Scholarship, New Media, and Building Bridges to Hebrew Culture" appears in the edited volume *What We Talk about When We Talk about Hebrew (And What It Means to Americans).*

Dr. Michal Raucher is Assistant Professor of Jewish Studies at Rutgers University. Her book, *Birthing Jewish Ethics,* about reproductive ethics among *charedi* women in Jerusalem, is forthcoming.

Rabbi Or Rose is Director of the Miller Center for Interreligious Learning & Leadership of Hebrew College. He is the co-editor of *Speaking Torah: Spiritual Teachings from Around the Maggid's Table.*

Dr. Judith Rosenbaum is Executive Director of the Jewish Women's Archive. She publishes regularly in both academic and popular journals and anthologies, including a recent article "Bread and Roses: Jewish Women Transform the American Labor Movement" in *The Sacred Exchange: Creating a Jewish Money Ethic.*

Rabbi Dr. Rachel Sabath Beit Halachmi has served as President's Scholar and Assistant Professor of Jewish Thought and Ethics at Hebrew Union College, as Vice President of the Shalom Hartman Institute, and as Rabbi of Congregation Shirat HaYam on Nantucket Island. She was ordained at HUC, received a PhD from the Jewish Theological Seminary, and speaks and writes on theology, Jewish peoplehood, Israel, gender, and ethics.

Dr. Jonathan D. Sarna is University Professor and the Joseph H. & Belle R. Braun Professor of American Jewish History at Brandeis University, where he directs the Schusterman Center for Israel Studies. He is also Chief Historian of the National Museum of American Jewish history and the author of *American Judaism: A History.*

Dr. Joshua Shanes is Associate Professor of Jewish Studies and Director of the Center for Israel Studies at the College of Charleston. He is the author of *Diaspora Nationalism and Jewish Identity in Habsburg Galicia* as well as dozens of publications on modern Jewish politics, religion, and identity.

Dr. Elana Stein Hain is Scholar in Residence and Director of Faculty at the Shalom Hartman Institute of North America. She is currently working on her first book, *Circumventing the Law: Rabbinic Approaches to Legal Loopholes and Fictions,* as well as "The Legal Parameters and Tools of Talmudic Interpretation," for the *Oxford Handbook of Jewish Law.*

Dr. Claire E. Sufrin is Associate Professor of Instruction and Assistant Director of Jewish Studies at the Crown Family Center for Jewish and Israel Studies at Northwestern University. She is the author of "Buber, the Bible, and Hebrew Humanism: Finding a Usable Past," published in *Modern Judaism.*

Dr. Daniel H. Weiss is the Polonsky-Coexist Senior Lecturer in Jewish Studies in the Faculty of Divinity at the University of Cambridge. His research examines the intersections between philosophical thought and classical Jewish texts, and he is the author of *Paradox and the Prophets: Hermann Cohen and the Indirect Communication of Religion*.

Rabbi David Wolkenfeld serves as Rabbi of Anshe Sholom B'nai Israel Congregation in Chicago's Lakeview neighborhood.

Dr. Wendy Zierler is the Sigmund Falk Professor of Modern Jewish Literature and Feminist Studies at HUC-JIR, New York, and author, most recently, of *Movies and Midrash: Popular Film and Jewish Religious Conversation*, a finalist for the National Jewish Book Award.

Rabbi Shlomo Zuckier is a PhD candidate in Ancient Judaism at Yale University, an AJS Dissertation Completion Fellow, and a member of RIETS's Kollel Elyon. He is the editor of the forthcoming *Contemporary Uses and Forms of Hasidut*.

Permissions

Index

CPSIA information can be obtained
at www.ICGtesting.com
Printed in the USA
LVHW051939240121
677312LV00001B/1